Lecture Notes in Computer Science 9013

Commenced Publication in 1973
Founding and Former Series Editors:
Gerhard Goos, Juris Hartmanis, and Jan van Leeuwen

More information about this series at http://www.springer.com/series/7408

Samuel A. Fricker · Kurt Schneider (Eds.)

Requirements Engineering: Foundation for Software Quality

21st International Working Conference, REFSQ 2015
Essen, Germany, March 23–26, 2015
Proceedings

 Springer

Editors
Samuel A. Fricker
Blekinge Institute of Technology
Software Engineering Research Laboratory
Karlskrona
Sweden

Kurt Schneider
Software Engineering Group
Leibniz Universität Hannover
Hannover
Germany

ISSN 0302-9743
Lecture Notes in Computer Science
ISBN 978-3-319-16100-6
DOI 10.1007/978-3-319-16101-3

ISSN 1611-3349   (electronic)

ISBN 978-3-319-16101-3   (eBook)

Library of Congress Control Number: 2015933158

LNCS Sublibrary: SL2 – Programming and Software Engineering

Springer Cham Heidelberg New York Dordrecht London
© Springer International Publishing Switzerland 2015

Printed on acid-free paper

Springer International Publishing AG Switzerland is part of Springer Science+Business Media
(www.springer.com)

Preface

Requirements Engineering is a dominant factor that influences the quality of software, systems, and services. The REFSQ working conference series is well established as one of the leading international forums for discussing RE and its many relations to quality. The first REFSQ took place in 1994, and since 2010 REFSQ has been organized as a stand-alone conference. During March 23–26, 2015, we welcomed participants at REFSQ 2015, which was held in Essen, Germany.

We chose "I heard it first at REFSQ" as the special theme for REFSQ 2015. The working conference is interested in the future of RE and in really new views on Requirements Engineering that are debated in the many interactive formats of REFSQ 2015. In addition to general papers on Requirements Engineering and quality, we therefore encouraged submissions that highlight the utilization of Requirements Engineering for solving our society's Grand Challenges, such as the aging population and the expected scarcity of energy. We need novel ways for utilizing emerging technologies such as smart networks, novel Internet architectures, and the wide availability of sensors and data sources. Contributions from further related areas, such as systems engineering, economics, and management, were also very welcome for the insights they provide to Requirements Engineering.

We are pleased to present here the REFSQ 2015 proceedings that feature 23 papers presented during the REFSQ 2015 conference. This collection of papers resulted from a thorough peer-review process. Eighty-one abstracts were initially submitted. Not all abstracts were followed-up by papers, and three contributions were withdrawn. Sixty-two papers entered into the formal review process. Each paper was reviewed by three members of the Program Committee. An extensive online discussion within the Program Committee considered and enriched reviews during the search for a final decision. During a physical Program Committee meeting, the papers were discussed and selected for inclusion in the conference proceedings. Selected authors of rejected papers were encouraged to submit their papers at the REFSQ workshop, or as an industry or research methodology track contribution, or as a poster.

The REFSQ 2015 conference was organized as a three-day symposium. Two conference days were devoted to presentation and discussion of scientific papers. The two days connected to the conference theme with a keynote, an invited talk, and poster presentations. The keynote was given by Christoph Thümmler from Edinburgh Napier University and from the Klinikum Rechts der Isar, the hospital of the Technical University of Munich. Christoph had a crucial role in large-scale requirements engineering to align European computing infrastructure with the needs of the healthcare sector. One conference day was devoted to presentation and discussion of RE research methodology and industry experience.

There were two parallel tracks on the third day: the Industry Track and the new Research Methodology Track. In a joint plenary researchers met with industry to debate innovation in the discipline of requirements engineering.

REFSQ 2015 would not have been possible without the engagement and support of many who contributed in many different ways. As Program Co-chairs, we would like to thank the Steering Committee, all the members of the Program Committee, and the organizing team.

- Tobias Kaufmann and Selda Saritas were invaluable in the organization of this conference.
- Klaus Pohl headed the background organization of the REFSQ conference series.
- Adrian Zwingli transferred experience from the Swiss Requirements Day, introduced the REFSQ ambassador program, and prepared the stimulating industry track.
- Barbara Paech and Roel Wieringa launched the research methodology track.
- Raimundas Matulevicius and Thorsten Weyer increased the number of workshops substantially.
- Eric Knauss and Anna Perini were responsible for the posters.
- Dan Berry and Xavier Franch were responsible for the doctoral symposium.

All the research papers can be found in this present proceedings. The publications associated with the satellite events can be found in the REFSQ workshop proceedings published at CEUR.

We hope the proceedings convey the inspiration of the REFSQ conference and conversations throughout the symposium. We hope you will find research results and really new ideas that you have first heard at REFSQ 2015!

January 2015   Samuel A. Fricker
                                                                            Kurt Schneider

Organization

Program Committee

Eya Ben Charrada — University of Zurich, Switzerland
Richard Berntsson Svensson — Chalmers and University of Gothenburg, Sweden
Daniel M. Berry — University of Waterloo, Canada
Sjaak Brinkkemper — Utrecht University, The Netherlands
David Callele — University of Saskatchewan, Canada
Nelly Condori Fernandez — Vrije Universiteit Amsterdam, The Netherlands
Oliver Creighton — Siemens AG, Germany
Daniela Damian — University of Victoria, Canada
Maya Daneva — University of Twente, The Netherlands
Joerg Doerr — Fraunhofer IESE, Germany
Xavier Franch — Universitat Politècnica de Catalunya, Spain
Vincenzo Gervasi — University of Pisa, Italy
Martin Glinz — University of Zurich, Switzerland
Tony Gorschek — Blekinge Institute of Technology, Sweden
Olly Gotel — Independent Researcher, USA
Paul Grünbacher — Johannes Kepler University Linz, Austria
Andrea Herrmann — Herrmann and Ehrlich, Germany
Patrick Heymans — University of Namur, Belgium
Frank Houdek — Daimler AG, Germany
Natalia Juristo — Universidad Politécnica de Madrid, Spain
Erik Kamsties — University of Applied Sciences and Arts Dortmund, Germany
Marjo Kauppinen — Aalto University, Finland
Eric Knauss — Chalmers and University of Gothenburg, Sweden
Eleni Kosta — Tilburg University, The Netherlands
Anne Koziolek — Karlsruhe Institute of Technology, Germany
Kim Lauenroth — Adesso AG, Germany
Nazim Madhavji — University of Western Ontario, Canada
Andrey Maglyas — Lappeenranta University of Technology, Finland
Sabrina Marczak — Pontifícia Universidade Católica do Rio Grande do Sul, Portugal
Raimundas Matulevicius — University of Tartu, Estonia
Raul Mazo Peña — University of Paris 1 Panthéon-Sorbonne, France
Oli Mival — Edinburgh Napier University, UK
John Mylopoulos — University of Trento, Italy
Cornelius Ncube — Bournemouth University, UK
Andreas Opdahl — University of Bergen, Norway

Barbara Paech	Universität Heidelberg, Germany
Oscar Pastor	Universitat Politécnica de València, Spain
Anna Perini	Fondazione Bruno Kessler, Italy
Anne Persson	University of Skövde, Sweden
Kai Petersen	Blekinge Institute of Technology, Sweden
Klaus Pohl	University of Duisburg-Essen, Germany
Rozilawati Razali	Universiti Kebangsaan Malaysia, Malaysia
Gil Regev	École Polytechnique Fédérale de Lausanne, Switzerland
Björn Regnell	Lund University, Sweden
Michael Rohs	Leibniz Universität Hannover, Germany
Camille Salinesi	Université Paris 1 Panthéon-Sorbonne, France
Kristian Sandahl	Linköping University, Sweden
Peter Sawyer	Lancaster University, UK
Norbert Seyff	University of Zurich, Switzerland
Guttorm Sindre	Norwegian University of Science and Technology, Norway
Inge van de Weerd	Vrije Universiteit Amsterdam, The Netherlands
Thorsten Weyer	University of Duisburg-Essen, Germany
Roel Wieringa	University of Twente, The Netherlands
Krzysztof Wnuk	Blekinge Institute of Technology, Sweden
Eric Yu	University of Toronto, Canada
Didar Zowghi	University of Technology, Sydney, Australia

Additional Reviewers

Adam, Sebastian	Knauss, Alessia
Bano, Muneera	Lucassen, Garm
Bex, Floris	Mahaux, Martin
Bourguiba, Imen	Miranskyy, Andriy
de La Vara, Jose Luis	Morales-Ramirez, Itzel
Ghazi, Parisa	Nass-Bauer, Claudia
Groen, Eduard	Nekvi, Rashed
Huebner, Paul	Perrouin, Gilles
Huber, Martina	Seiler, Marcus
Ionita, Dan	Sharifloo, Amir
Jabbari, Ramtin	Todoran, Irina
Kücherer, Christian	Van Der Werf, Jan Martijn
Keikkila, Ville	Wüest, Dustin
Klotins, Eriks	

Sponsors

Platinum Level Sponsors

The Ruhr Institute for Software Technology

Gold Level Sponsors

adesso | business. people. technology.

IREB International® Requirements Engineering Board

Silver Level Sponsors

accelerator

University of Applied Sciences and Arts Northwestern Switzerland
School of Engineering

Partners

BTH BLEKINGE TEKNISKA HÖGSKOLA

Leibniz Universität Hannover

Requirements Engineering for Digital Health Keynotes (Abstract)

Christoph Thümmler

Edinburgh Napier University, Edinburgh, United Kingdom,
and Technical University Munich, Munich, Germany
c.thuemmler@napier.ac.uk

What Is Digital Health and Why Is It important?

OECD countries are typically spending annually between 9% and 18% of their GDP on healthcare, whereby the increase in healthcare spending has been outperforming the growth in GDP over recent years. There is no indication what so ever that this trend may reverse in the foreseeable future. New, digital technologies are expected to increase the efficiency and effectiveness within the healthcare industry and have the potential to prevent a shortage or a drop in quality of care. One theory is, that disruptive digital technologies might enable less experienced and therefore less expensive professionals to "move upmarket" to progressively fill roles, which were previously filled by highly skilled experts.

Requirements Engineering and "Disruptive Technology Plots" in Digital Health – Definitely Maybe?

Tools have been proposed to identify and counteract on Disruptive Technologies in order to protect established companies and their products. However, time and time again established brands suffer huge losses or go under because of their seemingly inability to change. If (according to Christensen) neither asking the customer, nor asking the management is actually a helpful strategy, how can Requirements Engineering make a difference?

Requirements Engineering in Digital Health – Detecting the Soft Stuff

"Hard is Soft and Soft is Hard" is a famous phrase coined by Tom Peters in his study leading up to the landmark publication "In search of Excellence", when investigating the resilience of the American automotive industry against Asian competitors. Also openly invited and in a way hoped for by many leading politicians disruptive technologies seem not be able to penetrate health care systems and unfolding their efficiency boosting effects. Can Requirements Engineering explain this? Can Requirements Engineering help to find ways for new disruptive digital technologies to establish themselves in neo-conservative, highly controlled markets places.

Chances and Challenges with Regards to Requirements Engineering in Digital Health

Healthcare is the largest and fastest growing industry globally with a size ranging between 3% and 18% of national GDPs. Many technologies will have to be replaced in the near future in order to streamline healthcare systems and improve their suitability and their general resilience. According to study results investment in Requirements Engineering typically achieves excellent return hence why this market is of great interest. Requirements Engineering for Digital Health needs to consider highly relevant specific areas such as ethical, social and legal factors to support new and in particular disruptive digital technologies for the health care markets. This talk will discuss general strategies to capture trends in the health care industry using examples from a recent large scale European Research Project.

Contents

Experimental Validation of a Risk Assessment Method

Eelco Vriezekolk[1,3]([✉]), Sandro Etalle[2,3], and Roel Wieringa[3]

[1] Radiocommunications Agency Netherlands, Groningen, Netherlands
[2] Eindhoven University of Technology, Eindhoven, Netherlands
[3] University of Twente, Enschede, Netherlands
eelco.vriezekolk@agentschaptelecom.nl

Abstract. **[Context and motivation]** It is desirable that requirement engineering methods are reliable, that is, that methods can be repeated with the same results. Risk assessments methods, however, often have low reliability when they identify risk mitigations for a system based on expert judgement. **[Question/problem]** Our goal is to assess the reliability of an availability risk assessment method for telecom infrastructures, and to identify possibilities for improvement of its reliability. **[Principal ideas/results]** We propose an experimental validation of reliability, and report on its application. We give a detailed analysis of sources of variation, explain how we controlled them and validated their mitigations, and motivate the statistical procedure used to analyse the outcome. **[Contribution]** Our results can be used to improve the reliability of risk assessment methods. Our approach to validating reliability can be useful for the assessment of the reliability of other methods.

Keywords: Reliability · Risk assessment · Expert judgement · Experiment design · Telecommunications

1 Introduction

Risk assessment is the identification, analysis, and evaluation of risks, and provides the arguments for the choice and justification of risk mitigations [12]. It can be viewed as a way to transform high-level system goals (to avoid risks) into more detailed system requirements (to implement specific mitigations). For example, in security risk assessment, the high-level system goals of confidentiality and availability can be transformed into the more detailed system requirements that there be a firewall and that a function must be implemented redundantly.

Risks assessments are often performed by experts who assess (that is: identify, analyse and evaluate) risks on the basis of best available expert-knowledge of an architectural model. It is known that such expert judgements may have a low reliability [9]. We call a method reliable if it can be repeated with the same results [27]. Other terms in use for this concept are repeatability, stability, consistency, and reproducibility.

Testing the reliability of a risk assessment method is an important issue, which has however received very little attention in the literature. If a risk

© Springer International Publishing Switzerland 2015
S.A. Fricker and K. Schneider (Eds.): REFSQ 2015, LNCS 9013, pp. 1–16, 2015.
DOI: 10.1007/978-3-319-16101-3_1

assessment method is not quite reliable, then its results will always largely depend on the intuition and the expertise of the expert carrying it out. This weakens the ability of decision makers to justify risk mitigation actions that are based on such assessments.

In previous papers we have illustrated the RASTER method for assessing availability risks in telecom infrastructures [24]. A test of RASTER with real experts in a real assessment task has shown that RASTER can achieve useful results within limited time, but did not provide evidence about its reliability [22,23].

In this paper, we illustrate the method we have developed for validating RASTER's reliability. Our approach is based on an experiment, guided by a general checklist to ensure that all important aspects are adequately addressed [25]. Here, we illustrate the choices we have made and the methodologies we have applied to ensure a scientific assessment. We believe that our approach is sufficiently general to be applicable to other requirements engineering methods as well.

We describe risk assessment, and the RASTER method in particular, briefly in Sect. 2. Our approach to testing reliability of a method is presented in Sect. 3. In Sect. 4 and 5 we describe the design and outcome of an experiment using this approach. We discuss implications of this for practice and for research in Sect. 6.

2   Background and Related Work

In what follows, a telecom operator is a company that provides an infrastructure for communication, such as Deutsche Telekom in Germany. Examples of telecom services provided by an infrastructure are voice calling between two parties, internet access, virtual private networks, etc. End users are companies or individuals that use these services, such as banks, shops, police and emergency services, and citizens.

Nowadays, a typical telecom service uses the physical infrastructure and services of several independent telecom operators. These operators may not be aware that their infrastructure is used for the particular service. For example, an operator of fiber-optic transmission network typically leases capacity to other operators and will therefore not know what end-user services are being offered. The end-user organisations' availability requirements are therefore not (fully) known by the operators. Operators strive for high availability and resilience, but are not able to adapt their network to accommodate the availability requirements of individual end users. For some classes of users these availability requirements are very strong, for example for fire and emergency services. Reliable risk assessments can therefore be very important for telecom services.

To side-step the problem of low reliability of expert judgements, risk assessments are sometimes based on checklists and best practices, in what we call 'compliance-based methods'. These compliance-based methods are not sufficient for today's telecom networks, mainly because of three reasons. First, as explained above, telecom operators aim for local optimisations that may have detrimental effects on global availability. Second, the infrastructure is extremely complex, and composed of fixed and mobile networks, using PSTN, internet, wireless and cable

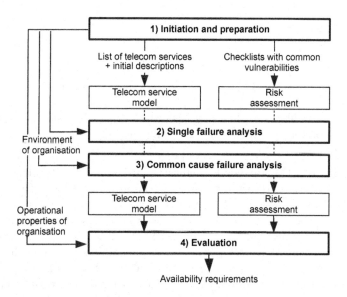

Fig. 1. The four stages of the RASTER method. Stages are shown in bold; documents and flow of information in standard lines.

infrastructures. Third, the infrastructure is in a state of continuous evolution, and threats to the infrastructure evolve as well. This makes compliance-based risk assessments even less effective than risk-based assessments.

Risk assessment methods can be quantitative (e.g. [2,16]) or qualitative (e.g. [3,11]). Quantitative methods estimate probability and impact of risks by ratio scales or interval scales, qualitative methods estimate probability or impact by an ordinal scale, for example 'Low–Medium–High'. Due to lack of information, availability risks for telecom infrastructures have to be estimated qualitatively. This means that expert judgement plays a crucial role. This reduces reliability of risk assessments, either because a single expert makes different estimates for the same object at different times, or because multiple experts make different estimates at the same time. Herrmann *et al.* argue that one reason why reliability is low is that risk estimation requires a lot of information [7,9]. They report that group discussions, although time consuming, have a moderating effect.

The goal of the RASTER method is to guide experts in doing an availability risk assessment on behalf of an end user, that is as reliable as possible, given the constraints of limited information about the target of assessment. The RASTER method is typically executed by a team of analysts comprising of telecom experts as well as domain experts from the end-users organisation [24]. The method consists of four stages (Fig. 1):

1. collect initial information and determine the scope of the analysis, mostly based on existing documentation from the end user and its telecom suppliers. The results include an initial architecture model and a list of common vulnerabilities;

2. analyse single failures (single incidents affecting a single architectural component, e.g. a cable break). After a few iterations, this results in an updated architecture model (see Fig. 2 for an example);

3. analyse common cause failures (single incidents affecting multiple components simultaneously, e.g. a faulty software update that has been applied to multiple routers);

4. perform the final risk evaluations, also considering other stakeholders' interests and possible reactions that may influence the range of acceptable risk mitigations.

Assessments in RASTER are mostly qualitative, using an ordinal scale, and explicitly take into account uncertainty, lack of consensus, and lack of information. Each vulnerability is assessed through two factors: Frequency (indicating likelihood of an incident because of this vulnerability) and Impact (indicating effects, repairability, and number of actors involved). The decision which mitigations to apply is out of scope of RASTER. These decisions are not made by the analysts but by a stakeholder responsible for the mitigation budget, who typically must trade off risk mitigation requirements against other kinds of requirement.

3   Our Approach to Testing Reliability of a Method

We define reliability as repeatability, and so we are interested in how much variation there is across different instances of using the method, where we will control all possible contextual sources of variation in results. We want to understand how to minimise the variation caused by the method itself. Internal causes are inherent to the method, and will be present in any application of the method. For example, the method may be ambiguously described or underspecified. Contextual causes of variation are due to the subject applying the method, the environment during application, or to other aspects of the context in which the method is applied. For example, the time available for application of the method may have been too short. Contextual causes of variation will be present regardless of any particular method being used. We consider a method to be reliable if the variation of the results of using it is small, when contextual causes of variation are held constant.

The sources of variation in an experiment are different from those in the field. We need to control variation in order to be able to draw conclusions from the experiment. Controls therefore only need to be effective within the setting of the experiment; it is not necessary that successful mitigations transfer to field settings.

We now describe our approach of keeping contextual causes of variation constant.

3.1   Controlling Variation

Mitigation of contextual causes of variation involves 1) identification and mitigation of contextual causes, and 2) validation of the effectiveness of mitigations.

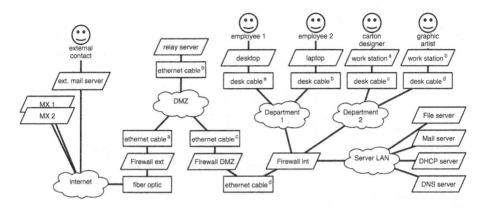

Fig. 2. Example of a telecommunication service model, showing the email service used by a company. Shapes indicate the type of components: equipment (rectangle), cables (parallelogram), and unknown links (cloud). Lines indicate that components are physically connected.

1) Identification and Mitigation. Contextual sources of variation can arise from three areas: a) from the subjects applying the method, b) from the case to which the method is applied, and c) from the circumstances and environment in which the method is applied. In practice it will be impossible to remove contextual causes altogether, but steps can be taken to reduce them, or to measure them so that we can reason about their possible influence on the outcome. Because contextual conditions are controlled, the testing of the reliability of a method will be a laboratory experiment.

a) Subjects Applying the Method. We identified three causes for variation arising from the participants in reliability experiments. Participants may not *understand* the task, not *be able* to perform the task, or not *be willing* to do so.

First, *misapplication and misunderstanding of the method by the participants* can cause variation. If the participants do not have a clear understanding of the method and the task at hand, then they may improvise in unpredictable ways. This can be mitigated by providing a clear and concise case which would be easy to explain, together with clear instructions and reference materials. Furthermore, the clarity of these instructions and the task itself can be tested in a try-out, in which the experiment is conducted with a few participants. Experiences from the try-out can then be used to improve the experiment setup.

Second, *lack of experience and expert knowledge* can cause variation. Even when participants understand the method, they still require skills and knowledge to apply the method properly. Researchers in empirical software engineering often use students as subjects in experiments. It is sometimes claimed that the use of students instead of professionals severely limits the validity of software engineering experiments, because students display behaviour that diverges from that of experts. However, it is valid to use students as a model for experts on the condition that students are representative with respect to the properties being investigated. Just like a paper model of a house can be used to study some (but not all) properties of a real house, students can be used to study some (but not all) properties of professionals applying software engineering methods [26]. Some studies have indeed found that certain kinds of behaviour are similar across experts and students [10,17,20]. Be this as it may, industry reality often precludes the use of experts in experiments, regardless of how desirable that would be from an experimenter's point of view. Testing with students is cheaper and less risky, and therefore increases the likelihood of successful technology transfer to industry [5]. In addition, in reliability experiments it is not the students' direct results that are of interest. Instead, it is the variation among their results that is relevant. It is therefore not automatically a problem if students achieve different results than professionals, as long as the experiment allows us to draw general conclusions about the method. In the lab (using students) and in the field (using experts) the participants to a reliability experiment should be as similar to each other as possible in background and experience.

Third, participants must *be sufficiently motivated* to apply the method to the best of their abilities. When tired or faced with a tedious and uninteresting task, the quality of the results will suffer. Experiments using students are sometimes conducted as part of a software engineering course. The experimentor then should consider whether compulsory participation offers sufficient motivation, or whether voluntary participation based on students' intrinsic motivation would be preferable. Furthermore, when the task at hand requires estimation (as will be the case for risk analysis), particular care should be given to avoid personal biases that can result in over- or underestimation. A frequently used way to control this bias is to employ teams instead of individuals. Discussion within the team can dampen individual biases.

b) Case to Which the Method is Applied. A method such as RASTER is not designed for a single case, but should perform well in a large variety of cases. If a case is ill-defined, then one cannot blame the method if it provides results with low reliability. Since testing of reliability requires a constructed laboratory experiment, the experimentor must carefully design the case to be used by the participants. The case should be representative of cases encountered in practice, but reduced to the essentials to make it fit to the limited time and setting available to laboratory experiments.

c) Environment During Application. Variation may also derive from *environmental conditions*, such as the meeting room, lighting, or time of day. First, the conditions should be as similar as possible between the different subjects to the experiment. Ideally, conditions should be identical. If the conditions differ, then any variation in results could be attributed to these conditions and does not necessarily indicate a lack of reliability. Secondly, the conditions should be as similar as possible between the experiment and real world applications of the method. For example, the experiment should, or should not be performed under pressure of time, depending on what is the case in practical applications. If the conditions differ, then it could be argued that variation in lab results would not occur in the field.

2) Validation of Effectiveness. When causes of contextual variation have been identified and mitigated, it is necessary to give a convincing argument that mitigation has been effective. The results of the method's application cannot be used in this argument, because the results may vary due to properties of the method rather than due to contextual factors. Instead, it will be necessary to make additional observations, using tools such as interviews, questionnaires, and observations. Therefore experiments to test reliability of a method will collect two kinds of data: measurements on the results of the method, and measurements on the usage of the method. We now discuss how we will analyse the results of the usage of the method.

3.2 Analysis of Measurements on the Results of the Method

The analysis of the reliability of a method can make use of several well-known statistical techniques for inter-rater reliability [6]. Inter-rater reliability is the amount of agreement between the scores of different subjects for the same set of items.

Well-known measures for inter-rater reliability are Cohen's kappa, Fleiss' kappa, Spearman's rho, Scott's pi and Krippendorff's alpha [15]. Cohen's kappa and Scott's pi are limited, in that they can only handle two raters. To test reliability, more than two outcomes are necessary in order to be able to draw conclusions. Fleiss' kappa can handle multiple raters but treats all data as nominal. Spearman's rho can take ordinality of data into account, but only works for two raters. Krippendorff's alpha works for any number of raters, and any type of scale. Furthermore, Krippendorff's alpha can accommodate partially incomplete data (e.g. when some raters have not rated some items). This makes Krippendorff's alpha a good choice for this domain. We will abbreviate 'Krippendorff's alpha' to 'alpha' in the remainder of this document.

Alpha is defined as $1 - D_o/D_e$, where D_o is the observed disagreement in the scores and D_e is the expected disagreement if raters assigned their scores randomly. If the raters have perfect agreement, the observed disagreement is 0 and alpha is 1. If the raters' scores are indistinguishable from random scores then $D_o = D_e$ and alpha is 0. If alpha < 0, then disagreement is larger than random disagreement. Alpha is therefore a measure for the amount of agreement that cannot be attributed to chance. Cohen's kappa and Scott's pi are basically defined in the same way as alpha, but differ in their computation of observed and expected (dis)agreement. For alpha and ordinal data, the disagreement between two scores s_1 and s_2 of an item depends on how often these scores occurred in the observed scores, as well as how often the levels between s_1 and s_2 have been used. The observed disagreement can thus be calculated by summation, and the expected disagreement can be computed based on the relative frequency of each ordinal level. More information is given in our internal report [21].

In order to compare the inter-rater reliability of two subsets of items, the calculations must be done carefully to ensure that the alphas are comparable. To be able to compare alphas on two subsets, we must ensure that the D_e value for both alphas is calculated over the complete set of scores, not over the their respective subsets [14]. In a subset the disagreement within the items may be large when seen in isolation, while that disagreement may be much smaller when compared to the totality of scores. Since the absolute values for D_o and D_e depend on the number of items over which they are calculated, a scale factor must be applied during calculation. This computational complexity is not a peculiarity of alpha alone; by analogy, the other measures of inter-rater reliability are affected by a similar issue.

4   Research Method

4.1   Experiment Design

We conducted a replicated experiment in which small teams of volunteers performed part of the RASTER method on a fictitious telecom service. Detailed information on the practical aspects of the experiment are given in our internal report [21]. The following description follows the checklist given by Wieringa [25].

Treatment Design.   Executing RASTER means that several activities need to be performed, ranging from collecting information to obtaining go-ahead from the executive sponsors of the risk assessment (see Fig. 1). Not all of these are relevant for reliability, because not all of them can contribute to variation in results. From previous research we know that different experts can create architecture diagrams in RASTER that are largely identical. We consider this part of the method reliable, and exclude it from our current experiment. In stage two, most of the expert assessments of frequencies and impacts of vulnerabilities are made, and so this stage is an important source of possible variation. Stages three and four add no other sources of variation. Including them in the experiment would greatly complicate the experiment without adding new knowledge about sources of variation, and so we decided to restrict our experiment to stage two.

Choice of Volunteers.   To ensure sufficient knowledge of information technology (IT) security, we recruited student volunteers from the Kerckhoffs Masters programme on computer and information security offered jointly by the University of Twente, Eindhoven University of Technology, and Radboud University Nijmegen [13]. Since our groups are not random but self-selected, our experiment is a quasi-experiment [18]. This creates systematic effects on the outcome, that we will discuss in our analysis of the outcomes.

RASTER is applied by a team of experts. This allows for pooling of knowledge and stimulates discussion. We acquired 18 volunteers, enabling us to form 6 groups. Our sample of groups is not randomly selected and is anyway too small for statistical inference, but we will use similarity-based reasoning to draw tentative generalisations to analogous cases [1,4,19,25].

Target of Assessment.   The telecom service for the experiment had to be small so that the task could be completed in single afternoon, but large enough to allow for realistic decisions and assessments. The choice of students imposed further restrictions; wireless telecommunication links had to be omitted (as students were unlikely to have sufficient knowledge on these), and a telecom service was chosen to be relatively heavy on information technology. The telecom service for the experiment was an email service for a small fictitious design company heavily dependent on IT systems (Fig. 2).

Measurement Design.   For measurement of the results of the method, we used the risk assessment scores by the groups. Groups were instructed to try to reach consensus on their scores. Each assessment was noted on a provided scoring form (one form per group). The possible scores form an ordinal scale. Detailed scoring instructions and descriptions of each of the values were included in the hand-out. In addition, groups could decide to abstain from assessment. Abstentions were allowed when the group could not reach consensus on their score, or when the group members agreed that information was insufficient to make a well-informed assessment.

For measurements on the usage of the method we used an exit questionnaire and our observations during the experiment. Each participant individually completed an exit questionnaire at the end of the experiment (Table 1).

4.2   Using our Approach to Testing Reliability

Subjects Applying the Method. Participants should understand the task, be able to perform the task, and be willing to do so. To mitigate lack of understanding, we provided a concise case which would be easy to explain; we prepared what we hoped were clear instructions and reference materials. We then tested the instructions (as well as the task itself) in a try-out. As a result of the try-out, we made small improvements to the instructions and to the case description. At the start of the experiment we invited questions from the participants and made sure to proceed only after all confirmed that they understood the task at hand. To mitigate lack of experience, we created a case that closely matched the expected experience of our students. As explained, we omitted wireless technologies, and emphasised IT systems in the case. To mitigate lack of motivation we recruited volunteers, offered the customary compensation, and raffled cinema tickets as a bonus.

Case to Which the Method is Applied. Two causes of variation drew our special concern. First, the *number of risk scenarios* could be too large. In the experiment, risks consist of the combination of an architectural component and a vulnerability, e.g. "power failure on the mail server". Many different scenarios can be devised for this risk to occur. For example, a power cable can be accidentally unplugged, the fans in the power supply unit may wear out and cause overheating, or the server can be switched off by a malicious engineer. A large number of risk scenarios will make the results overly dependent on the groups' ability to identify all relevant scenarios. Given the limited time available for the experiment, groups could not be expected to identify all possible ways in which a vulnerability could materialise. As a mitigation, we tried to offer clear and limited vulnerabilities in the case description.

Second, reliability cannot be achieved if there is *widespread disagreement on the 'true' risk* in society. Physical risk factors can in principle be assessed objectively, but some risk factors (such as fairness or voluntariness) are unavoidably subjective. We therefore use quotation marks for 'true'; in some cases no single, most valid risk assessment may exist. Such controversial risks do not lend themselves to impartial assessment. In our choice of the experiment's case we tried to avoid controversial risks.   -

Environment during Application. We did not identify important causes of variation that needed mitigating. We provided each team with a quiet and comfortable meeting room, in a setting not unlike real world applications of RASTER.

Verification of effectiveness. For each source of external variation thus identified, the questionnaire checked whether participants had the required knowledge, ability and motivation to apply the corresponding countermeasure. For example, for 'lack of knowledge or experience' we used these three questions: "I am knowledgeable of the technology behind office email services", "My knowledge of the technology behind office email services could be applied in the exercise", and "It was important that my knowledge of email services was used by the group".

We also used the opportunity to include four questions to test some internal sources of variation. In particular, we wanted to test whether the scales defined for Frequency and Impact were suitable, and whether the procedure to avoid intuitive and potentially biased assessments was effective.

5   Results

Each of the six teams scored 138 Frequency assessments and 138 Impact assessments. Our scale for each is ⟨*extremely low, low, moderate, high, extremely high*⟩, but groups were also instructed that they could abstain from scoring. The experiment results can therefore be described as having 6 raters that had to rate 276 items, and partially incomplete, ordinal data. We computed alpha over these items, but also computed alpha over subsets of items. Subsets included the Frequency scores and Impacts scores separately, the scores on a single architectural component, and the scores on a single vulnerability.

Detailed results can be found in [21]; anonymised copies of results can be made available on request.

5.1   Scoring Results

Over the entire set of items, alpha is 0.338. This is considered a very weak reliability; Krippendorff recommends alpha at least 0.667 for provisional conclusions, and alpha at least 0.8 for firm conclusions, although he stresses that these figures are guidelines only [15]. Over the Frequency scores alpha is 0.232; over the Impact scores alpha is slightly higher, at 0.436.

This relatively low level of agreement is in line with earlier findings about reliability of risk assessments [7,8]. To understand why the level of agreement is relatively low we turn to the exit questionnaires.

Table 1. Exit questionnaire questions. Answers were scored on a five-point scale (strongly disagree to strongly agree, unless indicated otherwise).

1. The instructions at the start of the exercise were (very unclear – very clear).
2. I knew what I needed to do during the exercise.
3. In the experiment I could practically apply the instructions that were given at the start of the exercise.
4. The instructions that were given at the start of the exercise were (mostly useless – very useful).
5. My knowledge of the technology behind office email services can be described as (non-existent – excellent).
6. My knowledge of the technology behind office email services could be applied in the exercise.
7. It was important that my knowledge of email services was used by the group.
8. Before the exercise I was instructed to make rational, calculated estimates.
9. During the experiment I knew how to avoid fast, intuitive estimates.
10. The instructions and procedures for avoiding fast, intuitive estimates were (very cumbersome – very easy to use).
11. When estimating Frequencies and Impacts of vulnerabilities, it is necessary to consider many possible incidents.
12. I could think of practical examples for most of the vulnerabilities.

13. When discussing vulnerabilities, other members of my group often gave examples that I would never have thought of.
14. In my group we mostly had the same ideas on the values of estimates.
15. The estimates made by other groups (compared to ours) will be (very different – very similar).
16. For all estimates, there exists a single best value (whether we identified it or not).
17. I was able to concentrate on the exercise and work comfortably.
18. The time to complete the exercise was (way too short – more than sufficient).
19. Participating in this experiment was (very tiresome – very interesting).
20. The scales for values of Frequency and Impact estimates were (very unclear – very clear).
21. In my group we hesitated between two adjacent Frequency and Impact values (almost always – almost never).
22. The scales of values for Frequency and Impact were suitable to this exercise.
23. The final answer of my group often equalled my immediate personal estimate.

5.2 Exit Questionnaire

The exit questionnaire is shown in Table 1; answers are summarised in Table 2. The following discussion also makes use of our observations of the participants during the experiment.

Answers to the questionnaire (q1–q4) indicate that participants believe they had the required knowledge, skill, and motivation to employ the method. Our observations during the experiment confirm that, except for a few isolated cases, the instructions were effectively included in the groups' deliberations. We conclude that our mitigations for lack of understanding were successful.

The answers to q5–q7 were mostly positive, but our observations showed a marked difference in practical experience between groups. Some participants, contrary to our expectations, did not fully understand the function and significance of basic IT infrastructure such as DNS servers. To check whether lack of knowledge did induce variation in the scores, we compared the inter-group variation for components that are relatively well-known (such as desktop and

Table 2. Total scores for each of the questions in the exit questionnaire (see Table 1).

Question	Strongly disagree	Disagree	Neither agree nor disagree	Agree	Strongly agree
1				IIIIIII	IIIIIIIIII
2			I	IIIIIIIIII	IIIIII
3			I	IIIIIIIIIIII	IIII
4				IIIIIII	IIIIIIIIII
5		I	III	IIIIIIIIIIII	II
6			III	IIIIIIIIIIII	II
7		III	IIIIIIIII	IIIIII	
8		II	I	IIIIIIIIIIIII	I
9			IIII	IIIIIIIIIIII	
10		II	IIII	IIIIIIIIIII	
11		I	I	IIIIIIIIIIIII	II
12			II	IIIIIIIIIIII	III
13		III	IIIIIIII	IIIIII	
14		I	II	IIIIIIIIIIIII	I
15		I	III	IIIIIIIIIIII	I
16	IIII	IIIIIIII	IIII	II	
17			III	IIIIII	IIIIIIII
18		IIIII	IIIIIII	III	II
19		II		IIIIIIIIIII	III
20		I	II	IIIIIIIIIIIIII	
21	I	IIIIIIIII	IIIII	II	
22		II	IIIIIIII	IIIIIII	
23		I	II	IIIIIIIIIIII	I

laptops), to that for components that are less familiar (such as firewalls and routers). Alphas over end-user components (0.383 for frequencies assessments, 0.448 for impact assessments, 0.416 combined) were indeed higher than the general scores (0.232, 0.436, 0.338 respectively). We therefore conclude that lack of experience can explain some of the variation in results.

The answers to q8-q10 suggest that participants succeeded in avoiding personal biases. This was confirmed by our observations. We therefore conclude that our mitigations for lack of motivation were successful.

Two causes of variation arising from the case were identified and mitigated: a high number of risk scenarios and widespread disagreement on the 'true' risk. On the number of risk scenarios answers to the questionnaire (q11–q13) and observations indicated that mitigations were successful. In cases when the number of scenarios seemed unlimited (e.g. the risk of a general cable break in the Internet), groups did not hesitate to abstain from answering. For the second cause ("no 'true' risk") the questionnaire results were mixed: positive on agreement within the group and expected agreement with other groups (q14–q15), but negative on whether a single best assessment is possible (q16). The positive results could be a reflection of pleasant, cooperative teamwork, but the negative result to q16 makes it clear that participants believe there is no true answer. Our observations are that most groups made assumptions that significantly affected their assessments. The one group that scored high on q7 ("It was important that my knowledge of email services was used by the group") also was the only group that scored positively on q16. This indicates that the participants probably recognised that their assumptions were somewhat arbitrary. The scoring forms had space for groups to mark important assumptions; none of these assumptions were extraordinary or unrealistic. We did observe that groups generally made many more assumptions than were noted on their forms, but these unrecorded assumptions were mostly natural or obvious. Based on the above, we conclude that variation in scores can be partly explained by the difference in assumptions made by groups.

Mitigation of causes of variation from environmental conditions appear to have been successful. Neither questionnaire (q17–q19) nor observations indicate that conditions affected the results unequally. One group finished within the time set for the task, others exceeded that time by a few minutes, although one group finished almost 45 minutes late. All groups completed their tasks.

To summarise, the measurements on the usage of the method indicate two unmitigated contextual causes for variation: participants' lack of experience and knowledge about IT systems, and different assumptions made by the groups. We now turn to sources of variation internal to the RASTER method itself. From these we discovered a third cause for variation.

The questionnaire (q20–q22) and our observations showed that groups often hesitated between two adjacent frequency or impact classes (recall that all assessments required the selection of a value from an ordinal scale). Participants also remarked that the range of the scales was large, and that the difference between adjacent steps was problematic. We observed that participants volunteered arguments pro and con, and referred to previous scores to ensure a consistent scoring. This was independent of the particular ordinal value; discussion was necessary for the extreme scores as well as for the moderate scores. It is likely that groups settled for different values in these discussions. A third, method-internal cause of variation in outcomes is therefore the difficulty in choosing between adjacent ordinal values.

5.3   Implications

We found three explanations for the variation in the assessments:

1. The lack of expert knowledge by the participants.
2. The difference in assumptions made by groups.
3. The need to make somewhat arbitrary choices between adjacent ordinal values.

In practical applications of RASTER the team of analysts would consist of industry professionals, and lack of knowledge (1) is therefore not expected. Also, in a field setting analysts have ways to deal with unavailable data other than making assumptions (2). For example, they can make additional observations, conduct inspections, actively look for further documentation, or interview actors to fill gaps in available information. The number and severity of assumptions would therefore likely be much lower in field settings. In practice the team of analysts will be larger than the in the experiment (three students), allowing for more interaction and deliberation in order to reach consensus. Again, this suggests that in practice reliability of RASTER may be higher. These differences between lab and field suggest that RASTER will produce less variable results in practice than in the lab. Our experiment provides insight in why this can happen; only further field studies can demonstrate whether this is indeed the case.

However, explanation (3) will also be present in the field, and therefore is a point for improvement in the RASTER method.

6   Discussion, Conclusion, and Future Work

We have presented an approach to validating and measuring the reliability of a method, presented a research design that used this approach, and discussed the result of using this for RASTER. Our approach to measuring reliability of methods does not mention risk assessment at all, and should be of use also in measuring the reliability of other methods. The research design too should be of use for measuring other properties of methods.

Our analysis confirms that reliability of expert judgements of likelihood and impact is low. Our results add to this a quantification of that lack of reliability, using statistical tools, and a careful explanation of all possible sources of this lack of reliability, in the method as well as in its context of use. We conclude from our quantitative analysis that reliability in risk assessment with scarce data, that has to rely on expert judgement, may not be able to reach the standards common in content analysis. It may very well be the case that it is not achievable for any method that requires a very high amount of expert knowledge.

If this is true, then experts performing such assessments retain a large responsibility for their results. Their risk assessments not only yield risk evaluations, but also justifications for these evaluations, along with best guesses of likelihood and impact. They have to communicate these limitations of their evaluations to decision-makers who use their evaluations.

Based on our results, we have identified several ways in which the RASTER method could be improved. For example, RASTER currently defines medium impact as "Partial temporary unavailability of the service for some actors"; high impact as "Long-term, but eventually repairable unavailability of the service for all actors." Participants struggled with assessing risks that, for example, led to *partial* unavailability for *all* actors. We are currently working on improvements of the scales that do away with these ambiguities, which we will validate in a follow-up experiment.

Acknowledgments. The paper benefited from early comments by Sjoert Fleurke on inter-rater reliability, and Nazim Madhavji on research goals and research design.

References

1. Bartha, P.: By Parallel Reasoning. Oxford University Press (2010)
2. Feather, M.S., Cornford, S.L.: Quantitative risk-based requirements reasoning. Requirements Engineering **8**(4), 248–265 (2003)
3. Franqueira, V.N., Tun, T.T., Yu, Y., Wieringa, R., Nuseibeh, B.: Risk and argument: a risk-based argumentation method for practical security. In: 2011 19th IEEE International Requirements Engineering Conference (RE), pp. 239–248. IEEE (2011)
4. Ghaisas, S., Rose, P., Daneva, M., Sikkel, K.: Generalizing by similarity: Lessons learnt from industrial case studies. In: 1st International Workshop on Conducting Empirical Studies in Industry (CESI), pp. 37–42 (2013)
5. Gorschek, T., Garre, P., Larsson, S., Wohlin, C.: A model for technology transfer in practice. IEEE Software **23**(6), 88–95 (2006)
6. Hallgren, K.A.: Computing inter-rater reliability for observational data: An overview and tutorial. Tutorials in Quantitative Methods for Psychology **8**(1), 23 (2012)
7. Herrmann, A.: Information need of IT risk estimation - qualitative results from experiments. In: Proceedings of the REFSQ 2011 RePriCo Workshop, pp. 72–84 (2011)
8. Herrmann, A.: REFSQ 2011 live experiment about risk-based requirements prioritization: The influence of wording and metrics. In: Proceedings of REFSQ 2011, pp. 176–194 (2011)
9. Herrmann, A., Paech, B.: Practical challenges of requirements prioritization based on risk estimation. Empirical Software Engineering **14**(6), 644–684 (2009)
10. Höst, M., Regnell, B., Wohlin, C.: Using students as subjects–a comparative study of students and professionals in lead-time impact assessment. Empirical Software Engineering **5**(3), 201–214 (2000)
11. IEC: Analysis techniques for system reliability - Procedure for failure mode and effects analysis (FMEA). International Standard 60812:2006 (2006)
12. ISO: Risk management - principles and guidelines. International Standard 31000 (2009)
13. Kerckhoffs Institute: The Kerckhoffs masters programme. http://www.kerchoffs-institute.org/ Last accessed 2014–07–10
14. Krippendorff, K.: Calculation of alpha over partitions (Private communication)
15. Krippendorff, K.: Content analysis: an introduction to its methodology. 2nd edn. Sage Publications (2004)
16. Ojameruaye, B., Bahsoon, R.: Systematic elaboration of compliance requirements using compliance debt and portfolio theory. In: Salinesi, C., van de Weerd, I. (eds.) REFSQ 2014. LNCS, vol. 8396, pp. 152–167. Springer, Heidelberg (2014)
17. Runeson, P.: Using students as experiment subjects–an analysis on graduate and freshmen student data. In: Proceedings of the 7th International Conference on Empirical Assessment in Software Engineering.-Keele University, UK, pp. 95–102. Citeseer (2003)
18. Shadish, W., Cook, T., Campbell, D.: Experimental and Quasi-Experimental Designs for Generalized Causal Inference. Houghton Mifflin Company (2002)
19. Sunstein, C.: On analogical reasoning. Harvard Law Review **106**, 741–790 (1993)
20. Svahnberg, M., Aurum, A., Wohlin, C.: Using students as subjects–an empirical evaluation. In: Proceedings of the Second ACM-IEEE International Symposium on Empirical Software Engineering and Measurement, pp. 288–290. ACM (2008)

21. Vriezekolk, E.: Testing reliability of Raster - report of experiment with Kerckhoffs students. Technical report, University of Twente (2014)
22. Vriezekolk, E., Wieringa, R., Etalle, S.: A new method to assess telecom service availability risks. In: Mendonca, D., Dugdale, J. (eds.) Proceedings of the 8th International Conference on Information Systems for Crisis Response and Management ISCRAM2011 (2011)
23. Vriezekolk, E., Wieringa, R., Etalle, S.: Design and initial validation of the Raster method for telecom service availability risk assessment. In: Rothkrantz, L., Ristvej, J., Franco, Z. (eds.) Proceedings of the 9th International Conference on Information Systems for Crisis Response and Management ISCRAM2012 (2012)
24. Vriezekolk, E.: Raster documentation website http://wwwhome.ewi.utwente.nl/~vriezekolk/Raster/
25. Wieringa, R.: Design Science Methodology for Information Systems and Software Engineering. Springer (2014)
26. Willner, P.: Methods for assessing the validity of animal models of human psychopathology. In: Boulton, A., Baker, G., Martin-Iverson, M. (eds.) Animal Models in Psychiatry, I, Neuromethods vol. 18, pp. 1–23. Humana Press (1991)
27. Yin, R.K.: Case study research: design and methods - fourth edition. Sage Publications (2009)

Supporting the Validation of Adequacy in Requirements-Based Hazard Mitigations

Bastian Tenbergen[✉], Thorsten Weyer, and Klaus Pohl

paluno – The Ruhr Institute for Software Technology,
University of Duisburg-Essen, Essen, Germany
{bastian.tenbergen,thorsten.weyer,klaus.pohl}@paluno.uni-due.de

Abstract. **[Context and motivation]** In practice, validating functional safety requirements is mainly done by means of reviews, which require large amounts of contextual information about hazards, such as safety goals or the operational conditions under which the hazard occurs. **[Question/problem]** This information is often scattered across a plethora of artifacts produced particularly during requirements engineering and safety assessment. In consequence, there is a risk that not all relevant information is considered during reviews, leading to subjective and misjudged results. **[Principal ideas/results]** In order to improve the consideration of all relevant information necessary to validate functional safety requirements, we propose a diagrammatic representation integrating all relevant contextual information. **[Contribution]** We hypothesize that reviewers are more likely to base their judgment on the relevant contextual information about the hazard, which increases objectivity and confidence in review results. To support this hypothesis, we report preliminary results of an empirical study.

Keywords: Safety requirements · Hazards · Validation · Safety assessment · Mitigation · Adequacy · Safety-critical embedded systems

1   Introduction

During the development of safety-critical embedded systems (hereinafter "systems"), particular emphasis must be placed on ensuring sufficient system safety, i.e. ensuring that during operation, the system's functionality does not lead to harm for human users, external systems, or the environment [1]. During development, safety assessment is concerned with providing objective assurance that all identified hazards are adequately mitigated, i.e. that any operational situation in which the system's functionality leads to harm is sufficiently improbable (cf. [2], [3], [4]). For this purpose, in early phases of safety assessment, initial requirements are subjected to hazard analyses (e.g., Functional Hazard Analysis, FHA [5]) to identify potential hazards and define possible safety goals (see [6], [7], [8]). Safety goals typically describe abstract conditions to be achieved [8], where the concrete implementation is left up to the developer [9]. Before such mitigations can be implemented into the system, it is necessary to refine safety goals into functional safety requirements, which document the conditions and capabilities to mitigate a hazard.

© Springer International Publishing Switzerland 2015
S.A. Fricker and K. Schneider (Eds.): REFSQ 2015, LNCS 9013, pp. 17–32, 2015.
DOI: 10.1007/978-3-319-16101-3_2

As Hatcliff et al. have recently illustrated in [10], "one of the biggest challenges in engineering certifiably safe software-dependent systems is to establish valid [functional safety] requirements," (see [10], p. 189). *Valid* in this sense means that the *right* capabilities and conditions (cf. [11]) have to be specified, which are *adequate* to mitigate the identified hazards. In accordance with [12], we prefer the term *adequacy* over *correctness* [13] in order to honor the non-binary nature of the suitability of requirements for this purpose. Inadequate safety requirements have severe repercussions for the system, as inadequacy may not only result in project delays and extraneous development cost like in non-safety-critical systems [14], but in worst case can result in death [10]. Therefore, Hatcliff et al. argue that "requirements engineering should facilitate the validation needed for [the assurance of system safety]" (see [10], p. 190).

From a requirements engineering perspective, however, therein lies a significant challenge. Validation is in practice often done through reviews, which require large amounts of contextual information about the hazard, i.e. safety goals from hazard analyses and the operational conditions under which the hazard is triggered. This contextual information is not only distributed among the requirements specification, but also across artifacts from safety assessment. Moreover, reviews often depend on the reviewers' understanding of the problem domain [15], [16] and development process [17], [18] as well as the availability and presentation of information to be reviewed [19]. In particular, the widespread use of natural language in development artifacts is seen as detrimental to validation due to inherently poor traceability and the sheer amount of documents to review [19]. Consequently, there is a risk that crucial information to conduct such a review is overlooked, leading to subjectivity and low confidence in review results as well as misjudged adequacy of functional safety requirements. Model-based representations have recently received attention to alleviate these risks by fostering artifact understandability, traceability, and communication about the contained information [20].

In this paper, we seek to support the consideration of the information relevant to review the adequacy of functional safety requirements. We propose a diagrammatic representation which integrates functional safety requirements, hazards, safety goals, and trigger conditions. We hypothesize that by using this integrated representation, more information relevant to the hazard is used during review. In the following, we introduce a running example in Section 2 and fundamental concepts in Section 3. The integrated representation is discussed in Section 4. In Section 5, we present results of a pilot study to support our hypothesis. Section 6 briefly reviews the related work and Section 7 summarizes this paper and gives an outlook on future work.

2   Running Example

We illustrate our modeling approach by means of a simplified Traffic Collision Avoidance System (TCAS) from the avionics industry. The main functionality of a TCAS is to survey the airspace surrounding the own aircraft, to warn the pilots of other aircraft in the vicinity, and to suggest collision threat resolutions. The activity diagram in Fig. 1 shows the functional requirements of the TCAS described in [21].

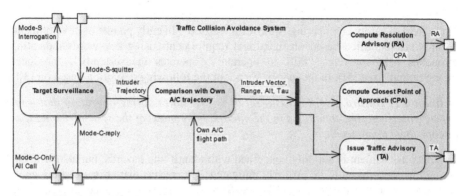

Fig. 1. Functional Requirements of the Traffic Collision Avoidance System

The TCAS consists of five basic functions: *Target Surveillance, Comparison with Own Aircraft (A/C) trajectory, Compute Closest Point of Approximation (CPA), Compute Resolution Advisory (RA),* and *Issue Traffic Advisory (TA).* The TCAS may request the own aircraft's transponder to issue a Mode-S-Interrogation, i.e. a signal which requests nearby traffic (such as passenger, cargo, or military aircraft), to reply with uniquely identifying information, course, and altitude (*Mode-S-squitter*). Traffic that is not equipped with Mode-S capability (e.g., some sport planes), will be surveyed using *Mode-C-Only All Call*, which is akin to a regular radar sweep and allows *Target Surveillance* to infer course and altitude from repeated *Mode-C-reply*. Once traffic is detected, the TCAS compares the trajectory of the possible intruder with the own aircraft's flight path and determines the intruder's altitude (*alt*), *range*, directions to the intruder (*intruder vector*), and the time to intercept (*tau*). This information is relayed to the function *Issue Traffic Advisory (TA),* which displays the information on a cockpit display, and the function *Compute Closest Point of Approach (CPA).* If this function determines that the intruder is a threat to be avoided, the resolution advisory (*RA*) is computed and audio-visually relayed to the pilots. While the TA merely informs the pilots of nearby traffic, the RA advises pilots to climb or descend at once in order to increase separation between the own aircraft and the intruder and prevent a collision. For more details on the functionality of an airworthy TCAS, see [21].

3   Fundamentals

The academic disciplines of requirements engineering and safety engineering[1] are closely related, yet, a consistent terminology between the two has not yet emerged. Therefore, in the following, the basic terms and definitions underlying our approach are introduced.

---

[1]   In the following, we use the term *safety engineering* for the academic discipline, while we use the term *safety assessment* for the activities carried out during development.

One term that is of particular importance, but differs across standards and authors in the field of safety engineering is the term "hazard". In early phases of development, hazards are identified based on functional requirements using key words indicating erroneous behavior (e.g., "fails to operate", "operates inadvertently", "produces wrong output", see [5]). In this paper, we adopt the following definition based on [3]:

Definition 1: Hazard. *A hazard is a set of system states during operation that – together with triggering conditions in the operational context of the system – could lead or contribute to an accident.*

Safety assessment is not only concerned with identifying hazards, but also with ensuring that these hazards are properly mitigated. This means that abstract safety goals conceived during early phase FHA (see Section 1) must be refined into concrete measures to mitigate a hazard. For the purpose of this paper, we will use the more general term "mitigation" and adopt the following definition based on [3]:

Definition 2: Mitigation. *A mitigation consists of a set of functional safety requirements that refine safety goals into concrete implementable measures to avoid a hazard or reduce its harmful effects.*

The term "functional safety requirement" is used in two distinct, but related ways: In some cases, a requirement is often considered safety-critical when it gives rise to a hazard (see, e.g., [2]). In contrast, especially requirements engineering literature often considers safety requirements a type of quality requirement (e.g., [22], [23]), which is in place to achieve a certain level of safety. However, safety can only be achieved when concrete functional safety requirements in the sense of [2] are in place, i.e. concrete conditions and capabilities that, when implemented entirely and without error, mitigate the hazard. To honor this dual role of requirements with regard to safety and to emphasize the functional nature of requirements documenting hazard mitigations, we hence adopt the following definitions inspired by [2]:

Definition 3: Hazard-Inducing Requirement. *A hazard-inducing requirement is a functional safety requirement in the sense of [2], which given triggering conditions in the operational context of the system, cause a hazard.*

Definition 4: Hazard-Mitigating Requirement. *A hazard-mitigating requirement is a functional safety requirement in the sense of [2], which, possibly together with other hazard-mitigating requirements, is part of a mitigation, and thus – when implemented entirely and without error – avoid a hazard or reduce its harmful effects* [2]

The relationship between these terms and concepts is visualized in Fig. 2 by means of the running example from Section 2. As can be seen, the functional requirements of the TCAS from Fig. 1 were subjected to hazard analyses. One hazard that was identified is that the resolution advisory incorporates a descent in low altitude, causing the plane to crash into the ground, potentially resulting in casualties. In this case,

---

[2] It is to note that hazard-mitigating requirements may themselves cause hazards. Therefore, safety standards (e.g., [6], [7]) demand iterative hazard identification and hazard mitigation.

"Compute Resolution Advisory" from Fig. 1 is a *hazard-inducing requirement* for the *hazard* "RA descend into terrain, causing crash". A possible *mitigation* for this would be to add requirements to achieve the safety goal "Monitor own altitude when computing RA". Following the changes indicated in the mitigation, a *hazard-mitigating requirement* was added which incorporates the barometric altitude (i.e. the altitude measured via air pressure differences): "The TCAS shall not issue DESCEND resolution advisories when barometric altitude is less than 6,000ft".

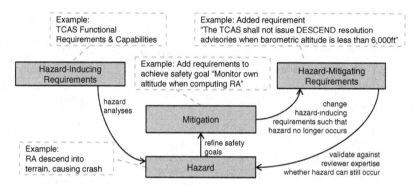

Fig. 2. The Relationship between relevant concepts illustrated through the TCAS Example

4   Supporting Validation through Hazard Relation Diagrams

In Section 4.1, we illustrate necessary development steps before validation of hazard-mitigating requirements can take place. We discuss the concepts needed to conduct validation in Section 4.2 before we introduce the ontology of an integrated representation called Hazard Relation Diagrams in Section 4.3. In Section 4.4 we present a visual notation for Hazard Relation Diagrams by means of the TCAS example.

4.1   Development Steps Prior to Modeling Hazard Relation Diagrams

In order to be able to create Hazard Relation Diagrams which support the validation of hazard-mitigating requirements, development must have progressed sufficiently far. Specifically, in accordance with safety standards (e.g., [6], [7]), the following development steps must have occurred:

Step 1: Functional Requirements Have Been Elicited and Documented by Means of Activity Diagrams. The basis of any development process is eliciting a set of system functions and documenting them by means of functional requirements. Model-based requirements documentation has been seen in the past as a promising avenue to manage complexity not just for safety-critical systems [20]. The advantage of activity diagrams like the one shown in Fig. 1 is that, in embedded systems development, they are particularly suitable to document the functional requirements [24] which are the basis for functional hazard analyses in the next step [5].

Step 2: Hazard Analyses Have Been Conducted. As outlined in Section 1, during early stages of safety assessment, the functional requirements from Step 1 are subjected to hazard analyses [3], [6], [7]. During hazard analyses, a set of hazards will be identified and documented in FHA result tables (see [5]). In particular, for each hazard, its hazard-inducing requirements, trigger conditions, and safety goals are documented. Table 1 shows an excerpt from a FHA of the function *Compute Resolution Advisory (RA)* from Fig. 1. The example hazard from Fig. 2 is shown as hazard H1.

Table 1. FHA of the *Function Compute Resolution Advisory (RA)* from Fig. 1 based on [5]

| Req. | Hazard | | Effect | Trigger Condition | Safety Goal | |
	ID	Description			ID	Description
Compute Resolution Advisory (RA)	H1	Descend into terrain	Impact with terrain, causing crash	Low altitude above ground	SG1	Monitor own current altitude while computing RA
	H2	Climb or descend into traffic trajectory	Fail to avoid intruder, causing collision	Intruder initiates climb or descend	SG2	Monitor intruder's climb or descend rate when computing RA
	H3	No RA issued		Failed to compute CPA	SG3	Announce loss of RA to crew

Step 3: For Each Hazard, Mitigations Are Defined and Documented. In this step, hazard-mitigating requirements are defined and documented which refine the safety goals from Step 2 into concrete mitigations (see, e.g., [6], [7]). This is done by modifying the existing hazard-inducing requirements. For example, the functional requirements from Fig. 1 can be modified by substituting the function *Compute Resolution Advisory (RA)* by a function *Compute Necessary Climb Rate to Achieve Separation Altitude*. Furthermore, a function *Compare with Own Altitude* could be added, which takes into account the current barometric altitude of the own aircraft and compares this information with the computed climb rate. The functional requirements can be modified further such that, if the altitude is less than the 6,000ft, the function *Compute Necessary Climb Rate to Achieve Separation Altitude* is run again with the constraint that the climb rate may not be negative, thereby preventing a descent. If the own current altitude is sufficient to allow descending or if the climb rate is positive, an *RA* can be issued.

4.2 Modeling Concepts for Validation of Hazard-Mitigating Requirements

As outlined above, the mitigations from Step 3 and the hazard-mitigating requirements subsumed therein must be adequate to ensure that the hazards from Step 2 no longer occur during operation. Validation in this sense does not only depend on the knowledge and experience of the reviewers (see, e.g., [16], [17]), but requires specific contextual information about the hazard against which the adequacy of hazard-mitigating requirements must be checked [11]:

- **Hazard.** In order to assess if hazard-mitigating requirements adequately prevent the hazard from occurring during operation (assuming the requirements have been implemented entirely and without error), it is necessary to have knowledge about what specific hazardous behavior may not occur [10]. Hence, the hazards identified during FHA must be taken into account.

- **Trigger Condition.** A hazard occurs when certain disadvantageous trigger conditions arise during operation [1]. These trigger conditions must be avoided or must be sufficiently unlikely in order for the hazard to be adequately mitigated and must hence also be taken into account.
- **Safety Goal.** Safety goals not only build the basis for safety arguments, they also specify abstract conditions, which must be achieved to mitigate a hazard [8]. Safety goals hence build the basis for mitigation and must be adequately fulfilled.
- **Mitigation.** Mitigations consist of a number of hazard-mitigating requirements, which refine one or more safety goals into concrete, implementable measures to avoid the hazard or reduce its harmful effects (see Definition 2). These must be made explicit in order for reviewers to be able to assess their adequacy.

4.3   Ontology for Hazard Relation Diagrams

In order to foster the validation of hazard-mitigating requirements, we propose integrating the concepts necessary for validation into one diagrammatic representation called Hazard Relation Diagrams. Hazard Relation Diagrams are an extension of UML/SysML activity diagrams, as shown in the ontology in Fig. 3.

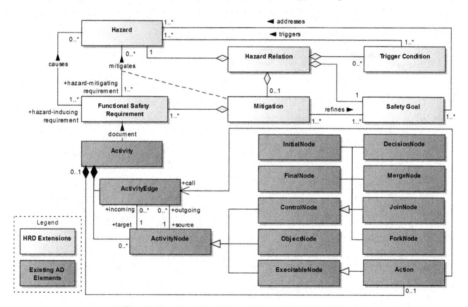

Fig. 3. Ontology for Hazard Relation Diagrams

The modeling constructs from Fig. 3 displayed in dark grey show the excerpt of the UML meta-model for activity diagrams presented in [25]. In order to document the contextual information about hazards, we have extended this excerpt by the modeling constructs and their relationships introduced in Section 4.2 (displayed in light grey). The resulting ontology shown in Fig. 3 defines the modeling foundation for Hazard Relation Diagrams. In Hazard Relation Diagrams, UML activities are used to document functional safety requirements. These may have two roles: Functional safety requirements can be *hazard-inducing requirements* (see Definition 3) or *hazard-mitigating requirements* (see Definition 4). As can be seen, the core of a Hazard Relation Diagram is a *Hazard Relation* which associates one *hazard* to its set of *trigger conditions*, *safety goals* (which specify what must be achieved to avoid the hazard), and at most one *mitigation*. A mitigation comprises a set of hazard-mitigating requirements (see Definition 2). Section 4.4 proposes a visual notation for this ontology. It is to note that functional requirements for a system are in practice not specified in a single but in multiple activity diagrams, which are furthermore not partitioned with respect to hazards. In consequence, mitigations could comprise hazard-mitigating requirements scattered across multiple diagrams.

4.4   Visual Notation for Hazard Relation Diagrams

We have defined a visual notation for the ontology from Section 4.3, which is shown in Fig. 4. In this case, the hazard mitigation has been defined entirely in a single Hazard Relation Diagram.

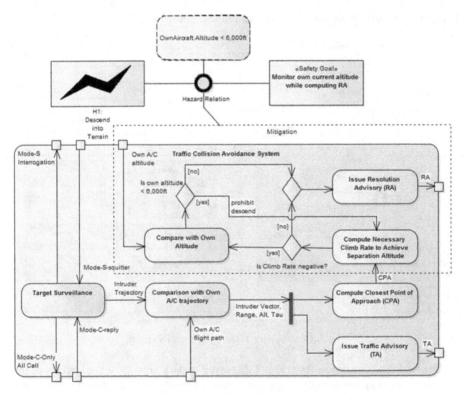

Fig. 4. Hazard Relation Diagram for Hazard H1 from Table 1

As can be seen, *Hazard Relations* are represented by a circle with a thick wall. *Safety goals* are represented as UML classes, stereotyped "<<Safety Goal>>" and containing its description. *Trigger conditions* are represented by dashed rounded rectangle shapes, similar to UML states. The *hazard-mitigating requirements* pertaining to the concrete *mitigation* are surrounded by a dashed partition, which in turn is associated with the Hazard Relation. The key idea of this representation is to focus on the dependencies between the contextual information necessary to validate hazard-mitigating requirements. Specifically, Fig. 4 shows the Hazard Relation Diagram for hazard H1 shown in Table 1. In this Hazard Relation Diagram, the hazard-mitigating requirements from Step 3 in Section 4.1 have been added to the TCAS specification from Fig. 1. As can be seen, instead of simply computing a *RA*, the TCAS will compute (positive or negative) climb rates based on the aircraft's own barometric altitude, thereby fulfilling the safety goal. During review, however, it may turn out, that the hazard-mitigating requirements contained in the mitigation are inadequate: A reviewer may notice that especially above mountains, the barometric altitude, i.e. the altitude measured through air pressure, can differ dramatically from the aircraft's altitude above ground. This means the trigger condition of the hazard is not avoided and may still cause the hazard during operation.

It is to note that in this simple example, only one mitigation for one hazard has been considered. In practice, it could be the case that there are several hazards which are addressed by the same mitigation. Similarly, multiple candidate mitigations could exist that present alternatives to address the same hazard (possibly with varying degrees of adequacy). The purpose of Hazard Relation Diagrams is to direct the attention of a reviewer on the adequacy of one mitigation with respect to one hazard. Therefore, it is necessary to review each candidate mitigation individually with respect to the corresponding hazard. In addition, it may often be the case that there are a number of hazard-mitigating requirements scattered across different activity diagrams (or, in case of large activity diagrams, in different positions within the same diagram). In this case, a Hazard Relation Diagram includes multiple mitigation partitions which surround any and all hazard-mitigating requirements that collectively make up the mitigation, thereby possibly aggregating several activity diagrams.

5   Impact of Hazard Relation Diagrams on Reviews

To investigate our hypothesis that by using Hazard Relation Diagrams, reviewers are more likely to base their adequacy judgment on contextual information about the hazard, we designed an empirical study, which is explained in Section 5.1. Section 5.2 reports on preliminary findings from a pilot test aimed to validate the study design. Section 5.3 reports on threats to validity.

5.1   Experiment Design

We designed a one-way between-subjects experiment [26]. We specifically opted for a between-subjects design because a repeated measures design would have significantly increased training overhead as participants needed instruction on a number of topics, i.e. safety engineering fundamentals, Hazard Relation Diagrams, and Functional Hazard Analysis. We therefore divided participants into treatment and control groups, where the treatment group was asked to perform a review of hazard-mitigating requirements by means of Hazard Relation Diagrams. The control group was asked to perform the review based on activity diagrams and FHA result tables.

Experimental Material. The experimental material consisted of a model-based requirements specification like the one in Fig. 1. The example system was that of an automotive Adaptive Cruise Control (ACC). The specification consisted of one activity diagram comprising five hazard-inducing requirements, for which a FHA was conducted (see Section 4.1). We specifically opted for a system from the automotive domain as in contrast to the TCAS example from Section 2, as participants are assumed to be familiar with automotive systems and hence required less instruction. The FHA yielded a total of ten hazards. Five of these hazards were randomly selected and *adequately* mitigated. To do so, for each hazard, a variation of the activity diagram was derived in which hazard-mitigating requirements have been documented that will avoid the hazard during operation. The remaining five hazards were *inadequately* mitigated. To do so, for each hazard, a variation of the activity diagram was derived in which hazard-mitigating requirements have been documented which contain semantic mistakes allowing the hazard to still occur during operation. For the treatment group, each adequate and inadequate activity diagram was extended into a corresponding Hazard Relation Diagram similar to Fig. 4.

Measurements. We measured a number of variables, including time needed to complete each review as well as the number of correctly and incorrectly assessed adequate and inadequate mitigations. In addition, we measured the self-reported confidence of a participant in the assessment for each review as well as several items from the Technology Acceptance Model 3 (TAM3, [27]) and Task Technology Fit (TTF, [28]) questionnaire. These self-report items were measured on a 5-point-Likert scale. Furthermore, participants were asked to issue a brief written rationale stating why participants assessed some mitigation as either adequate or inadequate.

Procedure. We conducted a pilot test in order to validate the experimental material as well as the experimental design. Before the pilot test, a short briefing was administered which instructed participants on how to perform the reviews. The order in which the ten hazard mitigations were presented was randomized for each participant to reduce primacy, recency, and carry-over effects [26]. In order to ensure that both participant groups reviewed approximately equally many information items, an effort was made to present only the one row from the FHA result relevant to one hazard to the control group participants at the time. The experimental procedure consisted of the following steps, as shown in Fig. 5:

- **Step 1: Introduction, Informed Consent, & Demographics.** The pilot test began with a brief introduction, where informed consent as well as demographic data was collected and participants were informed of their option to discontinue at any point.
- **Step 2: Separation into Groups.** Based on the demographic information, participants were then randomly assigned into treatment group and control group. An effort was made to distribute participants such that an equal number of participants with corresponding experience levels were assigned to each group.

- **Step 3: Instructions & "Dry Run".** Both groups were presented with instructions on how to review the experimental material once again. Furthermore, two example runs were performed in which the participants could rehearse the review task.
- **Step 4: Review of Hazard Mitigation & Self-Report Confidence.** Participants were asked to review hazard mitigations pertaining to one randomly selected hazard. Together with the subsequent step, this step was hence repeated ten times. For each randomly selected hazard, participants could review the experimental material for an indeterminate amount of time and indicate "yes" if they are of the opinion that the hazard may still occur during operation and "no" otherwise. In addition, participants were asked to rate their own confidence. Participants were able to change their assessment and self-reported confidence as often as they wished.
- **Step 5: Self-Report Rationale.** Participants were asked to state a brief reason why they chose "yes" or "no" in the previous step. This rationale was used by the experimenters to draw conclusions about the decision making process and assess what information was used to make the adequacy judgment. Participants were given the opportunity to return to the previous step and change their answer if thinking about the rationale made them change their mind. Furthermore, the experimental material along with their decision from the previous step was shown for reference.
- **Step 6: Post-Hoc Questionnaire.** Both groups were presented with several items from the TAM3 [27] and TTF [28] in order to gain data on the participants' experience during review, perceived usefulness of the respective notation, and the respective notation's ability to assist in the review process.

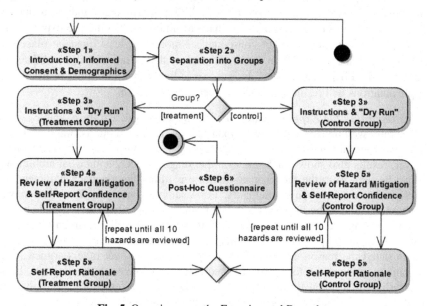

Fig. 5. Overview over the Experimental Procedure

Participants. Participants in the pilot test were researchers from the authors' research group. Most participants possessed or were in the process of obtaining a Master's or PhD degree in software engineering; only one participant already possessed a doctoral degree. All participants self-reported experience levels in requirements engineering and conceptual modeling from academic and industrial research projects and experience in static quality assurance from their daily academic work. A total of ten participants ranging from 25 to 36 years of age completed the study, yielding n = 5 per group. Albeit gender is not assumed to influence the experiment results, it is to note that no female participant participated in the study.

5.2   Preliminary Results from the Pilot Test

At the time of writing this manuscript, a detailed analysis of some of the measurements from Section 5.1 (e.g., analysis of correctness of participants' responses as well as an evaluation of TAM3 and TTF results) was still underway. Furthermore, the purpose of the pilot study was to validate the experimental design as well as the experimental material. In the following, we hence present findings regarding the suitability of design and material as well as some preliminary results on the impact of Hazard Relation Diagrams on reviews.

Insights regarding the Experimental Design. Experience from the pilot test indicates that training was a relevant concern, as participants were unfamiliar with the specific input/output-pin oriented notation of activity diagrams (cf. Fig. 1). During informal post-experimental discussions, one participant indicated that albeit he was familiar with this notation, he felt that more rigorous instruction about the specific semantics would have increased his understanding. In addition, participants indicated that the concept of *hazards* and *mitigations* were hard to understand in the pre-experimental briefing and introduction step. In consequence, more emphasis must be placed on explaining the used notations in detail. However, these findings also validate our choice of using a between-subjects design as it is likely that additional instruction in multiple notations will result in a much steeper learning curve.

Insights regarding the Experimental Material. Results show that the example system was generally well understood by participants. This confirmed our assumption that an example of the automotive industry is suitable for the purpose of the experiment. However, results also show that some example diagrams were somewhat ambiguous. This can be seen from the fact that rationales regarding the adequacy judgment differed significantly between participants. For example, one hazard mitigation was designated inadequate by the experimenters because it specified that a signal shall be considered during the operation of the ACC which is not available on any input pin. The reasons given by participants for their judgment varied considerably: Some participants stated the reason designated by the experimenters, yet others argued based on ambiguity in the execution order or based on syntactic flaws in the diagram. These findings show that albeit the example is suitable, some hazard mitigations must be revised in order to reduce variation in diagram comprehension.

Insights regarding Review Objectivity. We conducted a qualitative analysis of the rationales reported by the participants. This was done by reading the rationales given for each hazard mitigation (both adequate and inadequate) and classifying them with regard to the referenced information in the rationale. Specifically, we differentiated rationales being based on semantic properties (e.g., if a requirement is factually wrong), syntactic properties (e.g. if there was a syntactic mistake in the diagram), trigger conditions (e.g., if all trigger conditions were successfully avoided), and safety goals (e.g., if the safety goal was properly fulfilled). Results indicate that in the control group, out of a possible 50 rationales (five participants times ten hazards), 41 rationales were given. Of these 41 rationales, only six referenced trigger conditions. More strikingly, four out of these six rationales were given by the same participant. No rationale given by the control group referenced safety goals and one rationale stated syntactic mistakes. The majority of 34 stated semantic reasons. In contrast, in the treatment group, a total of 45 rationales were given. Of these 45 rationales, eleven referenced trigger conditions and six argued on the basis of safety goal fulfillment. Interestingly, all except one participant referenced trigger conditions at least once. Three rationales referenced syntactic mistakes and 25 rationales were based on semantic reasons. These results show that while the treatment group based their rationale more often on contextual information, the control group based their judgments almost entirely on activity diagram semantics, which supports our hypothesis.

5.3   Threats to Result Validity

As with any study, some threats to validity which impair the ability to draw conclusions from the experimental results remain. These are discussed in the following.

Internal and Construct Validity. One critical issue for the study at hand is the suitability of the experimental procedure and materials. To increase internal and construct validity, we conducted a pilot test. The pilot test yielded a few issues that warrant revisions to the experimental procedure and material, as outlined in Section 5.2.

Conclusion Validity. Only ten participants participated in the pilot test. In this case, such a small number of participants yield insufficient statistical power. Therefore, we emphasize that the results reported in Section 5.2 are preliminary and give mere indications in support of our hypothesis. Further testing with larger numbers of participants is expected to produce additional results and is subject of ongoing work.

External Validity. Neither participant population of the pilot nor experimental material is representative. Therefore, repetition studies with different populations and case studies with industry representatives ought to be carried out to ensure generalizability of results.

6   Related Work

A comprehensive overview over validation techniques that can be used to validate requirements is given in [29]. Albeit a number of techniques have been proposed to foster validation (e.g., inspection-like techniques [30], reading techniques [31], or prioritization techniques [32]), in practice, unstructured reviews remain the main vehicle to assess the adequacy of any type of requirement [24]. Furthermore, review techniques are typically generic in nature and support the developers in assessing requirements without particular focus on hazards. The methodology proposed in [29] improves upon this issue by combining in a joint process the identification of hazards and necessary changes to the requirements in order to mitigate the hazards. Formal quality assurance approaches such as [33], [34] place particular emphasis on ensuring that mitigations are formally correct. Such approaches focus on verifying system behavior and system design against behavioral constraints (e.g., real-time requirements).

A number of approaches propose joint safety/security processes, allowing for combined threat and hazard identification and resolution (e.g., [35], [36]). Most notably, misuse cases (e.g., [36], [37]) have been applied to safety in order to identify unsafe interaction between the system and its context and find candidate interactions to resolve them. Moreover, security threat analysis, safety hazard identification and subsequent requirements derivation have often been proposed to occur in a mutually beneficial manner (see [38] for a comprehensive comparison of techniques).

Goal-oriented (e.g., [39]) and scenario-based (e.g. [4]) approaches allow eliciting a set of safety requirements with regard to system hazards. For example, the KAOS approach [39] provides provably correct refinement patterns that can be used to refine hazard obstructions, i.e. obstructions that may arise during operation which impair safety-critical goal satisfaction, into operationalization resolving them. However, while this leads to a formally correct specification, whether or not the specification is adequate with regard to the semantic domain requires additional validation [40].

A wide range of non-goal-based formal approaches such as [35], [41], [42], [43], or [44] have been proposed. These require that at least some portion of the system has already been designed or even implemented and focus on analyzing timing constraints [44], behavioral constraints [35], design invariants [43], or event-based failure propagation [41] and can be used to deduce requirements which circumvent certain hazardous conditions. Hence, safety requirements that can be elicited using these approaches are more akin to technical constraints that become apparent during late development states rather than early phase requirements.

7   Conclusion and Outlook

In this paper, we have proposed a diagrammatic representation called Hazard Relation Diagrams which can be used during validation of hazard-mitigating functional safety requirements. Hazard Relation Diagrams combine functional requirements intended to mitigate a specific hazard with contextual information about the hazard, i.e. safety goals to be achieved and triggering conditions during operations under which the hazard occurs. We have shown how Hazard Relation Diagrams can be used during development and we have argued that using Hazard Relation Diagrams leads to increased consideration of contextual information when validating safety requirement adequacy by means of reviews. We have outlined an empirical study designed to investigate this claim and shown results from a pilot test. Findings indicate that participants using Hazard Relation Diagrams based their judgments more often on contextual information than the control group. Future work will entail revising instructional and experimental material and continue with the empirical investigation. Specifically, it is planned to carry out the experiment with students from an undergraduate requirements engineering course and students from a graduate quality assurance course.

Acknowledgments. This research was partly funded by the German Federal Ministry of Education and Research under grant number 01IS12005C. We thank Arnaud Boyer of Airbus Defence and Space for his consultation regarding TCAS and FHA and Dr. Kai Petersen, Marian Daun, and André Heuer for their feedback on the study design.

References

1. Leveson, L.: Safeware: System Safety and Computers. Addison-Wesley, Boston (1995)
2. Firesmith, D.: Engineering Safety Requirements, Safety Constraints, and Safety-Critical Requirements. J. Obj. Tech. **3**, 27–42 (2004)
3. Leveson, L.: Engineering a Safer World. MIT Press, Boston (2011)
4. Allenby, K., Kelly, T.: Deriving safety requirements using scenarios. In: Proc. 5th Int. Symp. Requirements Eng., pp. 228–235 (2001)
5. Ericson II, C.: Hazard Analysis Techniques for System Safety. Wiley, New York (2005)
6. ARP4761: Guidelines and Methods for Conducting the Safety Assessment Process on Civil Airborne Systems and Equipment. SAE International (1996)
7. ISO26262: Road Vehicles - Functional Safety. International Organization for Standardization (2011)
8. Bishop, P., Bloomfield, R., Guerra, S: The future of goal-based assurance cases. In: Proc. Workshop on Assurance Cases, pp. 390–395 (2004)
9. Whyte,D.: Moving the goalposts: the deregulation of safety in the post-piper alpha offshore oil industry. In: Proc. 47th Ann. Conf. Political Studies Assoc. of the UK (1997)
10. Hatcliff, J., Wayssyng, A., Kelly, T., Comar, C., Jones, P.: Certifiably safe software-dependent systems: challenges and directions. In: Proc. Future Softw. Eng., pp. 182–200 (2014)
11. Boehm, B.: Verifying and Validating Software Requirements and Design Specifications. IEEE Softw. **1**, 75–88 (1984)
12. Glinz, M.: Improving the quality of requirements with scenarios. In: Proc 2nd World Cong. Softw. Qual., pp. 55–60 (2000)
13. ISO/IEC 25010: Systems and software Quality Requirements and Evaluation (SQuaRE) – System and software quality models. International Organization for Standardization (2011)
14. Boehm, B.: Software Engineering Economics. Prentice Hall, Englewood Cliffs (1981)
15. Glinz, M., Fricker, S.: On Shared Understanding in Software Enigneering. Computer Sci. Res. Dev. doi:10.1007/s00450-014-0256-x
16. Gacitua, R., Ma, L., Nuseibeh, B., Piwek, P., de Roeck, A., Rouncefield, M., Sawyer, P., Willis, A., Yang, H.: Making tacit requirements explicit. In: Proc. 2nd Int. Workshop on Manag. Req. Knowl., pp. 85–88 (2009)
17. Lisagor, I., Sun, L., Kelly, T.: The illusion of method: challenges of model-based safety assessment. In: Proc. 28th Int. Syst. Safety Conf. (2010)
18. Sun, K.: Establishing Confidence in Safety Assessment Evidence. Dissertation, Univ. of York (2012)
19. Flynn, D., Warhurst, R.: An Empirical Study of the Validation Process within Requirements Determination. Inf. Syst. J. **4**, 185–212 (1994)
20. Davies, I., Green, P., Rosemann, M., Idulska, M., Gallo, S.: How do Practitioners use Conceptual Modeling in Practice? Data & Knowl. Eng. **58**, 358–380 (2006)
21. US FAA: Introduction to TCAS II, Version 7.1. (2011). http://goo.gl/EPCYzI
22. Glinz, M.: On non-functional requirements. In: Proc. IEEE Int. Requirements Eng. Conf., pp. 21–26 (2007)
23. Chung, L., Nixon, B., Yu, E., Mylopoulos, J.: Non-functional Requirements in Software Engineering. Kluwer, Boston (2000)

24. Sikora, E., Tenbergen, B., Pohl, K.: Industry Needs and Research Directions in Requirements Engineering for Embedded Systems. Requirements Eng. **17**, 57–78 (2012)

25. Störrle, H.: Semantics of UML 2.0 activities. In: Proc. IEEE Symp. Visual Lang. and Human-Centric Computing, pp.235–242 (2004)

26. Wohlin, C., Runeson, P., Höchst, M., Ohlson, M., Regnell, B., Wesslén, A.: Experimentation in Software Engineering – An Introduction. Springer, Heidelberg (2012)

27. Venkatesh, V., Bala, H.: Technology Acceptance Model 3 and a Research Agenda on Interventions. Decision Sci. **39**, 273–315 (2008)

28. Goodhue, D.: Development and Measurement Validity of a Task-Technology Fit Instrument for User Evaluations or Information Systems. Decision Sci. **29**, 105–138 (1998)

29. Denger, C.: SafeSpection — A Framework for Systematization and Customization of Software Hazard Identification by Applying Inspection Concepts. Dissertation, TU Kaiserslautern (2009)

30. Fagan, M.: Design and Code Inspections to Reduce Errors in Program Development. IBM Syst. J. **3**, 182–211 (1976)

31. Shull, F., Rus, I., Basili, V.: How Perspective-Based Reading Can Improve Requirements Inspections. IEEE Computer **33**, 73–79 (2000)

32. Li Q, Boehm B, Yang Y, Wang Q: A value-based review process for prioritizing artifacts. In: Proc. Int. Conf. Softw. Syst. Process, pp. 13–23 (2011)

33. Bitsch, F.: Safety patterns - the key to formal specification of safety requirements. In: Voges, U. (ed.) SAFECOMP 2001. LNCS, vol. 2187, pp. 176–189. Springer, Heidelberg (2001)

34. Heitmeyer, C., Kirby Jr., J., Labaw, B., Archer, M., Bharadwaj, R.: Using Abstraction and Model Checking to Detect Safety Violations in Requirements Specifications. IEEE TSE **24**, 927–948 (1998)

35. Zafar, S., Dromey, R.: Integrating safety and security requirements into design of an embedded system. In: Proc. 12th Asia-Pacific Soft. Eng. Conf., pp. 1530–1362 (2005)

36. Sindre, G.: A look at misuse cases for safety concerns. In: Ralyté, J., Brinkkemper, J., Henderson-Sellers, B. (eds.) Situational Method Engineering: Fundamentals and Experiences. IFIP, vol. 244, pp. 252–266. Springer, Heidelberg (2007)

37. Katta, V., Raspotnig, C., Karpati, P., Stålhane, T.: Requirements management in a combined process for safety and security assessments. In: Proc. Intl. Conf. on Availability, Rel., and Security, pp. 780–786 (2013)

38. Raspotnig, C., Opdahl, A.: Comparing Risk Identification Techniques for Safety and Security Requirements. J. Sys. Softw. **86**, 1124–1151 (2013)

39. van Lamsweerde, A.: Requirements Engineering: From System Goals to UML Models to Software Specifications. Wiley, New York (2009)

40. Letier, E., van Lamsweerde,A.: Deriving operational software specifications from system goals. In: Proc. Future of Softw. Eng., pp. 119–128 (2002)

41. Belli, F., Hollmann, A., Nissanke, N.: Modeling, analysis and testing of safety issues - an event-based approach and case study. In: Saglietti, F., Oster, N. (eds.) SAFECOMP 2007. LNCS, vol. 4680, pp. 276–282. Springer, Heidelberg (2007)

42. Chen, Z., Motet, G: Formalizing safety requirements using controlling automata. In: Proc. 2nd Int. Conf. Depend., pp. 81–86 (2009)

43. Guillerm, R., Sadou, N., Demmou,H.: Combining FMECA and fault trees for declining safety requirements of complex systems. In: Proc. Ann. Europ. Safety and Rel. Conf., pp. 1287–1293 (2011)

44. Hansen, K., Ravn, A., Stavridou, V.: From Safety Analysis to Software Requirements. IEEE TSE **24**, 573–584 (1998)

Metrics for the Evaluation of Feature Models in an Industrial Context: A Case Study at Opel

Olesia Oliinyk[1], Kai Petersen[2]([⊠]),
Manfred Schoelzke[3], Martin Becker[4], and Soeren Schneickert[4]

[1] Capgemini, Frankfurt, Germany
olesia.oliinyk@capgemini.com
[2] Blekinge Institute of Technology, Karlskrona, Sweden
kai.petersen@bth.se
[3] Adam Opel AG, Rüsselsheim, Germany
Manfred.Schoelzke@de.opel.com
[4] Fraunhofer Institute for Experimental Software Engineering,
Kaiserslautern, Germany
{martin.becker,soeren.schneickert}@iese.fraunhofer.de

Abstract. [**Context & motivation**] Feature models are used in product line engineering to document possible product configurations on the feature level. [**Problem**] In order to quantify the success of adopting feature modeling in practice, we need to understand the industry relevant metrics for feature model evaluation. [**Solution**] In order to identify the metrics a Goal-Question-Metric approach was used in the context of a case study conducted at Adam Opel AG. [**Contribution:**] We identified seven goals (quality criteria) we should strive for and evaluate when using feature models. Furthermore, we identified 18 sub-goals, 27 questions and corresponding metrics. The metrics were used to reflect on the feature modeling conducted at the company.

Keywords: Feature modelling · Evaluation · GQM · House of Quality · Automotive · Opel

1 Introduction

Feature models are an approach to structure the features in a Software Product Line (SPL) to show possible product configurations [1]. That is, feature models allow to represent mandatory features, alternative features, and also dependencies between them. Large organizations adopting feature modeling (FM) for the first time, or changing from one FM approach to another, would like to know whether the adoption or change was successful.

In order to quantify the success metrics are needed, which should be aligned with the goals of the organization when adopting FM. Understanding the metrics relevant for the industry is also of great benefit for researchers. The researchers can use the metrics to assess new approaches in, for example, experimental comparisons or industrial case studies.

© Springer International Publishing Switzerland 2015
S.A. Fricker and K. Schneider (Eds.): REFSQ 2015, LNCS 9013, pp. 33–48, 2015.
DOI: 10.1007/978-3-319-16101-3_3

Only few studies investigated metrics of feature models in practice, where the metrics often originate from academia, and the metrics are not properly defined [2]. Thus, this study complements the existing work determining quality goals as well as metrics to assess feature model usage, in particular from the point of view of practitioners. We were particularly interested in taking the industry perspective into account as this allows researchers to use practically relevant quality goals and metrics when evaluating feature modeling approaches empirically.

To address the research gap, we elicited the goals, questions, and associated metrics for feature modeling from the perspective of practitioners. The approaches used to guide the elicitation were the House of Quality [3] and the Goal-Question-Metric [4] approach. The context in which the elicitation took place was an automotive company (Opel AG), which was at the time of the study in the process of adopting feature modeling. The key stakeholders the for relevant perspectives were consulted. Furthermore, to illustrate the use of the metrics the feature modeling approach chosen for the company was analyzed.

The remainder of the paper is structured as follows: Section 2 presents related work. In Section 3 the research method is described. Section 4 presents the results, followed by the discussion in Section 5. Section 6 concludes the paper.

2 Related Work

Bezerra et al. [2] conducted a systematic mapping study to identify quality attributes and measures for the evaluation of feature models. A systematic mapping process [5] for study identification, inclusion as well exclusion, and analysis of studies was conducted. Furthermore, the study was very recent (available online in late 2014). Hence, it forms the basis to describe the current state of the art in the field. In total Bezerra et al. [2] identified 17 papers of interest.

Of the 17 papers only six were listed as being based on industry data. Other types of contributions were solution proposals with small application examples. No experience papers or experimental evaluations in the lab have been presented.

Seven quality characteristics (functional suitability, maintainability, usability, performance efficiency, portability, reliability, and security) were identified. Furthermore, 19 attributes were found. Many studies propose measures, but do not specify the measures (e.g. what unit of measurement to use). This leads to the need of identifying and defining measures in future work [2], for example how to measure ease of use has not been defined. Furthermore, the proposal of measures was mostly coming from the academic side, i.e. there is a need to investigate which metrics and qualities are important from the industrial perspective, in particular the automotive domain where a high degree of variability in the products exist [6,7].

3 Research Method

The research method used was case study [8] with the aim of improving the ability of the company to evaluate their feature models with metrics.

Research Questions: The following research questions were answered:

- *RQ1: Which goals should a feature model fulfill to be practically useful?* The answer to this research question highlighted the specific needs of practitioners with respect to feature models.
- *RQ2: Which questions need to be answered to assess the fulfillment of the goals, and which metrics are needed to answer the questions?* The answer to this question provided a foundation for future evaluations of feature modeling, and possibly other variability modeling approaches.

Sample/Subjects: In order to identify the goals, we elicited them from different perspectives. The high level goals were elicited from the perspective of the requirements engineer (Interviewee 2 in Table 1), validation engineer (Interviewee 4 in Table 1), and configuration and release manager (Interviewee 1 in Table 1). The interviewees have been selected with the help of the company, and were the main stakeholders to be considered essential when defining evaluation criteria for feature models.

Research Time-line: The data collection was done from May to September in 2012. The metrics for evaluation were identified in May/June, while the reflection was done in September of 2012. In the meantime it was defined how to structure the feature model. Then in June 2014 we contacted the company to learn about the progress after the initial research was completed, and learned that the approach has been implemented in multiple domains in the company, namely the E/E (Electric/Electronic) and Powertrain areas. Though, no baseline measures were available to determine the degree of improvement achieved.

Data Collection: The overall research process at the company was conducted in four steps.

1. Learn about the Company: Early in the research process we investigated the current state of capturing and documenting features at the company, including strengths, weaknesses, and improvement potential. This part was not the main goal of this study, and rather a need to get the collaboration starting; it was used to explain the context in this investigation. The five interviewees in Table 1

Table 1. Overview of Interviewees

ID	Role and description
1	**Configuration and Release manager:** This role has an overview of all the processes that are done throughout the development life-cycle, as the concerned person is responsible for providing and managing configurations for different customers and the management of software releases. The interviewee has 4 years in this role.
2	**Requirements Engineer:** The requirements engineer has insight of problems in requirements artifacts connected to SPL and feature modeling. He is responsible for collecting and documenting the requirements. The interviewee has 4 years in this role.
3	**Platform and Systems Engineer:** This interviewee is responsible for program management and has a high level view on the architecture and products of the whole system. The interviewee has 5 years
4	**Validation Engineer:** This role is connected to validation and diagnostics that is also an important part of the system. The interviewee has 2 years in this role.
5	**Subsystem Architect:** This role is responsible for modeling specific sub-system (feature) of the system. The concerned person works at another level of abstraction than platform and system engineers. That is why his view on the problem was also valuable. The interviewee has 1.5 years in this role.

were interviewed. The interviews lasted one hour, and were done individually. The interviewees were selected with the help of the company, the criteria were: expertise in the domain, which was reflected in the responsibilities the interviewees had at the company; an interest in collected measurements about feature models. The questions asked were: The current role and experience; The current situation with respect to modeling, such as how variability is documented currently, who are the main stakeholders of feature modeling (leading up to the choice who to involve in identifying the goals), and the process of adding and removing features; The challenges, e.g. in adopting, creating, and maintaining features and their relationships; Improvements, e.g. what the interviewees see as key improvements.

2. Identify the Goals, Questions, and Metrics Related to Feature Modeling: This step was done with three of the five practitioners, identified as the key stakeholders in the interviews. For the identification of the goals we used the House of Quality/Quality Function Deployment (QFD) approach [9]. The reasons for using the approach for goal identification were twofold: First, both GQM and House of quality/QFD are goal-driven approaches. That is, they complement each other well. In particular, QFD is a systematic approach of identifying an organization's goals. Second, the company has been using QFD intensively; hence using it for goal identification in this study was helping in making the goal elicitation process efficient. Each of the three stakeholders (1,2, and 4 in Table 1) filled in an empty Quality Function Deployment (QFD) template [9]. In particular they entered their statements of what they want to achieve individually, as well as the quality goals, and prioritizations. Thereafter, the results were merged, discussed, and revised. After having identified the goals, they have to be operationalized so that they can be measured. Hence, the previously involved three stakeholders answered the following questions:

 - Which sub-goals have to be fulfilled to achieve the higher level goals?
 - Which questions do you have to answer in order to determine whether the goals identified are fulfilled?
 - To answer the questions, which metrics do you need to collect?

3. Decide on the Feature Model and Pilot Implementation: Here the practitioners had to decide on how to structure the feature model, different strategies of modeling have been reflected on. The decision was made based on a structured review and discussion of the strategies. As the research question here is on how to evaluate and measure the feature model, and not on how to structure the model, Step 3 was not in the scope of this paper. After deciding on a structure, the feature model has been implemented for a particular part of the system (Park Assistant).

4. Using the Evaluation Approach/Measurements for Reflection: Based on the results of the implementation and the reflections made on the different strategies to structure the feature model, first we discussed the impact of the new feature model with interviewee 1 in Table 1 considering the identified metrics.

The discussion was documented capturing the expected impact with regard to his subjective reflections. Thereafter, the reflections on the impact were presented to all interviewees in Table 1, and their feedback was collected. The ability to reflect was facilitated by training the practitioners in product-line concepts, feature modeling, and requirements management. The duration of the training was 10 hours in the beginning of the research collaboration. Furthermore, we applied the selected strategies to model a part of their system (Park Assistant).

Analysis: We used the quality function deployment template [9] to structure the high-level goals and their priorities.

The results for capturing the goals have been structured using the Goal Question Metric (GQM) definition template and the GQM tree (cf. [4]). The GQM approach identifies the goals of the organization. In order to determine whether a goal is fulfilled one or more questions have to be answered through metrics, the questions representing what the stakeholders have to know to determine whether the goal has been achieved. The metrics should be quantifiable and need to be collected in order to answer the question. The relationships connecting goals, questions, and metrics form a tree-structure.

Furthermore, in order to evaluate whether the GQM result is sufficient to assess feature models in an industrial context, we applied it to a feature model of the Park Assistant system (see Section 4.3) at the company. The application was discussed in the case organization with the practitioners during a presentation to the working group (see interviewees 1 to 5 in Table 1) established at the company to conduct the transition to the new feature modeling approach.

4 Results

The results section is structured according to the research question. First, we present the goals with respect to feature modeling (Section 4.1). Second, sub-goals, questions to be answered to evaluate whether these are achieved, and metrics to answer the questions are presented (Section 4.2). Third, having an overview of the metrics we illustrate how the metrics were used in the company to reflect on the impact of introducing a new feature modeling approach (Section 4.3).

4.1 Goals of the Different Perspectives (RQ1)

We gathered the goal statements of the three perspectives, represented by the Configuration and Release Manager, Requirements Engineer, and Validation Engineer (see Table 1). The statements of the Requirements Engineer were:

- Wanted to *unambiguously* and *correctly* specify product variants and their associated requirements. Configurations of requirements have to be specified correctly as well. This also means that there should be a way to specify *needed types of dependencies* between features.

– Wanted an *"easy way"* to specify variation in the requirements. This should be supported by a tool. An easy way can also mean that the way of specifying requirements and variants is *precisely defined*. Everybody knows and can *understand* the process of adding variation to the requirements.
– Wanted a *uniform way* to specify variation in the requirements. The property of uniformity refers to the *standard* specified process. It should be defined how to address similar common situations during modeling. This contributes to better *understandability* and *reusability* of the variable information. This also should be more efficient, as the solutions for the most common problems are already defined, and people do not have to spend time for trying something out and then conducting rework.

The goal statements of Validation Engineer and Release Engineer were:

– Wanted an easy way to *understand* variation in the requirements. It is very important to be able to quickly understand the variations in the requirements and *dependencies* between them.
– Wanted to have *correct* and *complete* information regarding product variants and *their associated requirements*. As a user of created feature models, validation and release engineers need means to get information about product variants. This information should be *complete* and *correct* to avoid missing out important configurations or fault propagation.
– Wanted the variation information in a *uniform way*. When the same problems are similarly addressed, and in a standardized way, there is a better chance for a consistent interpretation of models across team borders.

Following the statements above, the quality goals listed below have been identified by the practitioners (see Step 2 in Section 3):

– **Understandability:** The introduction of feature model should contribute to understanding the variability of the system by giving an overview of the features, variants and dependencies. Considering Understandability as a property of a feature model means representation of information in a highly accessible way.
– **Correctness:** Model should not contradict reality. Reality here refers to requirements specification. Created Product Configurations should be a valid product.
– **Consistency (Traceability):** Traceability of variable information between artifacts, between elements of models in different levels of hierarchy
– **Completeness:** All the variants of a feature should be modeled. All the dependencies between features should be modeled. Also it should be possible to define all valid configurations.
– **Modularity:** Ideally feature models should be divided into a set of modules. The criteria for division could be different from semantics to number of dependencies.
– **Reusability:** Reusability here is used in the sense of avoiding redundant and duplicated information. Features (or parts of feature models) should not be copied, but rather used by reference.

- **Maintainability:** Evolution of feature models cannot be avoided. Though, the initial modeling should be done in the way that makes further maintaining manageable. The aspects of concern can be: no (or minimal) duplication of information, or separation of concerns.

In the following section the quality goals are further refined using GQM to be able to measure them.

4.2   Measurement Goals, Questions, and Metrics (RQ2)

The goal of GQM was to operationalize the above list of goals to become measurable, so that evaluation becomes possible. For the above goals we specified the overall goal of the performed GQM approach: *Evaluate* the Process and results of feature modeling *for the purpose of* Improvement *with respect to* Understandability, Correctness, Consistency, Completeness, Modularity, Reusability, and Maintainability *from the point of view* of the SPL engineers.

Each of the the quality goals is further discussed, stating the sub-goals associated to them, the questions to be answered in order to be able to follow up on the achievement of the sub-goals, as well as the measurements to be collected in order to answer the questions.

Understandability: The first goal G1 was to improve the understandability (see Table 2) of the system with respect to variability information.

Subgoal S1 deals with understandability during the specification of variants, and is based on expert opinion (Q1) and the time needed to specify the features (Q2). Better understandability is indicated by less time required to specify product variants.

Subgoal S2 defined understandability related to the usage of already specified product variants. How easily product variants can be captured in a subjective

Table 2. GQM Definition Template (G1: Understandability)

Subgoals	Questions	Metrics
S1: Easier specif. of product variants	Q1: Is specification of product variants easier?	Expert rating
	Q2: How efficient is spec. of product variability?	Time to specify features and their variants
S2. Understanding of product variants is better than before	Q3: In what artifacts is variability information described?	Types of artifacts
	Q4: How many artifacts is variability described in?	Number of Artifacts
	Q5: What is the time required to understand product variants?	Time required to understand
S3. Comprehensive overview of the high level features and their variants	Q6: Can features and variations be viewed at different level of abstraction?	Availability of abstraction levels for viewing
S4. Defined view according to point of interest	Q7. Can different views of the feature model be defined?	Availability of different views
S5. Dependencies between features and their variants can be analyzed	Q8. How much time is needed to understand dependencies between features?	Time to understand dependencies
	Q9. Does the approach describe possible dependencies between features and the way to express them?	Expert Based

measure. Questions Q3/Q4/Q5 focus on the speed of understanding and the amount of artifacts or documents that should be looked through to obtain relevant information. If information is understood faster than before, it is a positive indication for understandability.

Subgoal S3 stated that overall understandability will benefit if there is an option to get an overview of high level features and their variants.

Subgoal S4 contributed to better understandability by requiring the possibility of separating concerns with respect to stakeholder views. A mechanism of views for different roles and stakeholders could decrease the cognitive complexity, thus improving understandability.

Understandability is also influenced by how dependencies between features can be analyzed (see subgoal S5). Question Q8 aims to quantify the understandability of dependencies in terms of effort. An increased understanding of the relations between features improves the understandability of the system as a whole. Also to determine whether S5 is fulfilled we need to know whether the selected feature modeling approach describes relevant types of dependencies and how they should be expressed (Q9). The evaluation is done by experts based on their needs.

Correctness: Goal G2 (Table 3) was to improve the correctness of the feature model with respect to variability information. Subgoals S6, S7, S8 refined the meaning of correctness in this particular context. To answer questions Q10, Q11, Q12, Q13 inspections and review of models, product configurations and requirement specifications should be done by experts.

Consistency: One of the important problems noted was the traceability between different artifacts and descriptions of features on different abstraction levels. Goal G3 (Table 4) defines the property of consistency of variability information. G3 has been further refined with S9, S10, and S11 assuring that variability information is traceable between artifacts and levels of abstraction. Questions Q14 to Q17 should be answered by experts by evaluating the approach and the selected tools. To measure Q18 the number of identified patterns should be compared to the number of different solutions found.

Completeness: Completeness (G4, Table 5) depends both on the notation's capabilities, the selected structuring method, tool support and methodological

Table 3. GQM Definition Template (G2: Correctness)

Subgoals	Questions	Metrics
S6.Model should not contradict requirement specification(reality)	Q10. Does feature model contradict to the requirement specification documents?	Number of features that contradict specification
S7.Created Product Configurations should be a valid product	Q11. Can all valid products be described?	#valid products/ #Defined config.
	Q12. Is it possible to define a configuration that contradicts specification?	Expert based
S8.Specification of requirement variants is unambiguous	Q13. Is naming of features unambiguous?	Expert based

Table 4. GQM Definition Template (G3: Consistency)

Subgoals	Questions	Metrics
S9. Variable information should be traceable between different artifacts	Q14. Can the variability information be traceable between different artifacts?	Expert based
	Q15. Is traceability ensured by tool support?	Expert based
S10. Variable information should be traceable between different levels of abstraction	Q16. Can the variability information be traceable between different levels of abstraction?	Expert based
S11. Variability information should be described in the uniform way	Q17. Is the single notation used?	Expert based
	Q18. Are similar situations addressed similarly?	#identified patterns to #different solutions

Table 5. GQM Definition Template (G4: Completeness)

Subgoals	Questions	Metrics
S12. All possible variants of the feature should be modeled	Q19. How many variable features are described in Requirements Specification?	Number of feature variants in requirements specification
	Q20. How many variable features are modeled?	Number of variable features in the feature model
S13. All dependencies between features should be modeled	Q21. Is it possible to model all the dependencies?	Types of dependencies that should be modeled VS types of dependencies that are possible to model
	Q22. Are all the dependencies between features modeled?	Expert based

guidance provided. In this specific context completeness is examined from the two prospective (S12 and S13), i.e. modeling of all variants of a feature, and modeling of all dependencies between features. Moreover, we should divide between the possibility to model and whether everything was actually modeled. The first aspect should be ensured by the construction of the feature model. The second part is ensured by providing quality reviews of modeling results. Q19 and Q20 answer whether all the variants in the requirement specification were modeled by counting the number of variable features in both artifacts. To answer Q21 experts first should define the kinds of dependencies that are required. Afterwards, this information should be compared with the dependencies that can be technically described.

Modularity: Modularity (Table 6) is indicated by the locality of change when updating the feature model (change impact, such as adding, modifying, or removing features as well as the modification of relationships). To evaluate the locality of change three metrics should be gathered: 1) number of affected features, assertion and dependencies; 2) number of affected artifacts; 3) number of affected models. A low number of affected elements per change indicates good modularity. This measure could be used continuously to monitor the modularity, which also has a positive impact on maintainability. During the planning of features, one could also use this metric to reason on possible impacts of modularity when making structural decisions with regard to the model.

Reusability: Reusability is evaluated through reduced redundancy (Table 7) can be achieved by: uniformity of information representation (S15) and no duplicate information (S16). S16 is a property of the technical abilities of the used FM approach. To determine if the redundancy level is decreased, the number of copied parts of the feature model should be compared.

Maintainability: It is assumed that subgoals S10, S11, S14, as well as S16 contribute positively to maintainability (Table 8). In addition, we identified S17 and S18 as additional subgoals contributing to improved maintainability. Maintainability highly depends on work separation capabilities (S17). If the parts of the model can be maintained in parallel than the approach (together with its technical realization) is more efficient with respect to maintainability.

In summary, we identified 18 sub-goals, 27 questions and metrics answering the questions. In the following section the sub-goals, questions, and metrics were used to discuss the impact of the new feature model with the practitioners (see Section 3).

4.3   Application at the Company

Context - Introducing a New Feature Modeling Approach at Opel: At the time of the study, the company stored requirements specifications in MS word. No explicitly documented statement about common and variable parts of the requirements were available. Instead, they were spread across different systems (calibration files, use cases, and other artifacts).

Based on the reflections made by the practitioners (Table 1) the company chose multiple SPLs with modular feature models, which is illustrated in Figure 1. On the top level three SPLs are distinguished, and each SPL had different abstraction levels, L1 (customer features), L2 (subsystem features) and L3 (component functions).

The feature model itself was decomposed based on the functional architecture (e.g. the feature active safety is broken down into park assistant and cruise control).

The approach was supported by tools, as these were essential to record the information and keep track of traceability. The tools used at the time of study (May to September 2012) and the tool chain implemented later (since July 2014) are represented in Figure 2. The tool GEARS was used to structure the variability of the product-line and its features. DOORS was linked to GEARS and contained the requirements.

Table 6. GQM Definition Template (G5:Modularity)

Subgoals	Questions	Metrics
S14. Minimize impact of the change	Q23. Is impact of the change local?	Affected features, assertions, dependencies; affected artifacts and models

Table 7. GQM Definition Template (G6: Reusability)

Subgoals	Questions	Metrics
S16. Variability information should not be duplicated	Q24. Are there copied pieces of feature model?	Number of copied parts of feature model

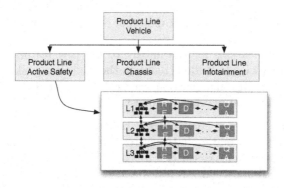

Fig. 1. SPL structure chosen by the company

This brief summary of the feature modeling approach evaluated with the existing measures should serve as a basis to understand the reflections provided in the following section.

Table 8. GQM Definition Template (G7: Maintainability)

Subgoals	Questions	Metrics
S17. Unnecessary complexity should be avoided	Q25. Can the patterns of unnecessary complexity be defined?	Types of complexities
	Q26. Are the defined complexities avoided?	Number of redundant complexities
S18. Separation of work should be allowed	Q27. Can model be used and developed in parallel?	Expert based

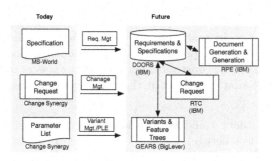

Fig. 2. Tool support used at the company

Evaluation of the Approach Using the Proposed Goals, Information Needs, and Metrics: In Section 4.1 the measurement goals of the stakeholders with respect to feature modeling were defined. With the defined questions and metrics (see Section 4.2) the results of the feature modeling adoption could be evaluated and compared with the previous situation. Some metrics were not possible to collect, as they require data collected over a longitudinal time period. Furthermore, to answer specific questions (e.g. *"Q2. How efficient is the specification of product variability?"*) historical data or data from controlled experiments was needed.

Nevertheless, indications for the impact of the new feature modeling approach at the company could be detected with the identified goals, questions, and metrics. Furthermore, if some questions cannot be answered, this indicates that some information may be relevant to collect.

Understandability: The first goal that was defined was to improve understandability of variability information in the system. With respect to making the specification of product variance easier (Q1 in Table 2) the practitioners agreed that providing clear decomposition strategies and tools has a positive effect. With respect to artifacts containing variability (Q3) and the number of artifacts (Q4), after the adoption of feature modeling variability information was consolidated in one place. Variability information was now described in feature models and profiles in GEARS tools. Information was not only in the single place, but was also in a structured form. Earlier it had been spread throughout the artifacts, such as requirements specifications, use cases, and additional documents. The exact time that was needed to understand product variants (Q5) was unknown. However, the functionality that was provided by the selected tool allowed a faster overview of what products are available and what are their differences. This was achieved by profiles and matrix combination, while before the practitioners relied on knowledge when studying the documentation in Word and Excel.

Correctness: The correctness of the specification of variability information cannot be assured automatically. A quality review process needed to be established and followed to assure correctness of modeling and product assembly. Whether the feature model contradicts the requirements specification (Q10) should only be answered after the modeling was done. But we can assume that defining rules of decomposition that correspond to the structure of requirement specifications may help to avoid confusion. By construction all valid products could be described (Q11). That is, products could be assembled from profiles of feature declarations. If all the constraints between features were modeled than any configuration (Q12) that contradicted these requirements was not possible to create.

Consistency: Consistency could be to a large extent ensured by construction. With the use of bridges between GEARS and other systems variability could be traced (Q14) from feature models to requirement specifications, design artifacts, test specification, which was supported by tools (Q15). Traceability between levels of abstraction (Q16) was not defined by the tool used, only traceability in the form of "requires" relationships could be established. A single notation (Q17) was used for feature modeling. Q18 was related to whether similar situations were addressed consistently. If the feature owners adhere to the strategies identified, then the situations could be addressed similarly. The formal metric for this question was the ratio between number of identified patterns and number of different solutions found.

Completeness: Another goal was the improvement of completeness with respect to variability information. The variability information was not structured and dependencies were not modeled explicitly. Nevertheless, we at least need to show that the information was as complete as it had been before the approach was introduced. To measure completeness, the model was to be further populated incrementally. Overall, checking completeness was supported by using a tool (GEARS), and making dependencies explicit (e.g. a feature without a link to requirements become visible).

Modularity: The proposed decomposition approach concentrated on the quality of modularity. By construction, the system was decomposed into SPLs and modular feature models. If the modularity was better than before cannot be evaluated, as there was no baseline defined with respect to the measures (see Q23).

Redundancy Reduction: The approach defined the concept of creating the context variability model with all the global variations. Feature declarations should be imported to other SPLs, in case they were referenced from more than one PL or asset. The tool allowed access to these features by reference from any other model or SPL. This assured that no information was reused by copying (Q24).

Maintainability: During the selection of structures and decomposition strategies the maintainability issue was taken into consideration. First of all monolithic feature models were discarded, because of too high complexity and consequently poor maintainability. Furthermore, better understandability also favored maintainability. The approach should define the complexity types, in the form of situations and patterns (Q25). A set of decomposition strategies were defined with the company. Whether complexities being present earlier were avoided (Q26) cannot be conclusively answered at this point in time, as this required to populate the model with more features and SPLs. The decomposition of the system into multi-SPLs supported parallel work (Q27) and separation of concerns. The improvement tendency of maintainability of variability information could be noticed. To get a precise comparison, a baseline should be established; measurements should be taken and compared to evaluate the magnitude of the improvement.

Overall, the measurements helped the company in the reflection and with that to decide to go ahead with the implementation beyond the Park Assistant, as many potential benefits could be identified. Opel implemented the solution as of July 2014 in parts of their organization (E/E (Electric/Electronic) and Powertrain areas). Hence, the measures have at least partially supported the technology transfer.

5   Discussion

The following reflections should be highlighted based on the results obtained.

Ability to Analyze: The questions identified for the goals can be quantified objectively in some cases (in particular metrics related to complexity [10,11]), but in other cases subjective measures have to be obtained. In case of expert based assessments, we propose to utilize categorical variables that allow practitioners to provide a rating based on their perception, as long as no well defined and countable unit of analysis exists. It would be a worthwhile effort to develop automated measurements for as many questions as possible that are based on well defined units of measures. These should be derived from the artifact itself, and from the configuration management system. The metrics proposed allowed the practitioners to reflect on feature modeling in their context, and supported them in their decision making.

Quality Goals and Their Relationships: We identified seven quality goals that were considered relevant by the practitioners. As pointed out by a few studies these quality goals are related (cause-effect and correlation) [12,13]. In order to achieve the quality goals that are important from a usage perspective (e.g. maintaining, reusing features and communicating features) we have to understand how these are impacted by other factors (e.g. completeness, correctness, and consistency). This research provides an initial input to such an analysis as it highlights what is important from an industrial perspective, and how this relates to individual quality goals.

Scope of the Metrics: The metrics were derived focusing on the feature model itself. Though, when the company wanted to reflect on entities beyond that (the ability of the modeling language and the modeling process including tool usage), the effect of those on the metrics could also be reflected upon. Thus, the metrics may have relevance for reflecting on feature modeling approaches as a whole (including modeling language, and modeling process) as these are not independent from the feature model.

Comparison with Related Work: When comparing with the classification suggested by Bezerra et al. [2] with the classifications provided by industry it is noteworthy that there were differences. As an example, level of abstraction contributes to understandability, and hence is linked to that goal, while it is classified differently in the literature (under the attribute "Variability" in the context of "Maintenance"). Given that the elicitation of metrics was goal-driven, the classification allows to directly identify what the main purpose of the metric is by linking it to the goals through the questions. Hence, the rational for decision making based on the measure also becomes more explicit.

The systematic literature study and our study performed at Opel have similarities, but also clear differences. Many goals and metrics are shared (e.g. maintainability, usability, complexity). Though, unique metrics have been identified in this study. Im particular, usability has only been defined as a goal/attribute in the literature [14], but no metrics were be proposed. Furthermore, the availability of views as a categorical measure has been added, as well as the goal of completeness. On the other hand, the mapping study identified measures that could be automatically derived from the feature model, and hence do not depend on expert opinion. As an example, solutions exist to assess the consistency of feature models [14]. Hence, the industry and academic view complement each other well. Given that there has been an overlap between the findings in our study and the literature, this indicates that the results are not unique to the feature modeling notation used. This is important as this means that feature models based on different notations could be compared using the metrics.

Validity Threats: External validity: The research has been conducted in one organization, which is a threat to external generalizability. Hence, potentially more goals, questions, and metrics may be relevant in other contexts. As this may be the case, this work builds a foundation to add questions to existing quality goals, and also define new metrics to better support the questions. A number of different contexts should be studied, as we did not find any existing studies with the main focus being on eliciting evaluation criteria for feature models from an industrial point of view. For example, studies should be conducted in a quite different domain, such as information systems. Also, within the company only few persons have been considered to provide the goals. These were the persons that would have been considered if the company would conduct the planning of collecting metrics, and hence represented the relevant stakeholders in that context. That is, the results were generalizable within the company.

Construct validity: Furthermore, there is always a threat that practitioners misunderstand the questions in the interviews, and researchers misinterpret the answers. Hence, all results were presented to the practitioners (member checking), confirming that we captured what they intended to communicate.

Internal validity: To what degree the metrics defined contributed to the actual adoption of the feature modeling structure presented here cannot be determined. What can be said is that it led to insightful discussions and reflections in the decision making process.

Reliability: To increase the reliability of the study, multiple research have been involved in the process of designing and reflecting on the data collected, reducing the threat of researcher bias.

6   Conclusion

Only few studies provided a set of measures and the goals to collect them in order to evaluate feature models. In order to address this research gap, we investigated the goals of feature model usage, the related information needs (questions) to assess whether the goals are fulfilled. Furthermore, metrics have been identified to answer the questions. The research has been conducted in collaboration with Opel. As a result, we identified seven quality goals/criteria, 18 sub-goals, 27 questions and the corresponding metrics. The application of the identified quality criteria to evaluate a new approach of applying feature modeling at the company demonstrated the ability to reflect on the impact of the new approach regarding goal fulfillment.

In future work, we encourage the research community to further extend the inventory of measurements presented here by studying further organizations.

References

1. Kang, K.C., Cohen, S.G., Hess, J.A., Novak, W.E., Peterson, A.S.: Feature-oriented domain analysis (foda) feasibility study. Technical report, DTIC Document (1990)
2. Bezerra, C.I.M., Andrade, R.M.C., Monteiro, J.M.S.: Measures for quality evaluation of feature models. In: Schaefer, I., Stamelos, I. (eds.) ICSR 2015. LNCS, vol. 8919, pp. 282–297. Springer, Heidelberg (2014)
3. Madu, C.N.: House of quality (QFD) in a minute: Quality function deployment. Chi Publishers Inc. (2006)
4. Caldiera, V.R.B.G., Rombach, H.D.: The goal question metric approach. Encyclopedia of Software Engineering 2(1994), 528–532 (1994)
5. Petersen, K., Feldt, R., Mujtaba, S., Mattsson, M.: Systematic mapping studies in software engineering. In: 12th International Conference on Evaluation and Assessment in Software Engineering, vol. 17, p. 1 (2008)
6. Sundmark, D., Petersen, K., Larsson, S.: An exploratory case study of testing in an automotive electrical system release process. In: 2011 6th IEEE International Symposium on Industrial Embedded Systems (SIES), Vasteras, Sweden, June 15–17, 2011, pp. 166–175 (2011)
7. Thiel, S., Hein, A.: Modeling and using product line variability in automotive systems. IEEE Software 19(4), 66–72 (2002)
8. Runeson, P., Höst, M.: Guidelines for conducting and reporting case study research in software engineering. Empirical Software Engineering 14(2), 131–164 (2009)
9. Pascoe, N.: Reliability Technology: Principles and Practice of Failure Prevention in Electronic Systems. John Wiley & Sons (2011)
10. Pohl, R., Stricker, V., Pohl, K.: Measuring the structural complexity of feature models. In: 2013 IEEE/ACM 28th International Conference on Automated Software Engineering (ASE), pp. 454–464. IEEE (2013)
11. Štuikys, V., Damaševicius, R.: Measuring complexity of domain models represented by feature diagrams. Information Technology and Control 38(3), 179–187 (2009)
12. Bagheri, E., Gasevic, D.: Assessing the maintainability of software product line feature models using structural metrics. Software Quality Journal 19(3), 579–612 (2011)
13. Berger, T., Guo, J.: Towards system analysis with variability model metrics. In: The Eighth International Workshop on Variability Modelling of Software-intensive Systems, VaMoS 2014, p. 23 (2014)
14. Benavides, D., Segura, S., Cortés, A.R.: Automated analysis of feature models 20 years later: A literature review. Inf. Syst. 35(6), 615–636 (2010)

Modeling and Reasoning About Information Quality Requirements

Mohamad Gharib(⊠) and Paolo Giorgini

University of Trento - DISI, 38123 Povo, Trento, Italy
{gharib,paolo.giorgini}@disi.unitn.it

Abstract. [**Context and motivation**] Information Quality (IQ) is a key success factor for the efficient performance of any system, and it becomes a vital issue for critical systems, where low-quality information may lead to disasters. [**Question/problem**] Despite this, most of the Requirements Engineering frameworks focus on "what" and "where" information is required, but not on the *intention* behind its use, which is essential to define the required level of quality that information should meets. [**Principal ideas/results**] In this paper, we propose a novel conceptual framework for modeling and reasoning about IQ at requirements level. [**Contribution**] The proposed framework is based on the secure Tropos methodology and extends it with the required concepts for modeling and analyzing IQ requirements since the early phases of software development. A running example concerning a U.S stock market crash (the May 6, 2010 Flash Crash) is used throughout the paper.

Keywords: Information quality · Requirements engineering · Modeling · Reasoning

1 Introduction

Information Quality (IQ) is a key success factor for organizations, since depending on low-quality information may cause severe consequences [1], or even disasters in the case of critical systems. Despite its importance, IQ is often loosely defined, or simply ignored [2]. In general, quality has been defined as "fitness for use" [3], or as in [4] the conformance to specifications, i.e., meeting or exceeding consumer expectations. For example, consider a stock market investor who uses his laptop to trade some securities, the level of IQ required by him concerning his trades is not the same as the IQ level required by a main stock market (e.g., NYSE, NASDAQ) that is responsible of managing thousands of trades in milliseconds simultaneously. In the first case, low-quality information can be accepted to a certain level, while in the second case it may result in a financial disaster (e.g., stock market crash, or at least loses of millions of dollars).

Several techniques for dealing with IQ have been proposed in the literature (e.g., integrity constraints). However, they mainly focus on technical aspects of IQ and do not solve problems that may rise at organizational or social levels.

© Springer International Publishing Switzerland 2015
S.A. Fricker and K. Schneider (Eds.): REFSQ 2015, LNCS 9013, pp. 49–64, 2015.
DOI: 10.1007/978-3-319-16101-3_4

More specifically, these techniques do not satisfy the needs of complex systems these days, such as socio-technical systems [5], where humans and organizations are integral part of the system along with the technical elements such as software and hardware (e.g., healthcare systems, smart cities, etc.). In these cases, requirements about IQ should be extended to a socio-technical analysis.

For example, the Flash Crash was not caused by a mere technical failure, but it was due to undetected vulnerabilities that manifested themselves in the interactions of the stock market systems that led to a failure in overall socio-technical system [6]. In particular, several reasons contributed to the Flash Crash were caused by socio-technical IQ related issues. For instance, according to [7] some traders intentionally provide falsified information. Others continue trading during the crash by forwarding their orders to the markets that did not halt their trading activities due to lake of coordination among the markets, where the lack of coordination resulted also from IQ related vulnerabilities. However, such failures could be avoided if the IQ requirements of the system-to-be were captured properly during the system design.

We advocate that answering "why" IQ related mechanisms and solutions are needed, and not just "what" mechanisms and solutions are needed to solve IQ related problems can provide a better understanding of stakeholders' needs that are beyond IQ requirements. The framework presented in this paper uses a Goal-Oriented Requirements Engineering (GORE) approach. Among the several GORE approaches offered in the literature (e.g., KAOS [8], i^* [9]), we adopted secure Tropos [10] as a baseline for our framework. Secure Tropos introduces primitives for modeling actors of the system along with their goals that can be refined through And/ Or decompositions. Resources are used to represent both physical and informational entities that are needed/ produced for/by the achievement of goals[1].

Moreover, it provides the notion of delegation to model the transfer of responsibilities among actors, and it adopts the notion of trust and distrust to capture the expectations of actors in one another. Our framework extends the conceptual framework of secure Tropos by providing the required concepts and constructs for modeling and reasoning about IQ requirements. It allows the analyst to identify clearly "why" a certain level of IQ is needed and not only "what" and "where" such information is needed.

The paper is organized as follows; Section (§2) describes our motivating example, while in Section (§3) we discuss the different problems related to capturing IQ. In Section (§4), we outline the limitation in secure Tropos for dealing with IQ, and then we propose the required extensions. In Section (§5), we present the reasoning techniques that our framework offers. Section (§6) implement and evaluates the proposed framework. Section (§7) presents the related work. Finally, we conclude and discuss the future work at Section (§8).

---

[1] NeededBy/ producedBy have been proposed in SI* [11], which is an extension of secure Tropos.

2   Motivating Example

Our motivating example concerns the May 6, 2010 U.S stock Flash Crash. Based on [7], we can identify several stakeholders including: *stock investors* are individuals or companies, who have a main goal of "making profit from trading securities", which is And decomposed into two goals "Produce sell/buy orders for targeted securities" and "Analyze the market for targeted securities", where the first goal produces "Inv- Sell/ Buy orders". While last goal is Or decomposed into two goals, "Analyze the market depending on trader" that needs to consume "Tr trading suggestions" (provided by a *trader*), and "Analyze the market depending on consulting firm" that needs to consume "Con trading suggestion" (provided by a *consulting firm*).

Stock traders are persons or companies involved in trading securities in *stock markets* with a main goal of "making profit by trading securities" either for their own sake or by trading on behalf of their *investors*. According to [7], *traders* can be classified under several categories, including: *Fundamental traders*: are able to either buy or sell a significant number of securities with a low trading frequency rate; *Market Makers*: facilitate trading on a particular security in the market, and they are able to trade large number of securities; *High-Frequency Traders (HFTs)*: are able to trade with very high trading frequency; *Small traders*: trade small amount of securities with very low trading frequency.

While *stock markets* are places where *traders* gather and trade securities, which have a main goal of "Make profit by facilitating the trades among stock traders" that is And decomposed into two sub goals "Manage order matching among traders" and "Ensure fair and stable trading environment", where the first intend to receive, match and perform orders from different *traders*, and the last is responsible of halting or slowing down the trading frequency in order to stabilize the trading environment when necessary. Moreover, *consulting firms* are firms specialized for providing professional advices concerning financial securities for a fee to *traders* and *investors*. Finally, *credit assessment ratings firms* are firms with a main objective of providing assessments of the credit worthiness of companies' securities, i.e., such firms help *traders* in deciding how risky it is to invest money in a certain security.

Figure 1 shows a portion of the secure Tropos representation of the stock market structure. Secure Tropos is able to capture the social/ organizational context of the system, but it does not offer primitives to model needs about IQ, i.e., it deals with information whether they are available or not and who is responsible about their delivery. For example, secure Tropos is able to model information provision between investors and traders, and between traders and markets. Yet, it does not provide concepts that enable to analyze the quality of the provided information (e.g., information is not falsified).

3   The Problem of Capturing Information Quality

The quality of information can be defined based on its "fitness for use", yet such definition does not explicitly capture the "fitness for use" for "what" and the

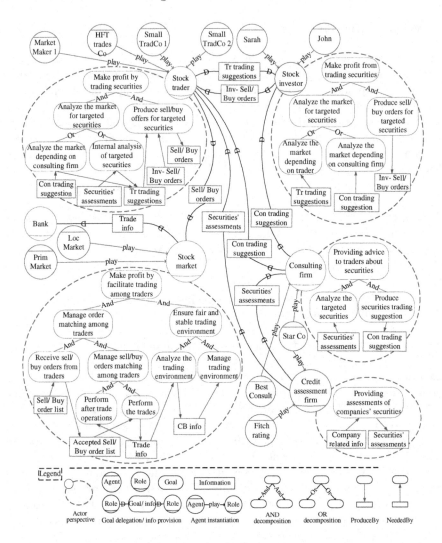

Fig. 1. A partial goal model concerning the U.S stock market structure

"fitness for use" of "who", which is very important when information has several
stakeholders, who may require different (might be conflicting) quality needs. In
other words, existing definitions of IQ miss the clear semantics to capture IQ
requirements taking into consideration the different needs of their stakeholders.
Without having such semantics, it is hard to determine whether IQ "fits for use"
or not.

Several IQ models and approaches have been propose [12,13], yet most of
them propose holistic methods for analyzing IQ (one size fits all), i.e., they
consider a user-centric view [14] without taking into consideration the relation
between information and its different purposes of usage. For example, in Figure 1

we can see a stock investor (e.g., John) who wants to send a sell/ buy order to a stock market through a stock trader. This simple scenario raises several questions: Do all the stakeholders (e.g., investor, trader, and stock market) have the same purpose of information usage? How we can define the quality of the buy/sell order based on the different purposes of usage? Should the stakeholders require the same quality of information? If not, how do their needs differ? Actually, the previous questions cannot be properly answered without defining a clear semantics among information, its quality, and the stakeholders' intended purposes of information usage.

Moreover, IQ can be characterized by different dimensions [15, 16] that can be used to analyze IQ, including: accuracy, completeness, consistency, timeliness, accessibility, trustworthiness, etc. However, we only focus on 4 IQ dimensions, namely: accuracy, completeness, timeliness and consistency, since they enable us to address the main IQ related problems that we consider in this paper. These dimensions can be defined as follows: **Accuracy**: means that information should be true or error free with respect to some known, designated or measured value[16]; **Completeness**: means that all parts of information should be available [15, 16]; **Timeliness**: means to which extent information is valid in term of time [13]; **Consistency**: means that multiple records of the same information should be the same across time [16].

After defining these dimensions, we need to ask several more questions, should the different stakeholders consider the same IQ dimensions for analyzing IQ? Do they analyze these dimensions by the same ways? For instance, can information validity be analyzed by an actor who requires to send information, and an actor who requires to receive (read) information by the same way? The same question can be asked about other dimensions. Moreover, most of the proposed IQ approaches ignore the social/ intentional aspects that underlie some of these IQ dimensions. Ignoring such aspects during the system design leaves the system open to different kinds of vulnerabilities that might lead to various kinds of failures (e.g., actors might intentionally provide falsified information).

4   Extending Secure Tropos with IQ Modeling Concepts

In order to capture the stakeholders' requirements concerning IQ, secure Tropos modeling language needs to be able to provide the required concepts and constructs for capturing the stakeholders' different purposes of information usage, and the different relations among the purposes of usage and IQ in terms of its dimensions. From this perspective, we extend the conceptual model of secure Tropos to accommodate the following concepts:

Goal-Information Interrelation: we need to provide the required concepts to capture the different relations between goals and information usage. Thus, we extend secure Tropos by introducing 3 different concepts that are able to capture such relations: **Produces**: indicates that an information item can be created by achieving the goal that is responsible of its creation process; **Reads**: indicates that a goal consume an information item. Reads relation can be strictly classified under, *Optional*: indicates that information is not required for the goal achievement, i.e., the goal can be achieved even such information has not been provided; *Required*: indicates that information is required for the goal achievement, i.e., the goal cannot be achieved without reading such information; **Sends**: indicates that the goal achievement depends on transferring an information item under predefined criteria to a specific destination.

For instance, in Figure 2 achieving the goal "Perform the trades" produces "Trade information". While the goal "Receive sell/buy orders from traders" optionally reads the "Sell/ Buy orders", since the goal will be achieved regardless the number of the received sell/buy orders. While goal "Manage trading environment" requires to read "Prim (CB) information". At the other hand, the goal "Perform after sale operations" needs to send "Trade info" to the bank that is responsible of finalizing the trade. These different relations are shown in Figure 2 as edges labeled with *produce*, *send[destination][time]*, *read [R]* and *read [O]* to represent produces, sends, optionally read and required read respectively.

Information Accuracy: we need to provide the required concepts that enable for deciding whether information is accurate or not from different perspectives of its stakeholders. In particular, information accuracy can be analyzed based on its production process, since information can be seen as product [17,18], and many of the product quality concepts can be applied to it. In other words, the accuracy of information is highly affected by its source [19]. Moreover, actors might depend on one another for information to be provided, and the provision process might also affect the accuracy of the provided information. More specifically, the accuracy of information can be analyzed based on its sources along with its provision process.

We rely on the notion of trust that has been proposed in secure Tropos to analyze the accuracy of information based on its source (trusted/distrusted source) and provision process (trusted /distrusted provision). For instance, a *market* considers information it receives as accurate, if a trust relation holds between the *market* and information source (e.g., *trader*), and if information has been provided through a trusted provision. The same can be applied to information that is send, i.e., send information is accurate from the perspective of its sender, if a trusted provision holds between the sender and the final destination of information. Such relation is shown in Figure 2 as edges labeled with T concerning the provided information ("Inv sell/buy orders") between John (*investor* and Small market Co1 (*stock market*).

Information Completeness: we need to provide the required concepts to capture the relation between an information item and its sub-items (if any), which enables us to decide whether information is complete or not. Thus, we rely on the *"part of"* concept that has been used in several areas (e.g., natural language, conceptual modeling, etc.) to model such relation. For example, one main reason of the Flash Crash was the effect of uncoordinated Circuit Breaker (CBs) [2] among the *markets*. Such failure resulted due to depending on incomplete information by *markets* for their CBs.

---

[2] Techniques used to slow or halt trading to prevent a potential market crash [20].

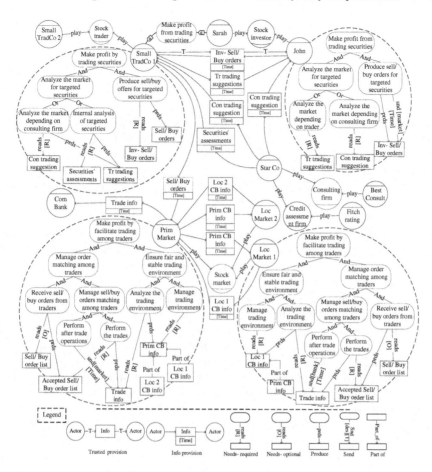

Fig. 2. A partial goal model of the Flash Crash extended with IQ related constructs

In particular, in stock market domain, the same securities might be traded in different markets. Thus, in order to coordinate the CBs between the different markets that trade the same security, markets should be aware of one another's activities concerning any change in the trading frequency. In other words, when a market halts or go into slow trading mode for a specific security, all markets trading the same security should do the same. This can be solved, if we consider the CB information that is used by any market is composed of the local CB information along with the CB information produced by the primary listing market (the main market for trading the security) to guarantee that all markets who trade the same securities will coordinate properly. Similarly, the main listing market should be aware of the different activities performed by the markets that trade the same securities. Such relation is shown in Figure 2 as edges labeled with *part of* between "Prim CB info" and both its sub-items "Loc 1 CB info" and "Loc 2 CB info".

Information Timeliness: we need to provide the required concepts that enable for deciding whether information is valid in terms of time for its purpose of usage. Since we already defined two different relations between goals and information that can be affected by time aspects (e.g., reads and sends), we need to define validity that fits the needs of each of these relations: **Read timeliness**: in order to ensure that information is valid for read, we need to ensure that its value in the system represents its value in the real world. Lack of timeliness leads to situations where the value of information in the system does not accurately reflects its value in the real world [15]. We rely on Ballou et al. [17] work to analyze the timeliness of read information depending on its *currency (age)*: the time interval between information creation (or update) to its usage time [13,14]) and its *volatility*: the change rate of information value [14], i.e., information is not valid, if its currency (age) is bigger than its volatility interval, otherwise it is valid. **Send timeliness:** is used to capture the validity of information at its destination in terms of time. In particular, it defines the allowed amount of time for information to reach its destination, which should be defined based on the needs of information sender.

Referring to Figure 2, the achievement of the goal "Perform after trade operations" is subject to the validity of "Trade info" at its destination [bank], if information was not valid (delivered within the defined send [time]), the goal will not be achieved. While the achievement of the *investor's* goal "Analyze the market depending on trader" depends on the validity of "Tr trading suggestions" that is provided by the *trader*, in order for such information to be valid, it should be provided within a time interval that is less than its volatility change rate.

Information Consistency: we need to provide the required concepts that enable for deciding whether information is consistent or not. Information consistency arises only when there are multiple records of the same information that are being used by several actors for *interdependent purposes (goals)*, and we call such actors as *interdependent readers*. While if actors use the same information for independent purposes, inconsistency will not be an issue since the actors' activities are independent. For example, CBs information should be consistent among all markets trade the same securities, since they depend on such information for controlling their trading environment (*interdependent purposes*). While the same information can be used by a *trader* for analyzing the market and make trading decision, yet inconsistency between information a *trader* use and the ones used by markets will not produce any problem, since such information is used for independent purposes.

Moreover, consistency in our work is a time related aspect [3], i.e., the value of information among its different *interdependent readers* might became inconsistent due to time related aspects. In particular, to ensure consistency among the different *interdependent readers*, we need to ensure that these readers depend on the same information value in term of time. Thus, we define *read-time* that indicates the actual read time by information *reader*, and by ensuring that all *interdependent readers* have the same *read-time*, we can ensure the consistency of

---

[3] In [14] consistency was used to refer to "representational consistency" of information.

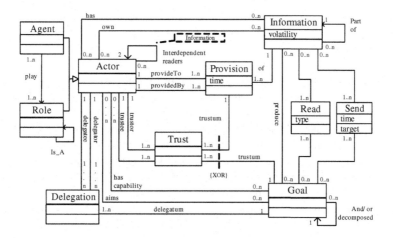

Fig. 3. Meta-model shows the extended version of secure Tropos

such information. Considering our example, to ensure the consistency of "Prime CB info" among all markets that trade the same security (*interdependent readers*), all of them should have the same *read-time*, i.e., such information should be provided to them in a way that ensure all of them have the same *read-time*

Actor's Social Interactions and IQ: actors' interactions might affect IQ. Thus, we need to provide the required concepts to capture how such interactions might affect IQ in terms of its different dimensions. To get better understanding of actors interactions and IQ, we depend on what is called *information provenances* [21], which enable us to capture any information that helps in determining the history of information, starting from its source and the process by which it has been delivered to its destination [22]. In particular, information accuracy can be influenced by the trustworthiness of information production along with its provision process (discussed earlier). At the other hand, information validity can also be affected by actors' interactions. More specifically, *information provision time* [4] might influence information read and send timeliness, or even information consistency, if there are *interdependent readers* of the provided information.

All new concepts along with the basic constructs of secure Tropos modeling language are structured in terms of a meta-model shown in Figure 3, where we identify: an actor that covers two concepts (role and agent) and it may have a set of goals, it aims for. Further, an actor may have the related capabilities for the achievement of goals. Actors can be interdependent readers concerning an information item. Moreover, actors may delegate goals to one another, and they may have information, and provides it to one another, where provision has a provision time. Goals can be and / or-decomposed, and they may produce, read, or send information; yet read can be descried by its type (e.g., optional or required), while send can be described by its both time and target attributes.

---

[4] The amount of time information transmission requires from source to destination (referred to as the transmission time in networks).

Information has volatility rate that is used to determine its validity. Further, information can be composed of several information items (*part of*). Finally, actors may trust one another for goal achievement / information provision.

Finally, in order to allow for the systematic design of the system-to-be, we propose an engineering methodology that underlies our extended framework. The process consists of several steps that should be followed by designers during the system design; each of these steps is described as follows: (1) *Actors modeling*: in which the stockholders of the system are identified and modeled along with their objectives, entitlements and capabilities; (2) *Goals modeling*: the stockholders' goals are identified and refined through And/ Or-decomposition, and based on the actors capabilities some goals might be delegated; (3) *Goals-information relations*: the different relations among goals and information are identified and modeled along with their IQ needs; (4) *Information modeling*: information is modeled, the structure of composed information is identified, and then information provisions are modeled; (5) *Trust modeling*: trust among actors concerning goal delegation, information producing and provisions are modeled; (6) *Analyzing the model*: at this step the model is analyzed to verify whether all the stakeholders' requirements are achieved or not; (7) *Refining the model*: during the model analysis, if some of the stockholders' requirements were not achieved, the analysis try to find solution for such issues at this step.

5   Reasoning about Information Quality Requirements

We use Datalog [23] to formalize the concepts that have been introduced, along with the required axioms[5]. Further, we define a set of properties (shown in Table 1) that are used to verify the correctness and consistency of the requirements model. These properties define constraints that the designers should consider during the system design.

Pro1: states that the model should not include any goal that is not *achieved* from the perspective of the actor, who has it within its objectives. Goal might not be achieved due to several reasons (e.g., delegating the goal with no trust chain, missing required information, IQ related issues, etc.). For example, in Figure 2 *Sarah* delegates the goal "making profit by trading securities" with no trust chain to *Small tradCom 1*. This leaves *Sarah* with no guarantee that its goal will be achieved.

Pro2-3: state that the model should not include any information unavailability related issues, i.e., senders / required readers should have the information they intend to send/ read. Note that capturing information availability is not a trivial task. For example, in Figure 2 if the goal "Perform the trades" was not achieved, information "Trade info" will not be produced, and both goals "Perform after trades operations" and "Analyzing the trading environment" will not be achieved as well, since both of them require to read "Trade info". Similarly, the effect of not achieving these goals might be propagated to other goals.

---

[5] The formalization of the concepts and axioms is omitted due to space limitation, yet they can be found in [24].

Table 1. Properties of the design

Pro1	:- objective(A, G), not achieved(A, G)
Pro2	:- sender(T, A, B, I), not has(A, I, Z)
Pro3	:- reader(required, P, A, I), not has(A, I, Z)
Pro4	:- reader(T, P, A, I), producer(B, I), prvChain(T, B, A, I), not trust(A, B, *produce*, I)
Pro5	:- reader(T, P, A, I), producer(B, I), prvChain(T, B, A, I), not trustChain(B, A, *provide*, I)
Pro6	:- reader(T, P, A, I), not complete(A, I)
Pro7	:- reader(T, P, A, I), prvChain(T, B, A, I), producer(B, I), info(I, V), not $T < V$
Pro8	:- reader(T, P, A, I), interdependent_reader(A, I), not consistent(A, I)
Pro9	:- sender(T, A, B, I), prvChain(T, A, B, I), not trustChain(A, B, *provide*, I)
Pro10	:- sender(T, A, B, I), prvChain(Tr, A, B, I), not $Tr < T$
Pro11	:- play(A, $R1$), play(A, $R2$), conflicting_roles($R1$, $R2$)

Pro4-5: state that the model should not include any inaccurate information from the perspectives of their readers, i.e., there is no guarantee that information is accurate for read, if it was not produced by a trusted source (**Pro4**), and provided by a trusted provision (**Pro5**). Intentionally falsified information (inaccurate from the reader's perspective) was a main reason that led to the Flash Crash. In particular, some HFTs were accused of providing orders that last very short time, which make them unavailable to most traders, in order to affect the prices of some securities before starting their real trades. Moreover, Market Makers and in order to fulfill their obligations concerning providing sell / buy orders in the market, provide what is called "stub quotes", which are orders with prices far away from the current market values. Such orders can also be considered as falsified information; since they are orders were not intended to be performed. During the Flash Crash, over 98% of all trades were executed at prices within 10% of their values before the crash because of "stub quotes" [7]. In particular, if orders that have been provided by both HFTs and Market Makers were not considered accurate for granted, such crash might be avoided.

Pro6: states that the model should not include information that is not complete from the perspective of its reader. For example, after considering "Prim CB info" as a part of "loc 1 CBs information", Pro6 is able to detect and notify the designer, if *Loc market 1* does not has "Prim CB info". While **Pro7** states that the model should not include any invalid information from the perspective of their readers. For example, a *Small Tradco 1* provides *John* with "Tr trading suggestions". Yet, the delivery time should not exceed the information volatility rate to be considered as valid. Otherwise, *John* may make wrong trading decisions based on invalid (old) information. **Pro8** states that the model should not include any *interdependent reader* that depend on inconsistent information. Considering our example, *Loc Market 1* and *Loc Market 2* are *interdependent readers* concerning "Prim CB info". Pro8 is able to detect and notify the designer, if "Prim CB info" is not consistent between them.

Pro9: states that the model should not include inaccurate information at their destination from the perspective of their senders, i.e., a trusted provision chain should hold between the sender and its intended destination. While **Pro10** states that the model should not include invalid information at their destination from

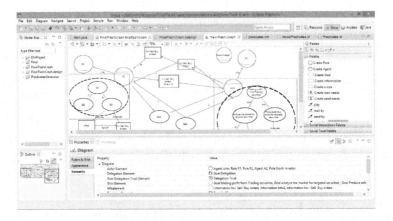

Fig. 4. Screenshot of the Eclipse-based tool

the perspective of their senders. For example, *stock traders* (e.g., *Small TradCo 1*) have different quality of services, including the time that orders require to reach the market (milliseconds might be very important). If a *Small TradCo 1* is not able to provide the time to market that *John* requires, his orders will not be considered as valid from his perspectives.

Pro11: states that the model should not include any agent that plays conflicting roles. In particular, it is used to ensure that the model manage separation of duties among its actors to avoid any conflict of interest that leaves the system open to various kinds of vulnerability. In Figure 2, we can see that *Star Co* is playing both roles "Credit assessment firm" and "Consulting firm". Such situation should be avoided, since we cannot trust a company for providing accurate consulting information considering the securities of a company that they get paid to perform their credit assessment. Pro11 can be used to capture similar situations, such as firms that provide accounting services along with auditing services to the same company (e.g., The Enron scandal [25]).

6 Implementation and Evaluation

Evaluation is an important aspect of any research proposal; it aims to demonstrate the utility, quality, and efficacy of a design artifact. Our framework belongs to the design science area. Hevner et al. [26] classify evaluation methods in design science under five categories: observational, analytical, experimental, testing, and descriptive. We aim to evaluate the applicability and effectiveness of our framework depending on simulation method (experimental), i.e., execute artifact with artificial data. To this end, we developed a prototype implementation of our framework[6] (Figure 4) to test its applicability and effectiveness for modeling and reasoning about IQ requirements. In what follows, we briefly describe the

---

[6] http://mohamadgharib.wordpress.com/

prototype, discuss its applicability and effectiveness over the Flash Crash scenario, and then test the scalability of its reasoning support.

Implementation: our prototype consist of 3 main parts: (1) a graphical user interface (GUI) developed using Sirius[7], which enable designers for drawing the model diagram by drag-and-drop modeling elements from palettes, and enables for specifying the properties of these elements along with their interrelations; (2) model-to-text transformation that supports the translating of the graphical models into Datalog formal specifications depending on Acceleo[8]; (3) automated reasoning support (DLV system[9]) takes the Datalog specification that resulted from translating the graphical model along with the reasoning axioms, and then verifies the correctness and completeness of the requirements model against the properties of the design.

Applicability and Effectiveness: is reported in [24], where the framework was applied to a big-size Flash Crash scenario. In particular, the Crash was not due to an attack or illegal activities, but some actors exploit undetected vulnerability in the system organizational structure, i.e., the design of the system allows for such failure. The framework was able to identify these vulnerabilities along with other vulnerability that manifested themselves in actors' interactions, or resulted from their conflict of interests. For example, a *stock market* considers information received from both *Market Marker 1* and *HFT trades Co* as inaccurate information, since no trust in information production holds between them at one hand and the *market* at the other. Moreover, information produced by *Star Co* is considered as inaccurate, since it plays two conflicting roles ("Credit assessment firm" and "Consulting firm"), i.e., we cannot trust a company for providing accurate consulting information considering the securities of a company that they get paid to perform their credit assessment.

At the other hand, "Prim CB info", "Loc 1 CBs info" and "Loc 2 CBs info" were identified as incomplete information from the perspectives of their readers, since they miss some sub parts related to the purpose of their use. Finally, it was able to detect the inconsistency concerning "Prim CB info" to both "Local market 1" and "Local market 1".

Experiments on Scalability: to test the scalability of the reasoning technique, we expanded the model shown in Figure 2 by increasing the number of its modeling elements from 188 to 1316 through 7 steps, and investigate the reasoning execution time at each step by repeating the reasoning execution 7 times, discarding the fastest and slowest ones, and then computed the average execution time of the rest. We have performed the experiment on laptop computer, Intel(R) core(TM) i3- 3227U CPU@ 190 GHz, 4GB RAM, OS Window 8, 64-bit. The result is shown in Figure 5, and it is easy to note that the relation between the size of the model (the number of its nodes) and the execution time is not exponential, i.e., the reasoning techniques should work fine with real world scenarios, where there sizes probably will not exceed the sizes we considered.

---

[7] https://projects.eclipse.org/projects/modeling.sirius
[8] https://projects.eclipse.org/projects/modeling.m2t.acceleo
[9] http://www.dlvsystem.com/dlv/

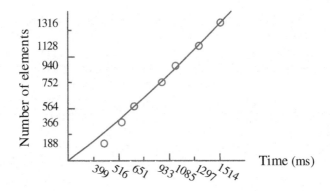

Fig. 5. Scalability results with increasing the number of modeling elements

7   Related Work

A large body of literature has focused on IQ. For instance, Wand and Wang [15] propose a theoretical approach to define information quality. While Wang and Strong [27] introduce the Total Data Quality Management (TDQM) methodology, with a main purpose of delivering high quality information products (IP) to information consumers. Ballou et al. [17] presented the Information Manufacturing System (IMS), which can be used to determine data quality in terms of timeliness, quality, etc. Moreover, Shankaranarayanan et al. [18] propose Information Product Map (IP-MAP) that extends IMS and offers a formal modeling method for creating Information Product (IP). Relying on the IP-MAP framework, Scannapieco et al. [28] introduce IP-UML approach that combines both data analysis and process analysis in order to assess the quality of data. However, all the previously mentioned approaches were not designed to capture neither the organizational nor the social aspects of the system-to-be, which are very important aspects in current complex systems.

At the other hand, RE community did not appropriately support modeling nor analyzing IQ requirements (e.g., [8,9]). For example, abuse frame [29] addresses integrity (IQ related aspect) related issues (modification) by preventing unauthorized actors from modifying information, or prevent authorized actors from doing unauthorized modifications. While, UMLsec [30] proposes concepts for modeling information integrity as a constraint, which can restrict unwanted modifications of information, but IQ can still be compromised in several other ways. Finally, secure Tropos [10] / SI* [11] seem to be sufficient to capture the functional, privacy and trust requirements of system-to-be, yet they provide no primitives for explicitly capturing IQ requirements.

8   Conclusions and Future Work

In this paper, we highlighted the importance of capturing IQ needs from the early phase of system development. Moreover, we argued that IQ is not only a technical problem, but it is also an organizational and social issue, and we showed how IQ can be analyzed depending on its different dimensions. Furthermore, we proposed framework that enables system designers to capture IQ requirements in terms of their different dimensions; taking into consideration the intended purposes of information usage. Further, it provides the required analysis techniques to verify whether the stakeholders' IQ requirements are met or not, and it enables designers to refine the system design until such requirements are met.

For the future work, we intend to extend the considered IQ dimensions (e.g., trustworthiness, believability, etc.), and investigate in more details the different interrelations among them. Further, information production process needs more investigation, since information might be produced depending on other information item(s), and the quality of the produced information might be influenced by the quality of the information item(s) that has/have been used in the production process. Moreover, we aim to enrich the trust analysis that is used to assess information accuracy by relying on actors' internal structure (their intentions, desires, etc.), which allows to clearly identify "why" an actor should trust/ distrust another one for information accuracy. Finally, we plan to provide IQ policy specification language, which can be used to clearly identify the permitted, forbidden and obligated action to be carried out by the actors of the systems.

Acknowledgment. This research was partially supported by the ERC advanced grant 267856, "Lucretius: Foundations for Software Evolution", http://www.lucretius.eu/.

References

1. Redman, T.: Improve data quality for competitive advantage. Sloan Management Review **36**, 99 (1995)
2. Fox, C., Levitin, A., Redman, T.: The notion of data and its quality dimensions. Information Processing & Management **30**(1), 9–19 (1994)
3. Juran, J., Gryna, F., Bingham, R.: Quality control handbook. McGraw-Hill, New York (1979)
4. Reeves, C.A., Bednar, D.A.: Defining quality: alternatives and implications. Academy of Management Review **19**(3), 419–445 (1994)
5. Emery, F., Trist, E.: Socio-technical systems. management sciences, models and techniques. churchman cw et al. (1960)
6. Sommerville, I., Cliff, D., Calinescu, R., Keen, J., Kelly, T., Kwiatkowska, M., Mcdermid, J., Paige, R.: Large-scale complex it systems. Communications of the ACM **55**(7), 71–77 (2012)
7. Kirilenko, A., Kyle, A.S., Samadi, M., Tuzun, T.: The flash crash: The impact of high frequency trading on an electronic market. Manuscript, U of Maryland (2011)
8. Dardenne, A., Van Lamsweerde, A., Fickas, S.: Goal-directed requirements acquisition. Science of Computer Programming **20**(1–2), 3–50 (1993)
9. Yu, E.S.K.: Modelling strategic relationships for process reengineering. PhD thesis, University of Toronto (1995)
10. Mouratidis, H., Giorgini, P.: Secure tropos: A security-oriented extension of the tropos methodology. International Journal of Software Engineering and Knowledge Engineering **17**(2), 285–309 (2007)

11. Zannone, N.: A requirements engineering methodology for trust, security, and privacy. PhD thesis, PhD thesis, University of Trento (2006)
12. Liu, L., Chi, L.: Evolutional data quality: A theory-specific view. In: IQ, pp. 292–304 (2002)
13. Pipino, L.L., Lee, Y.W., Wang, R.Y.: Data quality assessment. Communications of the ACM **45**(4), 211–218 (2002)
14. Wang, R., Strong, D.: Beyond accuracy: What data quality means to data consumers. Journal of Management Information Systems, 5–33 (1996)
15. Wand, Y., Wang, R.: Anchoring data quality dimensions in ontological foundations. Communications of the ACM **39**(11), 86–95 (1996)
16. Bovee, M., Srivastava, R.P., Mak, B.: A conceptual framework and belief-function approach to assessing overall information quality. International Journal of Intelligent Systems **18**(1), 51–74 (2003)
17. Ballou, D., Wang, R., Pazer, H., Tayi, G.K.: Modeling information manufacturing systems to determine information product quality. Management Science **44**(4), 462–484 (1998)
18. Shankaranarayanan, G., Wang, R., Ziad, M.: Ip-map: Representing the manufacture of an information product. In: Proceedings of the 2000 Conference on Information Quality, pp. 1–16 (2000)
19. Dragoni, A.: A model for belief revision in a multi-agent environment. Decentralized AI **3**, 103–112 (1992)
20. Gomber, Peter, Haferkorn, Martin, Lutat, Marco, Zimmermann, Kai: The Effect of Single-Stock Circuit Breakers on the Quality of Fragmented Markets. In: Rabhi, Fethi A., Gomber, Peter (eds.) FinanceCom 2012. LNBIP, vol. 135, pp. 71–87. Springer, Heidelberg (2013)
21. Simmhan, Y.L., Plale, B., Gannon, D.: A survey of data provenance in e-science. ACM Sigmod Record **34**(3), 31–36 (2005)
22. Sebastian-Coleman, L.: Measuring Data Quality for Ongoing Improvement: A Data Quality Assessment Framework. Newnes (2012)
23. Abiteboul, S., Hull, R., Vianu, V.: Foundations of databases, Citeseer (1995)
24. Gharib, M., Giorgini, P.: Detecting Conflicts in Information Quality Requirements: the May 6, 2010 Flash Crash, Università dgli studi di Trento (2014)
25. Petrick, J.A., Scherer, R.F.: The enron scandal and the neglect of management integrity capacity. American Journal of Business **18**(1), 37–50 (2003)
26. Hevner, A.R., March, S.T., Park, J., Ram, S.: Design science in information systems research. MIS Quarterly **28**(1), 75–105 (2004)
27. Wang, R.: A product perspective on total data quality management. Communications of the ACM **41**(2), 58–65 (1998)
28. Scannapieco, M., Pernici, B., Pierce, E.: Ip-uml: Towards a methodology for quality improvement based on the ip-map framework. In: 7th Int'l Conf. on Information Quality (ICIQ 2002), pp. 8–10 (2002)
29. Lin, L., Nuseibeh, B., Ince, D., Jackson, M., Moffett, J.: Introducing abuse frames for analysing security requirements (2003)
30. Jürjens, J.: Secure systems development with UML. Springer-Verlag New York Incorporated (2005)

Detecting and Correcting Outdated Requirements in Function-Centered Engineering of Embedded Systems

Marian Daun[✉], Thorsten Weyer, and Klaus Pohl

paluno – The Ruhr Institute for Software Technology,
University of Duisburg-Essen, Essen, Germany
{marian.daun,thorsten.weyer,klaus.pohl}@paluno.uni-due.de

Abstract. **[Context and Motivation]** In function-centered engineering of embedded systems, changes of stakeholder intentions are often directly incorporated in the functional design without updating the behavioral requirements accordingly. **[Question/Problem]** As a consequence, it is likely that the behavioral requirements of the system become outdated over the course of the engineering process. **[Principal Ideas/Results]** We propose a validation technique that aids the requirements engineer in detecting and correcting outdated behavioral requirements. The approach relies on a dedicated review model that represents a consolidated view of behavioral requirements and functional design. **[Contributions]** This paper reports on a semi-automated approach and presents first experimental results showing that our technique can significantly aid the requirements engineer in the detection and correction of outdated behavioral requirements.

Keywords: Behavioral requirements · Functional design · Function-centered engineering · Embedded systems · Outdated requirements · Review model

1 Introduction

It is widely acknowledged that the correctness of a system is determined by whether the system fulfills its requirements specification or not (cf. e.g., [1]). The correctness of the system presupposes that the requirements specification and each requirement therein satisfy certain quality criteria (cf. [2], [3]). The quality criteria correctness and completeness directly refer to how the requirements reflect the current consolidated stakeholder intentions with respect to the system to be built.

Stakeholder intentions change during the lifecycle of the system, e.g., due to external influences or due to knowledge gain (cf. [4], [5]). Accordingly, the ISO/IEC/IEEE Std. 29148 [6] requires that the requirements engineer has to guarantee that each requirement within a requirements specification "is currently applicable and has not been made obsolete by the passage of time". Thus, requirements must be kept up-to-date throughout the whole development lifespan.

In the development of embedded systems, function-centered engineering is a commonly used approach to cope with complexity of systems' software functions and their interdependencies (cf. [7]). Function-centered engineering focusses on the

© Springer International Publishing Switzerland 2015
S.A. Fricker and K. Schneider (Eds.): REFSQ 2015, LNCS 9013, pp. 65–80, 2015.
DOI: 10.1007/978-3-319-16101-3_5

functional design as the central development artifact throughout the whole engineering process. The functional design specifies the functions to be implemented, their hierarchical structure, and the intended behavior of each function (cf. [8], [9]). Moreover, it defines the interactions and dependencies between the functions in such a way that the interplay between different functions fulfills the behavioral properties documented in the behavioral requirements. Functionality is explicitly designed to emerge from functional interplay, e.g., to optimize the function deployment and minimize the number of expensive electronic control units, to avoid redundancies affecting maintainability, and to foster function re-use.

As the functional design serves as basis for most subsequent development artifacts, an effort is made in industrial practice to keep the functional design up-to-date. Hence, behavioral properties resulting from changed stakeholder intentions are directly incorporated into the functional design. In contrast, the behavioral requirements are not updated right away and become outdated. Outdated behavioral requirements have many negative consequences for the engineering process since, for instance, test cases cannot be derived properly, automated verification techniques are not applicable, and contractual agreements are violated.

1.1   Motivating Example

We use example steps of a function-centered engineering process for a lane keeping support (LKS) to illustrate how behavioral requirements could get outdated:

Step 1 - Elicit Stakeholder Intentions: Stakeholder discussions reveal that the LKS shall prohibit unintended lane exits. To this end, the stakeholders intend to use automated braking, as also used by the electronic stability program. Using automated braking interventions to keep the lane means that minor braking interventions to one single brake are initiated to force a change in the car's driving direction, thereby steering away from the road marking. In case only minor corrections are needed, the stakeholders favor automated interventions to the steering wheel in order to ensure a high degree of driving comfort. In contrast to braking interventions, steering interventions (which are provided by the electronic steering support) are perceived more smoothly by the driver, if at all.

Step 2 - Document Behavioral Requirements: The behavioral requirements are documented according to the stakeholder intentions by means of message sequence charts (MSC) – a commonly used language in the automotive domain (cf. [10]). Fig. 1(a) depicts the resulting MSC: Based on the aberration of 'yawrate' and 'lane angle', either the 'steering angle' is corrected, or braking is used to perform the intervention. Note that the system to be built is depicted as a black instance within the MSC while entities and values from the context are depicted as grey instances.

Step 3 - Specify the Functional Design: Based on the behavioral requirements, the function 'Steering Intervention' is specified. Fig. 1(b) shows a simplified version of the functional design of the LKS. Note that dashed lines indicate context functions.

Step 4 - Deploy the Functions to Hardware Parts: The engineers decide to deploy the function 'Steering Intervention' to two different control units. This is due to the fact that automated interventions to the brakes are provided by the electronic stability program, and automated interventions to the steering wheel by the electronic steering support.

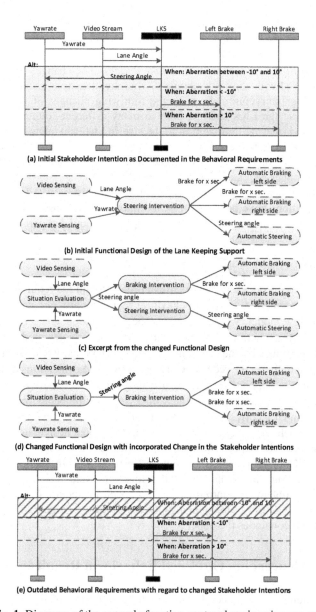

(a) Initial Stakeholder Intention as Documented in the Behavioral Requirements

(b) Initial Functional Design of the Lane Keeping Support

(c) Excerpt from the changed Functional Design

(d) Changed Functional Design with incorporated Change in the Stakeholder Intentions

(e) Outdated Behavioral Requirements with regard to changed Stakeholder Intentions

Fig. 1. Diagrams of the example function-centered engineering process

Step 5 - Update the Functional Design: The functional design is updated so that the function 'Steering Intervention' is split into two separate functions. One function is named 'Steering Intervention' as well and shall provide the functionality necessary for automated steering interventions to the steering wheel, the other function is named 'Braking Intervention' and provides the necessary functionality for automated steering interventions to the brakes. The interplay between the both functions is designed in such a way that the behavioral requirements are still fulfilled. Fig. 1(c) depicts an excerpt from the updated functional design. Now, the function 'Braking Intervention' can be deployed to the electronic stability program, and the function 'Steering Intervention' to the electronic steering support.

Step 6 - Negotiate Changes with the Stakeholders: The changes to the functional design are discussed with some stakeholders. Thereby, the explicit specification of the function 'Steering Intervention' leads to the following changes of the stakeholders' intentions: Because the LKS shall be sold in many different countries, it is noticed that the automated steering intervention to the steering wheel violates some countries' local laws. Hence, stakeholders agree that this function shall no longer be provided. As a result, the functional design is changed, and a steering intervention to the steering wheel is no longer provided. This is shown in Fig. 1(d).

Result of this process: The behavioral requirements are outdated. Changes of the stakeholder intentions have been incorporated into the functional design, but not into the corresponding requirements. Fig. 1(e) highlights the outdated parts from Fig. 1(a).

1.2   Contribution and Outline

In this paper, we propose a semi-automatic approach to aid the requirements engineer in detecting and correcting outdated behavioral requirements. The approach relies on a dedicated review model, which integrates the information given in the behavioral requirements and the functional design in one model. The review model is created in a fully automated manner by means of model-transformations, while the actual review is performed manually by the requirements engineer. First evaluations of the approach have shown that its application can significantly improve effectiveness, efficiency, reviewer's confidence, and supportiveness of reviews of the behavioral requirements. In addition, a manually corrected version of the review model can be used to automatically update the behavioral requirements and the functional design consistently.

The remainder of the paper is structured as follows: We describe the specific problem and its implications for possible solutions in Section 2. In Section 3, we give an overview of existing approaches from the literature, and discuss their suitability for the specific problem. We introduce our approach in Section 4. Section 5 reports on the major findings from the evaluation of our approach in an experimental setup. Finally, Section 6 concludes the paper.

2   Cases Concerning Outdated Behavioral Requirements

Stakeholder intentions, behavioral requirements, and functional design may differ with regard to particular behavioral properties in the course of function-centered engineering processes. This section introduces the different cases that lead to outdated behavioral requirements, as well as cases that need to be distinguished explicitly from cases that go along with outdated behavioral requirements. If only cases with outdated behavioral requirements were considered, a defect in the functional design that concerns a behavioral property could, for instance, lead to the wrong conclusion that the behavioral requirements must be updated, whereas the behavioral requirements are up-to-date and the functional design has to be corrected.

Table 1 shows relevant combinations of characteristics of stakeholder intentions, behavioral requirements and the functional design with respect to a particular behavioral property. For example, case ③ has to be read as: A behavioral property is desired by the stakeholders (✓), but is neither documented in the behavioral requirements (✗) nor in the functional design (✗), while both the behavioral requirements and the functional design are consistent with respect to that particular behavioral property though the behavioral requirements are outdated.

Table 1. Cases Concerning Outdated Behavioral Requirements

ID	A Particular Behavioral System Property is...			Consistency of Behavioral Req. and Funct. Design	Up-to-dateness of Behavioral Requirements
	... desired by the Stakeholder Intentions	... documented in the Behavioral Requirements	... specified in the Functional Design		
①	✓ (yes)	✓ (yes)	✓ (yes)	consistent	up-to-date
②	✓ (yes)	✓ (yes)	✗ (no)	inconsistent	up-to-date
③	✓ (yes)	✗ (no)	✗ (no)	consistent	outdated
④	✓ (yes)	✗ (no)	✓ (yes)	inconsistent	outdated
⑤	✗ (no)	✓ (yes)	✓ (yes)	consistent	outdated
⑥	✗ (no)	✓ (yes)	✗ (no)	inconsistent	outdated
⑦	✗ (no)	✗ (no)	✓ (yes)	inconsistent	up-to-date

In the following, we elaborate on exemplary situations showing that all of the cases from Table 1 can arise during function-centered engineering:

Situation 1 - Correct Behavioral Requirements lead to a correct Functional Design (case ①): The stakeholder intentions are elicited and a specific behavioral property is documented in the behavioral requirements. This property is also correctly realized in the functional design. The behavioral requirements and the functional design are consistent and the behavioral requirements are up-to-date. This situation represents an ideal situation during development.

Situation 2 - Changed Stakeholder Intentions lead to outdated Behavioral Requirements (cases ④ and ⑥): Stakeholder intentions change. These changes are incorporated in the functional design, but not in the behavioral requirements. As a consequence, the behavioral requirements are outdated, and behavioral requirements and functional design are inconsistent. This situation has already been described in the motivating example of Section 1.1.

Situation 3 - Requirements are forgotten or realized erroneously (cases ② and ⑦): Stakeholder intentions are elicited and documented in the behavioral requirements, but the corresponding behavioral property is not specified in the functional design. For example, stakeholders desire that the driver is informed when the LKS detects the need for a steering intervention. The stakeholders hence want an optical warning through cockpit instruments. During development of the functional design this requirement is either forgotten (case ②), or has been realized erroneously: Instead of an optical warning an acoustic warning is specified in the functional design. This results in cases ② and ⑦, since the optical warning is missing, and the acoustic warning is neither documented in the behavioral requirements nor desired by the stakeholders.

Situation 4 - Unnecessary Behavior is specified within the Functional Design (case ⑦):
Unnecessary behavioral properties are realized which do not result from the documented requirements and are not intended by the stakeholders. For example, the engineers decide to implement both, the optical warning and the undesired acoustical warning. This situation is an example of case ⑦ and is commonly known as gold plating. It is to note that in this situation the realization itself could change stakeholder intentions, resulting in desiring both warning mechanisms, which would then lead to case ④.

Situation 5 - Changed Stakeholder Intentions remain unnoticed (cases ③ or ⑤):
Assuming that the decision regarding in which target countries the LKS shall be used changes (e.g., the LKS should not only be sold in Europe but also in North America). Thereby, stakeholder intentions change, but have not been elicited: e.g., a law may enforce visual and acoustic warning in cases of automated steering interventions. This will lead to cases ③ or ⑤ depending on the fact whether a behavioral property is desired by the stakeholders. The functional design and the behavioral requirements are consistent but outdated at the same time.

In summary, it is required for a solution approach to support the detection of outdated behavioral requirements (cases ③, ④, ⑤, and ⑥) and incorrect realizations of the functional design (cases ②, ④, ⑥, and ⑦), as well as to support the explicit differentiation between the examined cases in order to aid the requirements engineer in correcting the artifacts consistently.

3   Potential Solutions from the State of the Art

This section reviews the state of the art in order to assess how existing techniques could aid in detecting and correcting outdated behavioral requirements. In the end, we have adopted and enhanced the most promising techniques that we have analyzed to be used within our solution approach.

Automated Verification. Verification techniques (e.g., [11], or [12]) aim at checking the correctness of a development artifact or the software. To do so, at least one correct artifact is needed as reference. By using automated verification techniques, cases ④ and ⑦ (see Table 1) can be detected, as behavioral properties in the functional design contradict the behavioral requirements. While both cases can be detected, fully automated techniques cannot distinguish between them, because automated techniques cannot take undocumented knowledge into account. Furthermore, model checking is only of limited use: Single counter examples in temporal logic or as finite state machines neither support the engineers in detecting the inconsistency in the original models nor in correcting the original models (cf. [13]).

Consistency Checking and Simulation. As an enhancement of model checking, consistency checking (e.g., [14], or [15]) can be used to detect inconsistencies between two models. Simulation is also often used to check for consistency between different executable models. Thereby, it is verified that all execution paths specified in one artifact are also executable in another artifact and, in order to ensure full consistency, vice versa. However, doing so does not aid in distinguishing between the different cases from Table 1, since it does not provide support in determining whether the behavioral requirements are outdated or the functional design is incorrect.

Similarly to the automated verification techniques, the stakeholder intentions are not taken into account.

Model Evolution. Another approach to keep track with changing requirements is model evolution, whereby one model is constructed from the information given by another model. Since manual approaches are time consuming and error prone, automated approaches can be used to update the behavioral requirements in order to reflect a changed functional design. Since one-way model transformation approaches result in the loss of the original behavioral requirements, model synchronization techniques (e.g., [16], or [17]) can be used to implement bidirectional model evolution (cf. [18]). While model evolution would benefit the development of consistent behavioral requirements and functional design, existing approaches do not consider whether a change of the functional design results from changed stakeholder intentions. In consequence, cases ③ and ⑤ can result from model evolution. In addition, other cases can be maltreated. For example, changing the functional design due to technical issues could contradict the behavioral requirements. Model synchronization would change the behavioral requirements accordingly. If this is not in correspondence with the stakeholder intentions, it would turn a case like ② into a case like ⑤.

Traceability. Establishing traceability links between requirements and design artifacts is often seen as a basis for continuous requirements engineering (cf. [19], [20]). Based on traceability links, changes to the functional design can be traced back to the requirements artifacts, and necessary changes to the requirements can be detected easily. This may be used as a trigger for the discussed model evolution techniques. In industrial practice the requirements are not continuously updated, and the requirements engineer is not involved in changes to the functional design. Hence, using traceability-centric approaches only fails to detect cases ② and ⑦. These cases could be misinterpreted in such a way that the behavioral requirements are changed as intended in the functional design, which would lead to the cases ③ and ⑤.

Validation and Review. Manual reviews can be performed to validate the up-to-dateness of the behavioral requirements and the correctness of the functional design. As part of the review, the requirements engineer will typically detect deficiencies in the original models and correct these deficiencies right away. Model-based review techniques have been evaluated as very effective and appropriate (cf. [21], [22]). Specializations such as perspective-based reviews (cf. [23], [24]) were partially evaluated as even more effective. Manual reviews performed by the requirements engineer, who has access to the stakeholders to check and elicit their intentions, can be used to detect all cases ① – ⑦, and to distinguish between them. Despite this advantage, the major disadvantages comprise the time-consuming nature of these manual approaches, and the likely occurrence of errors within the manual tasks.

In summary, automated approaches lack in decision making whether a property's documentation in the behavioral requirements or its specification in the functional design is correct and up-to-date. In addition, automated approaches cannot consider undocumented stakeholder intentions, which is necessary to determine if a behavioral requirement is up-to-date or outdated. Only manual reviews are able to consider all possible cases ① – ⑦, but they are time-consuming and potentially error prone. In view of the complementary benefits and drawbacks of automated and manual techniques, we propose the use of semi-automated enhancements to aid efficient (i.e., less time-consuming) and effective (i.e., less error-prone) reviews.

It is important to note that in addition to manual reviews, automated approaches for verification and consistency checking could be of use to determine inconsistencies between behavioral requirements and functional design. These approaches cannot aid in deciding whether the behavioral requirements or the functional design is correct by means of stakeholder intentions. Furthermore, these approaches cannot aid in detecting incorrect and outdated parts of the specification artifacts, which have been consistently documented in the behavioral requirements and in the functional design. Nevertheless, we intend to adopt such techniques in future work to guide the reviewers' attention during the review to obviously deficient parts of the specification artifacts.

4   Semi-automated Support for Detecting and Correcting Outdated Behavioral Requirements

Since manual review approaches can consider all of the seven cases from Table 1, we recommend conducting reviews after the functional design has been built. The requirements engineer will review the behavioral requirements and the functional design, and conduct further negotiations with the stakeholders to decide whether the behavioral requirements must be corrected, the functional design must be corrected, both artifacts must be changed, or everything is correct and up-to-date.

Figure 2 illustrates our overall solution concept for detection and correction of deficiencies in the behavioral requirements and in the functional design. The approach relies on a dedicated review model that integrates the information given by the behavioral requirements and the functional design. To aid the requirements engineer, the review model is documented in the same notation and keeps as far as possible to the same structure as the original behavioral requirements. Different diagrams within this review model display behavioral properties that are: 1) consistent in both artifacts; 2) only documented in the behavioral requirement; or 3) only specified in the functional design. Distinguishing these different kinds of diagrams aids the requirements engineer in detecting and correcting outdated behavioral requirements, as each kind is closely related to the cases described in Section 2.

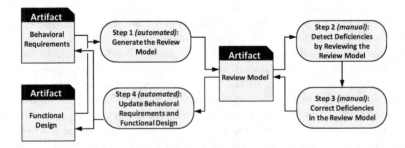

Fig. 2. Automated and Manual Parts of the Solution Concept

The review model can be derived by the use of model transformations in a first fully automated step (more information on the generation of the review model can be found in [25]). The review model is then subject to the review conducted by the requirements engineer, partially supported by the functional designer, to decide which behavioral properties are desired by the actual stakeholder intentions. When deficiencies are detected, we suggest incorporating the correction of these directly into the review model. Doing so allows for the application of automated model transformations to automatically update behavioral requirements and functional design consistently based on the corrected and up-to-date review model.

The review model basically features three kinds of diagrams to aid the review by the requirements engineer. These are:

o *Refinement diagrams.* Refinement diagrams describe behavioral properties that are in accordance with the behavioral requirements as well as with the functional design. We use automated refinements to enhance a diagram of the behavioral requirements with consistent, more detailed information from the functional design. This kind of diagram is needed, as the requirements engineer has to decide whether the behavioral property described must be considered as case ① or as case ⑤ (see Table 1). In case ⑤, the requirements engineer will simply remove the refinement diagram from the review model to update the behavioral requirements.

o *Diagrams of unrefinable requirements.* These diagrams depict behavioral properties documented in the requirements that are not part of the functional design and, as a consequence, cannot be automatically refined by the information given in the functional design. Thereby, the diagrams of the behavioral requirements that contain behavioral properties not specified in the functional design become part of the review model as well. These diagrams can result from forgotten requirements during the creation of the functional design (Table 1, case ②), but may also indicate unnecessary or erroneous requirements (case ⑥). In case ⑥, the requirements engineer removes the diagram from the review model. In case ②, the diagram has to be refined by the requirements engineer. The involved system functions must be identified, and the interactions between them specified. The requirements engineer will typically need the support of the function designer or other members of the development team due to the fact that solution details must be displayed.

o *Diagrams of unspecified requirements.* These diagrams depict behavioral properties that are only specified in the functional design and not in the behavioral requirements. Therefore, the relevant properties are identified within the functional design and translated into the notation of the review model. Unspecified requirements may, for example, display undesired features resulting from gold plating (Table 1, case ⑦), or are a consequence of changed or new requirements that have not been documented explicitly in the requirements specification (case ④). In case ⑦, the requirements engineer removes the diagram from the review model. In case ④, the requirements engineer simply accepts the diagram as correct and up-to-date for the review model.

Note that, of course, it is not conceivable that there are diagrams displaying case ③ because it is not possible to generate diagrams displaying behavioral properties that are desired by stakeholders but have never been documented elsewhere before. As a result, the requirements engineer will have to check the completeness of the entire review model in close cooperation with the stakeholders.

To support the requirements engineer, the review model preserves the original structure of the behavioral requirements. This is exemplarily shown in Fig. 3. The figure depicts a refinement diagram (Fig. 3(c)) derived from the behavioral requirements (Fig. 3(a)) and from the functional design (Fig. 3(b)) of the lane keeping support. It is to note that the excerpt taken from the original specification has a broader view than illustrated in Fig. 1. It is desired by the stakeholders that the driver of a car is able to stop any automated steering interventions. This is first documented within the behavioral requirements as a message sequence chart. Afterwards, this is specified in the functional design of the lane keeping support. In this case, the excerpt from the functional design of the LKS given in Fig. 3(b) only displays the structure between the functions. In addition, each function consists of its own behavior specification.

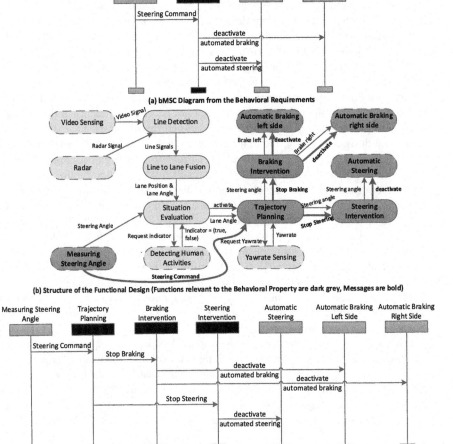

Fig. 3. Exemplary Refinement Diagram of the Review Model (c) and the corresponding Diagrams of Behavioral Requirements (a) and Functional Design (b)

The requirement is realized in the interplay of three system functions: 'Trajectory Planning', 'Steering Intervention', and 'Braking Intervention'. To check this behavioral property, the requirements engineer would have to review all three behavior specifications as well as their interplay in detail. To aid the requirements engineer, a refinement diagram of the review model is created (see Fig. 3(c)). As can be seen, this diagram enables the requirements engineer to decide whether this property is realized correctly and still in accordance with current stakeholder intentions.

5   Evaluation

We conducted a controlled experiment to determine effectiveness, efficiency, user confidence, and supportiveness of a reviewer using a dedicated review model as review artifact, compared to using the original behavioral requirements and the original functional design as review artifacts. The study employs perspective-based reviews of the behavior that is specified in behavioral requirements and functional design against the actual stakeholder intentions. This is carried out by deciding whether a stakeholder intention is correctly displayed in the behavioral requirements, in the functional design, in both artifacts, or is not displayed at all.

5.1   Study Design

In detail, as **independent variable**, we investigate two different *review styles* to validate the specified behavior against the actual stakeholder intentions:

o *Review Style SP (short: SP):* The participants will use the original specifications of behavioral requirements and functional design as review artifacts.
o *Review Style RM (short: RM):* The participants will use the automatically generated review model that integrates the information specified in the behavioral requirements and the functional design into one review artifact.

As **dependent variables**, we determined

o *effectiveness*: the ratio of correctly identified and rejected stakeholder intentions;
o *efficiency*: the average time spent on one correctly identified or rejected stakeholder intention;
o *user confidence*: the average confidence a participant claims for identifying and rejecting a stakeholder intention; and
o *subjective supportiveness:* average result of standardized questionnaire items from the Technology Acceptance Model version 3 (TAM 3) to rate *RM* against *SP* for *perceived usefulness, perceived ease of use,* and *computer self-efficacy.*

The **hypotheses** (null hypotheses and alternative hypotheses) are:

o **H1-0:** There is no significant difference between the effectiveness of *SP* and *RM*.
  H1-a: *RM* is significantly more effective than *SP*.
o **H2-0:** There is no significant difference between the efficiency of *SP* and *RM*.
  H2-a: *RM* is significantly more efficient than *SP*.
o **H3-0:** There is no significant difference between user confidence in *SP* and *RM*.
  H3-a: *RM* is significantly rated higher in user confidence than *SP*.

o **H4-0:** There is no significant difference between the subjective supportiveness of *SP* and *RM*.

H4-a: *RM* is significantly rated more supportive than *SP* by the users.

We conducted the experiment among 21 participants. The participants were junior researchers, student assistants, and master-level students, mainly holding degrees in 'Systems Engineering' (with emphasis on software engineering), 'Business Information Systems', or, in one case, 'Business Administration'.

To investigate effects resulting from participants' experience and knowledge, we also measure several covariates such as highest educational achievement, degree program, employment status, semester, age, gender, as well as the participant's self-rated experience in six ordinates related to conducting reviews in general, and the used modeling notations in particular.

The study is conducted as an online experiment. The study's experimental setup consists of an experiment (to determine effectiveness, efficiency, and user confidence) and a post-hoc questionnaire (to determine subjective supportiveness and the covariates). The experiment uses a within-subject design. Each participant conducts a review of an industrial sample specification in both review styles (*SP* and *RM*). The shown artifacts are designed to be comprehensible within one web page. For example, the review model consists of 11 diagrams. The order of the review style is randomized for each participant to avoid primacy, recency, and carry-over effects and to minimize habituation. Participants review the specifications against 12 stakeholder intentions. This means that each participant reviewed 24 stakeholder intentions, 12 in *SP*, and 12 in *RM*. Stakeholder intentions and their appearance in the depicted diagram is identical in *SP* and *RM*. In this setup reviewing means deciding whether a stakeholder intention is depicted in the behavioral requirements, in the functional design, in both specifications, or in no specification.

5.2   Results

The experiment results for effectiveness are given in Fig. 4, results for efficiency in Fig. 5, results for user confidence in Fig. 6, and results for subjective supportiveness in Fig. 7. For example, with respect to effectiveness it can be seen that the review of the review model was in mean more effective than the review of the original specifications. Results of a Student's-T test indicate high statistical significance. Also, power analyses (cf. [26]) show a high effect size and an adequate power. In conclusion, we are confident to say that:

o *RM* is significantly more effective than *SP*: we can reject H1-0 and accept H1-a.

In the same manner we can conclude from the results related to effectiveness and user confidence that:

o *RM* is significantly more efficient than *SP:* we can reject H2-0 and accept H2-a.
o *RM* is rated significantly higher in user confidence than *SP*: we can reject H3-0 and accept H3-a.

Regarding the results for supportiveness we must consider the experimental design. We used questions from the TAM 3 questionnaire in order to determine computer self-efficacy, perceived ease of use, and perceived usefulness. The original TAM 3 assumes the rating of one variable from low to high, while we used the questions to rate the two review styles against each other. To validate the reliability of our changed instrument, we determined Cronbach's α between the composed values and the single questions. For perceived usefulness: $\alpha(5)=0.892$; for perceived ease of use: $\alpha(4)=0.935$; for computer self-efficacy: $\alpha(4)=0.795$. In consequence, we are confident to claim reliability of the adopted questionnaire. Furthermore, we use all three measurements to determine supportiveness. In this case we also used Cronbach's α to validate the reliability of the composed measurement. With $\alpha(4)=0.884$ and under consideration of the results presented in Fig. 7 we can conclude that:

o *RM* is significantly more subjective supportive than *SP*: we can reject H4-0 and accept H4-a.

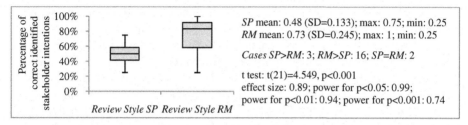

Fig. 4. Effectiveness

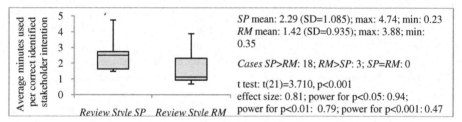

Fig. 5. Efficiency

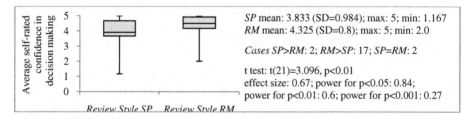

Fig. 6. User Confidence

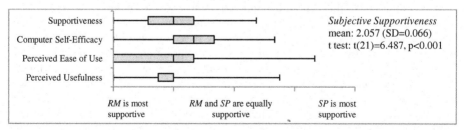

Fig. 7. Subjective Supportiveness

5.3   Threats to Validity

To mitigate relevant threats to validity that exist for this type of study (cf. [27] and [28]), we have employed certain strategies in the study design:

o To avoid bias in subject selection, statistical regression, or interaction effects, we did not select particular participants and use a within-subject design, where all participants are treated the same way and participate in the treatment and control conditions equally often. Of course, the recruitment of participants must still be considered as convenience sampling.

o To avoid threats with respect to testing or multiple treatments, we strictly use randomization to normalize test results. As we used a within-subject design there is still a risk that learning effects might occur. To evaluate these effects, we compared the dependent variables across the different orderings in which participants conducted the experiment. Since the values are equally distributed across both orderings, the value ranges do not differ, and differences are far from approaching significance, we are confident to say that habituation effects were minimal and can be considered not to have impacted the results.

o To avoid reactive or interaction effects of testing, as well as the 'John Henry Effect', we use naïve participants and did not give bonuses for participation in the experiment. We use no prehoc-questionnaire and conduct no upfront briefing.

o To avoid threats to construct validity, we have carefully designed the example specification in close collaboration with industry experts, and used a pretest group to validate the setup. In the post-hoc-questionnaire we keep to standardized questions suggested by the TAM 3.

o Since we did not use participants from industry, and the experiment material was adapted to suite the participants experience and knowledge, there is a threat to external validity. As suggested by [29], we aim at evaluating generalizability in an additional investigation. We already applied the proposed solution to industrial sample cases, and discussed the approach and its application with industry professionals (cf. [30]). Thereby we gained the insight that the solution is applicable in industrial engineering processes.

To avoid threats due to participatory history, maturation, or mortality, the experiment was designed to last only about 30–45 minutes. Results show that this amount of time was adequate, as most participants used 15-20 minutes for each review and additional 5 minutes for the post-hoc questionnaire. A further threat to validity is the setup of using an online experiment. In doing so, there is no knowledge about the actual time consumption for each decision taken. We measured time consumption for each page of the questionnaire (one example in one review style per page), but these values can be corrupted (e.g., by a participant taking a break during answering one page). This threat seriously affects the validity of the results regarding efficiency. As different experiences and knowledge factors of participants can also affect the results, we checked for significant correlations between dependent and independent variables and covariates. Results of Pearson's r indicate that some of the experience seems to have smaller impact on user confidence in both review styles. We could not determine effects related to effectiveness or efficiency.

6   Conclusion

In this paper, we presented an approach that aids the requirements engineer in detecting and correcting outdated behavioral requirements in function-centered engineering processes. We focused on the use of a review model, which represents a consolidated view of behavioral requirements and functional design, for detecting outdated behavioral requirements. Our evaluation showed that using our approach offers a substantial reduction of the manual effort and error rate of corresponding reviews.

Our work is part of a broader research agenda. Following this agenda, we will have to elaborate a more extensive support of manual reviews by increasing the amount of automation. We suppose that an enhanced version of our review model can also be used to support model evolution between behavioral requirements and functional design on the fly. For instance, when changing the functional design potential aberrations of the behavioral requirements can be detected and displayed immediately in a specific review model that depicts only the relevant parts of the artifacts affected by this change.

Acknowledgments. This research was partly funded by the *German Federal Ministry of Education and Research* (grant no. 01IS12005C). We thank Stefan Beck and Arnaud Boyer (Airbus Defence and Space) and Jens Höfflinger (Bosch) for their support regarding the adoption of industrial specifications to fit as experiment material.

References

1. ISO/IEC/IEEE: International Standard 24765: Systems and software engineering-Vocabulary (2010)
2. Davis, A., Overmyer, S., Jordan, K., Caruso, J., Dandashi, F., Dinh, A., Kincaid, G., Ledeboer, G., Reynolds, P., Sitaram, P., Ta, A., Theofanos, M.: Identifying and measuring quality in a software requirements specification. In: Proc. of IEEE Intl. Software Metrics Symposium, pp. 141–152 (1993)
3. Knauss, E., Schneider, K., Stapel, K.: Learning to write better requirements through heuristic critiques. In: Proc. of RE, pp. 387–388 (2009)
4. Nuseibeh, B.: Weaving together requirements and architectures. In: IEEE Computer, pp. 115–119 (2001)
5. Whalen, M., Murugesan, A., Heimdahl, M.: Your what is my how: why requirements and architectural design should be iterative. In: Proc. of Twin Peaks WS, pp. 36–40 (2012)
6. ISO/IEC/IEEE: International Standard 29148: Systems and software engineering - life cycle processes - Requirements engineering (2011)
7. Pretschner, A., Broy, M., Kruger, I., Stauner, T.: Software engineering for automotive systems: a roadmap. In: Proc. of Future of Software Engineering, pp. 55–71 (2007)
8. Brinkkemper, S., Pachidi, S.: Functional architecture modeling for the software product industry. In: Babar, M.A., Gorton, I. (eds.) ECSA 2010. LNCS, vol. 6285, pp. 198–213. Springer, Heidelberg (2010)
9. Jantsch, A., Sander, I.: On the roles of functions and objects in system specification. In: Proc. of Int. WS on Hardware/Software Codesign, pp. 8–12 (2000)

10. Weber, M., Weisbrod, J.: Requirements engineering in automotive development - experiences and challenges. In: Proc. of RE, pp. 331–340 (2002)
11. Clarke, E., Emerson, E., Sifakis, J.: Model checking: algorthmic verification and debugging. In: Commun. ACM, pp. 74–84 (2009)
12. Blanc, X., Mounier, I., Mougenot, A., Mens, T.: Detecting model inconsistency through operation-based model construction. In: Proc. of ICSE, pp. 511–520 (2008)
13. Borges, R., Garcez, A., Lamb, L.: Integrating model verification and self-adaptation. In: Proc. of ASE, pp. 317–320 (2010)
14. Fradet, P., Le Métayer, D., Périn, M.: Consistency checking for multiple view. In: Proc. of ESEC/FSE, pp. 410–428 (1999)
15. Paige, R., Brooke, P., Ostroff, J.: Metamodel-based model conformance and multiview consistency checking. In: TOSEM, pp. 1–49 (2007)
16. Van Paesschen, E., De Meuter, W., D'Hondt, M.: SelfSync: a dynamic round-trip engineering environment. In: Briand, L.C., Williams, C. (eds.) MoDELS 2005. LNCS, vol. 3713, pp. 633–647. Springer, Heidelberg (2005)
17. Malavolta, I., Muccini, H., Pelliccione, P., Tamburri, D.: Providing architectural languages and tools interoperability through model transformation technologies. In: TSE, pp. 119–140 (2010)
18. Giese, H., Wagner, R.: From model transformation to incremental bidirectional model synchronization. SoSyM Journal, 21–43 (2009)
19. Gotel, O., Finkelstein, A.: An analysis of the requirements traceability problem. In: Proc. of RE, pp. 94–101 (1994)
20. Winkler, S., Pilgrim, J.: A survey of traceability in requirements engineering and model-driven development. SoSyM Journal, 529–565 (2010)
21. Boehm, B., Basili, V.: Software defect reduction top 10 list. In: IEEE Computer, pp. 135–137 (2001)
22. Gilb, T., Graham, D.: Software Inspection, Addison-Wesley (1993)
23. Basili, V., Green, S., Laitenberger, O., Shull, F., Sorumgard, S., Zelkowski, M.: The empirical investigation of perspective-based reading. J. Empir. Softw. Eng., 133–164 (1996)
24. Shull, F., Basili, V., Zelkowitz, M., Boehm, B., Brown, A., Port, D., Rus, I., Tesoreiro, R.: What we have learned about fighting defects. In: Proc. of Intl. Symp. on Softw. Metrics, pp. 133–154 (2002)
25. Daun, M., Weyer, T., Pohl, K.: Validating the functional design of embedded systems against stakeholder intentions. In: Proc. of Intl. Conf. on Model-Driven Eng. and Softw. Dev., pp. 333–339 (2014)
26. Faul, F., Erdfelder, E., Lang, A., Buchner, A.: G*Power 3: A flexible statistical power analysis program for the social, behavioral, and biomedical sciences. Behavior Research Methods **39**, 175–191 (2007)
27. Campbell, D., Stanley, J.: Experimental and Quasi-Experimental Designs for Research. Houghton Mifflin Company, Boston (1963)
28. Cook, T., Campbell, D.: Quasi-Experimentation - Design and Analysis Issues for Field Settings. Houghton Mifflin Company (1979)
29. Wieringa, R.: Empirical research methods for technology validation: Scaling up to practice. J. Syst. Software, 19–31 (2014)
30. Daun, M., Höfflinger, J., Weyer, T.: Function-centered engineering of embedded systems: evaluating industry needs and possible solutions. In: Proc. of Intl. Conf. on Eval. of Novel Approaches to Softw. Eng., pp. 226–234 (2014)

Estimating the Implementation Risk of Requirements in Agile Software Development Projects with Traceability Metrics

Patrick Rempel[✉] and Patrick Mäder

Software Systems Group,
Technische Universität Ilmenau, Ilmenau, Germany
{patrick.rempel,patrick.maeder}@tu-ilmenau.de

Abstract. [**Context and Motivation**] Agile developments follow an iterative procedure with alternating requirements planning and implementation phases boxed into sprints. For every sprint, requirements from the product backlog are selected and appropriate test measures are chosen. [**Question/problem**] Both activities should carefully consider the implementation risk of each requirement. In favor of a successful project, risky requirements should either be deferred or extra test effort should be dedicated on them. Currently, estimating the implementation risk of requirements is mainly based on gut decisions. [**Principal ideas/ results**] The complexity of the graph spanned by dependency and decomposition relations across requirements can be an indicator of implementation risk. In this paper, we propose three metrics to assess and quantify requirement relations. We conducted a study with five industry-scale agile projects and found that the proposed metrics are in fact suitable for estimating implementation risk of requirements. [**Contribution**] Our study of heterogeneous, industrial development projects delivers for the first time evidence that the complexity of a requirements traceability graph is correlated with the error-proneness of the implementing source code. The proposed traceability metrics provide an indicator for requirements' implementation risks. This indicator supports product owners and developers in requirement prioritization and test measure selection.

Keywords: Agile development · Requirements prioritzation · Traceability metrics · Risk estimation

1 Introduction

Agile software development focuses on continuously delivering small but value-added software increments into an integrated baseline, enabling early verification of requirements and architectural assumptions [8]. At the beginning of every increment, requirements are prioritized and the highest-prioritized requirements are chosen for implementation. At the end of every increment, appropriate test measures are applied to verify the requirement implementation. Considering the

© Springer International Publishing Switzerland 2015
S.A. Fricker and K. Schneider (Eds.): REFSQ 2015, LNCS 9013, pp. 81–97, 2015.
DOI: 10.1007/978-3-319-16101-3_6

risk of requirement implementation is beneficial for both activities [4]. Requirements traceability provides support for understanding relations between requirements [21]. Due to our previous work on traceability assessment [26–28], we hypothesized that a systematic assessment of existing trace links can be used to estimate the implementation risk of requirements, and can thus support requirement prioritization and test measure selection in agile projects.

In this paper, we propose three metrics that can be used to systematically assess requirement traceability relations. We conducted an empirical study on five industry-scale agile software projects, each specified by at least 500 requirements artifacts, to investigate whether or not the proposed metrics are appropriate for estimating the implementation risk of individual requirements. The results of our study show that all three metrics are useful to estimate the implementation risk of requirements, and can thus be used to support requirement prioritization and test planning. Furthermore, the results of our study demonstrate that the traceability metrics can also be used as predictors for unseen projects without project-specific training of the predictor.

The remainder of the paper is organized as follows. In Section 2, we discuss why considering the implementation risk of requirements is beneficial for requirement prioritization and test planning in agile projects. In Section 3, we propose three requirements traceability metrics to estimate the implementation risk of requirements in software projects. The empirical study, which we conducted on five industry-scale projects is presented in Section 4, while the data analysis procedure and results are presented in Section 5. Section 6 discusses the results of our study. Potential threats to validity and how we mitigated them are discussed in Section 7. In Section 8, we discuss previous work that is closely related to our study and highlight similarities and differences to our work. We draw conclusions and outline future work in Section 9.

2   Agile Requirements

The idea of agile software development was established through the agile manifesto [2] containing twelve principles. The first two principles of this manifest clearly indicate that requirements in agile developments are treated differently than in plan-driven development processes.

- *Principle 1*: "Our highest priority is to satisfy the customer through early and continuous delivery of valuable software."
- *Principle 2*: "Welcome changing requirements, even late in development. Agile processes harness change for the customer's competitive advantage."

As highlighted by these principles, agile development focuses on continuously delivering small but value-added software increments into an integrated baseline to enable early verification of requirements and architectural assumptions. Thus, requirements need to be prioritized to decide which of them will be implemented with the next increment.

2.1 Requirement Prioritization

Agile approaches have in common that requirements are prioritized based on business value. Higher prioritized requirements are implemented in earlier development increments so that customers can realize the maximum business value [8]. Though, customers and product managers often struggle to perform a justified prioritization, because quantifying the business value is difficult [18,30]. To provide systematic guidance for this task, Cohn [9] identified two important determinants that should be considered when prioritizing agile requirements: the *financial value* of having a feature and the *cost* of developing and maintaining a feature. An important, yet often underestimated aspect are maintenance costs. In a typical life-cycle, 30% of the costs are spent for development and 70% for maintenance [3]. Empirical studies demonstrated that the error-proneness of implemented software is an important driver for maintenance cost [31]. Therefore, estimating the requirement implementation risk by predicting subsequent defects helps to better understand cost, and thus, support requirements prioritization.

2.2 Focusing Test Effort

Beside requirements prioritization, estimating requirement implementation risk is also beneficial for directing testing activities. As critically discussed by Boehm and Turner [4], most projects spend equal time and effort on testing software parts, no matter how risky these parts are. Instead, focusing test efforts on high-risk parts can save downstream maintenance time and effort. Thus, a reliable estimate of requirement implementation risks also supports focusing test efforts.

3 Estimating Implementation Risk of Requirements Through Traceability Metrics

Even though, agile requirements are typically captured in small entities, the *Agile Enterprise Big Picture* [18] illustrates that even simple stories belong to a bigger context and thus have numerous relationships with other requirements. Requirements traceability provides support to make these relationships explicit. Based on the characteristics of the *Agile Enterprise Big Picture* [18] we derived a traceability information model (TIM) [20] for agile requirements management as depicted in Figure 1. This model conceptualizes traceable artifacts and trace links within the context of agile software development. In addition to the decomposition relations, dependency relations may exist between requirement artifacts such as: one artifact conflicts with another artifact, or one artifact supports another artifact. Figure 2 exemplifies a traceability graph containing the four requirement types (epic, feature, story, and task) and the two requirement relation types (decomposition and dependency).

We hypothesize that existing requirement dependency and decomposition relations, materialized as trace links between requirements, can be used to quantify the complexity of relations between requirements in order to estimate the

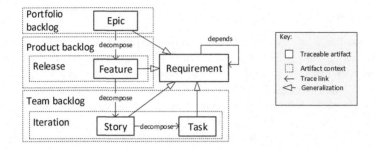

Fig. 1. A traceability information model (TIM) for agile requirements management

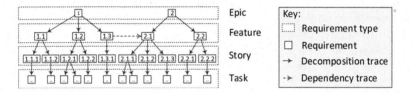

Fig. 2. An exemplary requirements traceability graph including dependencies and decompositions for an agile software development

implementation risk of requirements in agile projects. Therefore, we propose three requirements traceability metrics to assess and quantify the complexity of relationships between requirements. As requirements and trace links span a traceability graph, we aim to characterize the complexity of this graph. In general, a graph consists of vertices and edges, and thus, the complexity is driven by the number of vertices (Section 3.1), the distance between connected vertices (Section 3.2), and the number of edges (Section 3.3).

3.1 Number of Related Requirements (NRR)

Relationships between a requirement and other requirements typically mean that additional requirements and constraints must be considered when implementing that requirement. Thus, with every relation to another requirement, which can be direct or transitive, the complexity of the originated requirement increases. Additionally, a higher number of related requirements implies a higher potential of latent changes when a change request is raised against this requirement.

Definition: The *Number of Related Requirements* (*NRR*) is the number of requirements that are directly or transitively related to a requirement via decomposition or dependency trace links. A requirement r_j is related to a requirement r_i, if a path of trace links exist from r_i to r_j. RR_i is the set of related requirements of r_i.

$$NRR(r_i) = |RR_i| \qquad (1)$$

As exemplified in Figure 3-(A), metric $NRR_{1.3}$ for requirements artifact $r_{1.3}$ is 10 and $NRR_{2.2}$ for requirements artifact $r_{2.2}$ is 12, which means that artifact $r_{2.2}$ is related to more requirements than $r_{1.3}$. The NRR metric computes the same value for all vertices in a connected graph, which could be a limitation. In Figure 3-(A), NRR would be 10 for all requirements connected to $r_{1.3}$. However, new requirements arise continuously in agile projects and thus the traceability graph changes continuously. As the metric is only computed upon the creation or modification of a requirement r_i, NRR is able to discriminate the requirements artifacts of a connected graph.

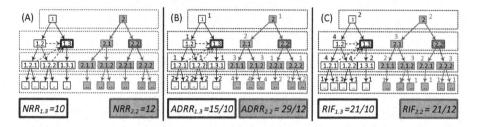

Fig. 3. Examples of the traceability metrics NRR, $ADRR$, and RIF for the requirement artifacts 1.3 and 2.2

3.2 Average Distance to Related Requirements (ADRR)

The distance between two related requirements r_i and r_{ij} indicates how many steps are necessary to traverse the path from r_i to r_{ij}. Longer average distances imply that on average more individual trace links need to be considered by a developer implementing this requirement. The effort for resolving and understanding these relationships increases with longer average distances.

Definition: The *Average Distance to Related Requirements* (*ADRR*) denotes the average number of trace links that need to be resolved to traverse from requirements artifact r_i to any related requirements artifact r_{ij}. The function d_{ij} denotes the distance from r_i to r_{ij}. If alternative paths exit between r_i and r_{ij}, the distance of the shortest path is used for calculation.

$$ADRR(r_i) = \frac{\sum\limits_{r_{ij} \in RR_i} d_{ij}}{|RR_i|} \tag{2}$$

As exemplified in Figure 3-(B), the $ADRR_{1.3}$ for requirement $r_{1.3}$ is $\frac{15}{10}$ and the $ADRR_{2.2}$ for requirement $r_{2.2}$ is $\frac{29}{12}$ suggesting that the average distance to related requirements from $r_{2.2}$ is ~ 0.9 steps longer from $r_{1.3}$.

3.3 Requirement Information Flow (RIF)

The requirement information flow is supposed to determine the coupling of related requirements, which we measure by counting the fan-in and the fan-out of a requirement. An increase in coupling, while assuming a constant number of related requirements, entails an increased number of trace links between the related requirements that must be understood by developers.

Definition: The *Requirement Information Flow (RIF)* of a requirement r_i is the average fan-in and fan-out of any related requirement r_{ij}. The fan-in of a requirement r_{ij} is the number of requirements that are directly connected through an inbound trace link. The fan-out of a requirement r_{ij} is the number of requirements that are directly connected through an outbound trace link. The set of related requirements is denoted as RR_i.

$$RIF(r_i) = \frac{\sum_{r_{ij} \in RR_i} fan\_in(r_{ij}) + fan\_out(r_{ij})}{|RR_i|} \tag{3}$$

As exemplified in Figure 3-(C), metric $RIF_{1.3}$ for requirements artifact $r_{1.3}$ is $\frac{21}{10}$ and metric $RIF_{2.2}$ for requirements artifact $r_{2.2}$ is $\frac{21}{12}$ suggesting that the information flow within the related requirements of $r_{1.3}$ is 0.35 trace links higher than the information flow within related requirements of $r_{2.2}$.

3.4 Research Questions

We hypothesize that the proposed traceability metrics can be used to estimate the requirements implementation risk in order to support the planning activities: requirements prioritization (see Section 2.1) and focusing tests (see Section 2.2). The number of defects at source code level is an accepted metric to quantify the error-proneness of developed software. Since source code is an immediate result of the implementation of requirements, we also consider the number of defects as valid quantification of the requirements error-proneness, and thus, for the requirement implementation risk. Our research questions are as follows:

1. *RQ-1*: Are requirements' *NRR*, *ADRR*, and *RIF* metrics associated with the requirements' defects?
2. *RQ-2*: Which, if any, combination of requirements traceability metrics can be used to predict requirements' defects within a project?
3. *RQ-3*: Can predictors, obtained from training projects, also be used to predict the number of defects for an unknown project?

4 Study Design

To investigate our research questions (see Section 3.4), we collected development artifacts and traceability data from five open-source software projects that apply an agile development approach.

4.1   Case Selection

Driven by our research goal to support the requirements prioritization (see Section 2.1) and test selection (see Section 2.2), we defined the following case selection criteria. A case to be included:

- shall apply an agile software development approach (e.g. XP, SCRUM),
- shall provide requirements artifacts at three or more refinement levels,
- shall provide defect artifacts associated to source code and requirements,
- shall provide traceability across requirements, and
- shall be in development for at least five years.

We started our search for potential cases from the list of open source projects[1] that use the ALM tool Jira [17] for requirements management.

4.2   Data Demographics

The five open source projects: CONNECT, Infinispan, jBPM, Weld, and Wild-Fly completely satisfy our case selection criteria and thus, were included in our study. CONNECT is a software project that was initiated by US federal agencies to support their health-related missions. It provides a solution for health information exchange locally and at the national level. Infinispan is a highly available key/value data store and data grid platform. The main purpose is exposing distributed and highly concurrent data structures. The business process management suite jBPM allows modeling and executing business processes. Weld is a reference implementation of the Java standard for dependency injection and contextual lifecycle management: Contexts and Dependency Injection for the Java EE platform. WildFly is a Java application runtime that supports the Java EE 7 standard.

Table 1. Characteristics of the five studied software projects

	Project	Requirements					Trace links		
		Epic	Feature	Impr.[1]	Task	$\sum$	Dec.[2]	Dep.[3]	$\sum$
A	CONNECT[A]	10	245	290	2,810	**3,355**	3,114	2,538	**5,652**
B	Infinispan[B]	–	850	522	666	**2,038**	372	1,716	**2,088**
C	jBPM[C]	–	1,146	112	1,007	**2,265**	472	1,168	**1,640**
D	Weld[D]	–	242	48	303	**593**	140	620	**760**
E	WildFly[E]	–	682	226	679	**1,587**	798	1,516	**2,314**

[A]www.connectopensource.org, [B]www.infinispan.org, [C]www.jbpm.org, [D]weld.cdi-spec.org, [E]www.wildfly.org, [1]Improvement, [2]Decomposition, [3]Dependency

---

[1] www.atlassian.com/opensource/overview

Table 1 provides an overview of the requirements artifacts and requirement traceability characteristics of the five studied projects. For all projects, we gained raw data by collecting all relevant project artifacts at the referenced websites created till Aug 16th, 2014. The *Requirements* column shows the number of requirements artifacts per refinement level and in total. The smallest project contains almost 600 requirements artifacts. The *Trace links* column shows the number of relations between requirement artifacts per relation type and in total. The smallest project contains 760 trace links.

4.3   Data Collection Process

Our data collection process consisted of three steps (see Figure 4).

Step 1: Parse Artifacts and Trace Links. All studied projects use the web-based application life-cycle management tool JIRA [17] to manage requirements, defects, and trace links. Every requirement features a unique identifier and trace links between requirements can be navigated forward and backward within the tool. Also, all projects used the source configuration management tool Git [13] to manage source code. We implemented a project artifact collection tool that automatically downloaded and parsed project artifacts and trace links at requirements and source code level. All studied projects were migrated from other requirements management tools to JIRA between 2005 and 2007. To avoid migration influences, we only considered requirements artifacts that were created at least one year after the project was migrated to JIRA.

Step 2: Generate Traceability Graph. Once all relevant artifacts and trace links had been captured by the artifact collection tool (Step 1), a traceability graph could be automatically generated. The generated traceability graph is directed. If a captured trace link is bi-directional, which is the case by default in JIRA, two directed edges are added to the traceability graph.

Step 3: Calculate Traceability Metrics. In the last step, we used the generated traceability graphs to calculate the introduced traceability metrics (see Section 3). Thereby, a data set of traceability metrics was calculated for every issued requirements addition and change. Additionally, we automatically counted the defects that occurred per requirement after this change. All studied projects used an issue tracker system to document defects and their resolution. Project contributors file their discovered defects as issues in this system and thereby support an automated analysis. However, the existence of a defect issue does not necessarily imply the existence of a software defect. Hence, we only considered defects from the issue tracker with the resolution types: *done, implemented,* and *fixed.* We excluded all defects with the resolution types: *cannotreproduce, communityanswered, duplicate, goneaway, incomplete, invalid, notaproblem, wontfix, worksasdesigned.* To correctly count the defects that occurred after a change, we needed to map the defect issues to the affected requirements by extracting two types of relationships. First, our tool analyzed all commit messages within the software configuration management system (SCM) for identifiers of defect issues filed in the issue tracker. Such an identifier means that with this software change the referred defect was addressed. We considered every changed source code file of such a commit to be affected by the defect. Second, our tool analyzed commit messages of the SCM system for identifiers that refer to requirements kept in the issue tracker. Such an identifier means that with this software change the referred requirement was implemented. We considered every changed source file of such a commit to be implementing the requirement. By chaining the extracted relationships: $requirement \xleftarrow{implements} source\text{-}code \xleftarrow{affects} defect$, we could map every defect to one or multiple affected requirements. To make this value comparable for different requirements changes, we always considered the number of defects that occurred within one year after the change. Further, we had to exclude requirement changes from the twelve months prior to our study, since the future defect information were incomplete for these requirements.

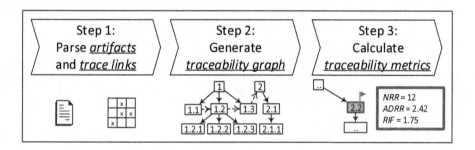

Fig. 4. Overview of the data collection process

5 Data Analysis

5.1 Statistical Model and Regression

As elaborated in Section 3.4, we want to investigate whether or not the proposed requirement traceability metrics NRR, $ADRR$, and RIF are associated with the number of defects occurring in the source code that implements a requirement. For this purpose we apply regression analysis to investigate how the traceability metrics NRR, $ADRR$, and RIF are related to the number of defects per requirement (DEF). That means, NRR, $ADRR$, and RIF are the independent variables and DEF is the dependent variable of our study. Table 2 summarizes the sample size as well as mean and standard deviation for every dependent and independent variable across all five projects.

Table 2. Summary statistics for the studied projects A–E

	N[1]	DEF		NRR		ADRR		RIF	
		$\bar{x}$	σ	$\bar{x}$	σ	$\bar{x}$	σ	$\bar{x}$	σ
A	42,278	0.428	1.269	19.489	46.387	3.451	2.677	14.221e+10	9.941e+11
B	22,754	2.61	5.148	10.525	13.583	1.354	1.062	16.874	82.229
C	12,449	0.216	0.676	1.685	1.284	0.442	0.56	2.167	2.615
D	31,024	0.92	2.85	4.863	9.312	1.21	0.471	0.307	0.228
E	59,333	0.538	2.948	2.169	3.524	1.694	0.796	0.597	0.145

[1]N refers to the number of changes calculated as: $\sum\limits_{i=1}^{commits}$ numberOfClasses(i)

Prior to deriving a statistical model explaining the effect of the independent on the dependent variable best, we assessed for every project whether the independent variables correlate with each other by calculating the Pearson correlation coefficient. The purpose was to determine whether or not our proposed traceability metrics are measuring the same characteristics of requirements relationships. If two metrics would strongly correlate with each other for all projects, one metric could be eliminated, because both metrics would measure the same characteristic. Table 3 summarizes the correlation coefficients (*rho*) and their significances (*p-value*). The table shows that no pair of independent variables strongly correlates for all projects. Thus, we considered all three metrics as a potential independent variable influencing the dependent variable.

Table 3. Pearson correlations between independent variables for all projects

	$cor(NRR, ADRR)$		$cor(NRR, RIF)$		$cor(ADRR, RIF)$	
	rho	p-value	rho	p-value	rho	p-value
A	0.621	< 0.001	0.739	< 0.001	0.513	< 0.001
B	0.572	< 0.001	0.249	< 0.001	0.411	< 0.001
C	0.428	< 0.001	0.197	< 0.001	0.239	< 0.001
D	0.636	< 0.001	0.624	< 0.001	0.73	< 0.001
E	0.462	< 0.001	0.95	< 0.001	0.179	< 0.001

To find a statistical model that describes the influence of the three independent variables on the dependent variable, we applied a stepwise model regression in forward direction. We added independent variables stepwise to the statistical model and compared the models of every step with the Akaike Information Criterion (AIC) [7]. With this approach we found that the following equation models the effect of the traceability metrics best for predicting *DEF*:

$$DEF = \beta_0 + \beta_1(NRR) + \beta_2(ADRR) + \beta_3(RIF) + \epsilon. \qquad (4)$$

In Equation 4, the parameters β_1, β_2, and β_3 capture the effect of NRR, $ADRR$, and RIF on DEF. While β_0 is the constant intercept, and ϵ is the error term. First, we estimated the empirical model for Equation 4 with Ordinary Least Square (OLS) regression. However, the Beusch-Pagan test [5] indicated heteroscedasticity for the estimated empirical model, which means that the assumption of homoscedasticity in the regression model was violated. To mitigate this violation, we opted for Weighted Least Square (WLS) regression for fitting the model. The results of the WLS regression are summarized in Table 4.

Table 4. WLS estimates for requirements of all projects

Independent Variable	Parameter	Coefficient	Std. error	p-value
Intercept	β_0	0.463 ***	0.009	0.000
NRR	β_1	0.257 ***	0.002	0.000
$ADRR$	β_2	0.352 ***	0.063	0.000
RIF	β_3	-0.068 ***	0.016	0.000

Significance codes for p-values: *** < 0.001, ** < 0.01, * < 0.05

5.2 Predicting Requirement Defects for Unseen Project Data

To assess the generalizability of our statistical model, we applied a leave-one-out cross-validation (LOOCV) strategy. We used the data-sets from four projects as the training sample and the fifth project as the hold-out sample. The regression is fitted on the training sample and applied to the hold-out sample. We repeated this procedure five times, every time with another project as hold-out sample. To evaluate the predictive power on the unseen data, we evaluated how well the predictor can assign a requirement to a risk category. To breakdown the prediction results into usable results, we adapted the traffic light system and distinguished three requirement risk categories:

- *low-risk*: requirement implementation entails 0..2 defects within one year
- *medium-risk*: requirement implementation entails 3..5 defects within one year
- *high-risk*: requirement implementation entails > 5 defects within one year

We considered a requirement risk prediction as correct if the traceability metric predicted the same risk category as we would derive from the actual project defects. Table 5 summarizes the percentage of correctly assigned requirement risk categories per predicted project.

Table 5. Prediction results for unseen project data with LOOCV

	A	B	C	D	E
Correctly predicted risk categories	79.85 %	73.72 %	97.82 %	87.92 %	94.79 %

6   Discussion

The results of the WLS regression for all projects, as shown in Table 4, indicate that the effect of NRR on requirement defects is positive and statistically significant (β_1 is positive and the p-value < 0.001). This result partially answers research question $RQ-1$. It suggest that the more requirements are directly or transitively related to a requirement the higher the defect rate of the requirement's implementation. This relation also implies a higher requirement implementation risk, assuming that all other independent variables remain constant. The WLS regression further indicates that an increase of $ADRR$ is associated with an increase of requirement defects ($\beta_2 = 0.352$), which provides another part to the answer to research question $RQ-1$. It suggests that the longer the average distance of a requirement to directly or transitively related requirements, the higher the requirement's implementation risk. The WLS regression also indicates that an increase of RIF is associated with a decrease of requirements defects ($\beta_3 = -0.068$), assuming that all other independent variables are constant.

The fact that none of the three traceability metrics were eliminated during stepwise regression with AIC and that all three metrics are statistically significant for the requirement defects implies that all three metrics have a significant effect on the defect rate in all five projects. This provides the answer to our research question $RQ-2$ suggesting that to properly estimate the implementation risk of a requirement, one should consider all three traceability metrics.

The results of the leave-one-out cross-validation (see Table 5) provide an answer to our research question $RQ-3$. For all five cases, our traceability metric predictor assigned requirements to the correct risk-level in unseen projects with at least 73.72 % correctness. For project C and E, the requirement risk predictions are even at a 95 % correctness level. These results suggest that the proposed traceability metrics can be used as an indicator for requirement implementation risks. For practitioners, it provides valuable support with prioritizing requirements as well as for deciding on which part of the implementation testing should be focused. Our proposed metrics can be used to provide recommendations for this tasks as well as to validate existing manual prioritizations.

7   Threats to Validity

A potential threat exists in the preparation and quality of the analyzed project data. Mitigating this threat, we carefully examined the available project artifact types and drew samples manually. These samples confirmed that every requirement artifact is stored as a database record with a unique identifier and trace links can be followed bi-directionally within Jira, from the source to the target requirement and vice versa. To avoid any manual bias during the project data preparation, we fully automated the process of project data collection and analysis. Although the process is fully automated, we carefully verified our tool that automates this process. Therefore we validated intermediate results of the process manually and cross-checked the data for inconsistencies and contradictions. Due to the public availability of the project artifacts and the fully automated collection and analysis process, our study can be replicated and additional projects could be included to further broaden the data corpus.

Another potential threat exists in the calculation of traceability metrics. The result of a traceability metric directly depends on the completeness and correctness of provided traceability data. In order to identify possible completeness problems, we performed completeness and correctness checks manually where possible. Based on the results of these manual checks, we concluded that all five projects are very mature developments and that the maintained artifacts and trace links are of high quality. Nonetheless, there remains a risk that we may have missed problems, especially incorrect trace links due to the large amount of data and our lack of project-specific domain expertise. Though, the great industrial acceptance and wide dissemination of the software products of all five projects supports our conclusions that all projects are of high maturity.

We analyzed five large scale projects to study the generalizability of our proposed traceability metrics for agile projects. There is a potential threat that one or multiple studied projects could follow an unusual development process which does not represent agile software development properly. To mitigate this threat, we defined project inclusion criteria as described in Section 4.1. Additionally, we manually assessed the project dashboards of all five projects to study the release cycles. We found that all projects follow the Scrum methodology, which is an accepted agile development methodology. We also found that all projects regularly develop and release small software increments in agile Sprints.

Furthermore, the number of defects in agile projects can vary between releases [23]. To mitigate this thread, we chose a rather long future defect observation period of twelve months. Every studied project created at least two releases within that period, meaning that we at least considered two release periods per analyzed project to capture potential post-release defect accumulations. Furthermore, the number of defects may be influenced by additional factors not been investigated within the current study, such as: the number of project members, the number of product end-users, or the experience of the development team. It remains a future exercise to study whether and how such additional factors influence the impact of the requirements complexity on the software defect rate, as measured by the proposed approach.

8   Related Work

Various researchers proposed traceability metrics to characterize traced software artifacts. For example, Pfleger and Bohner [25] proposed software maintenance metrics for traceability graphs. They distinguish vertical and horizontal traceability metrics. While vertical metrics are meant to characterize the developed product, horizontal metrics are meant to characterize the development process. To generically measure the complexity of requirements traceability, Costello et al. [10] proposed the use of statistic linkage metrics. Dick [11] extends the idea of analyzing traceability graphs by introducing trace link semantic, which he calls rich traceability. Main advantage of his approach is the applicability of propositional reasoning to analyze traceability relationships for consistency. Hull and Dick [15] advance the idea of rich traceability graphs and propose further metrics: *breadth* is related to the coverage, *depth* measures the number of layers making it a global metric, *growth* is related to the potential change impact, *balance* measures the distribution of growth factors, *latent change* measures the impact on a change. While all the proposed traceability metrics were meant to measure specific characteristics of the requirements traceability graph, little empirical evidence is available on how and to what extent these metrics support practitioners with activities such as prioritizing requirements or focusing tests.

Researchers also proposed a wide range of metrics to characterize software [12, 29,32] respectively software design [1,6,22]. In contrast to requirements traceability metrics, a wide range of studies provide empirical evidence for software and design metrics on how and to what extent these measures provide support during development. Nagappan et al. [24] as well as Graves et al. [14] study the appropriateness of software component complexity metrics to predict fault density. The implications of software design complexity measures on software defects are empirically investigated by Subramanyam et al. [31].

Although, the principles for measuring the characteristics of a graph are similar, no matter if it represents software (e.g., a software call graph), design (e.g., a component dependency graph), or requirements (e.g., a requirements traceability graph), empirical evidence of the practical benefit of requirement traceability metrics is lacking. As a first step, Mäder and Egyed [19] as well as Jaber et al. [16] conducted controlled experiments to investigate whether or not the existence of traceability data supports developers with software maintenance tasks. To the best of our knowledge, our study is the first to involve large scaled projects providing empirical evidence that requirement traceability metrics can be leveraged to systemically assess and predict the implementation risk of requirements.

9   Conclusions and Future Work

In this paper we focused on estimating the implementation risk of requirements through traceability in agile development projects. Estimating the implementation risk of requirements supports product managers and developers with prioritizing requirements and focusing tests on risky parts of the software.

Therefore, we proposed a set of three traceability metrics to estimate the implementation risk of requirements in this paper. To evaluate the applicability of our proposed metrics, we conducted an empirical study with five large scale agile development projects. The results of our study show that our proposed traceability metrics are suitable to estimate the implementation risk of requirements. We also found empirical evidence that our proposed metrics are generalizable, because the implementation risk of requirements could be estimated reliable in all five projects. Further, our LOOCV experiments show that our proposed traceability metrics can even be applied to unseen project data, making our proposed traceability metrics a potentially valuable tool to support practitioners with prioritizing requirements and making decisions on which part of the software the testing should focus.

Future work will focus on extending and improving the set of requirements traceability metrics to estimate requirement implementation risks. Especially, differences in the requirement structure such as different granularity levels shall be addressed with explicit metrics to improve the generalizability of our metrics. We also plan to extend our study to additional software development projects in order to gain more empirical evidence on the described findings. Finally, projects that do not follow agile development processes shall be included to gain further insights on whether or not the proposed metrics are also beneficial to estimate requirement implementation risks in plan-driven projects. The proposed approach and its evaluation were solely targeting agile development projects. While we hypothesize that the proposed traceability metrics are also applicable for other project types due to their generic nature, additional studies are required to investigate this hypothesis. We also plan to investigate additional potential influence factors such as: the number of project members, the number of product end-users, or the experience of the development team.

Acknowledgments. We are funded by the German Ministry of Education and Research (BMBF) grants: 16V0116, 01IS14026A and the excellence program of the TU Ilmenau.

References

1. Bansiya, J., Davis, C.G.: A hierarchical model for object-oriented design quality assessment. IEEE Transactions on Software Engineering **28**(1), 4–17 (2002)
2. Beck, K., Beedle, M., van Bennekum, A., Cockburn, A., Cunningham, W., Fowler, M., Grenning, J., Highsmith, J., Hunt, A., Jeffries, R., et al.: The agile manifesto (2001)
3. Boehm, B., Basili, V.R.: Software defect reduction top 10 list. Computer **34**(1), 135–137 (2001)
4. Boehm, B., Turner, R.: Using risk to balance agile and plan-driven methods. Computer **36**(6), 57–66 (2003)
5. Breusch, T.S., Pagan, A.R.: A simple test for heteroscedasticity and random coefficient variation. Econometrica: Journal of the Econometric Society, 1287–1294 (1979)
6. Briand, L.C., Wüst, J., Daly, J.W., Victor Porter, D.: Exploring the relationships between design measures and software quality in object-oriented systems. Journal of Systems and Software **51**(3), 245–273 (2000)

7. Burnham, K.P., Anderson, D.R., Huyvaert, K.P.: Aic model selection and multi-model inference in behavioral ecology: some background, observations, and comparisons. Behavioral Ecology and Sociobiology **65**(1), 23–35 (2011)
8. Cao, L., Ramesh, B.: Agile requirements engineering practices: An empirical study. IEEE Software **25**(1), 60–67 (2008)
9. Cohn, M.: Agile estimating and planning. Pearson Education (2006)
10. Costello, R.J., Liu, D.B.: Metrics for requirements engineering. Journal of Systems and Software **29**(1), 39–63 (1995)
11. Dick, J.: Rich traceability. In: Proc. of the 1st Int. Workshop on Traceability in Emerging Forms of Software Engineering, Edinburgh, Scotland, pp. 18–23 (2002)
12. Fenton, N.E., Pfleeger, S.L.: Software metrics: a rigorous and practical approach. PWS Publishing Co. (1998)
13. Git. http://git-scm.com/
14. Graves, T.L., Karr, A.F., Marron, J.S., Siy, H.: Predicting fault incidence using software change history. IEEE TSE **26**(7), 653–661 (2000)
15. Hull, E., Jackson, K., Dick, J.: Requirements engineering. Springer, London (2011)
16. Jaber, K., Sharif, B., Liu, C.: A study on the effect of traceability links in software maintenance. IEEE Access **1**, 726–741 (2013)
17. JIRA. https://www.atlassian.com/software/jira
18. Leffingwell, D.: Agile software requirements: lean requirements practices for teams, programs, and the enterprise. Addison-Wesley Professional (2010)
19. Mäder, P., Egyed, A.: Do developers benefit from requirements traceability when evolving and maintaining a software system? EmpSE, pp. 1–29 (2014)
20. Mäder, P., Gotel, O., Philippow, I.: Getting back to basics: promoting the use of a traceability information model in practice. In: ICSE Workshop on Traceability in Emerging Forms of Software Engineering, TEFSE, pp. 21–25. IEEE (2009)
21. Mäder, P., Gotel, O., Philippow, I.: Motivation matters in the traceability trenches. In: Proc. of the 17th IEEE RE conference, pp. 143–148. IEEE (2009)
22. Marinescu, R.: Measurement and quality in object-oriented design. In: Proc. of the 21st IEEE Int. Conference on Software Maintenance, pp. 701–704. IEEE (2005)
23. Murgia, A., Concas, G., Tonelli, R., Turnu, I.: Empirical study of software quality evolution in open source projects using agile practices. In: Proc. of the 1st International Symposium on Emerging Trends in Software Metrics, p. 11 (2009)
24. Nagappan, N., Ball, T., Zeller, A.: Mining metrics to predict component failures. In: Proc. of the 28th Int. Conf. on Software Engineering, pp. 452–461. ACM (2006)
25. Pfleeger, S.L., Bohner, S.A.: A framework for software maintenance metrics. In: Proc. of Software Maintenance conference, pp. 320–327. IEEE (1990)
26. Rempel, P., Mäder, P., Kuschke, T.: An empirical study on project-specific traceability strategies. In: Proceedings of the 21st IEEE International Requirements Engineering Conference (RE), pp. 195–204. IEEE (2013)
27. Rempel, P., Mäder, P., Kuschke, T., Cleland-Huang, J.: Mind the gap: assessing the conformance of software traceability to relevant guidelines. In: Proc. of the 36th International Conference on Software Engineering (ICSE), India (2014)
28. Rempel, P., Mäder, P., Kuschke, T., Philippow, I.: Requirements traceability across organizational boundaries - a survey and taxonomy. In: Doerr, J., Opdahl, A.L. (eds.) REFSQ 2013. LNCS, vol. 7830, pp. 125–140. Springer, Heidelberg (2013)
29. Sedigh-Ali, S., Ghafoor, A., Paul, R.A.: Software engineering metrics for cots-based systems. Computer **34**(5), 44–50 (2001)

30. Sillitti, A., Ceschi, M., Russo, B., Succi, G.: Managing uncertainty in requirements: a survey in documentation-driven and agile companies. In: 11th IEEE International Symposium on Software Metrics, p. 10. IEEE (2005)
31. Subramanyam, R., Krishnan, M.S.: Empirical analysis of ck metrics for object-oriented design complexity: Implications for software defects. IEEE Transactions on Software Engineering **29**(4), 297–310 (2003)
32. Washizaki, H., Yamamoto, H., Fukazawa, Y.: A metrics suite for measuring reusability of software components. In: Proceedings of the Ninth International of Software Metrics Symposium, pp. 211–223. IEEE (2003)

The Role of Catalogues of Threats and Security Controls in Security Risk Assessment: An Empirical Study with ATM Professionals

Martina de Gramatica[1], Katsiaryna Labunets[1(✉)], Fabio Massacci[1],
Federica Paci[1], and Alessandra Tedeschi[2]

[1] DISI, University of Trento, Trento, Italy
{martina.degramatica,katsiaryna.labunets,fabio.massacci,
federica.paci}@unitn.it
[2] Deep Blue srl, Roma, Italy
alessandra.tedeschi@dblue.it

Abstract. [**Context and motivation**] To remedy the lack of security expertise, industrial security risk assessment methods come with catalogues of threats and security controls. [**Question/problem**] We investigate in both qualitative and quantitative terms whether the use of catalogues of threats and security controls has an effect on the actual and perceived effectiveness of a security risk assessment method. In particular, we assessed the effect of using domain-specific versus domain-general catalogues on the actual and perceived efficacy of a security risk assessment method conducted by non-experts and compare it with the effect of running the same method by security experts but without catalogues.

[**Principal ideas/results**] The quantitative analysis shows that non-security experts who applied the method with catalogues identified threats and controls of the same quality of security experts without catalogues. The perceived ease of use was higher when participants used method without catalogues albeit only at 10% significance level. The qualitative analysis indicates that security experts have different expectations from a catalogue than non-experts. Non-experts are mostly worried about the difficulty of navigating through the catalogue (the larger and less specific the worse it was) while expert users found it mostly useful to get a common terminology and a checklist that nothing was forgotten.

[**Contribution**] This paper sheds light on the important features of the catalogues and discuss how they contribute into risk assessment process.

Keywords: Empirical study · Security risk assessment methods · MEM

1 Introduction

Security risk assessment is a key step in the design of critical systems. Yet, system architects often lack the necessary security knowledge to identify all security risks. Even experts focus on those risks which according to their experience were

© Springer International Publishing Switzerland 2015
S.A. Fricker and K. Schneider (Eds.): REFSQ 2015, LNCS 9013, pp. 98–114, 2015.
DOI: 10.1007/978-3-319-16101-3_7

critical in the past. Thus, they can forget to treat risks which are less interesting for them, although they might be relevant for the system. To alleviate this issue, industrial security risk assessment methods and standards come with catalogues of threats and security controls. The catalogues can be divided by size and specialization into domain-general catalogues like BSI IT-Grundschutz Catalogues [3], ISO/IEC 27002 [8], NIST 800-53 [20], and domain-specific catalogues like PCI DSS [23] (Banking domain) or EUROCONTROL ATM [6] (Air Traffic Management domain).

In this paper we report an empirical study on the role of catalogues of threats and controls in conducting security risk assessment. The goal of the study is to assess the *actual and perceived efficacy of catalogues* in performing a security risk assessment by non-experts (with the catalogues) and by experts (using the same method but without catalogues). Actual effectiveness has been quantitatively investigated as the quality of threats and security controls identified by the participants. Perception has been assessed both quantitatively via post-task questionnaire and qualitatively via focus group interviews with the participants.

The study involved 15 professionals in the Air Traffic Management (ATM) domain who worked individually to identify threats and security controls for the Remotely Operated Tower (ROT) application scenario. More than two third of the participants had more than 5 years of experience in the ATM, while the others had at least 2 years of specific experience.

The main findings are that domain experts that are not security experts can obtain almost the same results as domain experts without catalogues while applying a security risk assessment method. Regarding perceived efficacy, domain-specific catalogues were perceived to be easier to use than domain-general ones because they are easier to navigate and there is a clear mapping between threats and security controls.

In addition, the analysis of focus group interviews shows that non-experts and security experts have a different perception of catalogues. Non-experts found catalogues useful as starting point to identify threats and controls but at the same time they were concerned about the difficulty in navigating the catalogues because there were no link between threats and security controls. Security experts instead found catalogues mostly useful because they provide a common terminology to discuss about threats and controls and they can be used to check completeness of results.

In the remainder of the paper, Section 2 presents the research method; Section 3 presents the motivation of domain selection and Section 4 describes the setting of the study, whose findings are presented in Sections 5 and 6. Threats to validity to our study are discussed in Section 7 and Section 8 presents the related work on prior research in the area. The findings and conclusion are presented in Section 9.

2   Research Method

The goal of this study is to investigate whether catalogues of threats and security controls facilitate the execution of a security risk assessment process. In particular, we want to assess whether the use of catalogues has an effect on the actual and perceived efficacy of security risk assessment when used by people with no security expertise and comparing it with the effect of running the same assessment by security experts without catalogues. Accordingly, we formulated our research questions:

RQ1 *Does the use of domain specific or general catalogues improve the actual or perceived efficacy of a security risk assessment in comparison to each other and to the same assessment performed by experts without catalogues?*

RQ2 *Which are the qualitative features of a catalogue that impact actual or perceived efficacy?*

As our study is exploratory in nature, we applied a research approach combining both qualitative and quantitative methods. In particular, to address research questions *RQ1* on actual and perceived efficacy we used a quantitative approach and divided the participants into three groups: the first group conducted a security risk assessment with the support of a domain-specific catalogue (DOM CAT), the second group with the support of a domain-general (GEN CAT) one, while the third group worked without catalogue (NO CAT). All participants in the NO CAT group had security knowledge, while most of the participants in the DOM CAT and GEN CAT groups had limited or none security knowledge.

Then, we measured *actual efficacy* as the quality of results produced by the participants. Two security experts independently assessed the quality. They used a 5-item scale: *Bad* (1), when it is not clear which are the final threats or security controls for the scenario; *Poor* (2), when threats/security controls are not specific for the scenario; *Fair* (3), when *some* of them are related to the scenario; *Good* (4), threats/security controls are specific for the scenario; and *Excellent* (5), when the threats are significant for the scenario and security controls propose real solution for the scenario.

To measure *perceived efficacy* we asked the participants to fill in a post-task questionnaire along the Method Evaluation Model (MEM) [19]. According to MEM, we broke down perceived efficacy in *perceived ease of use (PEOU)* and *perceived usefulness (PU)*, and included the corresponding questions in the post-task questionnaire. The concrete post-task questions were adopted from the work of Opdahl and Sindre [21] in order to make comparison with related work easier. Questions were formulated as opposite statements with answers on a 5-point Likert scale. Table 3 in the appendix reports the post-task questionnaire.

To answer research question *RQ2* we involved participants in focus group interviews where they answered questions on the process followed to identify threats and controls and their perception of the method and the catalogues. We investigated the transcripts of the interviews through the open coding methodology [29, Chap. 8], on the basis of a pre-defined set of codes, slightly edited from a list of codes used in previous studies [12,13]. This selection of codes allowed to identify the most frequently mentioned topics in the interviews. We considered these topics as the most representative in the discussion. The qualitative analysis attempted to cast light on the catalogues' features affecting actual and perceived effectiveness of security risk assessment.

3   Domain Selection

One of the key issues to conduct our study is the selection of an appropriate domain. The ATM domain has been often used in Requirements Engineering. For example, see the work of Maiden and Robertson [14] for general Requirements Engineering and our own for Security Requirements Engineering [16]. We also selected this domain because security plays an important role to ensure the resilience of ATM Service provision. To this end, the SESAR (Single European Sky ATM Research Program) project 16.02.03 focuses on analyzing existing approaches for security risks identification and tailoring them to the ATM domain.

The SESAR ATM Security Risk Assessment Method (SecRAM), developed within the project 16.02.03 [25], is the " official " method applied by ATM professionals in the SESAR program. SESAR designed SecRAM as a simple, step-wise method that should be applicable to all the SESAR Operational Focus Areas (OFAs). The overall SecRAM process is divided into seven steps as follows: 1) primary asset identification and impact assessment, 2) supporting assets identification and evaluation, 3) threats scenarios identification, 4) impact evaluation, 5) likelihood evaluation, 6) risk level evaluation, and 7) risk treatment. The method should be clear to personnel with little expertise and background in security and risk management. It is also should support the integration and comparison of security risk assessment results from different SESAR OFAs. In order to support non-expert, ATM professionals considered catalogues of threats and security controls as a great added value to carry out efficient and effective security risk assessment in SESAR.

We selected SecRAM as a reference security risk assessment method under study aiming to compare its effectiveness with domain-specific and domain-general catalogues. As instances of domain-specific and domain-general catalogues we selected EUROCONTROL ATM catalogues and BSI IT Grundschutz catalogues, respectively.

The ATM catalogues were developed by EUROCONTROL to provide the best practices in security and safety analysis for ATM domain. They consist of three main parts: threats, pre and post security controls. The catalogues describe 32 threats of three types: Physical, Information and Procedural. The catalogues also propose 33 pre and 18 post controls to mitigate each threat. Each control is linked to the mitigated threats and a description of the security control procedure.

The BSI IT-Grundschutz standard was developed by Bundesamt für Sicherheit in der Informationstechnik (BSI[1]), and it is widely used in Germany. It is compatible with the ISO 2700x family of standards. The BSI IT-Grundschutz catalogues not only describe possible threats and what has to be done in general to mitigate them, but they also provide concrete examples on how security controls should be implemented. The catalogues describe 621 threats of the following types: Basic threats, Force Majeure, Organizational Shortcomings, Human

---

[1] Federal Office for Information Security (English).

Error, Technical Failure and Deliberate Acts. The safeguards catalogues describe 1444 security controls related to Infrastructure, Organization, Personnel, Hardware and software, Communication and Contingency planning.

The application scenario was chosen among one of the ATM new operational scenarios that have already been assessed by SESAR with the SecRAM methodology: the Remotely Operated Tower (ROT).

The Remote and Virtual Tower, is a new operational concept proposed by SESAR [26,27]. The main change with respect to current operations is that control tower operators will no longer be located at the aerodrome. They will move to a Remotely Operated Tower Center. Each tower module will be remotely connected to (at least) one airport and consist of one or several Controller Working Positions. The operator will be able to do all air traffic management tasks (e.g. authorize landing, departure, etc.) from this position. The idea is that operator will be able to control remotely more than one airport. The visual surveillance will be provided by a reproduction of the Out of The Window view, by using visual information capture and/or other sensors such as cameras with a 360-degree view, which will be able to zoom 36 times closer than current binoculars in all weather conditions. The visual reproduction can be overlaid with information from additional sources if available, for example, surface movement radar, surveillance radar, or other positioning and surveillance implementations providing the positions of moving object within the airport movement area and vicinity. The collected data, either from a single source or combined, is reproduced for the operator on data/monitor screens, projectors or similar technical solutions. The use of technologies will also enhance the visual reproduction in all visibility conditions (e.g., bad weather conditions).

This scenario presents relevant ATM and security issues and technological challenges that can benefit from a Security Risk Assessment. As apparent from the description, the ROT concept will be encompassed by data confidentiality, integrity and availability issues, also affecting airport safety, as well as physical security issues, like the on-site protection of the remotely located cameras, sensors and surveillance radars in the aerodrome, to be analyzed during our experiment.

4   Execution and Demographics

The study was run in May 2014 at Deep Blue premises and consisted of an empirical study with 15 professionals from several ATM Italian companies. As mentioned before the participants were divided into three groups and assigned to three different treatments. They were asked to apply individually the same method, namely SESAR SecRAM, with the support of domain-specific catalogues (EUROCONTROL ATM), general-domain catalogues (BSI IT-Grundschutz) or without any catalogues. Before starting, the participants were administered a questionnaire to collect information on their background and previous knowledge of other risk assessment methods.

The study was based on a step-wise process consisting of three interacting phases:

Table 1. Participants' Demographic Statistics

Variable	Scale	Mean	Distribution
Age	Years	33.1	20% were 25-29 years old; 53.3% were 30-39 years old; 20% were 40 and older
Gender	Sex		66.7% male; 33.3% female
Academic Degree			73.3% had MSc degree; 26.7% had PhD degree
Work Experience	Years	7.9	26.7% had $\geq$ 2 and <5 years; 46.7% had $\geq$ 5 and <10 years; 26.7% had $\geq$ 10 years
Experience in Risk Assessment	Years	0.67	Three participants had 2 years, 1.5 years and 0.25 years, respectively
Security/Privacy Knowledge	Yes/No	-	47% had experience; 53% had no experience

Training. The application scenario description was administered to participants for an individual reading. A frontal-training phase followed in which the method designer introduced the considered methodology process through a step by step tutorial.

Application. Each step of the method introduced in the tutorial, was forthwith applied individually on the case study until the completion of the last step.

Evaluation. Three evaluators independently judged the quality of the threats and security controls identified by the participants, providing marks and comments.

After the application phase we administered to the participants a post-task questionnaire to gather their perception of the method and the catalogues employed. They were later involved into focus groups, according to their treatment, to discuss drawbacks and benefits of the method and the catalogues under study. A list of questions guide the discussion that had been audio recorded for further analysis. The main positive and negative aspects generated in the focus groups then were reported on post-it notes.

The participants of the study were 15 practitioners from the different ATM companies. Table 1 presents descriptive statistics about the participants. Most of the participants (73.4%) reported that they had at least 5 years of working experience, some participants (26.7%) reported from 2 to 5 years of workings experience. In addition, almost half of participants (47%) reported that they had security/privacy knowledge, the rest did not report any similar knowledge. Three out of sixteen participants reported from 3 months up to 2 years experience in security risk assessment.

5 Quantitative Results

In this section we discuss the results on actual efficacy of the risk assessment and perceived efficacy of the method and catalogues. Tables 2a and 2b report the median values for Actual Efficacy, PU and PEOU of the method for each treatment. The detailed results of risk assessment delivered by the participants are reported in the Table 4. The detailed statistics on post-task questionnaire responses are reported in Table 5.

Table 2. Summary of Quantitative Results

(a) Threats				(b) Security Controls			

	DOM CAT	GEN CAT	NO CAT
AE	3.5	2.5	2.5
PU	4	4	4
PEOU	3	4	4

	DOM CAT	GEN CAT	NO CAT
AE	3.5	2.5	3
PU	4	4	4
PEOU	3	3	4

The AE row reports the medians of experts assessment of the threats and security controls produced by the participants. The PU (respectively PEOU) row reports the medians of participants' responses to a post-task questions about method's PU (PEOU). All values are on a 1-5 scale with 5 being the best score. The columns describe the type of task performed by the participants: risk assessment with a domain specific catalogue (DOM CAT), a generic catalogue (GEN CAT), or no catalogue by security experts (NOCAT).

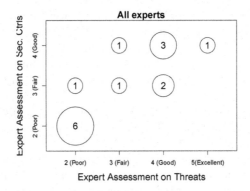

Fig. 1. Experts assessment of quality of threats and security controls

Actual Efficacy. As mentioned before we measured method's actual efficacy as a quality of threats and security controls identified by the participants. Two ATM security experts independently assessed the quality. They are reported a similar assessment for each group. Figure 1 illustrates the average of experts' evaluation for threats (reported on x-axis) and security controls (on y-axis). Six participants out of fifteen performed poorly. In terms of the final assessment we observed that: a) the experts marked bad participants the same way; b) they consistently marked moderately good participants; and c) they had a different evaluation only for the threats of one participant and for the security controls of another participant out of 15 participants.

We used Wilcoxon test to validate if the difference in experts' evaluation is statistically significant. The results showed that there is no statistically significant differences in the evaluations of two experts both for threats ($p = 0.09$) and controls ($p = 0.77$).

The first lines in Tables 2a and 2b report the quality of threats and security controls identified with three treatments. We used Kruskal-Wallis (KW) test to investigate the statically significant difference in the quality between treatments.

Table 2a shows that participants who used domain-specific catalogue to identify security controls performed as participants who did not use the catalogues.

While, the participants who applied the domain-general catalogue performed even worst than participants without catalogue. The difference in the quality of security controls is not statistically significant based on the results of KW test. Therefore we can conclude that there is no difference in the actual efficacy of a security risk assessment when used with catalogues by non-experts and without catalogues by security experts.

Perceived Efficacy. Table 2a shows that there is no difference in method's PU when the method is applied with or without catalogues of threats. Same results we have for method's PU regarding security controls identification (see Table 2b). Considering method's PEOU, the participants who conducted threats identification with domain-general catalogue of threats or without catalogue reported higher method's PEOU than participants who applied the domain-specific catalogues. While for method's PEOU for security controls identification only the participants who conducted risk assessment without catalogues reported higher perception. We also used non-parametric KW test to analyze the differences in participants PU and PEOU of the method. However, the results of KW test did not reveal any significant differences in PU and PEOU except one. The results of KW test showed: there is 10% significant difference in method's PEOU with respect to security controls identification (KW p =0.099). However, the post-hoc analysis with Mann-Whitney test with Holm correction [10, Chap. 14.2] did not show any significant differences between treatments. Therefore, we can conclude that there is no difference in the perceived efficacy of the method when used by non-experts with catalogues and by security experts without catalogues.

Exploring Correlations. We also explored possible correlations between actual and perceived efficacy with Kendall tau rank correlation coefficient. We used this test because our data are ordinal and have many ties. The correlation test revealed only one significant relation between the quality of threats and participants' answers to the question *"method helped me in brainstorming on the security controls"*. This is positive statistically significant correlation (p =0.04, $\tau = 0.45$).

6   Qualitative Results

In this section we report the analysis result of focus groups interviews and post-it notes sessions with the participants. The results explain the differences in the perception of two types of catalogues and outline the key features that effective catalogues must have.

Catalogue Structure. The analysis of interviews shows that the structure of catalogue is a key aspect in the identification of threats and security controls. Thanks to its basic layout, the clear tables and its relative length, the domain-specific catalogue is generally perceived by the participants as easier to browse and to read: *"I read only the titles* [namely the reference to the "Generic Threat" and the "Attack Threat"], *they were quite explanatory, therefore a very short* *consultation of the catalog allowed me to produce enough content"* [DOM CAT participant]. This is particularly true in comparison with the domain-general catalogue, consisting of a long list of items, perceived as *"not user-friendly at a first read"* [GEN CAT participant] and *"difficult to navigate and master due to its length and structure"* [GEN CAT participant].

Another relevant aspect in the structure of the domain-specific catalogues is the presence of linking references between threats and security controls. According to some participants this feature makes the identification of the controls an automatic mechanism: *"Once identified the threat, finding out controls was really a mechanical work"*[DOM CAT participant]. Even more so for security-novices, traceability is perceived as a fundamental feature in the structure of the catalogue. Because it provides a one-directional link between the two objects of interest, that makes the mistake quite impossible. In contrast, the domain-general catalogue does not provide this support and therefore the findings are affected: *"The identification of security controls was more difficult because you had to map them with the threats previously identified but there was no direct link in the catalogue. It was mainly due to a problem of usability of the catalogue"* [GEN CAT participant]. Examples, present in the specific-domain catalogue, are also perceived as helpful in the identification of threats and security controls.

Based on these findings we can conclude that a series of paths through structure of the catalogue will facilitate the threats and security controls identification. Thus, the usability of the catalogues is of capital importance mostly for security non-experts. The same we can said about navigability and traceability, two of the features that make the domain-specific catalogue a practical and useful tool for the risk assessment.

Catalogue Size and Coverage. If a catalogue is meant for security-novices the abstraction level should be kept low and just provide few critical threats and security controls. Otherwise, the security-novices can feel overwhelmed and not able to find any threat or security control at all. This is particularly the case of the general-domain catalogue, judged as: *"Very difficult to consult for non-technical people"*[GEN CAT participant] given the high number of threats and controls proposed. An interesting statement in this regard, comes from a participant who was not assigned to any catalogue but had the chance to glance at the general-domain catalogue. His opinion expresses the potential problem inherent to the use of a too complex catalogue: *"I saw people near to me; they were not able to find out stuff in the catalogue, they kept on getting lost in the pages and eventually they came up always with the same two or three items"*[NOCAT participant].

Regarding the coverage instead, considered in terms of specificity of the items , the opinion expressed by the participants was quite contrasting: this is particularly proven by the statements from the security experts claiming that the suggestions in both catalogues were very generic, rather than specific, precise and well-defined threats and controls: "[The catalogue provided a] *list of non-specific threats impacting the specific concept under investigation"* [GEN CAT participant] (from a security-expert user). The same result comes from the domain-specific catalogue: "*I found the catalogue useful, but I noticed that many threats were repeated*" [DOM CAT participant]. While security-novices did not support the idea and seems were in general more satisfied by the use of the catalogue. This is probably due to the fact that, without any experience any kind support is of great benefit. Security-novices than could not be able to judge the quality of the results achieved given their little past experience.

To be a useful tool for security experts the catalogue must provide specific threats and controls, otherwise it only allows to define generic and thus ineffective controls.

Catalogue as Common Language. One feature of the catalogue perceived as essential by every participant, irrespectively of the type of catalogue employed, is the fact that a catalogue by itself provides a common terminology for all users. As suggested by one participant, "*The catalogue could be seen as a useful tool, able to formalize the controls that have been formulated in an informal way, and to lead them back into a common nomenclature*" [DOM CAT participant]. "*The problem arises when we are in the same group and we use a different language*" [NOCAT participant]. The demand for a standard language caused by the need of sharing, discussing and presenting results that could be understood and therefore adopted by all participants of the risk assessment process. Unsurprisingly, this aspect is mostly perceived as important by participants who were not assigned to any catalogue.

Catalogue as Check-list. One tendency identified in the analysis is the difference in the opinion of security experts and security-novices about their general perception towards the catalogue. Security-novices indeed are more prone to express a positive judgment on the benefit of using the catalogue. While security-experts tend to be more uncertain about the real advantages of the catalogue. This could be explained by the fact that the catalogue represents an essential support for users without any (or with little) experience, as claimed here: "*The catalogue is really helpful if you do not have any background*" [DOM CAT participant]. While the added value for experienced users is not as higher as expected.

Furthermore, the statements collected from security-experts suggest an additional aspect: "*The first step is to use your own experience and then to use the catalogue to cover generic aspects that could be forgotten*"[NOCAT participant]. For security-experts the catalogue is perceived as a check-list, as something that can be used after a brainstorming session where user works based on his own experience. In this way, the catalogue is supposed to provide the verification of the efficiency and the coverage of the threats and security controls identified. For security-novices on the contrary, the catalogue represents: "*A good starting point for the evaluation of the threats and the controls.*" [DOM CAT participant].

Catalogue and Knowledge. Participants with security knowledge cared more about the quality of threats and security controls that they could identify with the support of the catalogues. That is mainly due to the fact that they used their expertise to evaluate the achieved results. Security experts based on their previous knowledge expected more specific results from the support of the catalogue. While security-novice were not able to judge the quality of the identified threats and controls. Therefore, they were more concerned about the usability of the catalogues, as demonstrated by their observations on the traceability and the navigability of the catalogues (see sections above).

7   Threats to Validity

The main threats to validity are related to internal, conclusion and external validity [30].

Another threat to internal validity could be the size of catalogues as the domain-general catalogues are significantly lager than the domain-specific ones in order to cover more grounds. We mitigated this threat by making the use of domain-general catalogues of similar difficulty as domain-specific one (155 pages) we prepare a short version of general catalogues (~55 pages) that contained only the list of available threats and security controls. But the participants still had access to the full version of the domain-general catalogues (~2500 pages).

The main threat to conclusion validity is related to the *sample size* that must be big enough to come to correct conclusions. We aware that due to the low number of participants (N=5 × 3) it is unlikely to draw any strong statistical results. But Meyer et al. [18] show that it is possible to have statistically significant results for the samples contain 3 and more observations. To control possible effect of participants' background on the results we collect information about participants' through demographics and background questionnaire at the beginning of the study. To mitigate possible effect of previous knowledge about object of the study the participants were given a step by step tutorial on the security risk assessment method and received textual description of the application scenario.

Another threat to conclusion validity could be the number of security risk assessment which produced low quality threats and controls based on the experts evaluation (6 out of 15). However, we think the level of quality reflects the diversity of participants' knowledge and expertise. It could be a threat to validity if we would have had all the risk assessment producing threats and controls of the same quality.

The main threat to external validity external validity is that both the risk assessment method and scenario were chosen within the ATM domain. However, the chosen risk assessment method is compliant with ISO 27005 standard that can be applied to different domains not just to the ATM. Therefore, this threat is not present in our study.

8   Related Work

In this section we reviewed the studies that relevant to our work that are studies comparing security methods and studies which investigated the role of structured knowledge in Requirement Engineering (RE).

Empirical Evaluation of Security Methods. There are many catalogues that describes existing security problems and countermeasure. We can divide them into general catalogues that describe Information Systems security practices like BSI IT-Grundschutz Catalogues [3], ISO/IEC 27002 and 27005 [7,8], NIST 800-30 and 800-53 [20,28], COBIT 5 [1,4], or domain-specific catalogues like PCI DSS [23] for banking security, or EATM for security and safety in ATM, OWASP [22] for web application security.

Yet, most of the studies evaluate the effectiveness of the risk assessment process detached from the security knowledge [9,11,12,21,24]. The effect of the use of catalogues on the actual and perceived effectiveness of risk assessment is not yet studied. And it is still a question which catalogues' aspects affect actual effectiveness of risk assessment and how they impact user perception.

Opdahl and Sindre [21] reported two controlled experiment with 28 and 35 students to compare attack trees and misuse cases. In [11] the same group of researchers reported the replication of the experiment with industrial professionals. Both experiments showed that attack trees help to identify more threats than misuse cases. In our study we adopted similar perception variables and post-task questions to measure them.

Jung et al. [9] reported two controlled experiments (7 PhD students and 11 practitioners) to compare two safety analysis methods, namely Fault Trees (FT) and Component Integrated Fault Trees (CFT). The methods were compared with respect to the quality of the results and participants' perception. The experiments showed that CFT could be beneficial for users without expertise in FT. Similar to this work, we adopted quality of results as a way to measure actual effectiveness of the method.

Among the experiments which studied industrial security assessment methodologies, Scandariato et al. [24] reported a descriptive study with 41 MSc students to observe how STRIDE works in laboratory conditions. The goal of this study was to assess STRIDE with respect to productivity of participants, and the correctness and completeness of the results. The participants were trained on STRIDE application during three lectures that is a reasonable time for training. As an application scenario was chosen a medium-scale distributed Digital Publishing System. The participants had 4 hours to apply STRIDE in the class and were allowed to finish the task as homework. The results of the experiment showed that precision of the results was acceptable but their productivity was quite low. In our study we selected a mix-method approach to evaluate both performance of the participants and their perception of risk assessment method and catalogues. We also completed our study with focus groups interview and post-it notes session in order to investigate the reasons behind quantitative results and shed light on the corresponding specific aspects of catalogues.

Labunets et al. [12] reported controlled experiment with 28 MSc students to compare the actual effectiveness and perception of visual (CORAS) and textual (SREP) methods for security risk assessment. The results of the experiment showed that visual method is more effective in identifying threats and better perceived by the participants than the textual one. Similar to previous study, the recent work of Labunets et al. [13] reported controlled experiment with 29 MSc students to compare textual (EUROCONTROL SecRAM) vs. visual (CORAS) industrial security risk assessment methods. The results showed that there is no difference in actual effectiveness of two methods, but the visual method had better perception. In our study we adopted similar experimental protocol proposed in [13]. We also adopted similar dependent variables (actual effectiveness, perceived usefulness and perceived ease of use). It is noteworthy to mention that in [13] participants reported that security risk assessment methods "would benefit from availability of catalogues of threats and security controls".

Considering similar empirical studies in the ATM domain it is worthy to mention the works of Maiden et al. [14,15]. They reported several case studies in ATM domain to evaluate the effectiveness of RESCUE, a scenario-driven requirements engineering method. The studies were conducted as series of RESCUE workshops with ATM professionals from different backgrounds. The participants applied method to gather requirements for the real complex ATM systems. The authors collected qualitative data by mean of post-it notes, color-coded idea cards and pin boards. The results of the studies demonstrated the effectiveness of the RESCUE method. Similar to Maiden et al., we conducted our study in form of two-days workshop with ATM professionals from different backgrounds. We concluded workshop with focus group interviews with participants to collect their opinion about most important aspects of the catalogues.

Empirical Studies on the Role of Structured Knowledge. The role of structured knowledge, i.e. catalogues, has not been investigated in the security community, but it has been investigated in RE community.

The work of Mavin and Maiden [17] is the closest to our study. This work aimed to investigate if structured knowledge have an effect on the effectiveness of walkthrough techniques and, therefore, led to better effectiveness in elicitation of stakeholder requirements. They also investigate if the domain-specific scenarios increase the effectiveness of requirements elicitation comparing to the other technique. The authors conducted a case study with a team of ATM professionals. The results showed that the use of walkthroughs with domain-specific scenarios doubled the number of elicited requirements comparing to the other method that was used by the team over the previous 6 months. In our study we also aimed to investigate the effect of knowledge on the effectiveness of the security risk assessment. In our case knowledge introduced into security risk assessment process in form of domain-specific or domain-general catalogues of threats and security controls.

To the best of our knowledge there is only one study aiming to investigate the effectiveness of using catalogues but in requirements engineering. Cysneiros [5] evaluated the effectiveness of using catalogues on nonfunctional requirements elicitation. The paper reported a controlled experiment with 12 fourth year students. The results of the experiment showed that the groups used catalogues with a method performed better than the others participants applied either method without catalogues or catalogues without method. However, there is no similar papers aiming to investigate effectiveness of catalogues of threats and security controls. In our study we compared the effect of using domain-specific and domain-general catalogues vs. using just security risk assessment method on the actual and perceived effectiveness.

9   Discussion and Conclusions

Security catalogue is an important part of security risk assessment process. Barnum and McGraw [2] admitted a crucial role of catalogues: *"as the [security] field evolves and establishes best practices, knowledge management can play a central role in encapsulating and spreading the emerging discipline more efficiently."*

The aim of catalogues of threats and security controls is to put best security practices into uniform document that can be re-used in security risk assessment. In this paper we have investigated in both qualitative and quantitative terms the effect of using domain-specific catalogues versus domain-general catalogues, and compare them with the effects of using the same method by security expert but without catalogues.

In quantitative terms there is no difference in the actual effectiveness of a security risk assessment method when used with catalogues by non-experts and without catalogues by security experts, albeit only few groups achieved a high quality score in terms of identified threats and security controls.

The qualitative analysis, carried with focus group interview and post-it notes session, showed that security experts have a different expectations from a catalogue than non-experts. Non-experts were mostly worried about the difficulty of navigating through the catalogue while expert users found it mostly useful to get a common terminology and a checklist that nothing was forgotten.

The catalogue alone does not facilitate the identification of threats and security controls. Participants without security knowledge were able to identify some threats and controls but these were not specific for the scenario under analysis. Participants who used the catalogues and had security knowledge were able to produce good threats and controls. Those who had security knowledge and did not use any catalogue performed the same or sometimes even worse than other participants. Catalogues could provide support for discussion among the analysts because they provide a common language for analysts with different background. They could also be used to check the completeness and coverage of the results.

In summary, the study show that with the use of the catalogues a satisfactory number of threats and controls can be identified. Results of higher quality can be better achieved through a combination of the catalogue and the added value of experience. If the latter is expensive to get, a domain-specific catalogue is your second best bet.

Acknowledgments. This work has been partly supported by the EU under grant agreement n.285223 (SECONOMICS) and by the SESAR JU WPE under contract 12-120610-C12 (EMFASE).

A   Additional information

Table 3. Post-task Questionnaire

Q#	Type	Question (positive statement)
1	PEOU	SecRAM helped me in brainstorming on the threats
2	PEOU	SecRAM helped me in brainstorming on the security controls
3	PEOU	I found SecRAM easy to use
4	PU	SecRAM process is well detailed
5	PEOU	SecRAM was difficult to master
6	PEOU	I was never confused about how to apply SecRAM to the application
7	PU	I would have found specific threats more quickly with the SecRAM
8	PU	I would have found specific security controls more quickly with the SecRAM
9	PU	SecRAM made the security analysis more systematic
10	PEOU	SecRAM made it easier to evaluate whether threats were appropriate to the context
11	PEOU	SecRAM made it easier to evaluate whether security controls were appropriate to the context
12	PU	SecRAM made the search for specific threats more systematic
13	PU	SecRAM made the search for specific security controls more systematic
14	PU	If I need to update the analysis it will be easier with SecRAM than with common sense
15	PU	SecRAM made the security analysis easier than an ad hoc approach
16	PU	SecRAM made me more productive in finding threats
17	PU	SecRAM made me more productive in finding security controls

Table reports post-task questions and their perception type, PU or PEOU (questions about intention to use and perceive leverage are omitted). Some questions do no specify whether the method was used for threats or for controls. In that case we have used the corresponding answers for both threats and controls.

Table 4. Participants, Their Results and Quality Assessment

ID	Security Knowledge	Working Experience	Education Length	Catalog	Quantity		Quality (Exp1)		Quality (Exp2)	
					Threats	SecCtrls	Threats	SecCtrls	Threats	SecCtrls
P01	No	6	MSC	GEN CAT	17	28	2	2	3	3
P02	No	5	PHD	GEN CAT	9	17	1	2	2	2
P03	Yes	4	MSC	GEN CAT	27	50	4	4	4	3
P04	No	5	MSC	GEN CAT	9	23	2	2	3	3
P05	Yes	4	PHD	GEN CAT	9	15	3	3	3	3
P06	No	8	DIPLOMA	DOM CAT	22	38	4	3	3	3
P07	No	4	MSC	DOM CAT	7	14	2	2	2	2
P08	No	5	PHD	DOM CAT	24	66	4	4	4	4
P09	Yes	2	MSC	DOM CAT	24	45	5	4	5	4
P10	No	7	PHD	DOM CAT	16	32	4	4	3	3
P11	No	5	MSC	NOCAT	10	13	2	1	3	3
P12	Yes	14	PHD	NOCAT	15	47	3	3	4	3
P13	Yes	17	MSC	NOCAT	15	19	2	3	3	3
P14	Yes	18	MSC	NOCAT	24	28	2	2	3	3
P15	Yes	15	MSC	NOCAT	6	13	2	4	4	3

Table presents the information about security knowledge, working experience and degree of participants; number of threats and security controls identified by participants and the assessment from two ATM experts on the quality of threats and security controls.

Table 5. Responses to the Post-task Questions

Q#	Type	DOM CAT		GEN CAT		NO CAT	
		Mean	Median	Mean	Median	Mean	Median
1	PEOU	4.2	4	4	4	3.2	3
2	PEOU	4.2	4	3.2	4	3.2	3
3	PEOU	3.4	3	3.2	4	4.2	4
4	PU	3.4	4	3.4	3	3.8	4
5	PEOU	3	3	3.4	4	3.8	4
6	PEOU	2.8	3	2.6	3	4	4
7	PU	3.4	3	2.4	2	3.2	3
8	PU	3.8	4	2.4	2	3.2	3
9	PU	3.8	4	4.2	4	4.2	5
10	PEOU	3.2	3	3.4	4	3	3
11	PEOU	2.8	3	2.6	2	3	3
12	PU	3.8	4	3.8	4	3.6	3
13	PU	3.4	3	3.6	4	3.6	4
14	PU	4	4	3.6	4	4.6	5
15	PU	2.8	3	2.6	3	3.6	4
16	PU	4.2	4	3	4	3.4	4
17	PU	4	4	3.4	4	3.4	3

Table reports mean and median value of participants' responses to each post-task question and the type of the question.

References

1. Information System Audit and Control Association: COBIT 5: A Business Framework for the Governance and Management of Enterprise IT (2012)
2. Barnum, S., McGraw, G.: Knowledge for software security. IEEE Security & Privacy **3**(2), 74–78 (2005)
3. BSI: IT-Grundschutz Catalogues (2005)
4. COBIT: Control Practices: Guidance to Achieve Control Objective for Successful IT Governance, 2nd edn. IT Governance Institute (2007)
5. Cysneiros, L.M.: Evaluating the effectiveness of using catalogues to elicit nonfunctional requirements. In: WER, pp. 107–115 (2007)
6. EATM: Threats, pre-controls and post-controls catalogues. European Organisation for the Safety of Air Navigation (2009)
7. ISO: Iso/iec 27005: Information technology security techniques - information security risk management (2012)
8. ISO: IEC 27002: 2013 (EN) Information technology-Security techniques-Code of practice for information security controls Switzerland. ISO/IEC (2013)
9. Jung, J., Hoefig, K., Domis, D., Jedlitschka, A., Hiller, M.: Experimental comparison of two safety analysis methods and its replication. In: 2013 ACM/IEEE International Symposium on Empirical Software Engineering and Measurement, pp. 223–232. IEEE (2013)
10. Juristo, N., Moreno, A.M.: Basics of software engineering experimentation. Springer Publishing Company, Incorporated (2010)
11. Karpati, P., Redda, Y., Opdahl, A.L., Sindre, G.: Comparing attack trees and misuse cases in an industrial setting. Inf. Soft. Technology **56**(3), 294–308 (2014)
12. Labunets, K., Massacci, F., Paci, F., Tran, L.M.: An experimental comparison of two risk-based security methods. In: Proc. of ESEM 2013, pp. 163–172 (2013)

13. Labunets, K., Paci, F., Massacci, F., Ruprai, R.: An experiment on comparing textual vs. visual industrial methods for security risk assessment. In: 2014 IEEE Fourth International Workshop on Empirical Requirements Engineering (EmpiRE), pp. 28–35. IEEE (2014)

14. Maiden, N., Robertson, S.: Integrating creativity into requirements processes: experiences with an air traffic management system. In: Proceedings of the 13th IEEE International Conference on Requirements Engineering, pp. 105–114. IEEE (2005)

15. Maiden, N.A.M., Jones, S.V., Manning, S., Greenwood, J., Renou, L.: Model-driven requirements engineering: synchronising models in an air traffic management case study. In: Persson, A., Stirna, J. (eds.) CAiSE 2004. LNCS, vol. 3084, pp. 368–383. Springer, Heidelberg (2004)

16. Massacci, F., Paci, F., Tran, L.M.S., Tedeschi, A.: Assessing a requirements evolution approach: Empirical studies in the air traffic management domain. Journal of Systems and Software (2013)

17. Mavin, A., Maiden, N.: Determining socio-technical systems requirements: experiences with generating and walking through scenarios. In: Proceedings of the 11th IEEE International on Requirements Engineering Conference, pp. 213–222. IEEE (2003)

18. Meyer, J.P., Seaman, M.A.: A comparison of the exact kruskal-wallis distribution to asymptotic approximations for all sample sizes up to 105. The Journal of Experimental Education $81(2)$, 139–156 (2013)

19. Moody, D.L.: The method evaluation model: a theoretical model for validating information systems design methods. In: Proceedings of the 11th European Conference of Information Systems (ECIS), pp. 1327–1336 (2003)

20. NIST: SP. 800-53. Recommended Security Controls for Federal Information Systems, 800-53 (2013)

21. Opdahl, A.L., Sindre, G.: Experimental comparison of attack trees and misuse cases for security threat identification. Inf. Soft. Technology $51(5)$, 916–932 (2009)

22. OWASP: The Ten Most Critical Web Application Security Risks 2013. The Open Web Application Security Project (2013)

23. PCI DSS: Payment Card Industry Data Security Standards. http://www.pcisecuritystandards.org

24. Scandariato, R., Wuyts, K., Joosen, W.: A descriptive study of microsoft's threat modeling technique. REJ, pp. 1–18 (2014)

25. SESAR: ATM Security Risk Assessment Methodology. SESAR WP16.02.03: ATM Security, February 2003

26. SESAR: Single Remote Tower Technical Specification Remotely Operated Tower Multiple Controlled Airports with Integrated Working Position - project P12.04.07 (2012)

27. SESAR: OSED for Remote Provision of ATS to Aerodromes - project P06.09.03 (2013)

28. Stoneburner, G., Goguen, A., Feringa, A.: Risk management guide for information technology systems. NIST special publication, 800-30 (2002)

29. Strauss, A., Corbin, J.M.: Basics of qualitative research: Grounded theory procedures and techniques. Sage Publications, Inc (1990)

30. Wohlin, C., Runeson, P., Höst, M., Ohlsson, M.C., Regnell, B., Wesslén, A.: Experimentation in software engineering. Springer (2012)

Analyzing and Enforcing Security Mechanisms on Requirements Specifications

Tong Li$^{(\boxtimes)}$, Jennifer Horkoff, and John Mylopoulos

University of Trento, Trento, Italy
{tong.li,horkoff,jm}@disi.unitn.it

Abstract. [**Context and motivation**] Security mechanisms, such as firewalls and encryption, operationalize security requirements, such as confidentiality and integrity. [**Question/problem**] Although previous work has pointed out that the application of a security mechanism affects system specifications, there is no systematic approach to describe and analyze this impact. [**Principal ideas/results**] In this paper, we investigate more than 40 security mechanisms that are well documented in security pattern repositories in order to better understand what they are and how they function. [**Contribution**] Based on this study, we propose a conceptual model for security mechanisms, and evaluate this model against 20 security mechanisms. Using the conceptual model, we provide a systematic process for analyzing and enforcing security mechanisms on system requirements. We also develop a prototype tool to facilitate the application and evaluation of our approach.

1 Introduction

Dealing with security requirements in the early stages of the system development has become an important topic in Requirements Engineering (RE) and Security research, as software companies have grown tired of spending millions to fix system flaws downstream. Security requirements analysis techniques, such as Misuse Cases [25], Obstacle analysis [26], Secure Tropos [18], involve eliciting security requirements and identifying security mechanisms to fulfill those requirements. Security mechanisms, such as firewalls and encryption, operationalize security requirements, such as confidentiality or integrity. As such, they do not function independently but interact and constrain parts of the system in specific ways. As a result, leveraging a security mechanism not only introduces new requirements to the system, but also inevitably modifies existing system requirements. Viewed as a cross-cutting concern [23], security mechanisms have global impact over the entire system.

Some approaches have claimed that leveraging security mechanisms influences system requirements specifications, which should be iteratively constructed by considering the application of security mechanisms [8,9]. However, these proposals only focus on new functional requirements that are introduced by a security mechanism and omit their impact on existing functional and non-funtional requirements. In other words, their approaches operationalize security requirements into only

© Springer International Publishing Switzerland 2015
S.A. Fricker and K. Schneider (Eds.): REFSQ 2015, LNCS 9013, pp. 115–131, 2015.
DOI: 10.1007/978-3-319-16101-3_8

individual functional requirements. In addition, there are neither systematic methods nor supporting tools available for analyzing and enforcing the impact of security mechanisms on system requirements.

We argue that system requirements specifications are not be complete unless they precisely capture such impacts. For example, when applying an access control mechanism to protect a data asset stored in a server, this mechanism imposes global constraints on all functional requirements that involve accessing the server, which should be reflected in the requirements specification in order to correctly develop a secure system. Moreover, the quality of the system functions are affected by the application of security mechanisms, which should be captured and taken into account in order to select the best functional alternatives. For instance, applying the access control mechanism to a specific system function will impair the usability and performance of all related functions provided by the system. Thus, we believe that a security mechanism is not a localized solution that can be independently decided upon over other elements of a requirements specification.

In this paper, we propose to capture and enforce the impact that security mechanisms impose over system requirements in order to completely and correctly account for their integration. Specifically, we investigate, in depth, a collection of security mechanisms that are well documented in security pattern repositories [5,22], and propose an approach to systematically and semi-automatically generate security-enhanced requirements specifications by analyzing the impact of applying security mechanisms. This work makes the following contributions:

- Presents a conceptual model which characterizes security mechanism from a requirements viewpoint.
- Proposes a systematic way to analyze and enforce the impact of a security mechanism imposed on system requirements. A set of corresponding logic rules are proposed to semi-automate the analysis process.
- Evaluates the expressiveness and effectiveness of our proposal by modeling 20 security mechanisms (selected from [5,22]) according to the proposed conceptual model and applying the obtained models to a real healthcare network scenario.
- A prototype tool has been developed to support the analysis process.

In the remainder of this paper, we introduce the background of this work (Section 2). We then present an illustrating example used throughout the paper in Section 3. In Section 4, we describe an enriched requirements specification, used as an input to our approach. We then present a conceptual model for security mechanisms in Section 5, along with a systematic process for analyzing the impact of security mechanisms (Section 6). After that we describe the evaluation of our approach in Section 7, and discuss related work in Section 8. In Section 9, we conclude the paper and discuss future work.

2   Background

In this section, we introduce the research baseline for our research.

Requirements Specification Concepts. Our previous work proposed a three-layer requirements analysis framework to analyze requirements, particularly security requirements, in different abstraction layers of Socio-Technical Systems (STS) [14]. This framework offers a holistic approach to analyze security issues in all layers, which takes into account the influences across layers. The requirements modeling language used in that work is based on the core ontology of RE [11], and is further expanded with social concepts that are adopted from i^* [27]. In addition, we use *security goals*, which are specializations of *softgoals*, to capture security requirements in the three-layer framework. Each security goal is specified with *importance, security property*, and *asset*, e.g., *"High data confidentiality [Clinical information]"*. A security goal is operationalized into a single security mechanism, which is treated as a specialization of a task. Fig. 1 shows a piece of a requirements model that is modeled in our three-layer framework.

In this paper, we specify requirements as in our previous work. In particular, we reuse the concepts: *goal (G), softgoal (SG), task (T)* (i.e., function), *domain assumption (DA)*, and the *refinement (REF)* and *contribution (CON)* relations, while adding a new concept *task constraint (TC)* in order to capture the impact of security mechanisms on existing tasks.

Security Knowledge Sources. With the aim of supporting non-security experts to carry out security requirements analysis and advancing the practical adoption of the analysis, we base our approach on existing security knowledge sources, namely, security patterns. Security patterns provide proven security solutions, through security mechanisms, for known security problems encountered in specific contexts. A number of security pattern repositories have been summarized in literature [5][22][7], which result in more than 100 security patterns in total. A security pattern is specified in a number of sections (depending on the selected pattern template), each of which addresses an aspect of the pattern. An example of the Virtual Private Network (VPN) security pattern is shown in Table 1, which follows the POSA (Pattern-Oriented Software Architecture) template [2] and presents a part of four sections, including *Context, Problem, Solution*, and *Consequence*.

In this paper, we extract security knowledge from well documented security patterns, specifically the work done by Fernandez et al. [5] and Scandariato et al. [22]. In particular, this paper exclusively focuses on the security mechanism (i.e. the solution) that is provided by each security pattern, while the reason for applying the security mechanism (i.e., the problem) was captured and analyzed in our previous work [15]. As we aim to analyze the impact of security mechanisms on system requirements, we mainly extract the knowledge of security mechanisms from the *Solution* section that specifies the requirements that need to be satisfied by a security mechanism, rather than the *Implementation* section that describes detailed design of a security mechanism.

Table 1. Part of the description of the Virtual Private Network pattern [5]

Context:
Users scattered in many fixed locations, who need to communicate securely with each other.
Problem:
How do we establish a secure channel for the end users of a network so that they can exchange messages through fixed points using an insecure network?
Solution:
Protect communications by establishing a cryptographic tunnel between endpoints on one of the layers of the communication protocol.
Consequence:
There is some overhead in the encryption process.

Modeling and Analyzing Security Patterns. Our previous work proposed to seamlessly integrate security patterns into security requirements analysis by modeling security patterns as contextual goal models, which facilitates the context-based selection among alternative security mechanisms [15]. After choosing the best security pattern, we apply its corresponding security mechanism that is modeled by using *tasks*, *domain assumptions*, and *softgoals*. In this method, the application of a security mechanism involves directly attaching the security mechanism model into the requirements model via refinement and contribution links.

However, this approach does not consider the impact of the mechanism on *existing* functional requirements, including how the impact further affects related non-functional requirements. Capturing and analyzing such impact is a non-trivial task. Take the VPN security mechanism as an example, which is described in the solution section in Table 1. This mechanism requires endpoints to communicate via a cryptographic tunnel, i.e., encrypting the communications. To correctly apply the mechanism, all the functional requirements that communicate confidential information should be constrained by this mechanism, and these requirements are not easy to identify. In addition, as described in the *Consequence*, the VPN mechanism impairs system performance. Thus, all the functional requirements that are constrained by VPN will have a negative influence on system performance, and this influence has to be taken into account when selecting alternative requirements.

In this paper, we propose a method which tackles the above challenges. In particular, we build upon our previous work and create a conceptual model for security mechanisms, which specializes tasks into security tasks, specifies security constraints post by security tasks, and captures the impact of security tasks on non-functional requirements. Based on this model, we are able to systematically analyze the impact of applying security mechanisms on existing requirements.

3   Scenario: The Healthcare Collaborative Network (HCN)

The HCN is a system that enables the exchange of healthcare messages and documents between and within organizations. The essential parts of the HCN include

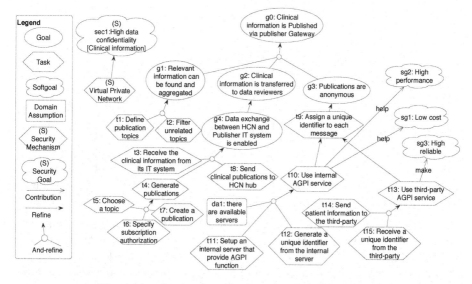

Fig. 1. A snippet of requirements goal model of HCN

an admin server and a message flow server, which communicate with gateways deployed at both the publisher side and the subscriber side. A full description of the HCN can be found online[1]. Fig. 1 shows part of the requirements goal model of the HCN, which captures the publisher gateway application, modeled using our existing framework [14]. Note that we assign unique identifiers to each node in the figure in order to facilitate the references in the remaining part of this paper.

4   An Enriched Requirements Specification

In this paper, we use an enriched requirements specification. Such specifications consist of not only goals (G), softgoals (SG), tasks (T), domain assumptions (DA), refinements (RE) and contributions (CON), but also task constraints (TC), which reflect the impact of security mechanisms on tasks. Thus, an enriched requirements specification is defined as a 7-tuple, i.e.,

$$\mathcal{R} = \{G, SG, T, DA, REF, CON, TC\}$$

A task constraint is specified in terms of task invariants and pre/post-conditions. The invariants describe properties that have to be true during the entire execution of the task. The pre/post-conditions describe properties that have to hold before/after the execution of the task. The value of a task constraint can be either a constant (e.g. *user_data*) or a predicate (e.g. *encrypted(user_data)*).

Fig. 1 presents an example of a requirements specification, including all these concepts except for task constraints. Note that the notation of the security mechanism shown in Fig. 1 (task with (S) annotation) is only used as a placeholder,

---

[1] http://www.redbooks.ibm.com/redbooks/SG246779

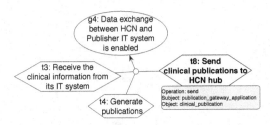

Fig. 2. An example of the enriched requirements elements

as described in our previous work [14]. This placeholder indicates a security mechanism is applied to achieve the security goal. In this work, this notation is replaced by detailed concepts of a security mechanism, as described in Section 5.

Expanded Attributes of Tasks. In order to better analyze the semantics of tasks, we associate each task with three attributes: its *subject*, *object*, and *operation*. For example, as shown in Fig. 2, we detail the selected task with a subject *publisher_gateway_application*, an object *clinical_publications*, and an operation *send*.

Such enriched requirements specifications are treated as the input of the analysis, i.e., each task has to be specified with a subject, an object, and an operation in order to be processed with our approach. During the requirements elicitation phase, there are two ways in which the above detailed information can be collected: firstly, interactively asking users when needed; secondly, automatically extracting the information from textual descriptions of tasks that have been elicited from stakeholders (with manual verification). For the second means, we leverage Nature Language Processing (NLP) as proposed in [13] to identify the roles of sentences, such as subjects, operations, and objects. In particular, we identify the Parts of Speech (POS) for each single word of a requirement statement. Then, we define a set of semantic patterns by using regular expression in order to capture the semantics of each sentence in terms of its subject, operation, and object. This technique has been implemented as part of our prototype tool (Section 7).

5   Modeling Security Mechanisms

In this section, we propose a conceptual model to characterize security mechanisms from a requirements perspective. In particular, a security mechanism is specified in terms of *security tasks*, *assumptions*, *security constraints*, and *quality influences*. As this paper exclusively analyzes the impact of security mechanisms imposed on the requirements specification that has been presented in Section 4, we map the concepts of the security mechanism to the requirements specification concepts as much as possible. In the reminder of this section, we describe each of the concepts that we use to model a security mechanism. An example of the VPN security mechanism is used for illustration, which is shown in Fig. 3.

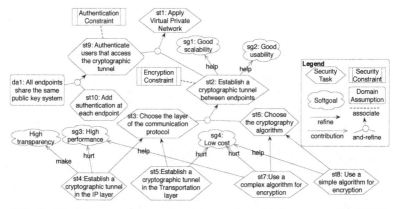

Fig. 3. Modeling security mechanism — virtual private network (VPN)

Security Tasks.

A *security task* is a detailed action performed by a system to achieve certain security goals. We define the security task as a specialization of *task*, and use T_S to represent the set of security tasks of a security mechanism. Each security task has an additional attribute *"asset"*, beyond the 3 attributes of regular tasks that are described in the previous section. This attribute specifies the asset that is protected by a security task, from which we can infer the impact of the security task. As the target asset of a security task depends on the application scenario of the security task, the obtention of this attribute is specified during the analysis process, described in Section 6.

As with all tasks, a composite security task can be decomposed into detailed security tasks, and we define the set of refinement relations between security tasks as REF_S. Note that we use the "root" security task to indicate the overall security mechanism, which can be repeatedly refined till reaching "leaf" security tasks, as shown in Fig. 3.

Assumptions.

An *assumption* specifies a expected state of affairs, under which the security mechanism can be applied correctly. Normally, these assumptions are captured during the refinements of security tasks, such as the assumption *"All endpoints share the same public key system"*, presented in Fig. 3. We map this concept to *domain assumption*, and use DA_S to represent the set of assumptions made in a security mechanism.

Security Constraints.

A security mechanism does not exist independently, but interacts and constrains existing system tasks in order to ensure that security requirements are satisfied. Thus, we explicitly capture such interactions between security tasks and tasks in the requirements model by using security constraints. We use SC to present the set of security constraints imposed by a security mechanism.

In this paper, we initially summarize 6 security constraints after investigating more than 40 reusable security mechanisms that are documented in a security pattern textbook [5] and a security pattern repository [22]. The 6 security constraints include *Encryption Constraint, Authentication Constraint, Permission*

Table 2. Security constraint rules

Global impact of security constraints
Rule_1: $constrain(ST, T) \leftarrow has\_operation(T, F) \wedge transfer\_operation(F)$ $\wedge has\_Object(T, O) \wedge protect(ST, O) \wedge has\_constraint(ST, encryption\_constraint)$
Rule_2: $constrain(ST, T) \leftarrow has\_operation(T, F) \wedge (protect(ST, F)$ $\vee (access\_operation(F) \wedge has\_object(T, O) \wedge protect(ST, O)))$ $\wedge has\_constraint(ST, authentication\_constraint)$
Rule_3: $constrain(ST, T) \leftarrow has\_operation(T, F) \wedge (protect(ST, F)$ $\vee (access\_operation(F) \wedge has\_object(T, O) \wedge protect(ST, O)))$ $\wedge has\_constraint(ST, authorization\_constraint)$
Rule_4: $constrain(ST, T) \leftarrow has\_operation(T, F) \wedge protect(ST, F)$ $\wedge has\_constraint(ST, centralization\_constraint)$
Rule_5: $constrain(ST, T) \leftarrow has\_operation(T, F) \wedge access\_operation(F)$ $\wedge has\_Object(T, O) \wedge protect(ST, O) \wedge has\_constraint(ST, protection\_constraint)$
Rule_6: $constrain(ST, T) \leftarrow (has\_function(T, F) \wedge protect(ST, F))$ $\vee (has\_Object(T, O) \wedge protect(ST, O)) \wedge has\_constraint(ST, auditing\_constraint)$

Constraint, Centralization Constraint, Protection Constraint, and *Auditing Constraint.* Each of these security constraints implies that a security task constrains specific tasks which have certain properties. Thus, regarding the meaning of each security constraint, we define security constraint rules for each particular security constraint to identify tasks that are constrained by a security task. The full list of security constraint rules are shown in Table 2. Take the *Rule 1* as an example: if a security task *ST* has an *encryption_constraint,* which targets the asset *O*, and there is a task *T* that has an operation *F*, which *transfers* the asset *O*, then the task *T* is constrained by the security task *ST*. Once having a list of security constraints, we need to go through each security task modeled before to identify whether it imposes certain security constraint. For example, as shown in Fig. 3, we identify that the security tasks *st2* and *st9* impose the *Encryption Constraint* and *Authentication Constraint,* respectively.

The proposed security constraints are not intended to be complete, but provide good coverage when considering the content of the 40 investigated security patterns. Additional constraints, together with their corresponding constraint rules (e.g. Table 2), can be incrementally integrated into our work.

Quality influences. Each security task not only changes functions of a system, but may also influence the qualities of the system, either positively or negatively. We use a set of *contribution* links to capture such quality influences, which are represented as CON_S. A contribution link is a triple, which specifies the influence imposed by a security task over system related quality (captured as a softgoal). We define the set of softgoals affected by a security mechanism as SG_S. Thus, the quality influences are defined as:

$$CON_S \subseteq T_S \times \{make, help, hurt, break\} \times SG_S$$

For example, in Fig. 3, the security task *"Establish a cryptographic tunnel in the IP layer"* makes the softgoal *"High transparency"*, while *hurts* another softgoal *"High performance"*.

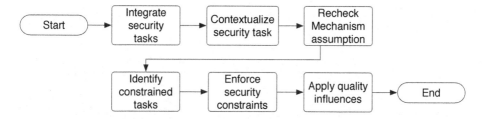

Fig. 4. The process for analyzing impact of security mechanisms

6 Analyzing the Impact of Security Mechanisms

In this section, we propose a systematic process to analyze and enforce the impact security mechanisms impose on the existing system requirements specification. We take the enriched requirements specification $\mathcal{R}$ and the to-be-applied security mechanism specification $\mathcal{M}$ as the input of our analysis, i.e.,

Input: $\mathcal{R} = \{G, SG, T, DA, REF, CON, TC\}$, $\mathcal{M} = \{T_S, REF_S, DA_S, \}$ SC, SG_S, CON_S

After systematically analyzing the impact of the security mechanism (Fig. 4), our approach will generate an updated requirements specification, $\mathcal{R}'$, which reflects all the impacts of the security mechanisms imposed on the requirements specification, i.e.,

Output: $\mathcal{R}' = \{G', SG', T', DA', REF', CON', TC'\}$

We illustrate the analysis process by analyzing the impact of the VPN mechanism (Fig. 3) imposed on the piece of requirements specification of the HCN scenario (Fig. 1). It is worth noting that if there are multiple security mechanisms need to be applied, all of them will be analyzed iteratively using the same approach.

Integrate Security Tasks. All security tasks, as a specialization of tasks, are directly incorporated into the initial requirements specification, as well as the refinements relations among them (if they exist). As such, the integration is defined as follows:

$$T = T \cup T_S \,,\, REF = REF \cup REF_S$$

As a security mechanism is applied to operationalize a security goal, the *root* security task of the security mechanism will replace the placeholder described in Fig. 1, and is directly linked to the security goal. In the illustrating example, the result of integrating security tasks of the VPN mechanism to the requirements specification is shown in the right part of Fig. 5 (*st1-st10*).

Contextualize Security Tasks. Once security tasks are integrated into the requirements and linked to a particular security goal, the target assets of security tasks should be determined in order to support the identification of constrained tasks in a later step. Each security goal in the requirements specification has already been specified an asset, such as the security goal *sec1* is specified with an asset "*clinical_information*" (Fig. 5). Thus, the security tasks that are applied to satisfy a security goal will inherit the asset from that security goal. In the

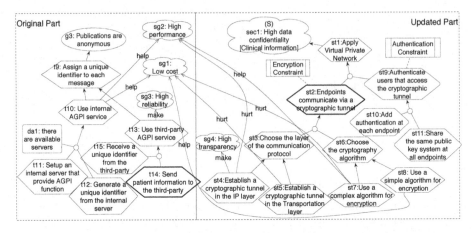

Fig. 5. Impact of the application of VPN (part)

illustrating example (Fig. 5), all the applied security tasks have the asset *"clinical_information"*, automatically derived from the security goal *sec1*.

Recheck Assumptions. When applying a security mechanism to a system within a particular domain, assumptions made in the mechanism should be further checked about whether or not it is still an assumption in the domain. Thus, a heuristic question can be asked, "Is the assumed phenomenon inside the boundary of system design now?" If so, we need to replace this assumption with a security task which "realizes" the assumption, and then add this security task to the set of tasks, i.e.,

$$T = T \cup \{a | \forall a \in DA_S, inside\_design\_boundary(a)\}$$

In this case, the newly added security tasks should be appropriately performed to ensure that the security mechanism is executed correctly. If the answer to the question is "No", the properties in the assumption keep being assumed to be held, and we add the assumption to the set of domain assumptions, i.e.,

$$DA = DA \cup \{a | \forall a \in DA_S, outside\_design\_boundary(a)\}$$

In our example, the assumption of the VPN mechanism *"All endpoints share the same public key system"* is determined to be inside the system design boundary. So we create a security task regarding this assumption (i.e., the *st11* in Fig. 5), and add this security task to the set of tasks.

Identify Constrained Tasks. After security tasks have been contextualized with the asset information, we now apply the security constraint rules (Table 2) to automatically identify the interactions between security tasks in the security mechanism and tasks in the requirements specification, i.e., identifying which tasks are constrained a security task.

During the above impact identification, we are concerned about not only the information derived from the two specifications (i.e., $\mathcal{R}$ and $\mathcal{M}$), but also additional domain knowledge models, such as data schemes (Fig. 6 (a)) and semantic hierarchies of words (Fig. 6 (b)). These models provide auxiliary rules to facilitate the analysis, e.g., the following rules:

Rule_7: protect(ST, A2) ← protect(ST, A1) ∧ part_of(A1, A2)
Rule_8: transfer_opertiona(O) ← send_operation(O)

Rule 7 indicates that if an asset needs to be protected, all the parts of this asset also should be protected. Rule 8 indicates that if an operation is of the type of "send", then it is also of the type of "transfer".

In our example, we use Rule 1 to infer, and identify three tasks {*t3, t8, t14*} (Fig. 1), which are constrained by the security task *st2*. Due to space limitation, Fig. 5 only represents part of the original requirements model that is related to *t14*.

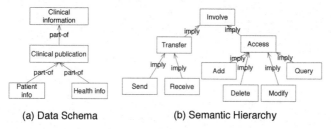

(a) Data Schema   (b) Semantic Hierarchy

Fig. 6. Examples of knowledge models

Enforce Security Constraints. After identifying all tasks that are constrained, we further enforce security constraints on those tasks. In particular, we propose specific enforcement measures for each of the 6 security constraints according to their meanings, which are detailed in Table 3. In this table, we first present the impact introduced by each security constraint. After that we describe the concrete enforcement measures, which are either adding task constraints or replacing tasks. For example, the *Encryption Constraint* adds a new pre-condition to the constrained task, the *Protection Constraint* adds a new invariant to the constrained task, and the Auditing *Constraint* adds a new post-condition to the constrained task. Apart from imposing task constraints, the *Centralization Constraint* replaces the constrained task with the corresponding security task. In this case, all the refinement relations that were linked to the constrained task are now redirected to the security task, and then the constrained task is removed.

According to the proposed enforcement measures, in our example, we enforce the encryption constraint on the constrained task *t14* (Fig. 5, i.e., adding a new pre-condition *performed(st2)* to this task.

Apply Quality Influences. Many requirements analysis techniques rely on qualities, which are normally captured as non-functional requirements (NFRs), to select alternative requirements [10]. Due to the interactions between security tasks and tasks, the quality influences introduced by security tasks may affect system requirements decisions, which need to be re-evaluated.

As the first step of applying quality influences, we correlate the softgoals in SG_S with the softgoals in SG, i.e. checking whether they are the same softgoals. As the same concept may be presented by different terms in different ways, this correlation analysis may require additional techniques, such as the Repertory Grid Technique (RGT) [19]. In the illustrating example, SG_S of the VPN mechanism involves several softgoals among which *"Low cost"* and *"High*

Table 3. Enforcement measures for the 6 security constraints

Security Constraints	impact	Enforcement
Encryption Constraint	the encryption security task should be done before the constrained task.	$add(performed(st),$ $t.precondition)$
Authentication Constraint	the authentication security task should be done before the constrained task.	$add(performed(st),$ $t.precondition)$
Permission Constraint	the authorization security task should be done before the constrained task.	$add(performed(st),$ $t.precondition)$
Centralization Constraint	the constrained task is replaced by the centralized security task.	$replace(t, st)$
Protection Constraint	the protection security task should be enforced to cover the whole execution period of the constrained task.	$add(cover\_by(st),$ $t.invariant)$
Auditing Constraint	the auditing security function should be done after the execution of the constrained task.	$add(need\_to\_perform$ $(st), t.postcondition)$

Remark: the st indicates the corresponding security task of a security constraint, while the t stands for the constrained task.

performance" have been correlated with softgoals in SG (in this particular case, the correlated softgoals have the same contents). For the softgoals in SG_S that are not correlated, the analyst needs to re-evaluate stakeholders' non-functional requirements to decide whether to include these softgoals. In our example, the uncorrelated softgoal "*High traceability*" is evaluated, and a decision is made to add it to the SG, shown in Fig. 5. This integration is defined below,

$$SG = SG \cup \{sg | \forall sg \in SG_S, uncorrelated(sg) \land decide\_include(sg)\}$$

However, the other uncorrelated softgoals, such as "*High usability*", are evaluated and are determined to not fit in with the current scenario. Once the above correlated softgoals and newly added softgoals are determined, all their corresponding contribution links in CON_S will be integrated into the requirements specification, i.e.,

$$CON = CON \cup \{contribute(st, inf, sg) | \forall contribute(st, inf, sg) \in CON_S, \exists sg \in SG\}$$

After correlating softgoals, we analyze the quality influences of a security task to its constrained tasks. Specifically, if a security task constrains a task, then all the quality influences introduced by this security task should be taken into account when evaluating the constrained task, especially if the constrained task is part of a requirements alternative. In the example (Fig. 5), since $t14$ is constrained by $st2$, the correct execution of $t14$ requires the appropriate interactions with $st2$. Thus, when evaluating the requirements alternatives that involve $t14$, such as the alternative tasks $\{t11, t12\}$ vs. $\{t14, t15\}$, the influences $st2$ imposed on the qualities (i.e., $sg1, sg2, sg4$) have to be taken into consideration.

7   Evaluation

Evaluate Expressiveness. We apply the proposed conceptual model to 20 security mechanisms, which are specified as reusable security solutions in the

Table 4. Statistics of applying the conceptual model to 20 security mechanisms

	Security Task	Assumption	Security Constraint	Quality Influence
Total	89	15	27	148
Average	4.45	0.75	1.35	7.4

security pattern textbook [5]. The statistics of applying the conceptual model to the 20 security mechanisms are presented in Table 4. The result of this evaluation shows that the 6 security constraints defined in this paper are enough to capture the semantics of these security mechanisms, and some security mechanisms impose more than one security constraint. On average each mechanism has more than 4 security tasks, which implies that security mechanisms are normally described at high abstraction level and can be further refined into detailed tasks. Moreover, the large number of quality influences further justify that security mechanisms can heavily affect the quality of systems, the impact of which should be carefully inspected. On the whole, by applying the conceptual model, a single security mechanism has around 14 nodes on average. Thus, the conceptual model is scalable to model a larger number of security mechanisms and include them into the repository.

Evaluate Effectiveness. We apply the proposed analysis approach to the full requirements model that we have built for the HCN scenario, which contains 23 goals, 8 softgoals, 67 tasks, and 75 refinement links. In particular, we analyze the impact of the VPN mechanism (Fig. 3), which has 9 security tasks, 1 assumption, 2 security constraints, and 8 quality influences. The application of this mechanism identifies 12 constrained tasks, each of which has applied 2 task constraints and 3 quality influences. This evaluation shows that our approach is able to identify and enforce the impact of security mechanisms, and it is scalable to a medium-size requirements model.

Tool Support. We have developed a prototype tool to support the evaluation and application of our approach. This prototype is built on top of our previous security requirements analysis tool MUSER [16]. Apart from the features provided by MUSER, e.g., graphically modeling requirements goal models, this prototype tool helps analysts to model security mechanisms and analyze their impact on requirements models. Specifically, the tool can infer the tasks that are constrained by specific security tasks according to the proposed rules. If certain information is missing during the reasoning process, the tool will interactively ask users to provide relevant information. Finally, as mentioned in Section 4, we leverage another tool to facilitate generating enriched requirements specification, which automatically extracts the *subject*, *object*, and *operation* from the description of a task by using NLP techniques [13].

8   Related Work

The interaction between requirements and architecture was first emphasized by Nuseibeh in [20], where he proposes a twin peaks model to show these interactions at an abstract level. Heyman et al. [9] and Okubo et al. [21] specialize the twin peaks model in the security area, respectively. They all outline a constructive process for co-developing secure software architectures and security requirements, but do not consider the impact secure architectures impose on other non-security requirements. In addition, none of these approaches has formalized the interactions between the twin peaks, and there is no tool developed to support the analysis process.

In Goal-Oriented Requirements Engineering (GORE), stakeholder's requirements, i.e., goals and softgoals should be operationalized into specific functions. As summarized by Dalpiaz et al. [3], there are several types of operationalization among existing GORE approaches, namely: functional requirements operationalization, qualitative operationalization, adaptation requirements operationalization, and behavior operationalization. Most of the existing work about security requirements operationalization falls into the first category, i.e., operationalizing security requirements into particular functions [8,14,17]. However, in this paper, we argue that any single category summarized above is not enough to characterize the operationalization of security requirements. Instead, our proposal aims to provide a new category of requirements operationalization, which focuses on capturing various changes on existing requirements specification.

Apart from the type of requirements operationalization, the means of doing the operationalization is also an essential step of the analysis. Letier and Lamsweerde have proposed to leverage operationalization patterns to guide the operationalization analysis [12], while Alrajeh et al. leverage machine learning techniques to operationalize goals [1]. As these approaches help to guarantee the correctness of the obtained operational specification, they can complement our work during the step of enforcing security constraints, specifically, validating the enforcement rules.

Security, as a cross-cutting concern, has been investigated in an aspect-oriented manner. Gunawan et al. model both systems functional designs and security mechanisms by using the collaboration-oriented behavior model, and propose to treat each security mechanism as a security aspect that can be inserted into different places of the system design [6]. Sousa et al. adapt the NFR framework to support aspect-oriented analysis [4]. Specifically, they illustrate their approach with a security requirements example, as they treat security requirements as a NFR. However, the above approaches do not consider the quality influences imposed by security mechanisms.

The impact of security mechanisms have been enforced by using model transformation techniques. Shiroma et al. focus on applying security mechanisms onto UML class diagrams [24]. They automatically enforce the security mechanism by defining transformation rules in ATLAS transformation language. However, this work focuses on the design phase and does not consider the impact on the system requirements. Yu et al. use i* constructs to model the context, problem, and solution of a security pattern, and automate the problem matching and application of the security solution by using ATL [28]. However, their approach highly depends on the semantics of the constructs of i*, such as dependencies and roles, and cannot be generalized for all security mechanisms, such as encryption.

9   Conclusions and Future Work

In this paper, we propose a conceptual model, which characterizes security mechanisms as security tasks, assumptions, security constraints, and quality influences. Using this conceptual model, we provide a systematic way to analyze and enforce the impact that security mechanisms impose over the system requirements. By defining related reasoning rules and implementing a prototype tool, the proposed analysis can be semi-automated. Finally, we evaluate the expressiveness of our conceptual model against 20 security mechanisms documented in existing security pattern repositories, and further evaluate the effectiveness of the analysis approach using a HCN scenario.

In the future, we want to generalize our approach to other goal-oriented security analysis approaches, such as Secure Tropos, KAOS. To this end, the proposed conceptual model of security mechanisms should be appropriately mapped to other types of goal-oriented requirements specifications, and the analysis process should also be adjusted accordingly. Another branch of the future work involves generalizing our approach to analyze and enforce the impact of all kinds of mechanisms (e.g., safety mechanisms, performance mechanisms, etc.) on the requirements specifications.

Apart from the above generalization of this work, we aim to collect more empirical evidence of the effectiveness of our solution, based on which we can further improve the approach. Firstly, beyond the 20 security mechanisms that have been specified in our conceptual model, we plan to analyze more security mechanisms to further check the coverage of the 6 security constraints proposed in this paper. Secondly, larger scale case studies will be done to better evaluate the effectiveness of our approach. Thirdly, we want to involve practitioners into the evaluation of the approach via controlled experiments to evaluate the potential of the practical adoption of our approach.

Acknowledgments. This work was supported in part by ERC advanced grant 267856, titled "Lucretius: Foundations for Software Evolution".

References

1. Alrajeh, D., Kramer, J., Russo, A., Uchitel, S.: Learning operational requirements from goal models. In: Proceedings of the 31st International Conference on Software Engineering, pp. 265–275 (2009)
2. Buschmann, F., Henney, K., Schimdt, D.: Pattern-oriented Software Architecture: On Patterns and Pattern Language, vol. 5. John Wiley & Sons (2007)

3. Dalpiaz, F., Souza, V.E.S., Mylopoulos, J.: The many faces of operationalization in goal-oriented requirements engineering. In: Proceedings of the Tenth Asia-Pacific Conference on Conceptual Modelling, vol. 154, pp. 3–7 (2014)
4. de Sousa, G.M.C., da Silva, I.G., de Castro, J.B.: Adapting the nfr framework to aspect-oriented requirements engineering. In: Proceeding of XVII Brazilian Symposium on Software Engineering, pp. 83–98 (2003)
5. Fernandez-Buglioni, E.: Security patterns in practice: designing secure architectures using software patterns. John Wiley & Sons (2013)
6. Gunawan, L.A., Herrmann, P., Kraemer, F.A.: Towards the integration of security aspects into system development using collaboration-oriented models. In: Ślęzak, D., Kim, T., Fang, W.-C., Arnett, K.P. (eds.) SecTech 2009. CCIS, vol. 58, pp. 72–85. Springer, Heidelberg (2009)
7. Hafiz, M., Adamczyk, P., Johnson, R.E.: Organizing security patterns. IEEE Software 24(4), 52–60 (2007)
8. Haley, C.B., Laney, R., Moffett, J.D., Nuseibeh, B.: Security requirements engineering: A framework for representation and analysis. IEEE Transactions on Software Engineering 34(1), 133–153 (2008)
9. Heyman, T., Yskout, K., Scandariato, R., Schmidt, H., Yu, Y.: The security twin peaks. In: Erlingsson, U., Wieringa, R., Zannone, N. (eds.) ESSoS 2011. LNCS, vol. 6542, pp. 167–180. Springer, Heidelberg (2011)
10. Horkoff, J., Yu, E.: Comparison and evaluation of goal-oriented satisfaction analysis techniques. Requirements Engineering 18(3), 199–222 (2013)
11. Jureta, I.J., Mylopoulos, J., Faulkner, S.: Revisiting the core ontology and problem in requirements engineering. In: 16th IEEE International Requirements Engineering, RE 2008, pp. 71–80. IEEE (2008)
12. Letier, E., van Lamsweerde, A.: Deriving operational software specifications from system goals. In: Proceedings of the 10th ACM SIGSOFT Symposium on Foundations of Software Engineering, pp. 119–128 (2002)
13. Li, J.-B., Li, T., Liu, L.: Chinese requirements analysis based on class diagram semantics. Acta Electronica Sinica, p. S1 (2011)
14. Li, T., Horkoff, J.: Dealing with security requirements for socio-technical systems: a holistic approach. In: Jarke, M., Mylopoulos, J., Quix, C., Rolland, C., Manolopoulos, Y., Mouratidis, H., Horkoff, J. (eds.) CAiSE 2014. LNCS, vol. 8484, pp. 285–300. Springer, Heidelberg (2014)
15. Li, T., Horkoff, J., Mylopoulos, J.: Integrating security patterns with security requirements analysis using contextual goal models. In: Frank, U., Loucopoulos, P., Pastor, Ó., Petrounias, I. (eds.) PoEM 2014. LNBIP, vol. 197, pp. 208–223. Springer, Heidelberg (2014)
16. Li, T., Horkoff, J., Mylopoulos, J.: A prototype tool for modeling and analyzing security requirements from a holistic viewpoint. In: The CAiSE 2014 Forum at the 26th International Conference on Advanced Information Systems Engineering (2014)
17. Mouratidis, H., Giorgini, P.: A natural extension of tropos methodology for modelling security. In: Proc. of the Agent Oriented Methodologies Workshop (OOPSLA 2002). Citeseer, Seattle-USA (2002)
18. Mouratidis, H., Giorgini, P.: Secure tropos: a security-oriented extension of the tropos methodology. International Journal of Software Engineering and Knowledge Engineering 17(02), 285–309 (2007)
19. Niu, N., Easterbrook, S.: So, you think you know others' goals? a repertory grid study. IEEE Software 24(2), 53–61 (2007)

20. Nuseibeh, B.: Weaving together requirements and architectures. Computer **34**(3), 115–119 (2001)
21. Okubo, T., Kaiya, H., Yoshioka, N.: Mutual refinement of security requirements and architecture using twin peaks model. In: Computer Software and Applications Conference Workshops (COMPSACW), pp. 367–372. IEEE (2012)
22. Scandariato, R., Yskout, K., Heyman, T., Joosen, W.: Architecting software with security patterns. Technical report, KU Leuven (2008)
23. Shah, V., Hill, F.: An aspect-oriented security framework. In: DARPA Information Survivability Conference and Exposition, vol. 2, pp. 143–145. IEEE (2003)
24. Shiroma, Y., Washizaki, H., Fukazawa, Y., Kubo, A., Yoshioka, N.: Model-driven security patterns application based on dependences among patterns. In: International Conference on Availability, Reliability, and Security, pp. 555–559 (February 2010)
25. Sindre, G., Opdahl, A.L.: Eliciting security requirements with misuse cases. Requirements Engineering **10**(1), 34–44 (2005)
26. Van Lamsweerde, A., Letier, E.: Handling obstacles in goal-oriented requirements engineering. IEEE Transactions on Software Engineering **26**(10), 978–1005 (2000)
27. Yu, E.: Towards modelling and reasoning support for early-phase requirements engineering, pp. 226–235. IEEE Computer Soc. Press (1997)
28. Yu, Y., Kaiya, H., Washizaki, H., Xiong, Y., Hu, Z., Yoshioka, N.: Enforcing a security pattern in stakeholder goal models. In: Proceedings of the 4th ACM Workshop on Quality of Protection,pp. 9–14 (2008)

How Artifacts Support and Impede Requirements Communication

Olga Liskin[(✉)]

Leibniz University Hannover, Hannover, Germany
olga.liskin@inf.uni-hannover.de

Abstract. **[Context & motivation]** Requirements artifacts, like specifications, diagrams, or user stories, are often used to support various activities related to requirements. How well an artifact can support a specific activity depends on the artifact's nature. For example, a plain text document can be adequate to provide contextual information, but is not well suited in terms of documenting changes. **[Questions / problem]** We wanted to understand how practitioners in various roles use requirements artifacts, how they manage to work with multiple artifacts at a time, and whether they use current practices for linking related artifacts. **[Principal ideas / results]** We have conducted an interview study with 21 practitioners from 6 companies. The interviews indicate that often a variety of artifact types is needed to successfully conduct a project. At the same time, using multiple artifacts causes problems like manual translation effort and inconsistencies. Mapping mechanisms that explicitly relate different artifacts are needed. However, existing methods are often not used. We investigate why these methods challenge developers in practice. **[Contribution]** We show challenges and chances of requirements artifacts. Our findings are grounded on true experiences from the industry. These experiences can support software developers in planning and improving their processes with regard to better requirements communication and researchers in making mapping methods more applicable in industry.

Keywords: Requirements artifacts · Requirements communication · User stories

1 Introduction

When Cockburn described the temperature of different communication channels [1], the hottest communication channel was not talking face-to-face, but *talking face-to-face at a whiteboard*. The reason is that writing down things helps clarify them. This is only one of many important powers of requirements artifacts. Moreover, they can help documenting information for later look-up, enable splitting requirements into explicit individual items for efficient management, and much more.

However, not all artifacts types are equally suited for all activities in software and requirements engineering. Artifacts like specifications, user stories, or GUI mockups foreground certain aspects of the set of requirements and hide others. This influences, for example, which information gets concretized or how well relations come into

© Springer International Publishing Switzerland 2015
S.A. Fricker and K. Schneider (Eds.): REFSQ 2015, LNCS 9013, pp. 132–147, 2015.
DOI: 10.1007/978-3-319-16101-3_9

view. Moreover, artifacts are used by many different persons, with various roles and different requests based on their individual work throughout the project. More and more companies strive to employ an iterative approach in the day-to-day development, requiring the appropriate artifacts. At the same time, teams following an agile approach realize with an increasing frequency that user stories and a backlog are not always enough. Especially in larger projects, having additional artifacts to integrate overall information, allow early general decisions, or meet regulatory needs, pans out.

Often, there is not one perfect kind of artifact that will serve the needs of all participants so that the project needs to deploy a whole variety of different artifacts. This, in turn, carries the risk of inconsistencies or inefficiencies emerging from the dependencies between multiple artifacts. Successful integration of requirements artifacts is an important matter in requirements engineering. In order to advance in this field, more research is needed to understand the challenges and chances of requirements representations. With the presented study, we contribute to improving this understanding.

2   Related Work

Several empirical studies have been conducted to study *requirements communication*. Bjarnason et al. [2], [3] and Abelein and Paech [4] have conducted interview studies on requirements communication in practice. They report on communication gaps in requirements engineering in general and on gaps in user-developer communication, respectively. Marczak et al. [5] conducted a field study where they regarded the communication network of developers working on related requirements. Knauss et al. [6] have developed a systematic scheme of requirements clarification patterns and report on a case study in which they investigated the patterns occurring in practice. Our paper extends this work on investigating requirements communication in practice by analyzing the facet of communication aided by artifacts.

Research on *requirements artifacts* addresses how they can be used to support software engineering activities and communication. Kumar and Wallace [7] describe communication patterns – including artifact facilitated discussion – and their outcome. Fernandez and Penzenstadler [8] research artifact based RE methods in contrast to activity based ones. They have designed and evaluated various artifact based RE models and then combined them into a domain-independent approach (AMDiRE). Gross and Doerr [9] analyze how artifacts and their contents should be constituted in order to support the needs of different roles in software engineering. Sharp et al. [10] use the distributed cognition approach to investigate the role of physical artifacts on communication within agile teams. Gallardo-Valencia et al. [11] explore whether agile requirements artifacts are sufficient for development and show that adding use cases can be beneficial.

The *mapping of requirements artifacts* has been repeatedly discussed in literature. Patton [12] describes techniques for (implicitly) mapping different story artifacts to each other. Imaz and Benyon [13] present an approach for enhancing relations between user stories and use cases. Antonino et al. [14] suggest a method for lightweight linking of requirements and development artifacts, which includes the mapping between user stories and individual requirements. Further research focuses on mapping requirements to more abstract items that are related to them. Abelein and Paech [15] describe the mapping of requirements to decisions. Rashid et al. [16] analyze how early aspects can be brought into requirements engineering and the according artifacts. Gotel et al. [17] describe how, in general, visualization of requirements and their connections could be used to improve software development. Creighton et al. [18] use sequences of video clips to visualize requirements in a user understandable way and then map these to more formal specification elements such as use case models and sequence diagrams. We investigate which of the available methods are actually applied in current practice and how they are working out. Our analysis contributes new knowledge to the field of mapping requirements artifacts by pointing out experiences and problematic areas.

The field of *tracing* provides many techniques to map requirements artifacts to subsequent project artifacts, like design artifacts, code, and tests. Boullion et al. [19] present scenarios in which requirements traceability is relevant in practice. Ben Charrada et al. [20] analyze code changes and then employ tracing tools to automatically identify outdated requirements. Research on improving tracing has many facets. For example, Anderson and Sherba [21] enhance automated management of traceability links by using open hypermedia techniques. Huffman-Hayes et al. [22] use information retrieval techniques to improve requirements tracing. Tracing mainly focuses on links between requirements artifacts and subsequent development artifacts, like architectural components, code, and tests. In contrast to that, we focus on enhancing links among requirements artifacts of the same or different kinds.

3   Study Design

Our objective is to study the usage of different artifacts in practice. We did this in two steps. First, we examined artifacts themselves and their support of development tasks. Then, we looked at the work with multiple types of artifacts at a time.

In the first phase of this study, our goal was to get an overview of how requirements artifacts are used in practice. We wanted to understand the values and impediments of different artifact types and the consequences of working with multiple artifacts at a time. The first two research questions guided this phase:

RQ1: What are the values and impediments practitioners see in different requirements artifacts? Throughout a project, different roles come into contact with requirements and perform different activities based on these. The requirements' representations can be more or less suited to support these activities. In conjunction with this research question, we create an overview of relevant activities and show which artifacts can or cannot support these.

RQ2: Which problems do practitioners face when using multiple different requirements artifacts within a project? Our study shows that oftentimes multiple different artifacts are used in order to support different activities. Often, artifacts have overlapping content, which can lead to inconsistencies. We want to find out which problems practitioners have actually experienced and consider relevant.

When working with multiple artifacts, many problems could be diminished if related parts within artifacts were explicitly mapped to each other. In the second phase, we focused on whether mapping methods are used in practice and what reasons prevent developers from implementing mapping methods. While still seeking insights and validation for the first two questions, we added the following two research questions:

RQ3: Which methods are used in industry to link multiple different requirements artifacts? Linking from one artifact to another one – for example simply by referring to the other artifact's ID – can help identify related content. This can be used to avoid inconsistencies when documenting changes. A more sophisticated method is to use clickable links that bring up additional content from a related artifact right away. Moreover, two artifacts could directly operate on the same content – serving as two views to the same content. It is not well known which of these methods are actually known or even used in industry. We want to close this gap with this research question.

RQ4: What challenges arise when linking multiple requirements artifacts? Often, only simple methods for artifact mapping are used. At the same time, developers find it challenging to work with multiple requirements artifacts. We want to find out what prevents practitioners from using more sophisticated requirements mapping methods. We want to know whether it is the creation of links that confronts them with problems or whether they see too little value in using links afterwards.

Table 1. Interview participants

Company Type	Company	Size	ID	Role
IT Service Provider	C1	500 - 1000	I1	Project Manager
	C2	1000 - 1500	I2	PO & Project Manager
In-House IT	C3	100 - 500	I3	Developer
			I4	Project Manager
			I5	Customer Rep.
			I6	Application Owner
			I7	Project Manager
			I8	Customer Rep.
			I9	Architect
			I10	Customer Rep.
			I11	Customer Rep.
			I12	Project Manager
			I13	Developer
	C4	1000 - 1500	I14	Process Engineer
			I15	Team Leader
			I16	Developer
			I17	Developer
			I18	Developer
Standard Software Producer	C5	<100	I19	Team Leader
	C6	<100	I20	Team Leader
			I21	Team Leader

Data Gathering and Analysis: We interviewed 21 practitioners from 6 companies. Table 1 shows an overview of the companies, projects, and roles of the participants. The company type influences the relation to the customer and therewith also requirements communication. Therefore, we interviewed persons from different company contexts. To ensure coverage of a wide range of requirements related activities, we interviewed people in different roles. We used semi-structured interviews, which mostly lasted about 75 minutes. We recorded and transcribed the interviews, and then coded and categorized the statements.

4   Results

4.1   Classification of Requirements Artifacts

The variety of requirements artifacts used in software projects is very high. Our interviewees mentioned mainly three types of artifacts: containers, individual elements, and solution models. In the course of the interviews, we found further characteristics of the artifacts that influenced their handling. We subdivide our artifact categories accordingly to accommodate these differences in the further analyses. Figure 1 depicts the categories of artifacts we found and the concrete artifacts that the practitioners reported to use.

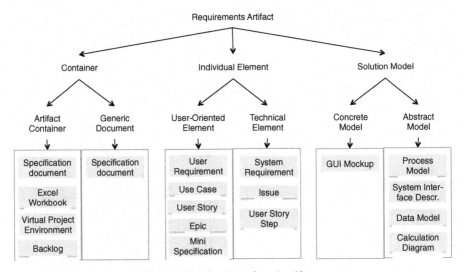

Fig. 1. Classification of used artifacts

Containers are characterized by their value to hold everything together in one place. We found that it makes a difference whether a container consists only of other artifacts (individual elements and solution models) or enables to include generic content. Generic elements make it easier to enter any important information quickly but at the same time carry the risk of the information being unsuitable for later tasks.

Virtual project environments and backlogs are artifact containers, while specification documents and excel workbooks can come in both forms. Generally, text documents are very generic and allow information to be entered in a variety of ways. Blocks of plain text can include one or several requirements at a time and mix them with goals, background information, or relevant policies. At the other end of the spectrum, documents can have a very strong formal structure, only consisting of elements that have a defined type and ID. Excel workbooks also provide very generic elements and could potentially be used to enter generic information. However, we have only seen it being used as an artifact container with each content element being a defined artifact like a user story, GUI mockup, or process model.

For *individual elements*, we found the most important aspect to be whether they are user oriented or not. It determines how well the users can contribute to the creation and assessment of that artifact. An element is considered user-oriented if it is clear to the user what will change with the completion of that element.

Elements referred to as *user stories* occurred in both forms, as user-oriented and technical elements. While user stories describe what users do as part of their job, technically oriented stories often describe smaller steps on the way towards a user story. A user can see, test, and comment them, but not understand them by herself (without translation by developers) because they do not clearly relate to the actual business tasks in the user's daily work. To distinguish such technical stories, we refer to them as *user story steps*.

Mini specifications are smaller specifications that describe just a part of a system instead of the whole system. They are used to gradually elaborate requirements details in iterative development or enhancement projects. The interviewees described mini specifications as easy to handle. Challenges emerge because a system possesses many such specifications, which are in addition interrelated. Therefore we classified them as elements instead of containers.

Solution models illustrate aspects of the future solution in the form of formal or graphical models. Concrete models directly relate to concrete situations a system's users experience. In contrast, abstract models show more universal generalizations of different concrete manifestations. For example, process models often show general abstract workflows spanning multiple roles and phases, while the step-by-step description of one specific partial path within this workflow is a concrete instantiation for a specific person. Our interviewees stated that they had experienced some user representatives to struggle with thinking in an abstract way. This influenced the models' effectiveness for aiding communication.

4.2   Values and Impediments of Different Requirements Artifacts (RQ1)

The main values of a requirements artifact lie in its ability to support a software engineering activity. We asked our participants which activities related to requirements they perform in their role throughout a project and which artifacts, if any, they use for them. Then, we inquired whether they had experienced an artifact to be supportive or troublesome for that activity.

Table 2 shows the activities that had come up in the interviews. In each cell, it displays how many interviewees mentioned that an artifact was supportive or troublesome for that activity. To better understand what led to the interviewees' assessments we also asked them about the relevant properties that made an artifact supportive or hindering. These properties are collected in Table 3.

One of the most strongly discussed activities was the *clarification of requirements details*. Many of the interviewees were struggling to find the right form of artifact for communication with the users. Although there are many templates and diagrams that are suggested for this activity, the interviewees reported that their customers could not work with most of them. It was considered helpful to use very concrete model artifacts for this communication. Users and user representatives were found to be best able to assess and contribute to requirements representations in the form of GUI-mockups or very concrete usage scenarios. Abstract models like flow charts of a process were considered helpful for some customers but dangerous for others. Customers who did not fully understand the notion or the abstract contents of such a model (and due to time pressure did not have time to address such problems), were

Table 2. Activities performed by interviewees. Numbers indicate number of interviewees who mentioned that artifact was suited for activity or could lead to problems, respectively.

ID	Activity	Artifact Container	Generic Document	User-Oriented Element	Technical Element	Abstract Model	Concrete Model	Verbal Comm., Email
A1	Understand & document overarching aspects	1 (p)	7 (s) 1 (p)	2 (s) 4 (p)	2 (s) 5 (p)		2 (s)	2 (s)
A2	General project planning		5 (s) 1 (p)				1 (p)	
A3	Collect requirements	2 (s)	6 (s) 1 (p)	7 (s)	1 (s) 1 (p)	1 (s) 2 (p)	4 (s)	1 (s)
A4	Reveal contradictions, inconsistencies	1 (s)	1 (s) 1 (p)	3 (s) 1 (p)		2 (s)	2 (s)	
A5	Prioritize Requirements		1 (s) 1 (p)	1 (s)	3 (s) 2 (p)			4 (s)
A6	Plan & control iteration		1 (s) 3 (p)	4 (s) 2 (p)	9 (s) 1 (p)	1 (s)		1 (s) 1 (p)
A7	Clarify requirements	1 (s)	1 (s) 2 (p)	7 (s) 2 (p)	2 (s) 2 (p)	4 (s) 6 (p)	7 (s)	2 (s)
A8	clarify requirements beyond analysis phase	1 (p)	1 (p)		1 (s)			5 (s)
A9	Manage requirements		3 (s) 4 (p)	4 (s) 4 (p)	4 (s) 2 (p)	1 (s) 1 (p)	1 (s)	4 (s) 6 (p)
A10	Review & report release completion		2 (s) 1 (p)		1 (s)	1 (s)	2 (s)	6 (s) 1 (p)
A11	Formal contract issues		4 (s)	1 (p)	1 (p)			1 (p)

(s) = # Int. mentioned that artifact was suited for activity　　(p) = # Int. mentioned potential problems with artifact

sometimes found to check it too superficially and to accept a presented model too quickly. This resulted in wrong assumptions and a false sense of security for the developers.

Interestingly, in most cases where user stories were employed, they were not well understandable for the users. Often, they were sliced in a way that they were not relating to the user's job tasks, but were too much on a system level. The team had drifted off to *user story steps* instead of user stories and lost some potential on involving users into the development and, most importantly, prioritization. This was partly compensated by communication, however at the price of additional translation effort (for explanation of user story steps).

Often, details also need to be *clarified beyond the analysis phase*, i.e. during implementation or testing. In these situations, very quick forms of communication and documentation, like emails or phone calls, were considered well suited. However this made later activities like *reconstructing a requirement's history* much harder or even impossible. Similarly, some interviewees stated that this activity was hard when working with a specification document. Besides the difficulties of finding a specific requirement within a document, relevant information like a requirement's creator or updater, the release it was shipped with, or the rationale behind it often simply were not recorded per requirement when using a specification document.

Table 3. Positive and negative properties of artifacts referred to by interviewees

Artifact	Positive Properties	# Int.	Negative Properties	# Int.
Container	collects everything in one central place	6		
	acceptable	4		
Artifact Container			new tool that needs to be learned	5
Generic Document	universal (everybody understands office documents)	1	difficult to search	6
	permits many ways to write down things	2	contents are too vague, generic	4
			contents are too detailed	4
Individual Element	divides big items into small manageable pieces	9	relations to overarching elements unclear	5
	good granularity for clarifying details	4	relations to other elements unclear	3
	easy to attach attributes (like author, release)	4	difficult to understand structure for persons who do not work with the elements regularly	3
User-Oriented Element	understandable for users	3	too coarse for development	2
Technical Element	good granularity for checking whether all necessary information is available	3	not understandable for users	6
			exact scope not clear	2
Solution Model	little room for interpretation	4	limited expressive power	1
	good for finding information quickly	4		
Concrete Model	best understood by customers	8		
Abstract Model			not understood by all customers	4

Planning and controlling implementation was reported to be well supported by elementary artifacts. Dividing the specification into elementary artifacts allows to attach additional information per artifact. Further, through the divide and conquer principle, it makes each element more tangible and manageable. This mostly aligns itself with what is known from literature on agile methods.

However, we also found activities that were considered problematic when only working with elements like user stories. The reported problems mostly relate to situations, which require more of an overall view on requirements. First, some interviewees mentioned that it was important to *understand and document the vision* of a project. They reported that sometimes, a requirement itself looked fine – for example, it was clear, self-contained, and had acceptance tests attached to it. However it was not making sense on a more general level because it was not solving the users' actual needs. To identify such situations, developers needed to understand the context of a story, like related stories or goals, which they not always were able to establish from their requirements artifacts.

A second important activity was to *develop tests that go beyond the scope of a single element* like a user story. For example, developers need to write automated tests that cover the collaboration of multiple stories. Similarly, acceptance testing for a release required additional information about general user goals. When just working with what was written on elementary requirements, they missed some connecting test cases. A third mentioned aspect was the *inclusion of strategic goals*. Strategic goals were mainly found to influence prioritization of work or introduce new requirements.

It was important to document such overarching information so that it does not get overlooked in the later project phases. However, it was considered difficult to document them just with elementary artifacts like user stories or use cases. Here, specification documents were considered helpful because of the high freedom they gave the author to note information. Sometimes, also slides with concrete or abstract models were kept as a reference for the overall vision and goals.

4.3 Problems Practitioners Face When Using Multiple Different Requirements Artifacts Within a Project (RQ2)

As the results in RQ1 indicate, many participants work with multiple different artifacts in order to be able to better support different activities. Another mentioned benefit was that displaying the same ideas in two different ways allowed the participants to better check whether they had interpreted requirements correctly. However, using multiple artifacts comes at the price of additional effort for creating, maintaining, translating, and preventing artifacts from inconsistencies. Table 4 shows the problems that were mentioned by the interviewees, as well as their reinforcers and effects. # Int. depicts the number of interviewees who mentioned an item. Some participants mentioned multiple items within a topic. Therefore, # Int. in the lines *reinforcers, problems and effects* displays the total number of interviewees who had talked about the according topic.

Table 4. Benefits and problems observed by interviewees when working with multiple artifacts

		# Int.
Reinforcers		5
R1	Some contents overlap, others are disjoint	2
R2	Non-trivial relations between (parts of) artifacts	5
Problems		15
Pr1	(R1 ->) Duplication of effort for creating multiple artifacts	3
Pr2	(R2 ->) Uncertainty about completeness of translation	6
Pr3	(R1 ->) Changes must be documented in multiple places	4
Pr4	(R1, R2 ->) Inconsistencies	3
Pr5	(R1, R2 ->) More difficult to find relevant information in multiple places	4
Effects		5
E1	Higher costs for performing tasks or preventing problems	2
E2	Higher costs when problems occur (mistakes, misunderstandings)	1
E3	Decreased trust in up-to-dateness of artifacts	2

We found that more than 70% of our interviewees had experienced problems when working with a variety of artifacts. Besides the extra effort for documenting and finding information in multiple places (Pr1, Pr3, Pr5), they had struggled with inconsistencies (Pr4). Further, they reported that it was difficult to check whether all (relevant) elements from one artifact type had been recorded in the other one (Pr2). Problems led to extra effort for preventing them (E1), but could not always be mitigated. If an inconsistency or other information was overlooked, misunderstandings or wrong assumptions occurred, which in turn potentially led to higher costs through mistakes (E2). Another reported effect was that people very quickly lost trust in a document (E3) – and hence stopped using it – if they repeatedly had found the contents to be not up-to-date or inconsistent.

In practice, two circumstances make working with multiple requirements artifacts particularly challenging. The artifacts do not just describe disjoint information, but various aspects of the same requirements (R1). Therefore, some – but also not all – information is contained in multiple artifacts. Further, artifacts are not always in a simple hierarchical one-to-many relationship, like when dividing a story into tasks (R2). For example, a process model and a set of user stories can have complex relations with the process model depicting the interaction of multiple stories, while at the same time, a subset of activities illustrating one user story.

4.4 Methods Used in Industry to Link Multiple Different Artifacts (RQ3)

We found different ways to map requirements artifacts that are used in industry. We have classified them into four kinds of mapping. Table 5 shows the kinds of mappings we found.

Table 5. Categories of mapping methods used in practice

ID	Mapping Method	# Int.
M1	Manual textual reference	6
M2	Attachment	10
M3	Link	3
M4	Generated artifact	1

The simplest way was to manually reference a related element by mentioning its ID in a textual way. This technique was mostly used to refer to parts of a specification document. For example, a change request contained the specification's chapter with the original requirements. Similarly, a developer who had translated a specification into User Stories, added the chapter with the original requirements to the stories. She reported that the specification's structure was changing, however, which rendered some of the references obsolete. In another project, the participants simply textually referred from User Stories to an overall GUI mockup and an overall flow chart.

Another common technique we found was to attach an element to another element. When working with the container element, the attachment can be directly accessed which makes it easy to obtain detailed information. However, the attached element only exists within the container element and cannot be accessed otherwise. Therefore, this technique is beneficial for hierarchical structures. Often, tools can create this kind of mapping automatically during the attachment process.

Linking two elements that exist by themselves was also used in the discussed projects, but only in very few cases. The direct link between the two elements allows to directly open one element from a referencing element. In one reported case, developers were managing their work iteratively, but based on technical tasks. They added a special type of artifact to represent user goals and linked the goal with all technical tasks that were necessary to fulfill it. This allowed the customers to see how the project was progressing on their goals, while the developers were still able to structure their work based on dependencies between development tasks.

Another mentioned technique is generating or constructing one artifact from multiple other artifacts. This technique is mostly used to create specification documents from requirements elements and models. It avoids the duplication of content by keeping the content in one place and just displaying it in another place. In order to use this technique, special attention to the arrangement of the elements must be paid.

4.5   Challenges of Linking Multiple Requirements Artifacts (RQ4)

We found indications for both, the effort for the creation of artifact links being perceived as too high as well as a too low perceived value. Table 6 presents challenges that interviewees mentioned to encumber or even prevent them from linking artifacts.

Table 6. Challenges of linking multiple requirements artifacts

ID	Challenge	# Int.
C1	Time pressure	5
C2	Interruption of other tasks	4
C3	Requires clear guidelines	1
C4	Difficult if requirements are not isolated from each other	2
C5	Manual links can become obsolete	2

When asked why they had not established an explicit link between particular artifacts, the interviewees' most common answer was that they had no time. We tried to find out more precisely, what it was that drove them not to want to spend time with such a task. One mentioned problem was that often the persons worked with related artifacts when they were in the middle of a different task. They were working on code or other artifacts when they had searched for additional information in artifacts. In this situation, they did not want to interrupt that task to create artifact links.

One interviewee, who had worked with links before, mentioned that clear guidelines are needed in order to establish a good linking structure. For example, it must be specified that each story has to be linked to a user goal. Thinking through such guidelines is an additional barrier that prevents practitioners from using linking structures.

Further, linking was considered challenging when the parts to link were not isolated. For example, if requirements are just contained in a block of plain text, or if a model element cannot be addressed isolated from the whole model, it is more challenging and imprecise to denote related elements. Whether it is easy to link parts of a model to other artifacts, mainly depends on the tooling used for creating the models. This is especially a problem in enhancement projects, where the developers have to build upon existing documentation.

Another mentioned demotivating factor was the high chance of breaking links on changes. One team had tried to maintain a set of links from user stories to detail chapters in a specification document. However, the chapters changed from time to time – rendering the links useless – so that the team ultimately gave up.

5   Discussion

Handling multiple requirements artifacts is challenging. Our results indicate that only one kind of requirements artifacts often is not enough for a software project. In most projects, multiple artifacts are used to support different requirements communication activities. However, our results also indicate that requirements artifacts often are not well integrated. Relations and dependencies between artifacts are not visible. If developers or customers do not keep them in mind or spend extra time to search artifacts, they miss important information.

Requirements communication with customers is not supported well. We see a strong need for more work on supporting customers or business analysts in communicating requirements. Customers are forced to create or accept artifacts in formats suited for developers. They cannot understand most of these languages and time pressure does not leave them the time anymore to learn them. Instead, they should communicate requirements in a form that is tangible for them and developers should be able to integrate these forms into later work items. User stories answer the purpose of making it easier for customers to communicate requirements and even participate in guiding development. However, often they are not used for this purpose. We have seen user stories being used as a means for developers to split work items and make work more manageable, having to be translated permanently for customer communication. In order to support the needs of both, developers and users, *stories at different levels of granularity are needed.* As suggested by interviewees, it makes sense to work with business user stories and technical user stories in combination.

Mapping requirements artifacts has a high potential. We have seen many problems that could be mitigated if requirements artifacts were used. A lot of effort could be saved for manually checking items for consistency, or proving that all items have been translated. In addition, several requirements engineering activities could also be improved. For example, developers could be warned about dependencies before they implement a story card or when user oriented elements are changed. If abstract models could be linked with concrete models or requirements elements, the requirements engineer could also use complex abstract models for customer communication. Parts of the abstract model could be directly translated to concrete models, providing an understandable view on the details. In the interviews, we got the impression that many of the potential benefits of mapping seem vague to most practitioners.

Good lightweight requirements communication is working well. Many interviewees reported that they were solving many tasks through direct communication. As Table 2 illustrates, many of the discussed activities were aided by direct communication. Many interviewees stated that they had intensified verbal communication between different roles – mostly through weekly or biweekly meetings – only in the last few years. They reported to have experienced many improvements since the introduction of such meetings. This is a good advancement. Lacking communication between the customer and development sites has been a problem for several years. However, we also saw new problems come up in the interviews when the reliance on verbal communication was too high. Interviewees reported that sometimes, the only way to detect a dependency or misunderstanding was when one particular person - who often was the only one having the necessary knowledge - brought it up in the according planning meeting. This strategy has worked out in many cases but is quite incidental. The described situations raise questions, like whether more means are needed to improve knowledge distribution in teams, and how such communication-reliant approaches can be scaled.

6   Threats to Validity

This section discusses threats to validity based on Runeson and Höst [23].

A threat to *construct validity* arises because the information provided by the participants is interpreted by the researcher to form categories. This categorization is not unique. The interview character of the study implied that not all questions were posed explicitly. By using interviews (in contrast to surveys, for instance) we were able to counteract misunderstandings with the participants.

Various aspects could influence the *internal validity* of our results. The types of a project and its customers greatly influence requirements communication and therewith the success of requirements engineering activities and utilized artifacts. To mitigate this threat, we interviewed practitioners from different types of companies and different projects. The participants were self-selected, i.e. they knew in advance that the interview would cover requirements artifacts and had agreed to participate in the study. We cannot rule out the possibility that they had a higher interest in requirements engineering practices and the usage of artifacts than the majority of software engineers. The methods they apply in requirements engineering, the artifacts they use and their perceptions of the benefits of those artifacts could be influenced by their general interest in RE.

The number of participants could influence *external validity*. We have interviewed only 21 practitioners, so it is likely that we have not covered all situations in requirements communication. Also, the participants are all from German companies. However, since we have spoken to people within different company settings, different projects, and different roles, the variety of covered perspectives is very high. In addition, we have reached a state in which answers were repetitive to insights from preceding interviews and further interviews lead to a diminishing number of results for our research questions (similar to theoretical saturation in Grounded Theory [24]).

Reliability is affected by the number of participants, which is too low to claim statistical significance, and the fact that the interviews and their analysis were conducted by one person. A different researcher could convey the questions and also interpret the answers differently.

We have used a qualitative research approach, which reflects subjective opinions and experiences of the participants. These cannot be generalized. Despite this and the above limitations, we believe that our results have a value for researchers and also for practitioners. They provide insights into the practice, increase the understanding of the employment of requirements artifacts, and indicate possible challenges.

7   Conclusions

We have interviewed 21 practitioners about their handling of requirements artifacts and report on their experiences, named challenges, and advances in using mapping techniques. We have found that various artifacts are needed. Developers require detailed items of fine granularity but also need to keep an eye on overarching aspects like the product vision and goals. Customers need very concrete artifacts to express their expectations. Project managers need a way to see the connections to the total amount of upcoming work.

The employment of multiple different artifacts imposes challenges like scattering of information, incomplete translations, or inconsistencies between artifacts. For these reasons, methods for mapping and linking requirements artifacts should be common proficiencies in requirements engineering. However, we have seen it rarely employed in practice. Most participants stated that they found explicit mapping or linking of artifacts too costly in their project context. Indeed, mapping is not necessary in all situations. However, if the methods and tools could be improved to better facilitate artifact mapping, this would assist in many software projects.

With our results, practitioners can get an increased understanding of an artifact's utility for different activities, get an overview on mapping techniques and understand what might prevent project members from using them. Researchers gain insights into the handling of requirements artifacts in practice and into challenges that need to be solved as well as investigated further.

In the future, we would like to work on improving facilitation of requirements mapping by building on the insights from this study. Further, we have seen that artifact mapping is not crucial in all kinds of projects. It would be interesting to investigate which project aspects constitute a need for mapping. Another interesting aspect is how to determine – especially in early project phases – which linking techniques and also which artifacts will be helpful in the project

Acknowledgments. I would like to thank all interview participants for their time, all the valuable insights, and the exceedingly interesting conversations.

References

1. Cockburn, A.: Agile Software Development. Addison Wesley (2002)
2. Bjarnason, E., Wnuk, K., Regnell, B.: Requirements are slipping through the gaps - a case study on causes & effects of communication gaps in large-scale software development. In: Requirements Engineering Conference (RE) (2011)
3. Bjarnason, E., Wnuk, K., Regnell, B.: Are you biting off more than you can chew? a case study on causes and effects of overscoping in large-scale software engineering. Information and Software Technology 54(10), 1107–1124 (2012)
4. Abelein, U., Paech, B.: State of practice of user-developer communication in large-scale IT projects. In: Salinesi, C., van de Weerd, I. (eds.) REFSQ 2014. LNCS, vol. 8396, pp. 95–111. Springer, Heidelberg (2014)
5. Marczak, S., Damian, D., Stege, U., Schroter, A.: Information brokers in requirement-dependency social networks. In: Requirements Engineering Conference (RE) (2008)
6. Knauss, E., Damian, D., Cleland-Huang, J., Helms, R.: Patterns of continuous requirements clarification. Requirements Engineering Journal (2014)
7. Kumar, S., Wallace, C.: A tale of two projects: a pattern based comparison of communication strategies in student software development. In: Frontiers in Education Conference. IEEE (2013)
8. Fernandez, D.M., Penzenstadler, B.: Artefact-based requirements engineering: the AMDiRE approach. Requirements Engineering Journal (2014)
9. Gross, A., Doerr, J.: What you need is what you get!: the vision of view-based requirements specifications. In: Requirements Engineering Conference (RE) (2012)

10. Sharp, H., Robinson, H., Petre, M.: The role of physical artefacts in agile software development: Two complementary perspectives. Interacting with Computers **21**(12), 108–116 (2009)
11. Gallardo-Valencia, R.E., Olivera, V., Sim, S.E.: Are use cases beneficial for developers using agile requirements?. In: Fifth International Workshop on Comparative Evaluation in Requirements Engineering (CERE) (2007)
12. Patton, J.: User Story Mapping. O'Reilly Media (2014)
13. Imaz, M., Benyon, D.: How stories capture interaction. In: INTERACT 1999, pp. 321–328. IOS Press (1999)
14. Antonino, P.O., Keuler, T., Germann, N., Cronauer, B.: A non-invasive approach to trace architecture design, requirements specification and agile artifacts. In: 23rd Australian Software Engineering Conference (ASWEC), pp. 220–229 (2014)
15. Abelein, U., Paech, B.: A proposal for enhancing user-developer communication in large IT projects. In: 5th International Workshop on Cooperative and Human Aspects of Software Engineering (CHASE), pp. 1–3 (2012)
16. Rashid, A., Sawyer, P., Moreira, A., Araujo, J.: Early aspects: a model for aspect-oriented requirements engineering. In: Requirements Engineering Conference (RE) (2002)
17. Gotel, O.C.Z., Marchese, F.T., Morris, S.J.: On requirements visualization. In: 2nd International Workshop on Requirements Engineering Visualization (REV) (2007)
18. Creighton, O., Ott, M., Bruegge, B.: Software cinema – video-based requirements engineering. In: Requirements Engineering Conference (RE) (2006)
19. Bouillon, E., Mäder, P., Philippow, I.: A survey on usage scenarios for requirements traceability in practice. In: Doerr, J., Opdahl, A.L. (eds.) REFSQ 2013. LNCS, vol. 7830, pp. 158–173. Springer, Heidelberg (2013)
20. Ben Charrada, E., Koziolek, A., Glinz, M.: Identifying outdated requirements based on source code changes. In: Requirements Engineering Conference (RE) (2012)
21. Anderson, K.M., Sherba, S.A.: Using open hypermedia to support information integration. In: Reich, S., Tzagarakis, M.M., De Bra, P.M.E. (eds.) AH-WS 2001, SC 2001, and OHS 2001. LNCS, vol. 2266, pp. 8–16. Springer, Heidelberg (2002)
22. Hayes, J.H., Dekhtyar, A., Osborne, J.: Improving requirements tracing via information retrieval. In: Requirements Engineering Conference (RE) (2003)
23. Runeson, P., Höst, M.: Guidelines for conducting and reporting case study research in software engineering. Empirical Software Engineering **14**(2), 131–164 (2009)
24. Glaser, B.G., Strauss, A.L.: The Discovery of Grounded Theory: Strategies for Qualitative Research. Observations (Chicago, Ill.). Aldine de Gruyter (1967)

Consonance Between Economic and IT Services: Finding the Balance Between Conflicting Requirements

Maryam Razavian[✉] and Jaap Gordijn

VU University Amsterdam, Amsterdam, The Netherlands
{m.razavian,j.gordijn}@vu.nl

Abstract. [**Context and motivation**] Service Orientation has been heralded as the solution for seamless alignment of the business and IT. [**Question/problem**] Alignment, however, remains far from being resolved. [**Principal ideas/results**] While alignment research typically concentrates on *mapping* the counterpart elements, this paper provides a case for what we coin *consonance*—the mutual adjustment of conflicting requirements between business and IT perspectives. In previous work, we have identified inherent discrepancies between the requirements of the business- and IT perspectives. [**Contribution**] In this paper, to better understand such discrepancies and the kind of support needed for their consonance, we have carried out a real-world example in the music industry. Moreover, we study consonance in a networked setting; both in terms of a business network of enterprises, and in terms of a cross-organizational IT network. The use of the consonance approach in this example reveals important lessons learned.

1 Introduction

Service orientation has transformed many traditional, internally focused, information systems into externally visible *e-services*—commercial services provided via information technology (IT) offering customer value in return for payment or something else of value. Consider for instance the music industry, our real-world example domain. When radio stations broadcast music, they have to pay to Intellectual Property Rights (IPR) societies, who in turn distribute money over IPR owners such as artists, sing & song writers, and producers. Clearing rights and repartitioning the collected money over the IPR owners are *commercial services*, enabled by IT, which are of value to the rights owners and the radio station. Usually, a music track entails a number of IPR owners which can live, to complicate things, in different countries. Consequently, more than one IPR society is involved if a radio station broadcasts a track, as societies are often organized per type of IPR owner, country and value adding activity (e.g., clearing or repartitioning). This case, thus, forms a *network* of enterprises and individuals (radio stations, IPRs, IPR owners), using each other's services. This network is both a *business* and *IT* network; a business network because the

© Springer International Publishing Switzerland 2015
S.A. Fricker and K. Schneider (Eds.): REFSQ 2015, LNCS 9013, pp. 148–163, 2015.
DOI: 10.1007/978-3-319-16101-3_10

parties involved exchange things of economic value with each other, and an IT network as IPR management is largely supported by cross-organizational IT.

This example illustrates that in order to design, manage and maintain requirements for e-services, multiple perspectives should be taken into account, including the strategic, economic, process, and IT perspective [1]. In this work we scope down to two perspectives: namely the *economic perspective* and *IT perspective*. These two perspectives view e-services very differently, pursue different goals, and focus on different requirements. For example, the economic perspective views the IPR e-service as a number of commercial services that are of economic value for IPR owners, therefore satisfy the requirement of a profitable company. The IT perspective, on the other hand, focuses on exposing the functionality and architecture of cross-organizational IPR information systems, and ensures that they are reusable and flexible. Although the economic and IT perspectives view e-services differently, they are also related. For instance, in the IPR case, payment by the radio station for the usage of a music track (economic perspective) should be properly supported by administration of granting the right and handling of payments (IT perspective).

In general, developing economic e-services requires a dialogue between the economic/commercial considerations and information technology choices. In other words, in the context of e-service design, *Requirements Engineering* as a discipline should not only cover information system requirements, but also economic considerations, and their interrelationships such as economic sustainability of the e-service to be developed.

Considering economic and IT requirements of e-services is vastly complex. In earlier work [2], we found that this complexity roots in the conflicting and even contradicting requirements of the two economic and IT perspectives. Intuitively, these conflicts necessitate trade-offs, which are in their own right new problems, potentially more complex than the originals. Although conflicting requirements are inherent in the service alignment endeavors, none of the existing approaches capture them explicitly. Because of the focus on requirements discrepancies, we refer to the term *consonance* to characterize our approach.

In this paper, we propose a *tractable, easily understandable*, and *model-based* approach to deal with such requirement conflicts—by treating them as *first class* citizens of the requirements engineering process for e-services. Tractability refers to the idea that our approach should be carried out rather easily, and in a short time frame, as most innovative e-service development projects due the competitive nature require fast execution. Understandability is an important concern because our approach has to deal both with commercial, business and IT-oriented stakeholders. Finally, our approach is model-based to be usable in an information system development follow-up project.

This approach has emerged from our experience in a real-world example with an IPR society, where it proved effective in understanding the *current state* of consonance. On the long term, our research goal is to provide an assessment instrument that evaluates whether a change in the economic perspective (e.g. a change in the value proposition) can still be supported by service oriented information technology, so considering the *future state* of consonance.

The contribution of this paper is threefold: (i) we provide a consonance app-roach that brings a series of discrepancies between economic-and IT perspectives into focus. (ii) we approach the consonance of business and IT from the customer value proposition point of view, as well as the economic value network. This is in contrast with many approaches on business/IT alignment (e.g. [3]) that usually start with an understanding of the business strategy or business goals (e.g. [4]) or even business processes. (iii) we distinguish ourselves by taking a *network* perspective on business and IT; as industrial practice often relies on networks of enterprises offering jointly a bundled service, rather than just a single enterprise offering a simple service.

2   Context and Groundwork

2.1   Multiple Perspectives on Services: A Balancing Act

Service-oriented requirements engineering can be perceived as developing at least the economic and IT perspectives on a *single artifact*, namely the service at hand. These two perspectives have different foci: the economic perspective con-centrates on *commercial services for whose provision someone has to pay*, while the IT perspective considers the *IT elements that* realize *the commercial services*. Following this observation, a service in the economic perspective, has a (number of) IT service counterpart(s) in the IT perspective; aligning the two perspectives 'only' requires to link the counterpart services between the two perspectives.

However, in earlier work [2] we found that this perception constitutes the major reason behind why service alignment is so difficult. In particular, we argue that the economic- and IT perspectives are *not* two faces of the same concept; instead they are *two very different concepts*, pursuing different and even con-flicting requirements, and are comprised of inherently different elements. For instance, the economic perspective refers to *commercial* services, whereas the IT perspective is about *web* services. Although web services may put commercial services into operatfion, from an ontological point of view they are very different citizens. Such fundamental conflicts and differences between the two perspectives makes the alignment a complex, wicked problem [5].

In the same earlier work [2] we proposed inherent *discrepancies* between the two perspectives highlighting their conflicting requirements. Addressing these conflicting requirements means making trade-offs. One example of such a trade-off is profitability/sustainability versus openness. For our example on IPR, on the one hand, a IPR society is supposed to be at least economically sustainable, thus operating at as low costs as possible, such that the maximum amount of collected money can be paid to the appropriate IPR owners. On the other hand, however, IPR societies should be open in terms of operating with other actors (both business- and IT-wise). Such openness comes with a price which is a pres-sure on sustainability, and at the end of the day, decreases the amount of money to be paid to IPR owners. In general, for the earlier mentioned discrepancies, we claim that the economic and IT-perspectives should explicitly address the con-flicting requirements in order to a find a balance. We refer to such a desired state as *consonance*—where the very different requirements are in harmony—rather than *alignment* (i.e., only linking the counterpart elements).

2.2   Our Consonance Approach

In this paper we capture the As-Is situation of the economic- and IT perspective of the IPR example and analyze the state of consonance between the two perspectives. We model the economic perspective using e^3value [6] and explain this perspective along the line of the IPR example in Section 3.1. We model the IT perspective using *SoaML* [7] and explain it in Section 3.2. We chose these notations because they (i) capture the relevant perspective adequately, (ii) are expected to satisfy our requirements with respect to tractability and understandability, and (iii) are model-based. However our consonance approach is notation agnostic; any modeling notation that fulfills the above goals and motivate conceptual overlap between the perspectives can be used.

To capture the state of consonance between the economic and IT perspectives, we need an effective common ground that closes the gap between the elements of the two perspectives. In [2] we provide such a common ground in the form of *core elements* of Service Orientation, including: *actor, service, interaction, and contract*. What these core elements imply, however, is very different in the two perspectives, rooting in the inherently different requirements of the two perspectives. Table 1 provides an overview of the conceptual discrepancies of the core elements in the two perspectives as well as their rationale.

Moreover, to make consonance between two perspectives, we must perform trade-offs among the various requirements classified as belonging to each of the two perspectives. The requirements of the two perspectives may influence each other in positive or negative manner. In our approach we directly focus on these influences and their associated trade-offs. In short, our consonance approach embraces the following steps:

– **Step 1.** The starting point is to model the the As-Is and To-Be states. For the economic perspective, we can construct a basic e^3value model for the e-service at hand that at least contain the the core elements: the most important "actors" (e.g., the e-service provider and its customers and suppliers); the most important "commercial services"; the "contracts" and the "interactions" between actors. For the IT perspective, we should model the service network architecture with the types of "actors" that collaborate to provide IT services, provided and consumed "services" expressed as "contracts", as well as the "interactions" between actors involved in a contract should be modeled too.
– **Step 2.** For each of the core elements, we evaluate to what extent the corresponding requirements of the two perspectives are fulfilled (see Table 1). For instance, focusing on "actors"—looking from the lenses of the economic perspective we check if they are economically sustainable (economic perspective)–looking from the lenses of IT perspective, we check if the IT enables the actors to come and go on-the-fly. For our example on IPR, we check if the IPR society

Table 1. Overview of the different requirements of the core elements between the two perspectives [2]

	Economic Perspective	IT Perspective
Actor	Actors instances who are profit-and-loss responsible legal entities. *Rationale: the economic perspective focuses on how each actor would make profit or increases its utility.*	Service provider or consumer that are open. *Rationale: This perspective cares for flexibility and openness (actors should be able to come and go on-the-fly).*
Service	Commercial services that for their provision an actor has to give something of value in return *Rationale: economic perspective deliberately focuses only on services that have direct economic value.*	Repeatable and reusable capabilities that can be invoked by various consumers. *Rationale: IT perspective cares for reusability of services enabling their economies of scale.*
Contract	Caring about how actors assign economic value to the obtained services. *Rationale: economic perspective cares about what an actor offers and what an actor requests in return.*	Agreements about how to technically interact, such as protocols. *Rationale: IT perspective cares about information needed for communication*
Interaction	Economic value transfers such as service outcome or transferring money. *Rationale: Economic perspective focuses on interactions that represent reciprocal value transfers—value transfers that represent a change in valuable rights, such as right to use a services or ownership.*	Message exchanges between participants. *Rationale: IT perspective cares for loosely coupled interactions to maximize independence of services as well as their providers and consumers.*

operates at lowest costs, such that the maximum amount of collected money can be paid to the appropriate IPR owners. From IT perspective, however, IPR societies should be open in terms of operating with other actors (IT-wise).

 – **Step 3.** We analyze the trade-offs required for *simultaneously* fulfilling the requirements of the two perspectives. The essence of this step is to explore and scope the consonance areas of concern, *broadly*. Then, one core element is selected, we go *deep* in both the economic- and the IT perspectives, and find the desired, possibly future, requirements of economic- and IT perspectives, e.g., having economically sustainable actors (Economic Perspective) that are open (IT perspective), *simultaneously*. At this stage, we should assess if such ideal state is possible; and if not we should do trade-offs. For trade-off analysis, one can follow the existing approaches such as ATAM [8]. While assessing the state of consonance in depth, we can regularly switch to breadth-first and explore the context of consonance again, and vice versa.

3   Running Example: Clearing and Repartitioning Intellectual Property Rights on Music

Our real-world example is on an *Intellectual Property Rights (IPR)* e-service. This e-service involves a large international network consisting of *IPR societies* as well as *IPR owners* (e.g. artists, producers) and *IPR users* (e.g. radio station, restaurants). In general, many different IPRs exist; however in this paper we focus on the *right to make content public*. Commercial entities (e.g. radio stations) have to pay IPR owners (e.g. artists) a fee for using intellectual property (e.g. a music track), if they make it public. The IPR society collects money from the IPR user (called *right clearance*) and pays money to the IPR owners (called *repartitioning*). *Clearance* and *repartitioning* are commercial services that are semi-automated. In the following, we explain the economic- and IT perspectives of the current state of IPR e-service, using the scenario of a restaurant playing background music.

The goal of our study was to get a close up reality of what is like when consonance is assessed from discrepancy and conflict point of view. We focused on the *Clearance* and *Repartitioning* commercial services of the IPR society. The *stakeholders*, who were experts in economic- or IT perspective, were the Chief IT and Chief Financial Officer of the IPR society. We organized a number of workshops where, together with stakeholders, we applied our consonance approach (see Section 2.2). We audio recorded and later analyzed the workshops.

3.1 Economic Perspective

Fig. 1 shows an $e^3 value$ model representing that a restaurant plays background music and has to clear intellectual property rights for that. The model shows the value transfers for a time period of one year.

As there are many restaurants, the **Restaurant** actor is modeled as a market segment. Usually, restaurants do not play background music themselves but obtain a stream of background music from a **Background music provider**. Because there are a number of background music providers to choose from, the provider is modeled as a market segment too.

The restaurant has to exchange objects of economic value with three parties: (1) the already mentioned **Background music provider**, and (2) two IPR societies (RS1 and RS2). Because the restaurant plays the music in public, the restaurant has to pay the relevant IPR societies for the right to make public (RTMP). The fee depends on the number of square meters of the restaurant.

In general, IPR societies differ in the right(s) they clear and for whom they do so. IPR societies can perform two tasks: **clearing**, and **repartitioning**. Clearing is about granting the right to the IPR user and getting paid for that. Repartitioning is about paying the collected fees to the IPR owners. Sometimes IPR societies can do both tasks, but they may also concentrate on one of these tasks.

In this study, we assume that there are two IPR societies involved to clear the rights to make public. For brevity, we detail only such a society, namely RS1.

Considering the **Background music provider**, we see that the background music provider also has to clear rights with the relevant IPR societies. This is because the background music provider also makes the music public (namely to the restaurants) and consequently has to pay for that. Again, the background music provider is charged, but now based on market research in combination with the playlist of the broadcasters and the background music suppliers. For playlist reporting, background music providers are supposed to behave as **Radio stations** reporting their playlists; consequently playlist reporting by the background music providers are not shown explicitly in the $e^3 value$ model.

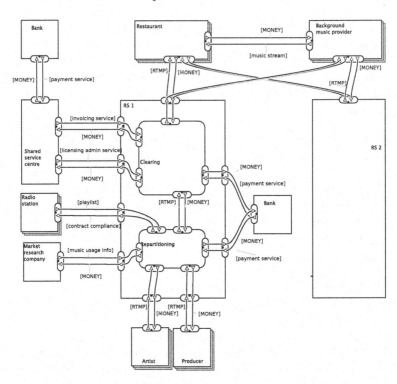

Fig. 1. As-Is value model for handling music rights - background music in restaurants

Considering RS1, we see that this society performs two value activities: (1) Clearing the right to make public, and (2) Repartitioning the right to make public.

The clearing activity obtains from each restaurant an amount of money *yearly*. The clearing activity obtains also money from the background music providers. Parts of performing the clearing activity are outsourced, in this case the licensing administration, and invoicing. Consequently, the results of these activities are modeled as separate value object services in the model, for which RS1 pays a fee. The shared service in turn uses a banking service to collect payments by the restaurants and background music providers. The repartitioning activity obtains the money pot build by the clearing activity, and divides the pot over the IPR owners. To do so, the IPR society obtains the playlists from a number of important radio stations. In order to obtain the playlists, the IPR societies offer legal contract compliance in return. Radio stations are obliged to give these playlists, as a result of their contracts with IPR societies. Additionally, market research is done to understand the tracks played by other IPR users than radio stations, so e.g. the restaurants. To this end, the IPR society hires a Market research company to perform the market research on music usage. The playlist and market research information is used to divide the money pot over the IPR owners. Finally, in order to do the actual payment, the IPR society uses a banking service, for which it pays a service fee.

3.2   IT Perspective

The IPR society operates its core activities, i.e., clearing and repartitioning, through a number of software systems, that are interconnected and are exposed to the outside world as services; and by consuming IT services provided by other actors. The interactions between the services are mainly message- and/or file-based.

With respect to the clearing service, Fig. 2.I shows that the restaurant uses an application, here called :BMuser, that invokes the streaming service (the service realizing the :Streaming contract in Fig. 2) of the :BMProvider. To pay the fee for broadcasting music to the IPR society both :BMuser application of the restaurant and the :BMProvider of background music provider invoke the :Clearing service. The bottom of Fig. 2.I shows that the IPR society carries out the clearance activity with two external parties: :SharedSeviceCenter and :InvoicingProvider. The IPR society has a software system called :UserLicenseSys that manages the licenses that music users (e.g., restaurants) obtain. In order to get the information about the new businesses the IPR society invokes the service enabling :LicenseAdministration of the :SharedSeviceCenter. For payments to be payed by music users, the clearance management system :ClearanceMngSys calls the :Payment service of the invoicing provider.

For the repartitioning service, the radio stations and the background music providers are obliged to provide playlist information to the IPR society. The IPR society provides the :Playlistinformation that music users can use to report the playlist information. To receive the playlist information gathered by the market research company the IPR society calls the :MusicUsage service. The IPR society (:RightSociety in Fig. 2) provides :Repertoire Info Service to the IPR owners in order to register intellectual work (e.g., a track in which they produced). That way IPR owners (e.g., record company) can invoke this service to manage repertoire information of their intellectual property.

4   Consonance between the Perspectives

We see consonance as a general problem aiming at relating the two economic- and IT perspectives and addressing a set of general trade-offs that cross-cut the two perspectives. Previous section presented the result of *Step 1* of our consonance approach where we modeled the economic and IT perspective of the IPR e-service. In this section we relate these two perspectives. First, we zoom into the different requirements of the two perspectives and the extent to which they are met (*Step 2*). Next, we present the resulting trade-offs of fulfilling both perspectives' requirements, simultaneously (*Step 3*). Due to space limitations, we only report the more interesting trade-offs related to actors and services.

4.1   Actors That Are Economically Sustainable and Open

Economic sustainability of actors From the economic perspective, we assessed whether and how each actor is economically sustainable. In particular, we looked

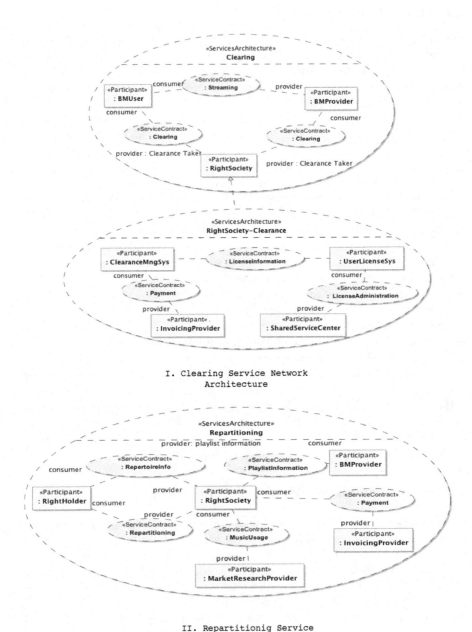

I. Clearing Service Network
Architecture

II. Repartitionig Service
Network Architecture

Fig. 2. As-Is IT architecture for handling music rights - background music in restaurants

at two main aspects: (i) if/how the actors create some sort of *profit* and (ii) if the economic model is *durable*.

Related to *profitability* of the IPR society, stakeholders emphasized that unlike what is normally the case with commercial entities, the goal is not maximizing the profit of RS itself. Instead, RS aims at maximizing the profit of the IPR owners (artists and producers). To this aim, RS seeks for minimizing its internal costs and maximizing the payment to the IPR owners.

Related to the *durability* of their economic model, RS aims at being economically independent, i.e., covering their costs and increase their value. The stakeholders noted that they include their costs in the calculation for repartitioning money to the IPR owners, meaning that the amount of incoming money (clearance fee) is always greater than the outgoing money. This ensures that they remain economically independent.

However, focusing on the *durability* of the economic model for the IPR owners (i.e., artists and producers), the stakeholders highlighted an important point of concern about the timing of payment. Currently, when a track of an artist is played on the radio, the artist will receive the money (for making that track public) approximately one year later. This implies that the artists loose one year of *interest* on their money. The same applies for the producers (e.g., record companies). The stakeholders emphasized that today these payments constitutes a significant part of the income of the producers.

Bottom Line: to ensure economic sustainability of IPR owners the timing of the payments should to be improved.

Openness of actors. From the IT perspective, we assessed to what extent the cross-organizational IT network allows the actors (service providers and consumers) to join and leave the network on-the-fly. In particular, we looked at whether the IT architecture (see Fig. 2) allows for addition of new types of actors.

The stakeholders emphasized that new technological advancements are introducing new type of actors in IPR societies. For example, internet-based technologies have introduced new types of music broadcasting such as Podcasting. Podcasting music allows the precise counting of music use if each listener reports track usage to a counting service. Reporting the music usage can be done through three types of actors (i) music users via their application, (ii) the podcasting music provider, and (iii) a third-party playlist provider. This implies that the IT perspective needs to be open enough to support addition of the new types of actors such as podcasting music provider or playlist provider. What hinders such openness, however, is the lack of use of open standards. Currently, in the IT architecture of IPR e-services the communication between actors is file-based, meaning that they have to agree upon and communicate based on a pre-defined format. A better alternative would be to use open, web-based standards such as WSDL and web service technology. The current IT architecture, however, does not support web service standards.

Moreover, currently IPR handling in many countries is a monopolistic activity as IPR societies are appointed and controlled by the local government. In the near future, however, it is expected that the private entities will be allowed to act as IPR societies. Music users, artists and producers may then select their preferred IPR society for clearance and repartitioning. To fulfill this requirement the IPR societies need to collaborate with each other and even collect fees for international IPR owners, rather than national ones. This introduces a new level of openness enabling actors to change roles and join and leave the IPR service network on-the-fly.

Bottom Line: lack of standardization has hampered the openness for actors which, according to the stakeholders, is absolutely necessary for the future needs of the IPR society.

Consonance between economically sustainable and open actors. In short term, there are trade-offs between the economic sustainability and openness of actors. Enabling the IT perspective to support openness does not come for free and requires significant investments. These investments initially might negatively affect economic sustainability. On long term, however, openness and economic sustainability can be synergic. If the actors are open (e.g. based on standards, web-services and alike), they can more easily, and so more cheaply, interact with IPR users (such as radio stations). Additionally, if international societies interact with each other using standards, it could be easier to exchange rights, payments, and playlist. Thus, more international rights could be cleared against lower costs. Therefore, the total amount of money to be paid increases as (i) increase in number of IPR owners leads to increase in amount of collected money, and (ii) standardization leads to lower costs. Therefore, the increase in amount of collected money and cost reductions results in higher payments to more IPR owners. Consequently, on the long term, there is no trade-off between sustainability and openness, rather they re-enforce each other.

4.2   Services That Are Value Adding and Reusable

Value-adding services From the economic perspective, we assessed whether the services *create value* for the consumers. Simply put, if the services are activities that consumers are willing to pay for. As shown in Fig. 1, there are two commercial services: Clearing and Repartitioning. The stakeholders indicated that two main factors determine the value of IPR services to the IPR owners: (i) high precision in repartitioning calculations, and (ii) maximizing the money being paid to the IPR owners. To ensure high precision, there are important manual actions, although the largest part of the two services is carried out automatically. For instance, matching a played track with the artists is carried out, partially, manually. Such manual operations, although benefiting the precision, however have some disadvantages: they increase human resources costs as more human effort is needed; they require skilled personnel, hence training costs; and they include faults caused by human mistakes (e.g., typos). Since manual operations have costs, they negatively affect the second value factor, i.e., maximizing the money being paid to the IPR owners.

Bottom Line: although precision in the repartitioning of collected money between the IPR owner is a good motivation for manual operation of some business activities, increasing the level of automation has obvious business benefits.

Reusability of services. From the IT perspective, we assessed if the services are *reused* in various business scenarios, and found that this is not the case for the IPR e-services, although there are many reuse opportunities. for instance, the stakeholders pinpointed that two of the main assets of the IPR society are (i) repository of repertoire information, and (ii) business licenses; with the IPR society's move to internationalization of their services, it becomes essential that the repertoire and licensing data services (i.e., services realizing :`RepertoireInfo` and :`LicenseAdministration` contracts in Fig. 2), are reusable by various international societies and in different business scenarios.

Bottom Line: future scenarios require higher levels of reuseability of services.

Consonance between value-adding and reusable services On one hand, there are trade-offs between high precision in the repartitioning calculations and maximizing the money being paid to the IPR owners. Our discussions with the stakeholders revealed that precision in the calculations is their highest priority. Thus, their current trade-off (semi-automated over fully automated services) remains unchanged. On the other hand, there are trade-offs between reusability and value creation of services, because reusability comes with a price, and decreases the amount of money being paid to the IPR owners.

5 Lessons Learned

In this work we focused on the conflicting requirements between the economic- and IT perspectives and addressed their consonance as the mutual adjustment of those conflicts. In what follows, we discuss our observations related to the application of our approach, lessons learned, and foreseen improvements.

5.1 Exposing Consonance Trade-offs

Observation. We observed that by focusing on the conflicting requirements, our approach makes the implicit trade-offs about consonance of the economic- and IT perspectives explicit. For example, by simultaneously focusing on the economic sustainability and openness of actors, we triggered stakeholders to identify various associated trade-offs. The e^3value and SoaML models are kept deliberately simple to facilitate the tractability and understandability requirements of our approach. We observed that the stakeholders understood the models, and used the two models and their corresponding differences as a starting point for identifying the trade-offs and design problems.

Lesson. In exposing trade-offs our approach showed to be effective. To do so, the used models should only capture the essentials and therefore be easy to understand. The approach directly revealed which conflicting requirements got higher weight, and whether this is desirable. In sum, it led to a lean and to-the-point approach to consonance where the primary focus is on trade-offs.

Improvement. The stakeholders showed interest in having views and viewpoints [9] that are specifically made for their domain. Those viewpoints should frame and highlight the conflicting requirements and visualize their possible prioritization.

5.2   Short-term Consonance Trade-offs Can be Long-term Synergies

Observation. We observed that although, in shorter period of time (e.g., 1 year), some of the conflicting requirements lead to trade-offs, in the long term (e.g., after 5 years) those requirements can be synergic. An example is the economic sustainability and openness of actors (see Section 4.1). Openness comes with a price that is a pressure on sustainability. On the long term, however, openness serves economic sustainability as it maximizes the amount of money to be paid to the right owners.

Lesson. Mainly in the reasoning leading to identification of trade-offs the notion of time remains implicit, although it is inherent in trade-off analysis and decision making [10]. In this work we learned that it is important to turn this situation around by explicitly capturing the timeframe of trade-offs.

Improvement. The stakeholders emphasized the importance of tools and techniques that explicitly capture and visualize consonance trade-offs, over time.

6   Discussion

6.1   Impact of Consonance on Requirements Engineering

Concerning our interpretation of e-services—*commercial* services which are provisioned via information technology—development of e-services obviously requires a software engineering effort, and as part of it, a requirements engineering process. Such a requirements engineering process entails the business development activity, too. This implies that requirements engineering for e-services is not limited to software system requirements only, but should incorporate economic requirements, such as economic sustainability of the e-service at hand for all actors involved also. This is already acknowledged by recent requirements engineering approaches [11], for instance in the field of goal modeling [12]. However, our approach recognizes specific goals such as economic sustainability.

In addition, early exploration of e-services needs development of both economic and IT requirements *in harmony*. IT requirements are important because e-services heavily rely on technology for their provisioning (most digital content services are in fact substantial IT operations). Economic considerations, such as economic sustainability are important because otherwise the commercial service would not be offered in the first place. Significant trade-offs between these two type of requirements need to be addressed early in the requirements engineering process because both economic sustainability and feasible information technology are needed for the e-service at the same time.

6.2   Related Work

Alignment has been researched in the fields of Requirements Engineering, Business Science, and Computer Science. In what follows we classify a number of recent approaches. What is common among these approaches is that they focus only on *mapping different elements*, and *balancing incompatible objectives* is *not* supported. This implies that the current focus consists of mapping the matching elements, rather than balancing discrepancies and conflicts. This work, to the best of our knowledge, is the first that externalizes the conflicting requirements and makes the trade-offs posed by such conflicts explicit.

Alignment Approaches in Requirements Engineering. Alignment in Requirements Engineering (RE) field is considered a form of requirements engineering. RE acknowledges that different stakeholders are involved, each with a different interest. Thus for proper requirements engineering, multiple perspectives have to be taken [13]—for example, an economic and IT perspective. From a requirements engineering point of view, these perspectives must represent the same system. Or in other words, the perspectives must be aligned [13]. Most of the approaches in RE *map* business elements to IT requirements (e.g., business strategy to requirements [12,14]). Our focus, however, is to treat the discrepancies as first class elements and balance conflicting requirements.

Alignment Approaches in Business Science. An analysis of over 150 articles reveals that most approaches in this field focus on integration between business- and IT strategies and requirements of a *single* enterprise [3]. In recent years, a number of approaches addressed alignment in networked organizations [11,15, 16]. Their IT perspective, however, is scoped down to high-level analysis models only (e.g., business and coordination process models [17]).

Alignment Approaches in Computer Science. Alignment in these approaches entails *mapping* different service-oriented elements. Some link service network- and business process models [18]; while others link business- and software service models [19]. Although the aforementioned approaches appear to be quite different, they all converge to a common perception of "business", i.e., activities or services that are eventually supported by IT services. In this sense, business services are higher-level abstractions of software services, the same as analysis models are higher level abstractions of design models. In practice, however, "business" does not entail higher level abstractions of IT services only. In turn, business might include elements that are in essence inconsistent with their corresponding IT elements. We argue that such simplistic perception of "business" is one of the main sources of confusion which make alignment especially challenging.

7   Conclusion

When Service Orientation was first introduced, many companies perceived it as providing *the solution* for the *old* alignment problem. After a decade, alignment still remains unsolved. Our consonance approach addresses a fundamental issue in the alignment problem: the implicit treatment of the important and difficult trade-offs between the two economic- and IT perspectives. Our approach, which brings the discrepancies and trade-offs into focus, can be adopted incrementally to make adjustments between the conflicting requirements. One way of addressing the consonance trade-offs is to guide the decision making using *conflict-centric architectural viewpoints*. In the requirements exploration phase, it is important to use tractable and easy understandable requirement representation formalisms, due to the limited time available due to the competitive nature of e-service projects, and the broad range of stakeholder interests. To this aim, future work will design viewpoints for aligning economic- and IT perspectives.

In this study we have relied on input and feedback from the stakeholders of IPR to study whether our consonance approach supports their reasoning. The feedback, although informal, has been positive. The consensus was that the models brings attention to what really matters in each perspective, and that the focus on discrepancies help their reasoning for alignment. Future work includes empirical validation of the effects of consonance approach in practitioners' reasoning. This requires engagement of a broad community of practitioners in e-service projects .

A limitation to generalizability of results is that the study was conducted at one company which means the findings are specific to this study. Two aspects, however, mitigate such limitation (i) to cover both economic- and IT perspectives, we chose stakeholders with different roles of he Chief IT and Chief Financial Officer of the IPR society, who hold extensive experience and are aware of requirements of each perspective. (ii) being heavily involved in collaboration with other sister IPR societies in Europe and United States, the stakeholders brought insight from IPR networks in those countries as well. Both aspects play in favor of generalizability of our results.

Acknowledgments. We would like to thank our real-world example provider for the meetings we had and the valuable feedback.

References

1. Derzsi, Z., Gordijn, J.: A framework for business/IT alignment in networked value constellations. In: Proceedings of the Workshops of the International Conference on Advanced Information Systems Engineering, pp. 219–226 (2006)
2. Razavian, M., Lago, P., Gordijn, J.: Why is aligning economic- and IT services so difficult? In: Snene, M., Leonard, M. (eds.) IESS 2014. LNBIP, vol. 169, pp. 92–107. Springer, Heidelberg (2014)
3. Henderson, J., Venkatraman, N.: Strategic alignment: Leveraging information technology for transforming organizations. IBM Systems Journal **32**(1), 472–484 (1993)

4. Yu, E.S.K.: Towards modeling and reasoning support for early-phase requirements engineering. In: Proceedings of the 3rd IEEE International Symposium on Requirements Engineering. RE 1997, pp. 226–235. IEEE Computer Society (1997)
5. Rittel, H.W., Webber, M.M.: Dilemmas in a General Theory of Planning. Policy sciences **4**(2), 155–169 (1973)
6. Gordijn, J., Akkermans, H.: Value based requirements engineering: Exploring innovative e-commerce idea. Requirements Engineering Journal **8**(2), 114–134 (2003)
7. OMG: Service oriented architecture modeling language (SoaML) specification. Technical report, Object Management Group (May 2012)
8. Kazman, R., Klein, M.H., Barbacci, M., Longstaff, T.A., Lipson, H.F., Carrière, S.J.: The architecture tradeoff analysis method. In: ICECCS, pp. 68–78 (1998)
9. International Organization Of Standardization: ISO/IEC/IEEE 42010:2011 - Systems and software engineering - Architecture description. Technical Report March, International Organization for Standardization (ISO) (2011)
10. Razavian, M., Lago, P.: A viewpoint for dealing with change in migration to services. In: Joint Working Conference on Software Architecture & 6th European Conference on Software Architecture, pp. 201–205. IEEE (2012)
11. Wieringa, R., Pijpers, V., Bodenstaff, L., Gordijn, J.: In: Value-Driven Coordination Process Design Using Physical Delivery Models, pp. 216–231. Springer (2008)
12. Singh, S.N., Woo, C.: Investigating Business-IT Alignment Through Multi-disciplinary Goal Concepts. Requir. Eng. **14**(3), 177–207 (2009)
13. Finkelstein, A., Kramer, J., Nuseibeh, B., Finkelstein, L., Goedicke, M.: Viewpoints: a framework for integrating multiple perspectives in system development. International Journal of Software Engineering and Knowledge Engineering 2 (1992)
14. Wegmann, A., Regev, G., Rychkova, I., Julia, P., Perroud, O.: Early requirements and business-IT alignment with SEAM for business. In: 15th IEEE International Requirements Engineering Conference. IEEE (2007)
15. Weigand, H., Johannesson, P., Andersson, B., Bergholtz, M.: Value-based service modeling and design: toward a unified view of services. In: van Eck, P., Gordijn, J., Wieringa, R. (eds.) CAiSE 2009. LNCS, vol. 5565, pp. 410–424. Springer, Heidelberg (2009)
16. Chen, H.M.: Towards service engineering: service orientation and business-it alignment. In: Hawaii International Conference on System Sciences. In: Proceedings of the 41st Annual, pp. 114–114. IEEE (2008)
17. Bodenstaff, L.: Managing dependency relations in inter-organizational models. PhD thesis, University of Twente (2010)
18. Danylevych, O., Karastoyanova, D., Leymann, F.: Service networks modelling: An SOA & BPM standpoint. Journal of Universal Computer Science **16**(13), 1668–1693 (2010)
19. Busi, N., Gorrieri, R., Guidi, C., Lucchi, R., Zavattaro, G.: Choreography and orchestration: A synergic approach for system design. Springer, pp. 228–240 (2005)

From Stakeholder Requirements to Formal Specifications Through Refinement

Feng-Lin Li[1(✉)], Jennifer Horkoff[2], Alexander Borgida[3], Giancarlo Guizzardi[4],
Lin Liu[5], and John Mylopoulos[1]

[1] Department of Information Engineering and Computer Science,
University of Trento, Trento, Italy
maillifenglin@gmail.com
[2] Centre for Human Computer Interaction Design, City University, London, UK
[3] Department of Computer Science, Rutgers University, New Brunswick, USA
[4] Computer Science Department, Federal University of Espírito Santo,
Vitória, Brazil
[5] School of Software, Tsinghua University, Beijing, China

Abstract. **[Context and motivation]** Stakeholder requirements are notoriously informal, vague, ambiguous and often unattainable. The requirements engineering problem is to formalize these requirements and then transform them through a systematic process into a formal specification that can be handed over to designers for downstream development. **[Question/problem]** This paper proposes a framework for transforming informal requirements to formal ones, and then to a specification. **[Principal ideas/results]** The framework consists of an ontology of requirements, a formal requirements modeling language for representing both functional and non-functional requirements, as well as a rich set of refinement operators whereby requirements are incrementally transformed into a formal, practically satisfiable and measurable specification. **[Contributions]** Our proposal includes a systematic, tool-supported methodology for conducting this transformation. For evaluation, we have applied our framework to a public requirements dataset. The results of our evaluation suggest that our ontology and modeling language are adequate for capturing requirements, and our methodology is effective in handling requirements in practice.

Keywords: Requirements modeling language · Functional requirements · Non-functional requirements · Ontologies

1 Introduction

Stakeholder requirements are notoriously informal, vague, ambiguous, and often unattainable. The requirements engineering problem is to formalize and transform these requirements through a systematic process into a formal, consistent and measurable specification that can be handed over to designers for downstream development. In fact, this is the core problem of Requirements Engineering (RE).

Predictably, there has been much work on transforming informal requirements to a formal specification, going back to the early 90s and before [1][2]. Some of this work exploits AI techniques such as expert systems and natural language processing (NLP)

© Springer International Publishing Switzerland 2015
S.A. Fricker and K. Schneider (Eds.): REFSQ 2015, LNCS 9013, pp. 164–180, 2015.
DOI: 10.1007/978-3-319-16101-3_11

[1]. Other proposals offer a systematic way for formalizing a specification [2]. However, the core problem has not been addressed effectively and has remained open, as attested by current requirements engineering practice, where word processors and spreadsheets continue to constitute the main tools for engineering requirements. For example, according to a webcast audience poll conducted by Blueprint Software System in 2014, more than 50% of the participants said that they are using documents and spreadsheets for conducting requirements[1] engineering. To address the poor support for collaboration, traceability, and management offered by such vanilla tools, there have been proposals for requirements-specific tools (e.g., Rational DOORS [3]) that support RE-specific activities, such as elicitation, modeling, specification and traceability management. However, these tools pay little attention to the derivation of requirements; instead, they focus more on the management of derived requirements.

Our work attacks the problem afresh, making the following contributions:

- Offers a comprehensive *ontology of requirements*, which consists of various kinds of goals: functional, quality and content goals (descriptions of world sates, i.e., properties of entities in the real world). In addition, our *specifications* include functions (aka tasks), functional constraints, quality constraints, state constraints (machine states that reflect world states) and domain assumptions.
- Proposes a requirements modeling language that can capture the kinds of requirements identified in our requirements ontology, as well as interrelations between them. We also provide a methodology for refining informal stakeholders requirements into formal specifications.
- Presents a three-pronged evaluation of our proposal using a prototype supporting tool and the PROMISE requirements set [4]. First, we classify the whole set of requirements according to our ontology in order to evaluate its coverage; second, we encode all the requirements in the set using our language to assess its adequacy; third, we apply our methodology to two case studies from the dataset, where formal specifications were derived from informal requirements for a *meeting scheduler* and a *nursing scheduler* exemplar[2].

The rest of the paper is structured as follows: Section 2 reviews related work, Section 3 outlines our research baseline, Section 4 presents our requirements ontology, Section 5 sketches the language for capturing requirements, Section 6 presents a methodology (including refinement operators) for deriving formal specification from informal stakeholder requirements, Section 7 presents the three-pronged evaluation, Section 8 summarizes contributions and offers a glimpse of forthcoming work.

2   Related Work

The transformation from informal requirements to formal specifications has been the subject of research for more than 25 years. Early work by Fraser et al. [5] proposed guidelines for developing VDM specifications from Structural Analysis (mostly Data

---

[1] http://www.blueprintsys.com/lp/the-business-impact-of-poor-requirements/

[2] Due to space limitations, only the meeting scheduler case study is presented in this paper. The two complete case studies are available at http://goo.gl/GGceBe.

Flow Diagrams). Giese at al. [6] tried to relate informal requirements (UML use case) to formal specifications written in Object Constraint Language (OCL). Seater et al. [7] have discussed how to derive system specifications from Problem Frame descriptions through a series of incremental steps (problem reduction). These approaches focus on functional requirements (FRs), and pay little attention to non-functional requirements (NFRs).

KAOS [2] constitutes a landmark goal-oriented methodology for deriving formal operational specifications from informal stakeholder requirements. In KAOS, goals elicited from stakeholders are formalized using Linear Temporal Logic (LTL), refined to sub-goals through a set of refinement patterns, and operationalized as specifications of system operations (pre-, post- and trigger conditions) by following a set of formal derivation rules [8]. This transformation process has been extended by many other researchers for deriving formal system specifications from KAOS goal models, as in [9]. The KAOS methodology does facilitate the derivation of functional system specification from stakeholder goals; however, it does not offer support for specifying and refining NFRs, and does not address ontological considerations for requirements.

The NFR Framework (NFR-F) [10] was the first proposal to treat NFRs in depth. NFR-F used softgoals (goals with no clear-cut criteria for success) to capture NFRs. Softgoals have the syntactic form "*type* [*topic*]" (e.g., "accuracy [account]", where "accuracy" is a type and "account" is a topic). The framework offers contribution links for linking software design elements to softgoals, and several operators for decomposing softgoals. Our work builds on these ideas, but aims to offer a comprehensive set of concepts for modeling and analyzing all requirements, not just NFRs.

Quality quantification has been used repeatedly to make NFRs measurable. In this regard, ISO 9126-2 [11] proposed a rich set of metrics for quantifying various quality attributes, while the P-language [12] suggested use of "scale and meters" to specify NFRs. However, these proposals do not offer guidelines or methodologies for deriving formal NFR specifications from informal ones. Techne [13] has proposed operationalizing softgoals into quality constraints which do come with clear-cut criteria for success. Techne facilitates the quantification of softgoals; however, like its NFR-F ancestor, it does not treat well existential dependencies between qualities and functional goals, a distinguishing feature of our proposal.

Ontologies, typically ontologies of specific domains for which requirements are desired, have been employed in RE mainly for activities or processes [14]. These efforts, however, are not proposals for an ontological analysis of requirements notions. In fact, few researchers have attempted to ontologically analyze requirements. Our goal here is in the ontological classification and conceptual clarification of different requirement kinds. In this spirit, the work that is strongly related to ours and receives the most attention in the literature is the Core Ontology for RE (aka CORE) [15]. Our work proposed in [16] and continued here is in line with CORE in several aspects. For instance, both proposals are founded on the premise that requirements are stakeholder goals and that NFRs should be interpreted as requirements that refer to qualities. However, there are also important differences between the two proposals. Firstly, CORE is based on the DOLCE foundational ontology, and ours is built on UFO [17]. As discussed in [16], UFO offers a richer set of categories to cover some important aspects of the RE domain, especially regarding the analysis of functional and quality requirements (as shown in Section 4). Secondly, CORE contains a number of deficiencies in handling NFRs [16]. For instance, it is unable to capture a class of requirements that refer to both function and quality, or neither qualities nor processes/events (in ontological term, perdurants), but entities (endurants), and it does not favor the expression of requirements that are vague but do not refer to qualities.

3   Research Baseline

This work builds on our recent work on quality requirements (QRs) [16][18], where we proposed an ontology for classifying, a formal language for modeling, and some refinement operators for refining QRs. Our existing requirements ontology (as shown in the unshaded part of Fig. 1) is based on a goal-oriented perspective where all requirements are goals of one sort or another. That ontology, however, focuses on quality goals (QGs) and quality constraints (QCs) that are used to capture quality requirements (QRs). These constitute the most important class of what has been traditionally called non-functional requirements (NFRs). The difference between a QG and a QC is that the former is vague while the latter comes with a clear-cut criterion for success.

According to [18], we treat a quality as a mapping from its subject to a quality region, and define a QR as a QG that requires a quality to map into values within a region QRG. Therefore, we write a QG as Q (*SubjT*): *QRG*, a syntactic abbreviation for $\forall x$. *instanceOf* $(x, SubjT) \rightarrow subregionOf (Q(x), QRG)$, meaning that for each individual subject x of type *SubjT*, the value of $Q(x)$ should be a sub-region of (including a point in) *QRG*. Note that the subject of a quality is not limited to an entity, function/task or process, but can also be a goal, as well as a collective of entities or processes (e.g., as in *"90% of all executions shall be within 5 sec."*).

Using this syntax, the requirement *"the product shall return (file) search results in an acceptable time"* can be captured as in Eq. 1.2. *Quality constraints* (QCs) that operationalize QGs use the same syntax, but must have a measurable region (see Eq. 1.3). For more interesting examples please refer to [16][18].

$$search' := search <actor:\{the\ product\}><object:\ file> \qquad (1.1)$$

$$QG1\text{-}1 := processing\ time\ (search')\ :\ acceptable \qquad (1.2)$$

$$QC1\text{-}2 := processing\ time\ (search')\ :\ \leq\ 8\ sec. \qquad (1.3)$$

In addition to the syntax, we provide operators for refining QGs/QCs, including *relax* and *focus*. *Relax* is used to make a requirement practically satisfiable or alleviate inconsistency between requirements. Specifically, we use U (universality), G (gradability), and A (agreement) operators to relax practically unsatisfiable requirements. For example, we weaken *"all the runs of file search"* to *"x% of the runs"* by using U, relax *"within 8 sec."* to *"nearly within 8 sec."* by using G, or relax *"(all the) web users shall report the UI is simple"* to *"y% of the web users"* by using A. *Focus* offers two ways to refine a QG: via the quality Q based on reference quality hierarchies (e.g., ISO/IEC 25010 [19]) or via the subject type *SubjT* according to the parts of an entity or the functional goal hierarchy. Take a *"security"* QG in a software development process for example, in the former case, stakeholders may lay particular emphasis on one of its sub-qualities, say *"integrity"*; in the latter case, we may not need to secure the entire system (e.g., the interface) but some important parts (e.g., the data transfer module).

4   An Ontology for Requirements

In this section, we extend the ontology of NFRs in our previous work [18] to a full-fledged ontology for requirements, with a focus on functional and content requirements. Our classification criteria is based on fundamental concepts such as *function*, *quality and subject* (the bearer of a quality function), along with the ontological semantics of the Unified Foundational Ontology (UFO) [17]. In general, both *functions* and *qualities* are existentially dependent characteristics that can only exist by inhering in their *subjects* (bearers). For example, the product search function or the reliability of an e-commerce website would depend on that specific system. Roughly, a *quality* is always manifested as long as it exists. In contrast, a *function* (capability, capacity) is ontologically a *disposition*, and is only manifested when certain *situations* hold. Function manifestations amount to happenings of *events* that bring about *effects* in the world.

In UFO, most perceived events are *polygenic*, i.e., when an event is occurring, there are a number of dispositions of different participants being manifested at the same time. For example, a manifestation event (i.e., a run) of the product search function will involve the capacities of both the system and a user. In software development, we can design the capacities of the system (a search function), but often make assumptions about the capacities of the user (e.g., the user is not visually impaired, the user masters a certain language). These kinds of requirements will be captured as functional goals and domain assumptions in our requirements ontology.

An overview of our extended requirements ontology is shown in Fig. 1, with new concepts shaded. A goal can be specialized into a functional goal (FG), quality goal (QG) or content goal (CTG), to be discussed in detail later. Note that a goal may belong to more than one category, such as FG and QG (e.g., "*the system shall collect real-time information*"), or FG and CTG (e.g., "*... display students records, which include ID, name, GPA, etc.*"). When this is the case, a goal is refined into FG and QG sub-goals, or FG and CTG ones. As in [18], a goal can also be operationalized by domain assumptions (DAs), which are assumptions about the operational environment of the system-to-be. E.g., "*The system will have a functioning power supply*".

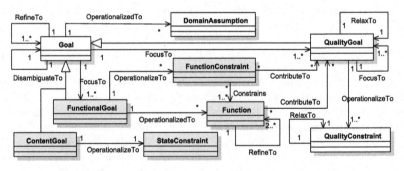

Fig. 1. The extended requirements ontology (based on [18])

Functional Goals, Functions and Functional Constraints. A *functional goal* (FG) represents a requirement that is fulfilled through one or more functions. Following the ontological underpinnings of our approach, an FG would come with the following associated information: (1) *function* — the nature of the required capability; (2) *situation* — the conditions under which the function can be activated; often this includes pre-conditions (characterizations of the situation), triggers (the event that brings about that situation), but also actors (agents), objects, targets, etc.; (3) *event* — the manifestations or occurrences of the function; (4) *effect* (post-conditions) — situations that are brought about after the execution of the function; and (5) *subject* — the individual(s) that the function inheres in. For example, in the requirement "*the system shall notify the realtor in a timely fashion when a seller or buyer responds to an appointment request*", the "*notify*" function, which inheres in "*the system*", will be activated by the situation "*when a seller or buyer responds to an appointment request*". Moreover, its manifestation, a notification event, is required to occur *in a timely fashion* (note this is not an effect, but a quality of the notification).

A *functional constraint* (FC) constrains the situation in which a function can be manifested. That is, an FC is usually stated as a restriction on the situation of a function. For example, in the FG "*users shall be able to update the time schedule*", one may impose a constraint "*only managers are allowed to perform the update*".

As we can see in these examples, FGs and FCs cannot be simply taken as propositions, as some goal modeling techniques have it. Rather, they are descriptions. Inspired by this observation, we use an "*attribute: descriptor*" language to capture them. E.g., the "*notify realtors*" and the "*update time scheduler*" examples can be captured as in Eq. 2 and Eq. 3, respectively. Note that the curly brackets indicate a singleton, and ':<' denotes description subsumption (e.g., Eq. 3 says that the update function is subsumed by things that only have managers as their actors).

$$FG2 := Notify <actor:\{the\ system\}><object:\ realtor><trigger:\ responds< \quad (2)$$
$$<actor:\ seller \lor buyer><target:\ appointment\ request>>$$

$$FC3 := Update <object:\ time\ schedule>:< <actor:\ only\ manager>>> \quad (3)$$

Content Goals and State Constraints. Content goals (CTGs) describe desired properties of world states, i.e., properties of entities in the real world. For example, a student in the real world has Id, name and GPA. To satisfy a CTG, the system-to-be must consist of states that reflect such world states. For example, to satisfy the aforementioned CTG, the student record database table of the system must include three columns: Id, name and GPA. Such desired machine states are termed *state constraints*.

Typically, CTGs are needed when defining: (1) data dictionaries, which describe required entities with associated attributes (e.g., the student example above); (2) multiple objects of a function, e.g., in "*the system shall display movie title, director, actor, etc.*", there is an implicit concept "*movie detail information*"; We show these two examples as in Eq. 4.1 and Eq. 4.2 below.

$$CTG4\text{-}1 := Student\ record :< <ID:\ String> <name:\ String> <GPA:\ Float> \quad (4.1)$$

$$CTG4\text{-}2 := Movie\ detail\ information :< <title:\ String> <director:\ String> \quad (4.2)$$
$$<actor:\ String>$$

Note that although CTG4-1 and CTG4-2 describe a set of attributes (and their associated value regions) that should be manipulated by the system, they are not QGs. The key point is that it is not descriptions of *qualities required to be present in the system-to-be*, but rather requirements on *desired properties of entities in the world*, to be fulfilled by the system-to-be.

5   A Requirements Modeling Language

We give the syntax of our language in Fig. 2 using Extended-BNF. Nonterminal are in italics, and terminals are quoted or derived from "...*Name*" nonterminal.

We start with the definition of *Attr*, an "*attribute: descriptor*" pair as shown in line 1. An attribute can relate an individual to more than one instance of the description, in which case we can use cardinality constraints "$\geq n$", "$\leq n$", "$= n$", "n" or "SOME" (n is a nonnegative integer, "SOME" means "≥ 1"). For example, "<*registerFor*: ≥ 3 *course*>" is a description of individuals who register for at least 3 courses. If the cardinality part is omitted, it is by default "$= 1$". The keyword "ONLY" implies that the attribute can only have individuals of type described by "*Descriptor*" as fillers. We currently do not provide a built-in set of attributes, which requires an ontology of software systems and of the application domain. That is, we allow engineers to invent new attributes when needed.

---

(01) *Attr* := '<' *AttrName* ':' [['$\geq$' | '$\leq$' | '='] n | 'SOME' | 'ONLY'] *Descriptor* '>'
(02) *Descriptor* := *atomicValue* | *automicDataType* | *SubjT*
(03) *SubjT* := *Entity* | *Function* | *Function*'.'*AttrName*
              | 'NOT' '(' *SubjT* ')' | *SubjT* '$\wedge$' *SubjT* | *SubjT* '$\vee$' *SubjT*
(04) *Entity* := *EntityName Attr** | *Attr$^+$* | '{' *IndividualName$^+$* '}'
(05) *Function* := *FuncName Attr**
(06) *Goal* := *GoalName*
(07) *FG* := *Function*
(08) *QG(QC)* := *QualityName* '(' *SubjT* ')' ':' *RegionExpr*
(09) *RegionExpr* := *region* | *QualityName* '(' *SubjT* ')'
(10) *CTG(SC)* := *Entity* ':<' *Attr$^+$*
(11) *FC* := *SubjT* ':<' *Attr$^+$*
(12) *DA* := *SubjT* (':<' | '$\equiv$') *SubjT*

Fig. 2. The Extended-BNF syntax for our language

The descriptor of an attribute can be an atomic value (e.g., "*Trento*" as the value of address, "5€" as the value of price), atomic data type (e.g., *String*, *Double*, and *Text*), or a subject type **SubjT** (line 2). A *SubjT* can be an entity, a function, a filler of an attribute in a function, the negation of a *SubjT*, the conjunction or union of *SubjTs* (line 3). Note that a *SubjT* is a type (or a class in object-oriented terms), and not an individual (instance). If the *SubjT* is a singleton, we wrap it with a curly bracket, e.g., {*the product*}. The constructors '*NOT*, '$\wedge$', and '$\vee$' applied to *SubjT* are standard set operations. An example can be "(*active* $\vee$ *outdated*) $\wedge$ *record*". Note that a function is treated as a type, having its runs as associated set.

An *entity* is composed of an optional entity name and a list of "*attribute*: *descriptor*" pairs, or a set of specific individuals (line 4). An anonymous entity is an entity with omitted name. For example, "<*accessedBy: manager*>" represents a type of entity that is accessed by managers. A *function* is represented in a similar way, but must have a function name (line 5). Since a *SubjT* (e.g., an entity or function) itself can be further qualified by attributes, resulting in nested descriptions (a trademark feature of Description Logics). For example, in "*the product shall record all the equipment that has been reserved*", "*equipment*" is the *object* of the function "*record*", and also has an attribute "*status*" (see FG6 in Eq. 6).

$$FG5 := Protect <actor: \{the\ system\}><object:\ user\ info \wedge private > \quad (5)$$

$$FG6 := Record <actor:\ \{the\ system\}> \\ <object:\ equipment <status:\ reserved>> \quad (6)$$

$$QG7 := understandability\ (\{the\ interface\}):\ intuitive \quad (7)$$

$$CTG8 := Non\text{-}clinical\ class :< <course\ name:\ String> \\ <lecture\ room\ requirements:\ Text> < instructor\ needs:\ Text> \quad (8)$$

In general, when a *goal* has not yet been specialized into sub-kinds like FG, QG or CTG, it can be simply written as a natural language string (Fig. 2, line 6). A *FG* is described as a required function (line 7). E.g., *"user private information shall be protected"* is captured as in Eq. 5. In line 8, a *QG/QC* is denoted in the form of "*Q (SubjT): QRG*" (adopted from our previous work [18]), where *QRG* can be either a *region* (e.g., low, fast, [80%, 95%]) in a value space or an expression that takes value/region from a value space (line 9). For instance, *"the product shall have an intuitive user interface"* is captured as in Eq. 7, in which *"the interface"* is a singleton.

Note that the syntactic form of QGs/QCs enables us to capture the important *inherence* relation between qualities and subjects: by "*Q (SubjT)*", we mean the quality Q inheres in an individual that is of type *SubjT* and, *SubjT* can be a function, an entity, or a goal. That is, a QG/QC in our framework is able to take a function or an entity involved in a function as its inhering subject. Capturing this inherence relation enables us to better manage QRs and FRs, as shown in our case study in Section 7.

A *CTG* (resp. SC) specifies the world (resp. machine) state of an entity through "*attribute: descriptor*" pairs. For example, the CTG *"a non-clinical class shall specify the course name, lecture room requirements, and instructor needs"* is captured as in Eq. 8. We use the subsumption relation (':<') instead of definition ('≡') because the specific entity could also have other properties not characterized at the moment. E.g., a non-clinical class may include extra attributes, such as *"course introduction"*. An *FC* is defined in a similar way, but can be imposed on either a function or an entity (type). E.g., *"only managers are allowed to access data tables"* can be captured as "*data table :< <accessedBy: ONLY manager>*". Finally, a DA assumes a *SubjT* to be subsumed by or equal to another *SubjT*. For instance, the DA *"the system will run on Windows"* can be encoded as "*{the system} :< <operation system: Windows>*". The definition relation ('≡') in DAs can be used to connect semantically equivalent concepts, e.g., *"list of class ≡ sequence of class"*.

The semantics of our language can be formalized by translation to a logic that has its own formal semantics already. As an example, interested readers can refer to our technical report available at http://goo.gl/GGceBe for a translation of our language to a Description Logic (DL) language, OWL [20] in this case .

6   A Methodology for Transforming Informal Requirements into a Formal Specification

In this section we first introduce two refinement operators that will be used for refining requirements, and then present a three-staged methodology for transforming informal requirements to a formal specification.

Refinement Operators. In our previous work [18], we have proposed *Relax* and *Focus* to refine QGs. Here we extend the set of refinement operators with *Operationalization* and *Contribution*, to facilitate the transformation process.

Operationalization. In our framework, *operationalization* transforms requirements to specifications. In general, a FG can be operationalized as function(s) and/or FC(s), a QG is operationalized by QC(s), and a CTG is operationalized by SC(s). FGs can be treated as the effect (post-condition) of functions: once the operationalizing functions are performed, the corresponding FG will be satisfied. To operationalize QGs, they must be made measurable — clear quality metrics and value regions must be defined. E.g., "*good security*" can be operationalized as "*monthly unauthorized access shall be less than* 3". For this purpose, standards like ISO/IEC 9126-2 [11] that have proposed a rich set of metrics for quantifying qualities are helpful. We make use of such standards in our methodology. To operationalize CTGs that describe world states, we need the system-to-be be in certain machine states (e.g., having a certain data base schema). Note that a goal (FG, QG or CTG) can be operationalized by domain assumptions (DAs). That is, it can be assumed true as long as the DAs hold.

Contribution. When QGs are operationalized as QCs, we only have the evaluation or success criteria for corresponding QGs. To meet these criteria, the system-to-be often needs to perform some functions, adopt certain designs, or impose suitable functional constraints. We use the classic contribution links "*help*", "*hurt*", "*make*" and "*break*" from NFR-F, to capture the relations between such functional elements and QGs. E.g., to achieve the "*good security*" QG above, we may need to include in our design functions such as "*authenticate users*" and "*authorize users*" to prevent unauthorized access. Note that contribution links are used to capture relations between functional elements and QGs at design-time, and QCs that measure QGs are evaluated at run-time. E.g., in the above example, at design time we may take that "*good security*" will be satisfied if the two contributing functions are present; at run-time, we need to monitor and check if "*monthly unauthorized access*" is less than 3 times (a QC).

A Three-Staged Methodology. Our methodology consists of three phases: (1) an informal phase, where informal requirements are disambiguated and broken down into goals representing single requirements; (2) a formalization phase, where each informal goal is formalized, along with its relationships to other goals; (3) a smithing phase, where refinement operators are iteratively applied on formally specified goals to derive unambiguous, satisfiable, mutually consistent and measurable specifications.

Informal Phase. Each requirement is treated here as a proposition and can be modeled and refined using existing goal modeling techniques (e.g., Techne [13]). The main tasks of requirement engineers in this phase are to: (1) identify key stakeholder concerns and classify them according to the requirements ontology of Fig. 1; (2) decouple composite concerns to make them atomic, and (3) refine high-level requirements to low-level ones and link functional elements to QGs in the spirit of goal-oriented refinement techniques.

Step 1: Identify key concerns and classify requirements. We ask the question "*what does a requirement r concern?*" to determine its classification, and provide some operational guidelines as follows:

- If *r* refers to both function and quality, then it is a composite goal. E.g., "*the system shall be able to interface with most DBMSs*" is composite since it refers to a function "*interface*" and a universality quality "*most*" over the set of DBMSs.

- If r refers to only function(s), then it is a FG.
- If r refers to only quality(-ies) and is vague (clear) for success, it is a QG (QC)
- If r constrains the situation of a function (e.g., actor, object, pre-condition, etc.), then it is a FC. E.g., *"the students added to a course shall be registered"*.
- If r makes an assumption about the environment of a system, then it is a DA. For example, *"the product will be used in an office environment"*.
- If r describes the attributes a real-world entity shall possess, then it is a CTG.

Step 2: Separate Concerns. In case a requirement r is a combination of concerns, they need to be separated:

- If r is a combination of function and quality, it can be focused into a FG and a QG. E.g., the DBMS example shall be decomposed into a FG *"the system shall be able to interface with DBMSs"* and a QG *"most of the DBMSs"*.
- If r refers to sibling functions/qualities, it shall be separated such that each resulting requirement concerns one function/quality. E.g., *"the system shall allow entering, storing and modifying product formulas"* shall be decomposed into *"the system shall allow entering ..."*, *"... storing ..."*, and *"... modifying ..."*.
- If r refers to nested qualities, we decouple them starting from the innermost layer. E.g., the QG *"at least 90% of the tasks shall be completed within 5 sec."* can be decoupled into two QGs: QG1 *"processing time within 5 sec."*, and QG2 *"QG1 shall be fulfilled for more than 90% of tasks"* (a universality QG).
- If r is a mix of function and content, it is suggested to define a CTG and a FG, respectively. E.g., for *"display date and time"*, we will have a CTG that defines an entity *"calendar"* with attributes date and time, and a FG *"display calendar"*.
- If r includes purposes or means, it shall be decomposed to different goals, which will be connected using refinements or contribution links. E.g., for *"the product shall create an exception log of product problems for analysis"*, we will have a FG *"analyze product problems"* being refined to *"create an exception log"*.

Step 3: Refine Requirements. In this step, we refine high-level goals to low-level ones by utilizing AND-*refine* or *refine*, and link functional elements to QGs through *contribution* links based on domain knowledge.

Formalization Phase. Here we formalize each goal in accordance with its classification. In the discussion below we focus on FGs, QGs and CTGs. As for other elements such as FCs and DAs, readers can refer to our syntax introduction in Section 5.

- *Functional Goals.* For FGs, we often need to find out its actor, object, and sometimes its target, pre-, post- and trigger conditions. For example, for *"when a conference room is reserved, the scheduler shall be updated"*, we can write *"update <object: scheduler> :< <trigger: reserve <object: room>>"*.
- *Quality goals.* The three key elements of a QG include quality, subject and desired quality region. Note that the subject can be either a bare function/entity or a complex description. For example, for *"90% of the maintainers shall be able to integrate new functionality into the product in 2 work days"*, there are two qualities: *"operating time"* for an integration process and *"universality"* for the set of maintainers. We thus define two QGs: *"QG1 := operating time (integrate <actor: maintainer> <object: new ∧ functionality> <target: {the product}>): 2 work days"*, and *"QG2 := U (QG1.actor): 90%"*.

- *Content Goals.* CTGs require the system-to-be to represent certain properties of entities in the real world. For example, *"the system shall display date and time"* will be captured as a CTG *"Calendar :< <hasDate: date> <hasTime: time>"* and a FG *"display <actor: {the system}><object: calendar>"*.

The encoding process facilitates the detection and resolution of ambiguity: if there is more than one way to encode a requirement, then there is ambiguity. E.g., *"notify users with email"* is ambiguous since it can be mapped into *"notify <object: user> <means: email>"* or *"notify <object: user <hasEmail: email>"*. In such situation, stakeholders have to identify the intended meaning(s).

Smithing Phase. Once goals have been formalized, we iteratively apply refinement operators relax, focus, operationalization, and contribution to derive satisfiable and measurable requirements specifications:

Step 1: Relax. In this step, we analyze whether a requirement is practically satisfiable or not, and use the three operators U, G, A, or a composition thereof to relax a requirement to an acceptable degree. For instance, the requirement *"all the tasks shall be finished within 5 sec."*, captured as *"QG1:= processing time (tasks): within 5 sec."*, can be relaxed by using G: *"QG2 := G (QG1): nearly"* (all the task shall be *nearly* within 5 sec.), or U: *"QG3 := U (QG1): 90%"* (*90% of the tasks* shall be within 5 sec.), or even both *"QG4 := U (QG2): 90%"* (*90% of the tasks shall be nearly within 5 sec.*). The A operator is mainly applied to subjective QGs, e.g., *"the interface shall be simple"*, captured as *"QG5 := appearance ({the interface}): simple"*, can be relaxed using A as *"QC6 := A (QG5): the majority of surveyed users"*.

Step 2: Focus. We focus QGs in two ways: via the quality Q or via the subject type SubjT. For example, the QG *"usability ({the product}): good"* can be focused into *"learnability ({the product}): good"* and *"operability ({the product}): good"* by following the quality hierarchy in ISO/IEC 25010. These quality goals can be further refined along subject hierarchy, e.g., a meeting scheduler often has functions like set up meeting and book conference room, so the quality *"learnability"* can be further applied to these functions, obtaining QGs *"learnability (set up meeting): easy"* and *"learnability (book conference room): easy"*.

Step 3: Operationalization. In this step, we operationalize FGs as functions, FCs, DAs or their combinations thereof, QGs as QCs, and CTGs as SCs. Our understanding of manifesting events of functions as polygenic enables us to systematically operationalize FGs. Take the example of *"the system shall notify realtors in a timely manner"*. What kind of effect is required to satisfy the FG? Is it the case that the goal is satisfied by merely a message being sent by the system? Or, alternatively, does the FG also require the message to be properly received by realtors? In the former case, we only need to design a *"send notification"* function and simply assume certain capacities on receiving (adding one or more DAs). However, in the latter case, we should design both the sending and receiving functions such that the joint manifestations of these functions have the desired quality (i.e., *"timely"*). When operationalizing QGs, vague by nature, to measurable QCs, we suggest using *"prototype values"* [16] to help define quality regions. For example, to operationalize the QG *"the learning time of meeting scheduler shall be short"*, we first ask stakeholders *"how long is short?"* Their answers provide prototype values. We can then employ mathematical techniques such as probability distribution or Collated Voronoi diagram, using the obtained prototype values to derive corresponding regions [16]. When operationalizing CTGs, properties of real-world entities being characterized will be mapped to corresponding machine states, often data base schemas. For example, the CTG "*Student :< <hasId: String> <hasName: String><hasGPA: Float>*" will be operationalized as a SC "*Student Record: <Id: varchar> <name: varchar> <GPA: float>*".

Step 4: *Contribution.* As discussed, we use contribution links to capture the relations between functional elements and QGs. Note that a functional element may help (make) some QGs but can also hurt (break) others, capturing trade-offs between requirements. For example, "*encrypt data*" can help a security QG while hurting a performance QG. In this case, we can further prioritize QGs through eliciting priorities from stakeholders [13]. Sometimes stakeholder requirements contain low-level concerns such as "*the system shall be developed using the J2EE runtime library*". In this case, it is necessary to consider refinements from a bottom-up perspective: often we ask "*why*" to elicit the implicit higher-level requirement, e.g., good interoperability with respect to different kinds of operation systems in this example.

7   Evaluation

We present results of our evaluation using the PROMISE (PRedictOr Models in Software Engineering) requirements set, which includes 625 requirements collected from 15 software projects [4]. This dataset comes with an original classification of requirements kinds: 255 items are marked as functional requirements (FRs) and the remaining 370 non-functional requirements items are classified into 11 categories such as security, usability and availability. The counts of original classifications are shown in the second column of Table 1.

The aims of our evaluation are: (1) evaluate the coverage of our requirements ontology by classifying the whole set of requirements; (2) evaluate the expressiveness of our language by formalizing all the 625 requirements using our syntax; (3) illustrate the effectiveness of our methodology by applying it to two case studies from the dataset: *meeting scheduler* and *nursing scheduler*. Due to space limitations, we present only statistics of our evaluation and the meeting scheduler case study here. The complete information of our classification and formal descriptions of the 625 requirements, the two case studies and our technical report can be found at http://goo.gl/GGceBe.

Evaluating Our Ontology. We went over the full dataset, identified the key concern of each requirement, and classified them by following the classification guidelines proposed in step 1 of the informal phase. We show our classification counts in Table 1, where we use '+' to indicate a combination of concerns within a requirement (e.g., FG+QG means a mix of FG and QG). These classification results extend the results over the 370 NFRs presented in our previous work [18].

From each row of table 1, we can see how the original categorization of requirements is distributed across our ontological classification. For example, from the original 255 FRs, we identified 183 FGs, 6 QGs, 9 FCs, 21 CTGs, 1 FG/FC+QG,

Table 1. The ontological classification of the 625 PROMISE Requirements

Requirements Category	Original	FG	QG	FC	CTG	FG/FC +QG	FG+FC	FG+ CTG	DA
Functional	255	183	6	9	21	1+0	6	29	0
Usability	67	7	46	2	0	11+1	0	0	0
Security	66	11	2	39	0	9+2	3	0	0
Operational	62	14	10	13	0	10+2	6	0	7
Performance	54	3	43	1	0	4+1	1	0	0
Look and Feel	38	9	20	0	1	6+2	0	0	0
Availability	21	0	20	1	0	0	0	0	0
Scalability	21	1	19	0	0	0	1	0	0
Maintainability	17	1	10	3	0	2+1	0	0	0
Legal	13	1	11	1	0	0	0	0	0
Fault tolerance	10	4	4	0	0	2	0	0	0
Portability	1	0	0	0	0	0	0	0	1
Total	625	234	191	69	22	46+9	17	29	8

6 FG+FC, and 29 FG+CTG. Here 51 out of the 255 (20.0%) of the FRs concern content. We found that most of the security related NFRs are often FG/FC related (the third row): 97% of them are identified as FGs, FCs, or combination with other concerns (11 FGs, 39 FCs, 11 FG/FC+QG, and 3 FG+FC). For example, for *"only managers are able to deactivate user accounts"* (originally classified as a security NFR, but in fact is an FC), the system needs to check whether the actor is a manager or not when the deactivation function is accessed. One can also see that many requirements (101/625, 16.2%) are a mix of concerns (with '+' in their labels).

Our evaluation shows that FCs, CTGs, and the mix of concerns such as FG+FC, FG +QG, and FG+CTG are not trivial and need more attention in practice. The results also provide evidence that our requirements ontology is adequate for covering requirements in practice.

Evaluating Our Language. After classification, we rewrote the set of all 625 requirements using our language to evaluate its expressiveness. In this step, we separated the concerns of a requirement if it was composite, and encoded it by following the guidelines presented in the formalization phase. Our syntax was able to capture all 625 requirements, resulting in 1276 statements (nearly double the amount of original requirements), including 419 FGs/Fs, 313 FCs, 375 QGs, 90 CTGs and 79 DAs. Note that there are 7 instance-level constraints (7/625, 1.12%) identified in our evaluation. We are able to express these constraints by using the *"same_as"* DL constructor [21]; however, the use of *"same_as"* imposes severe limitations on reasoning.

The count of each type of statement in our language does not strictly correspond to the classification counts in Table 1. For example, we have 22 CTG and 29 FG+CTG in Table 1, but ultimately 90 rather than 51 CTGs. This is because the original dataset includes many composite and nested requirements, e.g., sibling functions, nested qualities and content, and we broke these up into separate requirements when encoding them. In addition, we treat domain knowledge as domain assumption(s). For instance, *"Open source examples include Apache web server Tomcat"* was captured as "DA := *Tomcat :< web server ∧ open source"*.

Our language and guidelines facilitate the identification of ambiguity. During the formalization process, we identified 24 ambiguous requirements (3.84%), and eliminated the ambiguity by choosing the most likely interpretation. For example, *"notify users with email"* will be encoded as *"notify <object: user> <means: email>"*. Note that although we could have found some ambiguities by reading natural language requirements text, using a more ad-hoc, less systematic approach, such an approach would likely cause us to miss many ambiguities; as such naïve approaches do not force the user to carefully analyze and classify the text. Furthermore, once ambiguities are found, an ad-hoc approach would not tell us what to do when an ambiguous requirement is found. Our approach provides a systematic way for not only identifying but also dealing with ambiguities in requirements.

Our guidelines also contribute to making requirements accurate and concise. E.g., for a rather informal statement *"the product shall make the users want to use it"*, we can identify its focus by asking the question *"what does it concern?"*, and restate it as a QG *"attractiveness ({the product}): good"*, which can be further refined, .e.g., *"number of users ({the product} <period: one week after its launch>) : ≥ 1000"*.

Evaluating our Methodology. We performed two case studies on the meeting scheduler (MS) and nursing scheduler (NS) project, adopted from the PROMISE data set. Here we present the MS case study.

The Meeting Scheduler (MS) project has 74 requirements, including 27 FRs and 47 NFRs. A meeting scheduler is required to create meetings, send invitations, book conference rooms, book room equipment, etc. We classified the 74 requirements according to our ontology, separated the concerns of requirements when needed, encoded them by using our syntax. Next, we refined quality goals using the set of provided operators, including relax, focus, and operationalization, to make them practically satisfiable and measurable. Finally, we obtained a specification, which consists of 67 functions, 67 QCs, 8 FCs, 3SCs, and 10 DAs (155 in total).

We kept the requirements (goals, FGs, QGs and CTGs), specifications (functions, QCs, FCs, SCs and DAs), and the derivation process (refinement, operationalization, contribution, etc.) in a textual goal model, and then translated the whole model to OWL. To support this process, we developed a translation tool based on the OWL API, and used it to systematically and automatically translate the resulting requirements specification into an OWL-ontology.

The major benefit of translating a requirements specification to an OWL-ontology is the convenience of obtaining an overview of concerns, such as quality, function, and entity: we are able to ask a list of questions as shown in table 2 (technically, these questions will be translated into DL queries) [3]. For instance, we can ask *"<inheresIn: {the product}>"* (an instantiation of Q2) to retrieve the set of qualities that inhere in *"the product"*. Note that these questions are not exhaustive. If desired, we can ask more complex questions like *"what functions are required to finish within 5 sec.?"* in the form of *"<hasQuality: ProcessingTime <hasValueIn: within 5 sec.>>"*.

---

[3] Note that we are not using the full expressive and reasoning power of OWL. We are currently investigating translation to other logics and extending our language to allow more interesting forms of reasoning.

Table 2. Example useful queries over the requirements specification

ID	Concerned Questions	Syntax
Q1	What kinds of subjects does a quality refer to?	*<hasQuality: QualityName>*
Q2	What qualities are of concern for a subject?	*<inheresIn: SubjT>*
Q3	Who performs the function?	*<isActorOf: FG>*
Q4	What is the function operating on?	*<isObjectOf: FG>*
Q5	What functions do a subject is involved in?	*<object: SubjT>*

Threats to Validity. In our evaluation, the ontological classification of requirements and the encoding of natural language requirements as formal descriptions are performed by experienced modelers (the authors). In the future work, we intend to have others use our requirements ontology and modeling language to confirm their adequacy in capturing requirements. Also, although we have evaluated our requirements ontology and language on only one requirements dataset, the threat to our evaluation is low: (1) the size of the dataset we used is large (including 625 items); (2) the data set is collected by a third-party for software engineering research, hence not biased by ourselves. As for the case study, the meeting scheduler example we used (i) is one of the requirements exemplars for evaluating different kinds of research approaches [22] (ii) is able to demonstrate the different kinds of concepts and operators proposed in our approach (e.g., many of its NFRs need the relaxation and focus refinement; it does include ambiguous requirements that need to be disambiguated). We are also planning to evaluate our framework on industrial examples.

8   Discussion and Conclusions

We propose a framework for transforming informal requirements to formal requirements specifications. Our proposal includes three key contributions to the state-of-the-art: (i) a novel requirements ontology, (ii) a description-based requirements modeling language, and (iii) a methodology (including a set of refinement operators) for transformation purposes.

Our proposal also addresses several important challenges associated with NFRs [23]: (1) NFRs are often vaguely stated and hard to measure; (2) it is hard to specify crosscutting concerns for NFRs; (3) it is difficult to get an overview of NFRs that are associated with a FR; (4) it is not obvious where to document NFRs, etc. Our methodology addresses the first issue. Our treatment of NFRs captures the inherence (existential dependency) between NFRs and FRs, together with our language and tool support, we can easily know what subjects does an NFR refer to and what qualities are of concern with regarding to a subject, thus addressing the second and third issue. In fact, capturing the inherence relation also contributes to resolving the fourth issue: we can define a FR as a subject and relate concerned NFRs with it through the inherence link, turning the whole requirements to a structurally connected graph. In this way, NFRs and FRs are not separated anymore, as they are in the IEEE 830-1998 standard.

Note that our language is designed for requirements engineers rather than stakeholders. Users of our language need to have necessary knowledge and/or need to be trained. Moreover, our approach has limitations on handling temporal constraints. We currently represent temporal constraints with attributes such as *"before"*, *"after"*, and *"concurrent"*. However, the reasoning part of such representations is severely limited. Finally, our language is unable to capture algebraic constraints such as "given an initial balance a, after a withdrawal of b, the balance shall be $a - b = c$".

Several issues remain open, notably inconsistency handling. The resolution of inconsistency may require one to prioritize, relax (e.g., relax the quality region, adding pre-condition) or even drop requirements. This interesting point will certainly be further explored within our framework. Another important issue is how to effectively manage requirements evolution. Currently, we are capturing interrelations between FRs and QRs. It will be very interesting to see how a requirements knowledge base evolves with changing requirements, a major topic in Software Engineering for the next decade.

Acknowledgment. This research has been partially funded by ERC advanced grant 267856 "Lucretius: Foundations for Software Evolution", unfolding during the period of April 2011 - March 2016. It also supported by the Key Project of National Natural Science Foundation of China (no. 61432020), and the Key Project in the National Science & Technology Pillar Program during the Twelfth Five-year Plan Period (No. 2015BAH14F02).

References

1. Rolland, C., Proix, C.: A natural language approach for requirements engineering. In: Loucopoulos, P. (ed.) CAiSE 1992. LNCS, vol. 593, pp. 257–277. Springer, Heidelberg (1992)
2. Dardenne, A., Van Lamsweerde, A., Fickas, S.: Goal-directed requirements acquisition. Sci. Comput. Program. **20**(1–2), 3–50 (1993)
3. IBM - Rational DOORS. http://www-03.ibm.com/software/products/en/ratidoor
4. Menzies, T., Caglayan, B., He, Z., Kocaguneli, E., Krall, J., Peters, F., Turhan, B.: The PROMISE Repository of empirical software engineering data. http://promisedata.googlecode.com
5. Fraser, M.D., Kumar, K., Vaishnavi, V.K.: Informal and formal requirements specification languages: bridging the gap. IEEE Trans. on Softw. Eng. **17**(5), 454–466 (1991)
6. Giese, M., Heldal, R.: From informal to formal specifications in UML. In: Baar, T., Strohmeier, A., Moreira, A., Mellor, S.J. (eds.) UML 2004. LNCS, vol. 3273, pp. 197–211. Springer, Heidelberg (2004)
7. Seater, R., Jackson, D., Gheyi, R.: Requirement progression in problem frames: deriving specifications from requirements. Requir. Eng. **12**(2), 77–102 (2007)
8. Letier, E., Van Lamsweerde, A.: Deriving operational software specifications from system goals. In: FSE, ACM SIGSOFT Symposium, pp. 119–128 (2002)
9. Aziz, B., Arenas, A., Bicarregui, J., Ponsard, C., Massonet, P.: From goal-oriented requirements to Event-B specifications. In: NFM (2009)
10. Chung, L., Nixon, B.A., Yu, E.: Non-Functional Requirements in Software Engineering, vol. 5. Kluwer Academic Pub. (2000)

11. ISO/IEC, ISO/IEC TR 9126-2 Software engineering - Product quality - Part 2: External metrics, ISO/IEC (2003)
12. Gilb, T.: Competitive engineering: a handbook for systems engineering, requirements engineering, and software engineering using Planguage. Butterworth-Heinemann (2005)
13. Jureta, I., Borgida, A., Ernst, N.A., Mylopoulos, J.: Techne: Towards a new generation of requirements modeling languages with goals, preferences, and inconsistency handling. In: RE, pp. 115–124 (2010)
14. Kaiya, H., Saeki, M.: Using domain ontology as domain knowledge for requirements elicitation. In: RE, pp. 189–198 (2006)
15. Jureta, I.J., Mylopoulos, J., Faulkner, S.: A core ontology for requirements. Appl. Ontol. 4(3), 169–244 (2009)
16. Guizzardi, R., Li, F.-L., Borgida, A., Guizzardi, G., Horkoff, J., Mylopoulos, J.: An ontological interpretation of non-functional requirements. In: FOIS (2014)
17. Guizzardi, G.: Ontological foundations for structural conceptual models. CTIT, Centre for Telematics and Information Technology (2005)
18. Li, F.-L., Horkoff, J., Mylopoulos, J., Guizzardi, R.S., Guizzardi, G., Borgida, A., Liu, L.: Non-functional requirements as qualities, with a spice of ontology. In: RE (2014)
19. ISO/IEC 25010:2011, Systems and software engineering – Systems and software Quality Requirements and Evaluation (SQuaRE) – System and software quality models (2011)
20. McGuinness, D.L., Van Harmelen, F., et al.: OWL web ontology language overview. W3C Recomm. 10(10), 2004 (2004)
21. Cohen, W.W., Hirsh, H.: Learning the classic description logic: theoretical and experimental results. In: KR, vol. 94, pp. 121–133 (1994)
22. Feather, M.S., Fickas, S., Finkelstein, A., Van Lamsweerde, A.: Requirements and specification exemplars. Autom. Softw. Eng. 4(4), 419–438 (1997)
23. Berntsson Svensson, R., Olsson, T., Regnell, B.: An investigation of how quality requirements are specified in industrial practice. Inf. Softw. Technol. 55(7), 1224–1236 (2013)

Towards More Efficient Requirements Formalization: A Study

Wenbin Li[✉], Jane Huffman Hayes, and Mirosław Truszczyński

Department of Computer Science, University of Kentucky,
Lexington, KY 40506-0495, USA
wenbin.li@uky.edu, {hayes,mirek}@cs.uky.edu

Abstract. [**Context and motivation**] Validating natural language requirements is an important but difficult task. Although there are techniques available for validating formalized requirements, the gap between natural language requirements and formalism is huge. [**Question/ problem**] As part of a larger piece of work on temporal requirements consistency checking, we developed a front end to semi-automatically translate natural language requirements into an formal language called Temporal Action Language or *TeAL*. This work is based on an underlying assumption that human analysts can assist us in filling in the missing pieces as we translate natural language temporal requirements to *TeAL*.[**Principal ideas/results**] We performed a study to validate this assumption. We found that using the statements generated by our front-end tool appears to be more effective and efficient than a manual process. [**Contribution**] We present the design of our front-end and a study that measures the performance of human analysts in formalizing requirements with the help of an automated tool.

Keywords: Formal specification · Temporal requirements · Translation · Requirement comprehension

1 Introduction

Temporal requirements specify the temporal properties of the system, such as temporal dependency or timing constraints of different tasks. Such temporal requirements play an important role in the software systems that involve time critical data, instrumentation, and guidance control. A mission-critical financial trading system requires that certain transactions occur within a certain amount of time of other transactions (such as posting the proceeds of a stock sale or logging realized dividend payments). An e-commerce system requires that a payment be received prior to submitting an order for processing. A safety-critical pacemaker system requires that pacing occur within milliseconds of certain detected events.

As these examples suggest, errors in specifying, interpreting, or implementing temporal requirements can lead to disastrous consequences. If one or more requirements related to the pacing of the heart are in conflict, a negative heart

© Springer International Publishing Switzerland 2015
S.A. Fricker and K. Schneider (Eds.): REFSQ 2015, LNCS 9013, pp. 181–197, 2015.
DOI: 10.1007/978-3-319-16101-3_12

event might not trigger a required life-saving pacing event. To address such issues, we undertake consistency checking of temporal requirements. This is a labor intensive and tedious task, however. Indeed, it is possible that a specification of a system contains so many temporal requirements (and related contextual requirements) that it is not possible to check them manually. Hence we look to automation for assistance.

Many powerful formal languages and specification techniques have been offered to support temporal consistency checking [5,12,17]. Nonetheless, the main challenge for the automation of temporal requirement consistency checking is that they are typically represented as natural language text. There are several reasons for the use of text. Text is highly expressive, there is little to no learning required to use it and, when carefully used, natural text is precise and unambiguous. Yet, fully automated processing of textual requirements remains a distant goal. To take advantage of the power of formal methods in analyzing requirements specified in text, we need ways to translate the natural language requirements into some formal language. However, every attempt to do so runs into the question of whether the formal representation correctly captures the intended meaning of the natural language requirements.

To address this long-standing criticism of formal methods, we have developed an intermediate language to bridge the syntactically significant gap between low-level formalisms and natural language temporal requirements: the Temporal Action Language (*TeAL*) [20]. We developed fully automated methods to translate *TeAL* to low-level logic formalisms such as answer-set programming (*ASP*) [22,24] programs and linear temporal logic (*LTL*) [13] theories (the translation is the subject of another publication [19]). That reduces the overall problem of consistency checking to that of producing correct *TeAL* theories from the natural language representations of temporal (and contextual) requirements, and brings up a key question: how can *TeAL* theories be created more efficiently?

We introduce a semi-automated method that translates natural language to *TeAL*. The natural language requirements are taken from real datasets such as CM1 [1], a set of requirement documents produced by NASA. Sample requirements taken from CM1 follow:

- R1: If the value is not received, then a NAK message will be transmitted to the ICU within a second.
- R2: The DPU-SCUI shall be capable of deliverying one STPDU to the SCU every M milliseconds.
- R3: The DPU-CCM shall process real-time non-deferred commands within B ms of receipt from the ICU or the SCU.

The efficiency of this method rests on the assumption that humans can assist us during the translation. We performed a study to validate this assumption. We found that our tool is more effective and efficient at the translation task than a manual process. We posit the following research questions:

- RQ1: Does the front-end produce outputs that improve the effectiveness of generating correct *TeAL* statements?
- RQ2: Does the front-end produce outputs that improve the efficiency of generating correct *TeAL* statements?

RQ1 and RQ2 are important as they directly evaluate the quality of the method we developed and implemented for generating *AlmostTeAL* statements in an automated way. For RQ1, we measure how many *TeAL* statements written by the participants are correct (*Precision*), how many correct *TeAL* statements are written (*Recall*), and how many edits are required to change the statements generated by participants to correct *TeAL* statements (*Temporal Error Rate*). We also measure the participants' subjective opinion about the difficulty of the task. For RQ2 we measure the time spent on the task. The null hypothesis for RQ1 and RQ2 is that there is no difference in these measures with or without the statements generated by the front-end.

This paper represents the first study to evaluate human ability to assist with semi-automated translation to a formal language. Measures used in other fields such as foreign language translation have been applied in the study in order to gauge human ability to assist with *TeAL* translation. The paper is organized as follows. Section 2 briefly describes the formal representations studied. Section 3 discusses the related work. Section 4 presents our approach to natural language temporal requirement translation. Sections 5 and 6 discuss validation and results, respectively. Sections 7 and 8 analyze the results and the feedback we collected from participants. Section 9 provides conclusions and a look at future work.

2   Formal Representation of Temporal Requirements

Earlier, we introduced Temporal Action Language (*TeAL*) as a formal language for supporting software requirement analysis [20]. The *TeAL* language is an extension of Action Language *AL* [4], a language designed for modeling actions and their effects and for reasoning about ways in which a system can evolve. The *TeAL* language retains all the features of *AL* and can also be used to specify temporal constraints. Because *TeAL* is used to bridge the gap between natural language requirements and low-level logic formalism, we designed its syntax to be as close to natural language as possible to minimize analysts' time and effort. We briefly describe the syntax below (see [20] for a full description).

The basic components of *TeAL* are actions, fluents, and temporal conditions. Actions change the state of the system. They are performed by agents. For example, the *TeAL* expression *connect(serA,nodeA)* represents an action to establish a connection to *nodeA*; *serA* is the agent that performs this action. Fluents represent atomic (boolean) properties of the system. Complete and consistent sets of (possibly negated) fluents describe the state of the system. For example, the fluent *connected(serA,nodeA)* represents that the server *serA* is connected to the node *nodeA*. Temporal conditions specify temporal relationships on times when events occur. Such events include the start and end of actions as well as the changes of system properties (fluents). In *TeAL*, we use two prompts: **commence** *Act* and **terminate** *Act*, to represent the time when action *Act* starts and successfully finishes. In *TeAL* one can also relate two consecutive occurrences of the same action to each other. To distinguish between them, *TeAL* provides the keywords **previous** and **next**, as in: **commence previous** *Act* and **terminate next** *Act*. A fluent appearing in temporal conditions represents the time when this fluent becomes true. Similarly, the negation of a fluent in temporal conditions represents the time when this fluent becomes false. Additionally, we view the start of the system as a special event; **startTime** represents when it happens.

Time moments represented by actions and fluents are connected by temporal relationships. Given two time moments, *t1* and *t2*, the basic relationship between them can be: "*t1 before/after t2*," or "*t1 and t2 are at the same time*." Additionally, requirements may specify more information, such as "*t1 before t2 for some amount of time*." *TeAL* provides eight keyword phrases to represent temporal relationships. Most types of temporal relationships specify both time moments explicitly as, for example, in the expression

$$received(server, message, node) \textbf{ within } 5 \; second \textbf{ after}$$
$$\textbf{terminate } send(node, message, server)$$

which encodes the requirement "*the message is received by the server within 5 seconds after it is sent by the node*." Such elementary relationships between time points are called *temporal conditions*.

The keywords **and, or**, and **not**, as well as the **if** ... **then** ... phrase, can be used together with temporal conditions to represent their boolean combinations, called *temporal constraints*. The specific form of a temporal constraint used in *TeAL* is

$$\textbf{if } A_1 \textbf{ and } \ldots \textbf{ and } A_k, \textbf{ then } B_1 \textbf{ or } \ldots \textbf{ or } B_m; \tag{1}$$

where A_1 **and** ... **and** A_k and B_1 **or** ... **or** B_m are temporal conditions or their negations. An example of a temporal constraint in *TeAL* is an expression:

$$\textbf{if not commence } print(server, message) \textbf{ within } 5 \; second$$
$$\textbf{after } received(server, message, node)$$
$$\textbf{then terminate } send(server, alarm) \textbf{ within next } 2 \; second;$$

It captures the constraint "*if a message is not printed within 5 seconds after it is received, the server shall send an alarm within 2 seconds*."

3 Related Works

Our research is closely related to natural language understanding, a major task in natural language processing (*NLP*) [28]. This task focuses on converting natural language text into formal representations so that programs can handle them. Applications that accept natural language text as input often perform parsing of the text and then represent the parsed text as a logic set. These logic sets can be processed and used to assess the semantics of the text. Natural language processing toolkits such as Stanford parser [7,14] and *OpenNLP* library [3] support most of the common *NLP* tasks, including chunking, parsing, speech tagging, and tokenizing. It should be noted that the Stanford parser also extracts dependencies, which are the grammatical relations between words. This type of information is very useful for our research, the details will be given in the introduction of our proposed approach.

Another *NLP* task that is important to our research is Semantic Role Labeling (*SRL*) [11]. The *SRL* technique detects the semantic arguments of verbs or predicates and the roles of these arguments. For example, given "*a system updates data,*" *SRL* finds the verb *update* with *system* as its agent and *data* as its object. The *SRL* technique proves to be very useful in extracting actions and fluents from natural language. Such information is necessary for building *TeAL* theories.

NLP has been used to validate natural language software requirements. Fliedl et al. [10] introduced an approach for the linguistic analysis of requirements texts. This approach uses semantic tagging and chunk-parsing techniques to identify system information from natural language text. Deeptimahanti and Babar [8] developed a tool for generating UML models from natural language requirements, extracting the necessary information *actors* and their *actions* using *NLP* techniques. Weston et al. [30] proposed a tool framework for automatically processing natural language requirements into a formalized model. This tool framework uses grammatical patterns to identify the parts of a program that affect other parts of the system in natural language documents. In the approach introduced in this paper, we also use natural language processing tools to identify information such as *agent, precondition*, and phrases with specific patterns (e.g., *within* followed by a time period). The details will be discussed below.

We address only a subset of the research on assisting analysts to specify temporal properties due to space constraints. Dwyer et al. [9] found that most properties related to time can be classified into a set of patterns. Smith et al. [26] developed a tool *Propel* for assisting analysts to precisely capture temporal properties based on these patterns. *Propel* offers restricted natural language templates to help analysts specify the properties. Konrad and Cheng [15] introduced another tool *SPIDER* for instantiating system properties. The key component of *SPIDER* is a set of patterns for real-time properties and a structured natural language grammar that supports these properties [16]. *SPIDER* assists analysts in deriving the natural language properties using the correct phrases based on the grammar. Mondragon and Gates developed *Prospec* [23] for specifying properties that can be classified in Dwyer et al.'s patterns. *Prospec* supports composite patterns, but analysts cannot specify the properties in natural language. In the approach introduced in this paper, we collected a set of phrases that are closely related to temporal information and try to identify them from natural language requirements automatically. The construction of *AlmostTeAL* statements using such information is also automated so that analysts' task is reduced to validating the *AlmostTeAL* statements.

4   Translation from Natural Language Requirements

We aim to create a semi-automated approach for checking temporal consistency of requirements given in natural language. Our idea is to translate the requirements into a theory in a low-level formal system, which can be analyzed automatically. As mentioned earlier, the *"distance"* between natural language and low-level formal methods is substantial. We propose to use an intermediate language, *TeAL*, to bridge the gap. Thus, to translate text requirements into a low-level formal system we needs to translate from text to *TeAL*. We present and study one such method in this paper.

The method decomposes the task into four steps, presented below (Figure 1):

- Step 1: extract relevant requirements
- Step 2: identify system information
- Step 3: generate *AlmostTeAL* statements
- Step 4: build a *TeAL* theory that models the system

The first three steps are fully automated and generate a collection of *AlmostTeAL* statements. The last step requires the involvement of an analyst whose task is to convert *AlmostTeAL* statements to *TeAL* statements that correctly represent input requirements. Once a correct *TeAL* theory is generated, the result of process can be fully automated. The theory is translated into *ASP* using our translator [19]. The *ASP* program is then processed using existing tools, and the results illustrate if the requirements are consistent or not.

Step 1 (extract relevant requirements): Temporal requirements, such as *"R1: If the value is not received, then a NAK message will be transmitted to the ICU within a second.,"* must be identified and extracted from the collection of requirements. Most temporal requirements contain keywords such as *before* and *within*, or patterns such as *"do action every x seconds."* It is viable to detect many, if not all, of the temporal requirements based on these keywords and patterns. The technique described by Nikora [25] and *NLP* techniques [6] can be used to address this task and have been incorporated into our front-end translator. The limitation of this method is that temporal requirements with typos or grammatical errors (e.g., *wthin*) cannot be identified.

Given a set of temporal requirements, we also need to identify non-temporal requirements that are related to them and that might contain relevant system information. The same techniques as listed above can be used here because typically these non-temporal requirements share terms such as entity names with the temporal requirements (not temporal ones that are already found). We employ these techniques in our tool. By the end of this step, the tool has identified all requirements that are necessary for modeling the system.

Step 2 (identify system information): Given a list of requirements found in Step 1, several types of system elements must be identified: vocabulary and constraints.

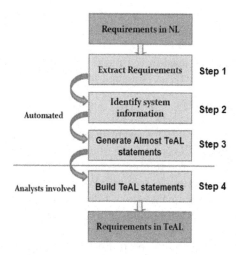

Fig. 1. Steps for Generating TeAL Statements

The vocabulary consists of the names of objects of the system and their properties. It also includes names of fluents and actions. Our front-end tool uses the semantic role labeling (*SRL*) technique and Stanford Parser to assist in extracting the vocabulary. As mentioned earlier, *SRL* finds actions and represents them as predicates such as: *transmit(NAK message,ICU)*. Some fluents, such as *received(Receiver,Msg,Sender)*, can also be found in this way. However, *SRL* cannot detect any fluent from the text "*system is in safe mode,*" while there is a fluent *in(system,safeMode)*. Therefore, our tool uses Stanford Parser to extract fluents such as this one. The parser generates a set of typed dependencies for given texts. Each typed dependency represents a relationship between two words. In this case, the useful dependencies are: *nsubj*(*is, system*) and *prep_in*(*is, mode*). These two dependencies illustrate that the system is "*in a mode,*" and this should be modeled as a fluent. Our tool also uses these typed dependencies to decide the types of the semantic arguments. For example, with the typed dependency *prep_from*(*receiver, sender*), our tool decides that the *received* action has an argument whose type is *receive_from*. Typed dependencies are useful because requirements often lack information on all of the arguments. For example, given the phrase "*if the value is not received,*" *SRL* will consider that the action *receive* only has one argument: the value. But if there is another requirement with the typed dependency *prep_from*(*receiver, sender*), the tool can infer that the *receive* action has another argument, and the generated action will be:

$$receive(\_, value, \_)$$

When the tool generates a translation such as this, analysts are alerted that something is missing.

Constraints can be temporal or non-temporal. Temporal constraints often contain patterns for specifying temporal relationships among events. For example, *"do action within x seconds after"* and *"do action every x seconds"* are patterns that are commonly used in temporal requirements. These patterns can be represented by Tregex Patterns [18] such as

$$(PP < ((IN < within)..(CD\$ + NNS)))$$

for the within pattern, where *PP* is prepositional phrase, *IN* is preposition or subordinating conjunction, *CD* is cardinal number, and *NNS* is plural noun. We use these patterns to extract the temporal constraints like *"a NAK message will be transmitted to the ICU within a second."* We collected a list of such patterns by reviewing requirement documents from different areas (the full list of patterns can be found at http://progit.netlab.uky.edu/frontend).

Additionally, we need to identify the relationships among actions, fluents, and temporal events. For example, we need to find out if a fluent is the precondition or the effect of an action, if two temporal relationships are disjunctive with each other, or whether a temporal relationship is a precondition or not. Our tool uses patterns and typed dependencies mentioned above for this task. The useful dependencies are *neg*, *conj_or*, and *conj_and*, which correspond to negation, disjunction, and conjunction. The patterns

$$(SBAR < ((IN < if)\$ + S))$$

and

$$(SBAR < ((WHADVP < (WRB < when))\$ + S))$$

are used for matching texts of the form *"if something"* or *"when something."* The temporal relationships and fluents that are included in these texts will be marked as preconditions. Given the sample requirement above: *"If the value is not received, then a NAK message will be transmitted to the ICU within a second."* our tool finds the following information: *receive(value)* and *transmit(NAK message,ICU)* are actions, and

$$transmit(NAK\ message, ICU)\ within\ a\ second$$

is a temporal relationship. In addition, the tool establishes that *receive(value)* is to be included in the precondition. Because there is negation in the precondition, the precondition becomes *not receive(value)*. Besides, if there are other requirements that contain the information of *"receive from somewhere,"* the tool will update the action to:

$$receive(\_, value, \_)$$

It should be noted that many non-temporal constraints are treated as *"common sense"* or tacit knowledge, and they will not appear in the requirements. For example, no requirement will specify that *"a message cannot be received if it has not been sent."* However, such common sense knowledge is necessary for modeling a system. One possible way to further automate the identification of such unspecified information is by using some kind of *"common sense library."* A possible choice is *ConceptNet* [21], a commonsense knowledge base that focuses on physical, temporal, and social aspects. It is also possible to use libraries that are domain specific, such libraries should cover the fundamental constraints in the domain.

Step 3 (generate *AlmostTeAL* statements): Our front-end tool builds *AlmostTeAL* statements based on the information generated in Step 2. For instance, for each action, the tool analyzes the information extracted in Step 2 to find this action's possible effects and preconditions, connect them with the conjunction or disjunction operator, and use them to construct precondition and effect statements. The tool also analyzes related temporal relationships to organize them into the *"if . . . then . . ."* expressions.

As mentioned above, some data may still be missing in the representation and some data may be unspecified. Given the sample output of Step 2, our tool generates:

> **if not** *receive*(_, *value*, _)
>
>   **then** *transmit*(*NAK message*, *ICU*) **within** *a second*;

Step 4 (build a *TeAL* theory that models the system): Analysts need to generate *TeAL* statements based on the outputs of the front-end tool. More specifically, analysts need to perform the following tasks:

- Read the *AlmostTeAL* statement to decide what it means.
- Compare the *AlmostTeAL* statement and its corresponding natural language and generate a correct *TeAL* statement.

Given the sample output of Step 3, analysts need to remove all errors in that *AlmostTeAL* statement and complete it to form a *TeAL* statement:

> **if not** *receive*(*receiver*, *value*, *sender*)
>
>   **then** *transmit*(*NAK message*, *ICU*) **within** 1 *second*;

In this case the analysts need to specify whether the constraint concerns the time when actions are commenced or when they are terminated. Also, analysts need to add the arguments for the receive action: the entities that receives and sends the value (here denoted by *receiver* and *sender*). However, the *AlmostTeAL* statement is very close to the *TeAL* statement we want to generate. And it is also close to natural language text, so the analyst's task is manageable and ultimately may even be further automated.

5   Empirical Evaluation

This section addresses validation of the usefulness of *TeAL* and of the *AlmostTeAL* tool. As mentioned earlier, our semi-automated method requires analysts' involvement before correct *TeAL* theories are generated. This involvement takes place in

Step 4, as Steps 1 - 3 are fully automated in our front-end tool that generates *AlmostTeAL* statements. Once *AlmostTeAL* output is available, analysts must add missing elements and remove inaccuracies in these statements so that a correct *TeAL* theory can be passed to the fully automated step of translating into a low-level formal system. The effectiveness and efficiency of this step greatly affects the effectiveness and efficiency of the entire method and is the focus of this paper.

Dependent and Independent Variables. This study uses one independent variable: *Method* (abbreviated as *M*)). There are two levels of this variable: *TeAL*, and *TeAL* with the assistance of *AlmostTeAL*.

Th research question RQ1 addresses the effectiveness of generating *TeAL* statements. The dependent variables that address RQ1 are: Precision (**Prec1**), Recall (**Rec1**), and F-measure (**F1**) of predicates and temporal relationships (*send, received, within next 10 second*); Precision (**Prec2**), Recall (**Rec2**), F-measure (**F2**) of arguments (e.g., *node, message, server* as arguments of *send* and *received*), Translation Error Rate (**TER**)[27], and Translation Difficulty Score (**TDS**).

The basic structure of *TeAL* statements is represented by predicates (*Pred*) and temporal relationships (*Temp*). Identifying predicates and temporal relationships is the key component of our front-end tool because the basic structure of *TeAL* statements is represented by these two types of information. For instance, *received within 10 seconds after send* is intuitive, though it needs more detail to be a correct *TeAL* statement.

The measure **Rec1** is defined as the percentage of correct *Pred/Temp* that are written, while the measure **Prec1** is the percentage of written *Pred/Temp* that are correct.

$$\mathbf{Rec1} \; = \; \frac{\#\; of\; correct\; Pred/Temp\; written}{\#\; of\; correct\; Pred/Temp}$$

$$\mathbf{Prec1} \; = \; \frac{\#\; of\; correct\; Pred/Temp\; written}{\#\; of\; Pred/Temp\; written}$$

The measure **F1** is a harmonic mean of **Prec1** and **Rec1**:

$$\mathbf{F1} \; = \; \frac{2 * \mathbf{Prec1} * \mathbf{Rec1}}{\mathbf{Prec1} + \mathbf{Rec1}}$$

The above formula puts equal importance to both **Prec1** and **Rec1**.

Our tool also identifies arguments. Arguments are necessary for generating correct *TeAL* statements. For instance, the example above needs the arguments of *send* and *received*.

Similar to the measures above, **Prec2** defines the percentage of correct arguments that are written, **Rec2** defines the percentage of written arguments that are correct, and **F2** is a harmonic mean of **Prec2** and **Rec2**.

We also use **TER** to measure how close a generated *TeAL* statement is to the *TeAL* statement that correctly specifies the system. The measure **TER** is an error metric for machine translation that measures the number of edits required to change a system output into a target text:

$$\mathbf{TER} \; = \; \frac{\# \; of \; edits}{average \; \# \; of \; words \; in \; target \; text}$$

where possible edits include the insertion, deletion, substitution of single words, and shifts of word sequences. We convert each *TeAL* statement into a sequence of words so that we can use this measure. For instance, we will convert

> *received*(*node*, *msg*, *server*)
>
> **within** 10 *second* **after terminate** *send*(*server*, *msg*, *node*)

into: *received node msg server within 10 second after terminate send server msg node* and then compare this sequence of words to the answer set to determine how many insertions, deletions, can changes are required.

The measure **TDS** is a rating on a scale from 1 to 5 indicating the participants' subjective opinion about the difficulty of translating from natural language to *TeAL* with/without *AlmostTeAL*. The dependent variable that address RQ2 is the average time (**T**) spent on each question. The measure **T**, or **Time**, evaluates the efficiency of the method.

Hypothesis. The null hypothesis for RQ1(H_{0RQ1}) is that there is no difference in the **Prec1**, **Rec1**, **F1**, **Prec2**, **Rec2**, **F2**, **TER**, and **TDS** between **TeAL** and **ATeAL**. The alternative hypothesis (H_{1RQ1}) is that there is a difference between the two methods.

Similarly, the null hypothesis for RQ2 (H_{0RQ2}) is that there is no difference in the measure **T** of **TeAL** and **ATeAL**. The alternative hypothesis (H_{1RQ2}) is that there is a difference.

Study Design. We conducted a study that evaluated effectiveness and efficiency with and without *AlmostTeAL*. The study involved thirty four participants, all students in computer science courses at the University of Kentucky. A pre-study questionnaire was given to all the consenting (per IRB regulations) participants in order to gauge prior experience and comfort with requirement analysis and formal languages. Additionally, each participant received a ten minute introduction about the background of the experiment. Participants were also given a fourteen minute training video and a training document. The training video introduced the syntax and semantics of *TeAL*. It focused on the representation of actions, fluents, and temporal relationships. The video includes *AlmostTeAL* as well. The training document covered everything in the video. The participants were required to watch the video or read the document before the main study task.

After the introduction, the main study assignment was administered. Each participant received a user ID. Each participant received a set of eight questions during the main study task:

– Given a natural language requirement (with/without *AlmostTeAL*), write down its corresponding *TeAL* statement.

We broke the participants into two groups based on their experience in requirements and formal languages. We randomly divided the participants of each experience level into two groups of the same size. One group wrote *TeAL* statements with the help of *AlmostTeAL*, another group did not have *AlmostTeAL* statements.

Participants were asked to complete the tasks in the classroom. They were also asked to record the time they spent on each question. After completing the main study task, participants were asked to submit a hardcopy of the results and complete a post-study questionnaire that asked for their reaction to requirement analysis and formal languages. The study used examples from two datasets: 511 Regional Real-Time Transit Information System Requirements (511phone) [2] and CM1 [1]. The 511phone dataset presents the system requirements for the Bay Area 511 Regional Real-Time Transit Information System (available open source). The requirements are primarily focused on the performance of the 511 System and data transfers with the transit agencies. The CM1 dataset is a requirement document produced by NASA for one of its science instruments. The document was released by NASA for use by the software engineering research community. The full requirement package is available upon request.

Threats to Validity. Our study was subject to a number of threats to validity, mitigated to the best of our ability. A threat to internal validity is the limited amount of time given to the participants to learn *TeAL*. The fourteen minute video and a document may not be enough for students to acquire the notation of *TeAL*. We were constrained by the amount of time available in the class period. To address this, we separated the training session and the experiment into separate sessions (separate consecutive class periods). This allowed the participants more time to understand *TeAL* and *AlmostTeAL* by using the training video and document. Another threat to internal validity is that we created answers for the questions and used them as the golden answer set. Because we designed *TeAL* and have much experience in creating *TeAL* statements from natural language requirements, the quality of the golden answer set can be assured.

Our work with student participants represented a threat to external validity. However, these students all have at least three years of background in computer science and they understand the concepts of software engineering and requirements engineering. Their background allows them to perform small tasks of requirement analysis the same as professionals with no significant differences [29]. Another threat to validity deals with our use of two datasets. Though both 511phone and CM1 datasets are from real projects, the study results may differ for different datasets in different domains. One solution is repeating the experiment with other datasets from other domains. The third threat to external validity is the motivation of the participants. Students were given extra credit to participate. This did not ensure that they answered all questions *"seriously"* or thoughtfully. We noticed that two participants read the training document during the experiment before they answered the questions. It is possible that they had not read it before the experiment. This could affect the correctness of their answers and the time it took for them to answer.

Dependent variable issues that threaten construct validity were reduced by the use of standard measures. We address this validity threat by using different sets of measures: precision, recall, F-measure, **TER**, and **TDS**, to analyze different aspects of "the effectiveness of generating *TeAL*." We use **Prec1/Rec1/F1** to measure the effectiveness of identifying predicates and temporal relationships, **Prec2/Rec2/F2** for the effectiveness of identifying arguments, **TER** for the edits required from generated *TeAL* statements to correct answers, and **TDS** for the subjective point of view from participants. Another threat to construct validity is that participants may have guessed the research hypothesis, that is, they may have assumed that *AlmostTeAL* was the focus of the research with an aim to improve effectiveness and efficiency before they worked on the main study assignment. We addressed this validity threat by not telling them that *TeAL* and *AlmostTeAL* are our research areas.

6   Results

Table 1 presents the results of the study whether using **ATeAL** is more effective than generating **TeAL** expressions directly (RQ1) and whether using **ATeAL** is more efficient than using **TeAL** directly (RQ2).

Table 1. Mean values of **Prec1**, **Rec1**, **F1**, **Prec2**, **Rec2**, **F2**, **TER**, **TDS** and **T**

	Prec1	Rec1	F1	Prec2	Rec2	F2	TER	TDS	T
TeAL	84.13%	85.63%	84.58%	65.25%	58.31%	60.96%	52.75%	3.38	282 sec
ATeAL	89.39%	89.28%	89.11%	84.89%	83.28%	83.97%	25.11%	4.33	167 sec

Specifically, Table 1 shows the mean values of precision (**Prec1**), recall (**Rec1**), and F-measure (**F1**) for predicates and temporal relationships. When **ATeAL** is used, the results are better in all aspects than when **TeAL** is used alone. However, the results are very close in this part of the study. The values of **Prec1**, **Rec1**, and **F1** also illustrate that participants performed well in capturing the general structure of **TeAL** statements, but the possibility of incorrect or missing predicates/temporal relationships cannot be ignored, no matter what target language is used.

Table 1 also shows the mean values of precision (**Prec2**), recall (**Rec2**), and F-measure (**F2**) for arguments. The **ATeAL** method is better than **TeAL** for 20% in precision and 25% in recall. The results show that it was much more difficult for the participants to generate correct and complete arguments without the help of *AlmostTeAL*.

The results of **TER**, **TDS**, and **T** show that the participants wrote better **TeAL** with the help of *AlmostTeAL* statements: the number of edits required from the generated **TeAL** statements to the correct **TeAL** was halved. The results on **TDS** illustrate that the participants generally felt more comfortable and found it easier to write **TeAL** statements with *AlmostTeAL* statements presented. Finally, participants reduced time spent by 40% with the help of *AlmostTeAL* statements.

7 Discussion

Based on the results above, it is clear that the *AlmostTeAL* statements generated by our front-end tool improve the process of generating *TeAL* statements in both effectiveness and efficiency.

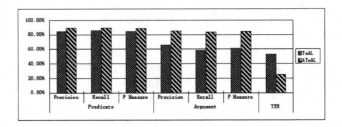

Fig. 2. Results of Objective Measures

Figure 2 compares between **TeAL** and **ATeAL** with regard to the objective measures concerning effectiveness: **Prec1,Rec1,F1,Prec2,Rec2,F2**, and **TER**.

Though there were practical differences in the **Prec1** and **Rec1** of our study, the differences were not statistically significant. The high **Rec1** and **Prec1** values (84%-89%) show that one possibility is that these elements can be identified without the help of *AlmostTeAL*. Yet the performance of **ATeAL** is still slightly better than **TeAL**.

The results of **Prec2** and **Rec2** show that participants had a hard time in identifying arguments without *AlmostTeAL*: they missed about 40% of arguments, while 35% of the arguments they identified were incorrect. The *AlmostTeAL* statements greatly improved both precision and recall to 83%-84%. The differences in the **Prec2** and **Rec2** measures are extremely significant. It appears that *AlmostTeAL* finds more correct arguments than the participants. Additionally, the missing pieces in *AlmostTeAL* can remind participants what information to look for when they read natural language requirements. Participants also reduced time spent by 40% and halved their error rate with the help of *AlmostTeAL* statements. The differences in the **TER** and **T** measures are also extremely significant. The decrease of **TER**, together with the increase of **Prec2** and **Rec2**, proves the effectiveness of **ATeAL**.

Additionally, the feedback from participants proves that they prefer **ATeAL** to **TeAL**. On the one hand, 56% of the participants thought it was difficult to write *TeAL* statements without any hints (**TDS** $\leq$ 3); on the other hand, 83% of the participants felt the presence of *AlmostTeAL* provides useful information (**TDS** $\geq$ 4).

Returning to the questions of interest, based on the study we found that:

– RQ1: Appears to be yes. While the differences in **Prec1** and **Rec1** are not significant, the differences in other measures are all extremely significant.

The *AlmostTeAL* statements generated by the automated method help analysts to produce *TeAL* with fewer errors. Analysts also prefer the **ATeAL** method. It is not clear if we have sufficient evidence to reject the null hypothesis.

- RQ2: Yes. The *AlmostTeAL* statements generated by the automated method reduces the time needed for this process. We can reject the null hypothesis in favor of the alternative (H_{1RQ2}).

8   Feedback

We get several comments from the post-study questionnaire about *TeAL*. There are positive comments such as: *"The syntax and order of arguments felt natural"* and *"TeAL provides a consistent and precise structure for interpreting requirements and relationships.* There are also comments that point out problems, such as: *"It was a little unclear how much was always required to be strict about things," "it was hard to be certain about if I was successfully stating things in perfect TeAL,"* and *"Sometimes I wasn't sure what words to use."* These comments remind us to further improve the effectiveness of step 2 and step 3, as better *AlmostTeAL* statements will solve/partially solve these problems. Additionally, we are considering providing other information together with *AlmostTeAL*, such as reminding analysts that certain parts of the *AlmostTeAL* statements are incomplete, or presenting a list of possible values for arguments.

9   Conclusion and Future Work

This work tackles a fundamental problem of requirements engineering. Requirements are most often given as natural language text and so are prone to ambiguities, incompleteness, and inconsistencies. To manually analyze requirements for correctness is hard and error-prone itself. The solution is in automation of the process. However, the distance between a natural language and a low-level formal one for which automated reasoning tools are available is large. We proposed to bridge the gap by means of an intermediate-level formal language *TeAL*. We use our translator tool to generates expressions in *"AlmostTeAL"* that are close to the correct ones in *TeAL* so that we can significantly ease the analyst task to produce final correct *TeAL* results. The effectiveness of the proposed approach largely depends on the help that *AlmostTeAL* can provide. We performed an experiment to study this problem and provided evidence that suggests that using the *AlmostTeAL* generated by our front-end improved efficiency of analysts and helps with accuracy.

We leaves several interesting questions for the future. First, we plan to enhance our translator tool by developing modules of common (tacit) knowledge that we expect will improve the accuracy of the translation process in Steps 1-3. Second, we are looking for methods to demonstrate possible incompleteness and ambiguity in *AlmostTeAL*. Third, our experience with the front-end translator to *AlmostTeAL* demonstrates it can be enhanced to provide analysts with feedback on obvious problems with the requirements (some entities never defined, missing terms, etc.). Thus, the quality of the input requirements can be improved even before they are translated into low-level formalism for consistency analysis. We plan to explore this direction in depth. Finally, because in this empirical study we only had very limited time for training, and the participants were non-experts, we plan a second study with professionals with adequate training.

Acknowledgment. This work is funded in part by the National Science Foundation grant CCF-0811140. This work was previously sponsored by NASA grant NNG05GQ58G. We thank the anonymous participants. We thank Mark Hays for statistics assistance.

References

1. CM-1 Dataset PROMISE Website. http://promisedata.org/promised/trunk/pro-mised/trunk/promisedata.org/data/cm1-maintain/cm1-maintain.txt, (accessed: April 18, 2013)
2. Regional real-time transit information system system requirements version 3.0 (2012). http://www.mtc.ca.gov/planning/tcip/Real-Time_TransitSystemRequire-ments_v3.0.pdf, (accessed: April 18, 2013)
3. Baldridge, J.: The opennlp project. http://opennlp.apache.org/index.html (accessed February 2, 2012) (2005)
4. Baral, C., Gelfond, M.: Reasoning agents in dynamic domains. In: Logic-Based Artificial Intelligence, pp. 257–279. Springer (2000)
5. Cimatti, A., Giunchiglia, E., Pistore, M., Roveri, M., Sebastiani, R., Tacchella, A.: Integrating BDD-based and SAT-based symbolic model checking. In: Armando, A. (ed.) FroCos 2002. LNCS (LNAI), vol. 2309, pp. 49–56. Springer, Heidelberg (2002)
6. Cleland-Huang, J., Settimi, R., Zou, X., Solc, P.: The detection and classification of non-functional requirements with application to early aspects. In: 14th IEEE International Conference on Requirements Engineering, pp. 39–48. IEEE (2006)
7. De Marneffe, M.C., MacCartney, B., Manning, C.D., et al.: Generating typed dependency parses from phrase structure parses. Proceedings of LREC **6**, 449–454 (2006)
8. Deeptimahanti, D.K., Babar, M.A.: An automated tool for generating uml models from natural language requirements. In: 24th IEEE/ACM International Conference on Automated Software Engineering, ASE 2009, pp. 680–682. IEEE (2009)
9. Dwyer, M.B., Avrunin, G.S., Corbett, J.C.: Patterns in property specifications for finite-state verification. In: Proceedings of the 1999 International Conference on Software Engineering, pp. 411–420. IEEE (1999)
10. Fliedl, G., Kop, C., Mayr, H.C., Winkler, C., Weber, G., Salbrechter, A.: Semantic tagging and chunk-parsing in dynamic modeling. In: Meziane, F., Métais, E. (eds.) NLDB 2004. LNCS, vol. 3136, pp. 421–426. Springer, Heidelberg (2004)
11. Gildea, D., Jurafsky, D.: Automatic labeling of semantic roles. Computational Linguistics **28**(3), 245–288 (2002)
12. Holzmann, G.J.: The model checker spin. IEEE Transactions on Software Engineering **23**(5), 279–295 (1997)
13. Huth, M., Ryan, M.: Logic in Computer Science: Modelling and reasoning about systems. Cambridge University Press (2004)

14. Klein, D., Manning, C.D.: Accurate unlexicalized parsing. In: Proceedings of the 41st Annual Meeting on Association for Computational Linguistics, vol. 1. pp. 423–430. Association for Computational Linguistics (2003)
15. Konrad, S., Cheng, B.H.: Facilitating the construction of specification pattern-based properties. In: Proceedings of the 13th IEEE International Conference on Requirements Engineering, pp. 329–338. IEEE (2005)
16. Konrad, S., Cheng, B.H.: Real-time specification patterns. In: Proceedings of the 27th International Conference on Software Engineering. pp. 372–381. ACM (2005)
17. Larsen, K.G., Pettersson, P., Yi, W.: Uppaal in a nutshell. International Journal on Software Tools for Technology Transfer (STTT) 1(1), 134–152 (1997)
18. Levy, R., Andrew, G.: Tregex and tsurgeon: Tools for querying and manipulating tree data structures. In: Proceedings of the Fifth International Conference on Language Resources And Evaluation. pp. 2231–2234. Citeseer (2006)
19. Li, W., Brown, D., Hayes, J.H., Truszczynski, M.: Answer-set programming in requirements engineering. In: Salinesi, C., van de Weerd, I. (eds.) REFSQ 2014. LNCS, vol. 8396, pp. 168–183. Springer, Heidelberg (2014)
20. Li, W., Hayes, J.H., Truszczyński, M.: Temporal Action Language (TAL): A controlled language for consistency checking of natural language temporal requirements. In: Goodloe, A.E., Person, S. (eds.) NFM 2012. LNCS, vol. 7226, pp. 162–167. Springer, Heidelberg (2012)
21. Marcus, M.P., Marcinkiewicz, M.A., Santorini, B.: Building a large annotated corpus of english: The penn treebank. Computational Linguistics 19(2), 313–330 (1993)
22. Marek, V.W., Truszczyński, M.: Stable models and an alternative logic programming paradigm. In: The Logic Programming Paradigm, pp. 375–398. Springer (1999)
23. Mondragon, O.A., Gates, A.Q.: Supporting elicitation and specification of software properties through patterns and composite propositions. International Journal of Software Engineering and Knowledge Engineering 14(01), 21–41 (2004)
24. Niemelä, I.: Logic programs with stable model semantics as a constraint programming paradigm. Annals of Mathematics and Artificial Intelligence 25(3–4), 241–273 (1999)
25. Nikora, A.P., Balcom, G.: Automated identification of ltl patterns in natural language requirements. In: 20th International Symposium onSoftware Reliability Engineering, ISSRE 2009, pp. 185–194. IEEE (2009)
26. Smith, R.L., Avrunin, G.S., Clarke, L.A., Osterweil, L.J.: Propel: An approach supporting property elucidation. In: Proceedings of the 24th International Conference on Software Engineering, pp. 11–21. ACM (2002)
27. Snover, M., Dorr, B., Schwartz, R., Micciulla, L., Makhoul, J.: A study of translation edit rate with targeted human annotation. In: Proceedings of Association for Machine Translation in the Americas, pp. 223–231 (2006)
28. Spyns, P.: Natural language processing. Methods of Information in Medicine 35(4), 285–301 (1996)
29. Tichy, W.F., Padberg, F.: Empirical methods in software engineering research. In: 29th International Conference on Software Engineering-Companion, ICSE 2007 Companion, pp. 163–164. IEEE (2007)
30. Weston, N., Chitchyan, R., Rashid, A.: A framework for constructing semantically composable feature models from natural language requirements. In: Proceedings of the 13th International Software Product Line Conference, pp. 211–220. Carnegie Mellon University (2009)

The Emerging Requirement for Digital Addiction Labels

Raian Ali[✉], Nan Jiang, Keith Phalp, Sarah Muir, and John McAlaney

Faculty of Science and Technology, Bournemouth University, Dorset, UK
{rali,njiang,kphalp,swilliams,jmcalaney}@bournemouth.ac.uk

Abstract. [**Context & motivation**] Digital Addiction, e.g. to social networks sites and games, is becoming a public interest issue which has a variety of socio-economic effects. Recent studies have shown correlation between Digital Addiction and certain negative consequences such as depression, reduced creativity and productivity, lack of sleep and disconnection from reality. Other research showed that Digital Addiction has withdrawal symptoms similar to those found in drug, tobacco, and alcohol addiction. [**Question/problem**] While industries like tobacco and alcohol are required by certain laws to have a label to raise awareness of the potential consequences of the use, we still do not have the same for addictive software. [**Principal ideas/results**] In this study, we advocate the need for Digital Addiction labels as an emerging ethical and professional requirement. We investigate the design of such labels from a user's perspective through an empirical study, following a mixed-methods approach, and report on the results. [**Contribution**] Our ultimate goal is to introduce the need for labelling to both researchers and developers and provide a checklist of questions to consider when handling this non-functional requirement.

Keywords: Digital addiction · Ethical and professional requirements · NFR

1 Introduction

Digital Addiction (hereafter DA) is becoming a serious issue which has a variety of consequences such as reduced involvement with their real life communities [1] and lower Grade Point Averages due to its negative impact including procrastination, distraction, and poor time-management [2]. People who feel insecure in real life often try to compensate in the digital world [3]. When that later option fails, it reduces even more their self-confidence and self-esteem [4]. Studies showed that addiction to Facebook has a negative impact on romantic relationships (leading to divorce in some cases) due to disclosure of private information, cyber-stalking and electronic surveillance by one's partner [5].

Young [6] classifies online addiction into five types: Computer (games) addiction, Information overload, Net compulsions, Cyber-sexual addiction, and Cyber-relationship addiction. Social network addiction, which is relatively new, would map to the last category but it may still include elements of the others, e.g. games. Such DA has characteristics similar to those found in "traditional" addiction such as mood modification, salience, tolerance, withdrawal symptoms, conflict, and relapse [7]. This paper will take social networks and games as exemplar addictive software.

© Springer International Publishing Switzerland 2015
S.A. Fricker and K. Schneider (Eds.): REFSQ 2015, LNCS 9013, pp. 198–213, 2015.
DOI: 10.1007/978-3-319-16101-3_13

However, in spite of this increasing recognition of the phenomenon of DA, there is still not enough data to decide whether the medium, in this case software and online space, has the main responsibility for addiction or whether personal characteristics is the genuine source and the medium is just a facilitator or a tool [4,5,7]. That is, the fundamental reason, at least in the beginning, may not be necessarily the subject of addiction, i.e. the software in our case. In all cases, awareness that a medium could facilitate an addictive behaviour should be a moral requirement if not a legal one.

DA is still an under-researched concept especially in the software engineering community. In our previous work [8], we defined DA from a requirements engineering perspective as "the excessive use of certain software-mediated operations to reach certain requirements. This includes the case when the use itself is compulsive or impulsive and also the case when the user cannot switch to other available alternatives to reach the same requirements without a good reason". The impulsive and compulsive use could lead to unconscious and hasty actions, which exacerbate the consequences and necessitate even more a sort of warning and awareness messages.

In this paper we explore the responsibility of the software industry in raising awareness of the potentially addictive nature of their products. Unlike industries like tobacco[1] and alcohol, which are required by law to raise such awareness through labels, software is still not seen subject to such social and ethical requirement. We confirm and enhance our initial argument and discuss thoughts on utilising the perception of users to best design DA labels. We follow a mixed-methods approach starting with a qualitative interview-based phase and following with a quantitative survey-based phase. We draw conclusions that we believe will inform further research on the topic and draw attention to this emerging professional non-functional requirement.

The paper is structured as follows. In Section 2 we describe the study design phases. In section 3, we report on the results of the first phase together with the degree of agreement of the larger samples involved in the quantitative phase. In Section 4, we present a set of research challenges with regard to the engineering of the labelling requirement. We conclude the paper and present future work in Section 6.

2   The Study Design

We study DA labels from a user perspective. Users are the ultimate target of such warning or awareness messages and thus their perspective is premium. Labelling is different from controlling. Labelling is to raise awareness and aid certain perceptions and behaviour change. Thus, it is a sort of recommendation similar to the Nudge approach to behaviour change in the health and social field where the recommender attempts to encourage people to make a better choice but do not actually attempt to control them. An example is to put health warnings on cigarettes but not make smoking illegal [14]. In [9] we conducted a study to understand how users would like recommendation messages to be delivered. The study concluded that besides the basic feature of having a relevant *message in terms of content and presentation,* users

---

[1] http://www.tobaccolabels.ca

require three other features: *control*, *awareness*, and *adaptivity*. These features guided the design of our interview questions and the following survey quantitative phase.

- **Message**. Users would like to see relevant content, i.e. content which addresses their particular needs rather than generic messages. The presentation and the medium used to deliver the content are an integral part of the message.
- **Control**. Users would like to be able to specify when and how a label should be shown and when to leave that decision to software. This includes the content, the presentation, the time and the inference strategy software follows to come up with a suitable label.
- **Awareness**. Users would like to be informed of the reasons why a label is being shown to them and what was collected about them to form it. It is a mixture of privacy and curiosity concerns. In other words, this relates to the meta-data users would like to know about the label and its development process.
- **Adaptivity**. Although users would like a certain degree of control, they would still like software to reason on their behalf and choose the best way to deliver the labels according to their dynamic context.

11 participants, five male and six female, aged between 19 and 35 years old, were recruited for the interview where four were professionals and seven were students studying Computing (four) and Psychology (three). Seven of them were selected after a pre-selection survey as they were all flagged up after the survey that they felt they would like to be assisted by labelling and warning messages to control their usage. For counter balancing, four participants, who did not feel the labelling was an efficient idea, were also invited to be interviewed. These four participants gave us an idea of what could be obstacles to achieving users' acceptance of DA labels. Each interview lasted about 30 minutes and the conversation was audio recorded and transcribed after acquiring the consent from the participants.

To confirm and enhance the results obtained through the content analysis of the interview, we designed a survey of nine questions, each covering some of the findings related to the Content, Presentation, Control, Awareness and Adaptivity of the DA labelling. The survey was disseminated through mailing lists to students at Bournemouth University, BCS-HCI mailing list, the social media and mailing lists of the authors. The survey started with a test question informed by the CAGE questionnaire [15] to detect whether a participant has any sort of addictive usage. 16 participants did not pass the test questions and their survey was terminated. 72 participants completed the survey (35 male, 36 female, and one preferred not to say). The age bands distribution was 18-25 (47%), 26-34 (33%), 35-44 (6%), 45-54 (4%), 55-64 (8%), 65+ (0%), and 2% preferred not to answer. The survey was tested on three participants before being disseminated.

3   Findings

In addition to the four facets of the DA message described in Section 2, we also aimed to get users' general view of the concept. This is due to the novelty of the concept itself, which makes the investigation of its feasibility and potentials important per se before delving into the details of how it should be developed.

3.1   General View

The term Digital Addiction did not raise any concerns to any of the interviewees and survey participants. The interview participants felt that DA is a sort of addiction although it may not have the same physiological consequences as substance addiction. Interviewees emphasized the social and mental well-being as the area in which DA has major effects. However, we are still unsure whether people will still like to be called "addicts" in the labels directed to them. One participant warned that the term may put some people off and may make them react negatively unless an appealing argument is made for their particular usage. 32% of the survey participants thought DA labelling is certainly needed, 50% thought is likely a good idea, 15% thought it is unlikely to be useful and 3% thought it is not going to work. This shows the high potential of investigating the topic.

Interestingly, according to the participants' comments, addiction is not only that related to the excessive usage, compulsively and/or impulsively, it is also about the actions a person would do in a hasty and non-thoughtful style with little resistance to the temptation for that. E.g. in a party a user may take pictures and post without thinking of the consequences. The ease of the process and the speed and the scale of information spread become over-attractive and encourage hasty actions to certain people. In addition to this observation, DA in its intuitive sense of over-spending time on digital media is not necessarily to achieve some sort of entertainment (called infotainment). DA may be caused by the fact that users feel the need to be online all the time to ensure the sanity of their social presence, e.g. no one is annoyed by their posts or felt ignored if they did not respond.

The concept of DA labelling is seen a powerful tool for a number of reasons. The first is that many people are simply unaware of how much they use social networks and games. A warning message would inform them in the first place even without any other content other than the time they spent. The label is also needed when there is a significant risk that the usage interrupts and distracts other activities, e.g. students having a "cyber-break" during a lecture. The label has particular value when users are unaware of potential withdrawal symptoms. E.g. some people feel lost without their connection to their social network or gaming community which could often happen not only because of technical errors but also due to social reasons, such as being banned by a group, or losing online fans, etc. For certain vulnerable groups, e.g. children, the label is not only important for the user but also for their carer. Finally, although it is generally agreed that software, like social networks and games typically aim to attract more users, labelling remains a moral and ethical responsibility which will inspire users trust in the software and increase their loyalty.

In spite of that, certain cases would hinder the feasibility and meaningfulness of such a label. Some of our participants emphasized that it is not purely a decision of the individuals to control their usage when everyone else is using it and they need to react. This means DA label targeting and advising the individuals needs to be aware of that. DA is in part a collective responsibility. One interviewee said that "if everyone posts what is needed only, people would not feel the need to check often and spend much time. It is like offering a person a drink". It is also stated that the label is secondary to the software design itself. It would be seen awkward to have a very tempting design and then show a label warning of the consequences of use. This view argues that it will be more sensible to embed the control of use in the design itself and aid users technically in moderating their excessive use instead of the labels. In an extension to that, DA label should not mean exempting developers from the responsibility of a deliberate inclusion of addictive elements in their software. Finally, a label is seen as ineffective when the original reason for DA is more than a careless usage. Depression and tension could lead to people spending hours and hours on games and social networks. Warning messages would look like a noise in that case. Similarly, introverts in real life could find compensation online and their excessive usage is the norm where their engagement in real-world in-person is seen the exception. Labels may mean little to them.

An interesting observation about DA label is the possibility to turn it to a social label in two ways. It could compare to other users who agreed to share their statistics of usage and, also, it could be generated by colleagues instead of software. This is similar to the case when friends try to warn someone to stop drinking in a party. There is still a space for dual use here which needs research, e.g. competing on drinking more.

3.2   Message: Content and Presentation

Regardless of the information content and the way it is presented, it is generally agreed that positive and gentle approach should be followed until it is an extremely excessive usage. This positive labelling will not put users off so they may stop the usage of the software all together. An encouraging approach would not leave a negative effect on the self-esteem, e.g. feeling over-guilty especially those who are unaware of the whole concept. Finally, judging a person usage to be a sort of addiction is an approximation so it may be wise to avoid confirmation and being so strict. In the following, we list the elements which could form the content of DA messages. Throughout the paper, the percentages represent the number of survey participants who ticked the option

Usage Related:

— Time already spent on the software (86%)
— The number of times I checked/visited the software (56%)
— Usage "bill", like mobile bills and bank statements (47%)
— The features which I heavily used (e.g., Like, tagging, messaging etc.) (17%)

Consequence Related:

— Consequences on real social life (e.g., relations breakdown) (51%)
— Effects on physiological and mental health (e.g., eye strains, tension etc.) (50%)
— Damage on your public profile (potentially seen by employer, etc.) (39%)
— The ease and speed of information spread once shared (32%)
— Potential risks on you, e.g. when you use social networks in excessive, hasty and unthoughtful way (29%)

— Consequences on your on-line relationship with others (e.g., hasty and not thoughtful interactions could be misinterpreted etc.) (29%)
— Consequences on online contacts (e.g., hasty and excessive tagging and sharing could affect the privacy of people involved in the posts) (19%)

Advice Related:

— Suggestion/advice on potentially interesting real life activities based on your usage, e.g. going to a social event which matches your detected online interests (44%)
— Factual and proved statements about the benefits of regulating usage styles (38%)
— Suggestions/advice on how to regulate the usage style, e.g. using filters to reduce the amount of feeds/notifications (33%)

By analysing the comments in both phases, the features offered by software and cause DA falls into four categories which are similar to the game elements categories proposed by Bartle's specification explained in [10].

— *Achievement*: when the software feature drives the user to achieve more, e.g. users who keep checking and posting to increase their rank and social capital.
— *Exploration*: when the feature keeps the degree of curiosity high and drives the person to keep connected to know what is next.
— *Socializing*: when the wealth of connectivity features and ease of access make one overly a socializer. This is sometimes due to a sort of escalating commitments where people are online, not because of the pleasure, but to see what others would require from them and whether they upset someone or got negative comments.
— *Killing*: which is more obvious in the case of gaming where a mental satisfaction and stress relief are achieved when one causes harm, virtually, to someone else.

On top of the four features, there are meta-features that increase the addictive nature of software. This includes the ease of use, the real-time nature, the scale of communication and vast diversity of information in an easily navigable cyberspace. These features mean additional attraction which would encourage addictive usage style.

In terms of presentation, DA messages could be delivered via various modes. Each one depends on different factors such as the device used, the activity being done, the stage of addiction and the personality type. We identified eight ways such messages could be delivered. The percentages reflect the amount of survey users who wanted it. An investigation of when to use each delivery method is still to be researched:

— Time-based progress status (e.g., clock/timers for your usage amount) (61%)
— Dynamic colouring of interfaces to reflect your degree of usage (e.g., Green bar for reasonable use, Red bar for excessive use, etc.) (53%)
— Pop-up notifications (44%)
— Personalised metaphors (e.g., an avatar of you when being overly engaged) (31%)
— Hardware based interactions (e.g., vibration and flickering on mobile phones or 3D glasses of gamers) (26%)
— Sounds (e.g., beeping when you overly play a game or check Facebook) (21%)
— Offline notifications, e.g. sent as a message or email (19%)
— Analogy to traditional addiction (e.g., a metaphor of consumption of number of "digital" alcohol glasses) (18%)

The participants emphasized a number of characteristics DA labels should enjoy in order to have a positive reaction from the users. This included:

— *Supportive content (61%)*. DA labels may not be necessarily in the form of a warning form. For example, when losing a game, a user would like a message moderating that feeling which will reduce the desire to start another round. Encouraging the healthy use is also part of this case.
— *Non-repetitive content (54%)*. Users will tend to ignore DA labelling if when it issues messages with similar content and presentation style.
— *Not overly-negative content (51%)*. Users do not like to be overly-warned as this could lead to disrupt their healthy usage. This is similar to the case where gambling is overly associated with people losing their properties and savings, time and social position while it is still possible that people use it moderately as an entertainment tool.
— *Socially-generated content (36%)*. It appeared that messages could be made by friends and this would increase their exciting nature for some users. It is similar to the case when one receives a friendly comment to stop drinking. Similarly the software would need to offer friends to do the same.
— *Precautionary content (36%)*. This is a proactive approach to DA labels. E.g. the message may not be about the current excessive use but the potential to get it or about the high-dependency on software which may lead to serious consequences when lost, e.g. when the connection or a password is lost, a page is closed, a membership is terminated, etc.

3.3   Control

The control aspect relates to what decisions users would like to have over DA labelling and how to express that to software. As a general principle, the interviewees emphasized that labelling, and following what is suggested in it, should remain a choice of the user (or a carer in the case of minors). Unlike alcohol and tobacco, the label could also trigger mechanisms to react to an addictive usage style, e.g. blocking for few hours or reducing some features such as limiting the amount of posts one can make per day. Although this is possible, interview participants' agreed that a user would always find a way, probably other software, when overly warned and controlled. Thus, we excluded this option and we would consider it part of a more like parental control than warning.

In terms of *What*, users would like to be able to control. 36% of the survey participants would like the software to be highly autonomous in forming and delivering labels once they enabled the labelling service. Still, the participants have preferences about being able to control the various settings of labelling:

— The frequency of sending labels (60%),
— How the label should be presented (graphics, sound, email, etc.) (50%),
— The time(s) the label should be delivered (44%),
— The actions that trigger a label (e.g., the things when used/done would require a generation and delivery of a label) (40%),

- The type of information the label could contain (39%),
- The accepted sources of the label (e.g., accept labels designed by certain developers, institutions or people) (38%),
- The strategy through which the labelling is decided (proactive or reactive to my usage style, comparative/relative to others or absolute) (31%).

In terms of *How*, it seems there is a degree of complexity in how users makes decisions. Besides the technical complexity of deciding what to control and what to leave to software, users have a *paradoxical requirement* to be looked after by a trusted hand, whether software or friends, but without being controlled and overly warned at the same time. An interviewee gave an interesting analogy saying that "it is similar to the feeling when one takes the bottle of wine from you because you have to drive or to go to work the day after". This point could be divided into two facets:

- *Resistance to change.* This is a challenge to handle during the initial period of issuing the labels. An analogy to that is the resistance to tobacco labels and smoking designated areas. Interviewees expected that, by time, people will accept DA labels as part of the new online norms. From engineering perspective, the management of that change is a socio-technical problem which is exacerbated by the current view of social media of being an indicator of trendiness by many people. This is analogous to the stereotype of smokers and drinkers in old marketing adverts and classical movies till laws prohibited that considering it a sort of manipulation.
- *Calibrated agreement.* Users tend to accept software to take decision on issuing DA labels and even enacting some sort of precautionary procedures, e.g. cooling-off period, when trust is established. Interviewees indicated that they would like to start with a clear separation of decisions and calibrate the relation over time so that a mutual understanding between their personal preferences and software reasoning is eventually established. This is similar to a supervision relationship, in business and academia, which calibrates overtime and eventually yields a mutual agreement through a sort of natural selection of a range of attitudes and treatments. The importance of this comes from the need to avoid making DA labelling specification a burden on users' experience which is the focus of the rest of this section.

In terms of the technical specification of DA labels, interviewees indicated the need for a range of facilities which would make labelling both accepted and efficient. Interviewees indicated that they are already involved in a plenty of other configurations, such as security and privacy, and adding yet another one for DA labels will be another threat to their comfortable usage. This is not only about setting up the labelling configuration but also the worry of how this would work given the newness of the concept. We identified various aspects on DA label specification:

- *Time-based specification.* The basic form of permission given to software, in relation to issuing the DA label, is time-based. This includes both the time to issue the label, e.g. when users exceed a certain time, and the time to present it, e.g. once users log in/out. The threshold is not necessary on the amount of time and the amount of checks but also on the nature of the actions. It is also context dependent, e.g. "extra use" meaning in holidays is different from it in work days.

— *Features-based specification*. Certain features of software seem to be highly addictive and lead to a hasty and excessive usage style, which, in turn, could also lead to consequences not only for the user but also their community. Users appreciate the control given to the software in issuing the warning label in relation to those features. E.g. sharing and tagging are examples of features where people may feel unable to control at certain point. An interviewee mentioned that "it is so easy and tempting to press the button, but once it goes you may not be able to retract".

— *Complementary actions*. The label should be seen as a part of an integrated process of a usage regulation, i.e. it is not a standalone treatment. This is especially true in the case of social software where there could be social consequences of not being online and such as losing attention and being missed when needed. The label should be complemented with supplementary procedure, which avoids the case that the new usage style harms the basic requirements, e.g. turning the profile message to explain absence to close friends. These actions could be part of the configuration and control of DA labels which make the process more holistic.

— *Social Control*. An interesting observation is that people would accept warning messages to come from their friends and contacts. This is not necessarily done on a one-to-one or direct basis. A person could generate messages to be shown to all friends or group members who exceed a certain limit. Although this idea seems futuristic, it stimulated interesting discussions. Some participants indicated that groups could nominate a guard or agree on norms of usage and DA labels should follow that mutual agreement and could be shown as a positive social pressure. This is a sort of blended control where software, users and the group take part of it.

— *Specification reuse*. Specifying DA labels and how this should be inferred and presented would add additional overhead. The idea of reusing labelling patterns suggested by trusted social entities, such as health institutes or close friends, seems to be interesting. This is similar to eating style proposed by reputed diet specialists.

3.4   Awareness

In [9], we showed that people would like to know why a certain recommendation is being delivered to them at a certain time. This is mainly for privacy and curiosity concerns and others sorts of meta-data to describe the label. People would like to know, or be offered to know, how the DA labels are processed for them and why a message is presented in a certain format and language. This becomes more of an issue when trust has not been established yet and when labelling is conducted as social activity, e.g. recommendations coming from colleagues as described in 3.3.

A general view is that the usage of online software, especially social networks, entails that certain usage data are collected about the user. Interviewees agreed that seeing a label warning about a usage style does not raise unusual privacy concerns in comparison to those already recognized. For example, it is commonly known that data about the amount a user spends on a certain page are sometimes used to infer the market trends and preferences of certain populations. However, in the case of the labelling, and given the fact it is typically to aid users, these typical concerns could have consequences on the efficiency and acceptance of the label itself and users experience with the software in general. The following points elaborate that further.

— *Trust*. People would start to question how DA labels were inferred when the software does not inspire their trust in the first place. Building a trust relation seems to be superior to warning the user of their addictive usage, no matter how right the warning is. Participants indicated that, besides the baseline trust with the software as a whole, the labelling-related trust is typically built through (i) factual correctness, e.g. by giving accurate and unbiased information, (ii) treatment, e.g. the language used and (iii) transparency of inference, i.e. the possibility to see what and how data were used. Some users would increase their level of trust in the software when they become aware that it is careful about them and it is putting its popularity at risk (knowing that they may simply leave it) to keep their usage within healthy levels. That is, the message would need to convey this caring attitude.

— *Loss of relationship*. As a continuation of the previous point, labelling could lead to a loss of closeness between users and software. Some participants stated that at times they may feel someone is picking on them. It is important to choose the right wording and graphics, e.g. loss vs. gain framing [11]. Being positive seems to moderate the negative feeling of being overly unhealthy at least for those who are unaware of the whole concept of DA and its potential consequences.

— *Moderate labelling*. The users should be made aware of the approximate and potentially imprecise nature of the label. Unlike tobacco and alcohol, where the consequences are pretty tangible and measurable, the consequences of DA are not necessarily visible and may not be the same for every person. The consequences are to a large extent related to the social and mental well-being rather than physiological. Awareness of the users about the approximate nature of the label is also an ethical principle, at least currently, due to the lack of experiments on DA.

— *Informed consent, iteratively*. People should be made aware that DA labelling is going to be installed and they should have the right to choose or exclude it. An explanation of the data which are going to be collected will inspire trust. For each label, a link to the stats which explain how the label was generated will be likely appreciated. Although this may not be interesting to many, but the fact it exists will increase trust and transparency and it will be consistent with the fact that labelling is ultimately an ethical and professional practice.

— *Indirect disclosure*. Users should know how their usage data will inform the design of others labels, e.g. when calculating the usage of an average user. This may not be always clear. For example, when a label contains a comparison of a person usage to the friends in a certain group, this in part implies how that group is collectively using it. This, in some cases, could mean much knowledge about individuals. In the case of social control of labelling the situation becomes paradoxical where a user would need to balance between giving the group some control over the labelling and being at the same time reserved on sharing usage information.

— *Developers' awareness*. Another interesting point was raised about the need to educate developers themselves to appreciate the dual usage of their software product. Their awareness will be the first step before they can raise users' awareness. 70% of the survey users believed that this is not a main concern of developers. Some survey participants who disagreed or remain neutral gave a contradicted view saying that making the software addictive is a deliberate goal in certain cases.

Table 1 shows the survey results on the same aspect (SA: Strongly Agree, A: Agree, N: Neither Agree nor Disagree, D: Disagree, SD: Strongly Disagree).

Table 1. Users view on the awareness dimension of DA label

Statement	SA	A	N	D	SD
Software needs to inspire my trust before I accept labelling.	31%	54%	13%	3%	0%
Labelling may lead to less natural use of software and make me lose closeness with it (no matter how useful labelling is).	4%	26%	44%	22%	3%
Software can only have approximation and estimation about my usage, so it should always make labels less confirmatory.	4%	50%	35%	8%	3%
I should be able to know how the label was generated and why; this will increase my acceptance of it.	25%	58%	8%	6%	3%
I need to be able know how my usage data and reactions to labels are used even if this is to enhance the labelling service.	14%	54%	22%	8%	1%
I feel software developers/industries are often unaware of, or uninterested in, the addictive nature of their software and its consequences	24%	46%	11%	11%	8%

3.5   Adaptivity

Adaptivity, in essence, means the ability to change the labelling as a response to some independent variable, called an adaptation driver. Adaptivity is a cross-cutting aspect which relates to the content of the message, its presentation, and the switch between the different styles of controlling the labelling process. We here discuss the adaptation drivers and what they affect in the labelling elements.

— *Stage of addiction.* The grade of DA should be taken into account when deciding the friendliness of the language used in the message, gain vs. loss framing, the medium of presentation, the persistent of the message, and ultimately the amount of control given to the software. It is not always straightforward to measure the stage of addiction. Time spent and hasty actions are not the only measure to consider. Participants mentioned cases where people could leave the windows open without being really engaged with it. Other usages could relate in part to their daily work updates. That is, the weight of the usage time should be different.

— *Computing device.* People demonstrate different addiction patterns depending on the computing device they use. For example while checking a mobile phone frequently is just a way to let time pass in the waiting room, refreshing a website on a PC in the same way would not be often a typical use. The computing device also affects the feasibility of each way to deliver the warning message. For example, much illustration is unlikely recommended on mobile devices. The context of use in the case of mobile devices is a factor while it is moderately an important factor in the case of stationary access. For example, a warning would need to check whether a person is walking when mobile phones are used to estimate the risk and issue a suitable label. The same check would not be needed in the case of a PC.

— *Time*. The time of usage is also an important factor to consider when adjusting the label. Using social networks at night is typically more acceptable than using during the day. Weekends and holidays are also known for leisure activities including the infotainment and relatively higher usage of social media.

— *Social context*. It seems that one of the important factors is also the seasonal engagement with software which may not be a sign of excessive usage. E.g. in a festival time people tend to use social media more and sometime in exaggerated style. This is analogous to some tolerance in food and drinking style in a festival period.

— *Personal profile*. This includes mainly the age. In the case of children, the label would may even need to be addressed, or at least a copy of it, to some guardian, though again this introduces further ethical and perhaps legal dimensions. It appears there may also be some personality traits that lead to the acceptance of the language used in the label and the persistent nature of that label. Although we cannot confirm any correlation without further investigation, we could make few observations. For example, some participants liked the idea that the label is persistent so that they take it seriously while others did not like that. Some participants preferred to be called by their own names as a sign of respect while others saw that irrelevant especially when it is coming from software. The presentation as a pop-up seems to be necessary for certain people while others prefers a less direct style such as the light and the colour based alert. Although these settings are adjustable by the user, an intelligent inference and a mapping of individual users to Personas seems to be necessary at least to suggest a default option to users.

Table 2 shows the survey results on the same aspect.

Table 2. Users view on the adaptivity dimensions DA label

Statement	SA	A	N	D	SD
The progress or stage of my addictive or excessive or hasty use (e.g., by changing the language and frequency accordingly)	25%	67%	7%	0%	1%
The type of devices I am using (e.g., my usage patterns and preferences on labelling may differ between mobile devices and computers)	24%	61%	8%	7%	0%
The time aspect (e.g., weekends and night time are probably peak time for using social software but it does not mean my usage would be excessive)	29%	49%	13%	8%	1%
My social context (e.g., in holidays or parties, one may post more on a social network)	15%	53%	18%	11%	3%
My personal profile (e.g., age, profession and sociability are all factors when judging whether it is an addictive use)	18%	40%	22%	17%	3%

4   Engineering Challenges for DA Labelling Requirement

Labelling is fundamentally a requirements engineering problem. It is an ethical and professional practice requirement and, given the clear consequences in certain cases and feedback from users groups it may be eventually enshrined in law [12]. In terms of beneficiaries, and in addition to the users themselves, software developers also gain potential benefits from implementing labelling, regardless of the existence of laws and social norms. As we explained in Section 3.4, users tend to trust the software more when it cares about their healthy usage and trust would typically increase their loyalty level. Obviously, we still need to study the fine line between carefulness and annoyance and how software should reason about that. Health and Welfare Services, both public and private sector, are further examples of "off-stage" actors where there is already growing interest in the possibility of using addiction-aware software to maintain the mental and social-wellbeing of users [13].

Our study identified four paradoxical requirements of users which DA labelling process would need to handle:

- *Control vs. autonomy paradox*: users would like software to be autonomous in measuring their usage and issuing the labels. At the same time, they would like to have a control over the process. Almost all the survey participants who chose to give the autonomy to software chose also to control certain aspects over the label-ling (Section 3.3). While the comfort is the motivation for the first, the effort needed for the second is clearly an obstacle to the design of such software. We proposed the notion of calibrated agreement as a sort of natural selection to elect the best control strategies between users and software over time. While this could also be the case for other kinds of requirements, e.g. privacy and security, there is an extra motivation in the case of DA labelling. This is mainly due to the supervi-sion and mentorship nature of this requirement unlike the classical case where us-ers use a sort of control panel to specify their software settings. Also, DA labels are not necessarily generated and sent by software but could also be sent by social enti-ties, individuals and groups, which would add a social dimension to the control.

- *Appreciation vs. Annoyance paradox:* users stated that their level of trust in the software would increase when it offered the labelling service. This will be still true even if they do not like this service all the time. From the interview comments and also those provided in the text entries in the survey, we observed that users would still have a complex set of requirements on how labelling should work, which makes it relatively easy for the labelling to become an annoyance. While this re-lates to the previous paradox in part, software industries would be still sceptical about introducing a label and unsure of at what stage this should be done. Man-agement of the change when introducing the labels to existing software is one fur-ther challenge. Introducing it with new software, as one of the interviewees said, may be a better option as "if it appears as part of the terms and conditions, one would both appreciate and be prepared to see it in the future".

- *Being cared vs. privacy.* Seven of the interviewees and 36% of the survey partici-pants found the idea of socially generated labels interesting and would want to make the control of software usage a sort of 'enjoyable' social activity. Knowing that more information about their usage will help others to give more meaningful DA labels, though privacy concerns are still clearly an obstacle. Interestingly users tended to have different preferences depending on whether the carer was 'just' software or a social entity. The space for negotiation and changing perception in sharing as a mutual care and community-related activity is still worthy of further work. This is particularly true given the novelty of the concept.

- *Individual vs. collective paradox.* Users indicated that the reason why they may excessively be online is mainly because others are online and that they feel they might be missing something if they stop. We may think of the DA label in this case as a label directed to a community rather than to an individual all the times. However, the border between the two is blurred.

DA labelling requires a multidisciplinary research by nature. A requirements engineer would need to understand how users and other stakeholders like these labels to be designed, deduced and presented for specific software. While these decisions may still relate to the nature of that software and its design objectives, they would not be achievable simply by consulting users and probably the entity who will own the software. These decisions require foundational research which is in part a requirements engineering research. Amongst other areas, this should include the following:

— *Generating factually correct DA labels content*, e.g. proven consequences. While this is clear in substance addiction, the research on DA is still in the early stages.
— *Laws and code of ethics.* It is becoming regular news on the media that the use of certain software features, e.g. the Selfie and games, is causing harm to people. The laws and also software engineering code of ethics would need to be updated to handle the peculiarities of the addictive nature of software. DA labels are still seen an option rather than a norm or even professional practice.
— *Fuzziness and metrics.* Monitoring usage and judging its addictive nature will need metrics that manage to represent a complex set of behaviours, particularly given the fuzzy nature of the concept. For example, 78% of users wanted software to appreciate that in holidays and at certain time of the day their usage could follow a different pattern to their normal levels. Similarly, as with physical addictions, such as to alcohol, some people have different thresholds of what an excessive use is, and this is further complicated by the fact that the amount, say consumed, is not always the sole indicator of dependence. For this reason, only 11% of our users disagreed that solely measuring their usage is never going to be sufficient as a predictor of addiction, and, therefore, DA labels would need to be less confirmative; one alternative being some kind of individual calibration.
— *Alignment.* We can view the DA labelling as an alignment problem in which the software has a requirement to align with health and social care regulations. However, although we use the term "addiction", the phenomenon of the excessive, impulsive and compulsive usage of software is still not formally considered a sort of addiction or disorder. We would still need a multidisciplinary research to come up with metrics for the healthy usage and what properties to ensure in the software design to maintain it.

In the case of DA labelling, and DA in general, requirements elicitation has a particularly private nature. To add weight to our argument, our pre-selection survey enabled us to interview only those who declared a sort of addictive usage. However, during the interview, participants moderated quite significantly their description of their usage style. People would typically feel uncomfortable declaring their true usage style when they are identified. This will call to a requirements elicitation which is a mixture of psychology and software engineering practice, in order to tackle DA labelling.

5   Conclusions

We advocated the need for Digital Addiction labels and studied how this should be implemented from a user's perspective through an empirical study. The vast majority of participants, +80%, confirmed it is potentially a good idea to aid them regulate their usage style. Besides the results which one would intuitively speculate about the content and presentation (time spent and clock, etc.), our study led to interesting findings. These are mainly in the area of the paradoxical need for freedom and being supervised in the same time, the novel ways of generating and communicating the label, the private nature of this requirement, the need for metrics for addictive usage, to name a few. Our future will delve into the details of each of these challenges from the perspectives of both requirements engineering and cyber-psychology.

Acknowledgment. The research was supported by an FP7 Marie Curie CIG grant (the SOCIAD Project) and by Bournemouth University through the Fusion Investment Fund.

References

1. Nyland, R., Marvez, R., Beck, J.: MySpace: social networking or social isolation?. In: AEJMC Midwinter Conference, pp. 23–24, (2007)
2. Kirschner, P.A., Karpinski, A.C.: Facebook and academic performance. Comput. Hum. Behav. **26**, 1237–1245 (2010)
3. Barker, V.: Older adolescents motivations for social network site use: The influence of gender, group identity, and collective self-esteem. CyberPsychol. Behav. **12**, 209–213 (2009)
4. Ellison, N.B., Steinfield, C., Lampe, C.: The benefits of facebook "friends": social capital and college students use of online social network sites. Comput-Mediat. Comm. **12** (2007)
5. Kuss, D.J., Griffiths, M.D.: Online social networking and addiction - a review of the psychological literature. Environmental research and public health **8**(9), 3528–3552 (2011)
6. Young, K.: Internet addiction: Evaluation and treatment. Student Brit. Med. **7**, 351–352 (1999)
7. Griffiths, M.D.: Components model of addiction within a bio-psychosocial framework. J. Subst. Use **10**, 191–197 (2005)
8. Alrobai, A., Phalp, K., Ali, R.: Digital addiction: a requirements engineering perspective. In: Salinesi, C., van de Weerd, I. (eds.) REFSQ 2014. LNCS, vol. 8396, pp. 112–118. Springer, Heidelberg (2014)

9. Jiang, N., Ali, R.: On the delivery of recommendations in social software: a user's perspective. In: Sauer, S., Bogdan, C., Forbrig, P., Bernhaupt, R., Winckler, M. (eds.) HCSE 2014. LNCS, vol. 8742, pp. 275–282. Springer, Heidelberg (2014)
10. Zichermann, G., Cunningham, C.: Gamification by design: Implementing game mechanics in web and mobile apps. O'Reilly Media, Inc. (2011)
11. Tversky, A., Kahneman, D.: Advances in prospect theory: Cumulative representation of uncertainty. Journal of Risk and Uncertainty 5, 297–323 (1992)
12. Da Zhan, J., Chan, H.C.: Government regulation of online game addiction. Communications of the Association for Information Systems 30 (2012).
13. Kim, K.: Internet addiction in Korean adolescents and its relation to depression and suicidal ideation: a questionnaire survey. Intl. journal of nursing studies 43(2), 185–192 (2006)
14. Thaler, R.H., Sunstein, C.R.: Nudge: Improving Decisions About Health. Yale University Press, Wealth and Happiness (2009)
15. Ewing, J.A.: Detecting alcoholism: the CAGE questionnaire. Jama 252(14), 1905–1907 (1984)

Challenges of the Customer Organization's Requirements Engineering Process in the Outsourced Environment – A Case Study

Heli Hiisilä[✉], Marjo Kauppinen, and Sari Kujala

Aalto University, Espoo, Finland
heli.hiisila@iki.fi, {marjo.kauppinen,sari.kujala}@aalto.fi

Abstract. **[Context and motivation]** The increasingly complex business and development environment brings challenges to IT system development and requirements engineering (RE) activities. **[Question/problem]** The goal of the case study was to investigate what the challenges of a customer organization's RE process are in the outsourced development environment and what demands these challenges bring to RE process development. The case study was conducted in a Finnish insurance company. **[Principal ideas/results]** The results are based on 17 interviews and the analysis of 15 large projects. The case study indicates that one of the biggest challenges is to develop business and IT as a whole. When combining business process and IT system development, requirements are an important tool. Another critical challenge in the outsourced environment is that the RE process is distributed between the customer organization and the supplier. Furthermore, highly integrated IT systems and enterprise architecture bring demands to RE process. **[Contribution]** The paper describes a complex environment in which the customer organization develops IT systems, and systematically defines challenges related to the RE process.

Keywords: RE process · Outsourced environment · Large complex projects

1 Introduction

Companies invest millions every year in IT system development aiming at adding business value to achieve strategic goals. IT projects consume customer organizations' resources and are seldom finished in accordance with their original schedule and budget or deliver the benefits expected [1]. To improve project outcomes, requirements engineering has been identified as one of the success factors in software projects [2] [3].

Today, many companies focus on core business and software development is outsourced to external suppliers. In outsourced processes, high-quality requirements are needed in acquisition, customer-supplier relationships need to be established and knowledge must be transferred between the customer and the supplier. The development environment has also become increasingly complex, and new themes have emerged in the RE field such as business process focus, systems transparency,

© Springer International Publishing Switzerland 2015
S.A. Fricker and K. Schneider (Eds.): REFSQ 2015, LNCS 9013, pp. 214–229, 2015.
DOI: 10.1007/978-3-319-16101-3_14

integration focus, distributed requirements, layers of requirements, packaged software, centrality of architecture and interdependent complexity [4]. Requirements are a notable risk for causing project failure [5] [6] [7] [8]. Most of the research of the outsourced project risks is focused on the vendor side of a project, but the client perspective has been ignored [8].

Large-scale and outsourced development projects can be a challenge for non-technical customer organizations and also the case study organization has faced these challenges in the large development projects. As a solution, the aim was to develop RE processes to better support projects. Straight forward answers to customer organization's RE process development issues were not available in the RE text books. Therefore, there is a need to understand current state of the customer organization to develop new RE processes and practices. The research question of the case study is: *What are the challenges of customer organizations' RE processes in the outsourced environment and what demands do these challenges bring to RE process development?*

2   Related Work

To understand the role of the customer in the RE processes, we studied definitions of the term "customer". One definition points out that requirements are specified and thus owned by the customer: "An individual or organization who specifies the requirements and formally accepts delivery of a new or modified hardware or software product and its documentation" [9]. Wiegers defines customer as "an individual or organization who derives either direct or indirect benefit from a product" [10].

The term "acquirer" is also used in the IEEE Software lifecycle processes standard [11] and the definition of the acquisition process includes, among others requirements definition, solution selection, RFQ (Request for Quotation) preparation and acceptance of the solution. However, we prefer the term "customer organization" to point out that, in addition to the acquirer part of the organization, the involvement of many stakeholders such as management, requirements analysts, business specialists, users and enterprise architects is needed.

Based on our literature review, RE of in-house development and product development has been studied (e.g., [3] [4] [12] [13] [14] [15] [16]). However, customer's viewpoint seems to be less discussed. Wiegers [10] defines requirements as a cornerstone of the outsourced development process. Hull et al. [17] identified stakeholder requirements management as the acquisition organization's main concern. Also RE challenges have been studied in the offshore outsourcing context. Bhat et al. [5] identified conflicting vendor-client goals, low client involvement, conflicting RE approaches, disagreements in tool selection, and communication and sign-off issues as challenges in a global IT-services organization. Furthermore, based on three case studies, Abdullah and Verner [7] [8] identified conflicting, over-specified, inadequate, incorrect and unclear requirements as project risk factors. The significance of different RE practices in the outsourced projects [18] and coordination of vendor and client of outsourced development projects have also been studied[19].

3   Research Method

3.1   Case Study Organization

The case study organization was an insurance company that specializes in statutory pension security in Finland. The company has more than 560 employees. Its business is information centric and legislated. The number of IT systems is 210 and these systems are highly integrated. In the past, the company had an internal IT department that was responsible for the development, maintenance and production of IT systems and also knew the business part well. IT system development was outsourced 2006 and is nowadays provided by external suppliers. Most of the suppliers are well known international software suppliers.

The RE process of the case study organization was defined during the years 2006-2007. The RE process description and guidelines are simple. They include basic activities such as requirements elicitation, analysis, specification, validation, and management. A small set of RE practices such as requirements collection workshops, usage of Office templates to document requirements and requirements reviews are recommended and they are used in most of the IT development projects.

3.2   Data Collection and Analysis

The research was performed based on interviews, document reviews and validation workshops (Table 1). The interviews were semi-structured and they were conducted in Finnish. The themes of the interview questions were

- changes in the development environment and effects upon RE
- RE experiences from large development projects
- demands and development ideas to improve the RE process

Table 1. Summary of data collection methods

Method	Data collection
Interviews	17 interviewees were selected based on the organizational and project roles to comprehensively represent different kinds of projects and organizational functions responsible for RE and project work.
Documenta- tion review	The requirements and project documentation of 15 large strategic outsourced projects were studied.
Validation workshops	To validate the findings, 5 workshops were performed with the inter- viewees and other RE practitioners of the case study company.

The questions that have been translated into English are available in the interview guide [20]. The interviewees included five business developers/specialists, three steering group members of IT development projects, two requirements definition specialists, two process developers, two IT managers, two IT architects, and one project manager. The duration of the individual interviews was approximately an hour. All the interviews were recorded and transcribed.

In addition to the interviews, requirements documents, project plans and final reports of 15 large projects were studied from the RE point of view. These projects covered all strategically important outsourced IT system development of the case study company during 2006-2014 and they were typically delivered by multiple suppliers. The costs of the projects varied from 1M€ to 35M€.

The interview data was analyzed iteratively. The unit of analysis was large IT development projects and the focus of the investigation was to analyze RE challenges. We analyzed the interview data with open-coding content analysis [21]. A large number of challenges and background information was identified based on the interviews and they were analyzed together with the challenges identified from the project documentation. The challenges were clustered to categories and modelled further based on validation feedback. The first author of the paper was responsible for the analysis She had worked in the organization in a wide variety of roles and, therefore had practical experience with the company's RE practices and development projects.

Five workshops were organized to validate the findings with the interviewees and IT management. During the validation workshops, the first author presented the results of the analysis and the participants gave feedback on the results. The validation workshops lasted 2-4 hours. The results of the analysis were also validated iteratively by the two researchers. The second author had participated in a previous RE process development project of the case study company and had, therefore, some background knowledge about the customer organization. The third author did not know the case study organization and her role was to act as an external reviewer of the findings. This paper was also reviewed by two IT executives.

4   Challenges and Demands of RE Processes at Customer Organization

Based on the study, we identified 42 challenges that established demands upon the RE process development. These challenges were categorized during the analysis phase into seven themes that are presented in Figure 1. The following subsections describe the challenges and demands related to the seven themes.

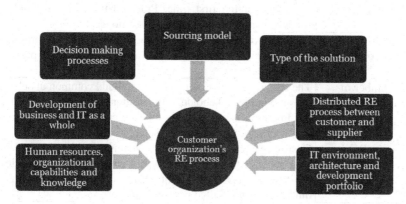

Fig. 1. Categories of the challenges related to the customer organization's RE process

4.1   Human Resources, Organizational Capabilities and Knowledge

Human resources, organizational capabilities and knowledge of the individuals in the project team was one of the main themes identified. The main focus of the customer organization is on the business and, therefore, there are only a limited number of professional developers. As most of the practitioners participate in development part-time, RE processes, practices and tools needed to be adapted to the resources of the semi-professional business organization.

Based on the study, the amount of time, resources, knowledge and skills needed for requirements definition in large-scale projects came by a surprise to the interviewees. The importance of requirements was underestimated or misunderstood by the business people and there was a hurry to move on to implementation of the project. Furthermore, knowledge and willingness to use practices varied in the organization.

In the highly integrated IT system environment, the amount of internal stakeholders tends to grow large: business management, end users, specialists in different business units, process or business developers, IT architects and IT management. Customer organizations have political aspects to be considered, as different stakeholders often have conflicting requirements based on their organizational responsibilities. In the studied projects, a large amount of external stakeholders was also identified: officials, legislators, external business partners, and other companies in the field with common IT solutions. The importance of taking customer needs (customer of the customer organization) into account has also been a trend. Challenges and related demands are summarized in Table 2.

Table 2. Summary of the challenges related to human resources, capabilities and knowledge

Challenges	Demands for RE process development
Semi-professional practitioners	RE process documentation, models and tools must be understandable for business practitioners without extensive technical training and skills.
Limited development resources	With the resources available, best-fitting RE processes and practices should be selected to maximize the benefits.
Need for support of the RE process	Practitioners require support when utilizing new RE practices and tools for the first time. Practical training and hands-on-support were preferred by the practitioners.
Cultural differences inside the organization	Organizational change management is needed to communicate the importance of requirements and implement RE processes in practice.
Large number of stakeholders	The RE process is needed as a tool to build common understanding among the stakeholders. In addition to internal stakeholders, the importance of external stakeholders and customers of the customer organization has also increased.
Selecting a RE project team	Customer organizations' project teams should consist of business specialists with in-depth and comprehensive knowledge of business processes, requirements analysts gathering requirements and skilled project managers.

4.2   Business Development and IT as Whole

In the case study organization, IT development is seen as one part of business development and the best total effectiveness has been achieved in programs developing both business and IT. Previously the business development has been IT-intensive, and more focused on improvement of the current state. Now, the focus is on development of the whole operating model and making strategic transformations via development programs. Challenges related are summarized in Table 3.

Table 3. Summary of the challenges related to business development and IT as whole

Challenges	Demands for RE process development
Development of the whole operation model instead of only IT	IT development was seen as a part of the development toolbox. Customer organizations' scope is to improve and develop business as a whole; i.e., business processes and services, organization and IT.
Steering projects based on strategic goals	Development programs and projects are seen as an important tool to accomplish company strategies through strategic transformation. Strategic development goals were seen as high-level requirements steering the project. Requirements gathered from users and other stakeholders should be prioritized by the goals defined.
Combining business process development and IT system development	Business process development brings requirements to system development and IT system development opportunities and limitations to business process development. Requirements are a tool to combine both approaches. Also, Business Driven Development (BDD) [22] was utilized in the subject organization in four development projects.
Managing organizational change and business transformation	Customers' project scope includes also organizational change management, business transformation and other activities related to changing the software tools used in the business processes. The supplier implementing the system has the project scope.
Long lifecycle of requirements	Customers' RE processes begin much earlier than software project and last to the end of the solutions lifecycle – from the development idea to business benefits. The lifecycle of a requirement may last for a quarter of a century. In an ideal case, requirements are up to date and a part of maintenance documentation.
Traceability from the business requirement to the benefits received	Requirements have a major impact upon the business benefits delivered. In the projects studied, IT development did not always deliver solutions that fulfilled the requirements and targeted business benefits were compromised. In an ideal case, traceability exists from a business requirement to implementation. The interviewees emphasized that being active in requirements management is important for delivering the expected benefits.

4.3   Decision-Making Processes

Connecting requirements engineering to the decision-making processes of the customer organization was identified one of the important themes. The connection to procurement and project management processes was identified: the project scope is defined by requirements; solutions fulfilling the requirements should be selected, as well as the software supplier. Also, a link to the customer organization's financial processes exists: requirements have major impacts upon development costs, maintenance costs and business value delivered. Challenges related to decision-making processes are summarized in Table 4.

Table 4. Summary of the challenges related to decision-making processes

Challenges	Demands for RE process development
Scoping and planning the project	Well-defined requirements scope the project and concretize the project goals. Requirements are a useful tool in project task planning.
Linking requirements to business case	Business case estimation and investment calculation were seen as tools to link the goals, scope, requirements, development and maintenance costs, and expected benefits together. Good requirements are so concrete that benefit and cost estimation can be done. An iterative approach has been useful because the organization learns during the requirements definitions, procurement state and implementation of the project.
Involving management and making decisions	Management should define goals as well as review and accept high-level requirements. Requirements management should be actively performed to analyze possible changes to goals and desired benefits.
Prioritization of requirements and requirements sets	The importance of prioritization of requirements was emphasized to focus upon strategic development, limit scope and improve cost efficiency. To maximize the benefits received from the development, requirements delivering the highest benefits should be implemented. Investment calculation for each requirement of a large project is impossible, but a rough estimation of costs and benefits is also useful.
Selecting the supplier and solutions that meet the requirements	When selecting the supplier to deliver the implementation project, bids should be evaluated based on the requirements. In addition to high quality and low costs, solution should meet the requirements.
Acceptance of the solution delivery based on the requirements	Acceptance testing and validation of the delivery should be done based on the requirements. However, in most of the projects studied, more detailed design specifications replaced original requirements in test planning.
Managing actively requirements	Requirements management should be performed actively during the procurement and project. Requirements should be up-to-date throughout the project.

4.4   Sourcing Model

Based on the study, the company's sourcing model has a major impact upon the RE processes, techniques, tools and resources needed. Three sourcing models were identified from the projects studied: 1) in-house, 2) outsourced partnership, 3) outsourced development with procurement procedures. In addition to three models, most of the projects/programs studied had multiple suppliers, up to 15; and, as a specialty of the business field, common IT system development projects between several customer organizations exist. A summary of the related challenges is defined in Table 5.

Table 5. Summary of the challenges related to sourcing model

Challenges	Demands for RE process development
In-house development	The organization has an internal common RE process, informal and close cooperation between its business and IT people, internal development costs and decision making.
Outsourced partnership development	Established RE processes with the customer and IT development partner; cooperation usually begins in the early phases of the requirements definition, which eases the work of customer organization; external development costs limit the use of partner organization specialists; partner has business and IT environment knowledge.
Outsourced development with procurement procedures	Customer organizations need to define high-quality requirements independently for the procurement/RFQ process; cooperation with the supplier begins after procurement; new supplier needs to learn the business and IT environment; common RE process must be established during the first project; and, in the projects studied, subsequent projects are easier as the partnership is established.
Multi-supplier projects	Customer organizations have a role as an integrator of the whole; several suppliers deliver components for the solution; one business requirement often has dependencies upon many projects and good requirements management practices are needed to support projects; utilizing tools in requirements management has been beneficial; requirements management must be effectively performed to keep track of solutions delivered by different suppliers; well defined and managed requirements are needed to glue all the parts into the solution to deliver business value.
Multi-customer projects	Negotiation of requirements between the customers is important. Combining business needs, IT environment and systems for common interfaces, registers and system logic.

4.5   Type of Solution

Based on the interviews and study of the projects, five categories of solution types were characteristic: 1) tailored software implementation, 2) implementation of software product (COTS), 3) software as service (SaaS) or buying outsourced services, including IT, 4) development of current IT systems, 5) integration work. Based on the study, the selection of a solution had an impact upon the RE tasks; amount of work and cooperation with the supplier and support for different kind of solutions were required from the RE process. Different solution types identified in the projects are summarized in Table 6.

Table 6. Summary of the challenges related to type of the solution

Challenges	Demands for RE process development
Tailored software implementation	In the large-scale tailored implementation projects, requirements definition work demands a lot of time, resources and modeling skills. All the functional and non-functional requirements needed must be defined. Cooperation between the customer and supplier is vital to share the knowledge and workload of large-scale requirements definition work. As an advantage, the process may be defined based on the business needs. Previously most of the solutions were tailor made; today, however, this is rare.
Software product implementation (COTS)	Business requirements and, usually, functional and non-functional requirements are needed to compare software products. From the customer point of view, it is vital to understand how requirements may be fulfilled (basic functionality vs. configurations vs. modification) and cooperation with suppliers is needed. In addition to software product implementation projects, the solution usually requires modifications to other systems and integrations – requirements for these parts should also be defined. Usually, the company's own business processes are adjusted to the processes supported by the software product, instead of modifying the product, to avoid increased maintenance cost.
Software as a Service or buying an outsourced service	Requirements are needed to compare the services offered by different service providers. The organization's internal process is adjusted to the process supported by the standard service.
Development of current IT systems	Large-scale projects were implemented to current IT systems due, for example, to changes in legislation or increases in automation level. Understanding of the current solution is needed and system documentation is used as a basis of the requirements definition work. Cooperation with the supplier in the early phases of requirements definition was seen as beneficial.
Integration work	All programs studied included integration work, from 10% up to 100% of total workload. Both business- and architecture-related requirements are relevant.

4.6   Distributed RE Process between Customer and Suppliers

Requirements engineering is cooperation between the customer and the supplier organization. The customer organization owns the requirements and has the business knowledge. The supplier has technical knowledge. In the projects studied, the customer had the main responsibility of defining high-level requirements, while the supplier was responsible for more detailed specifications. The challenges related to distributed RE processes are summarized in Table 7.

Table 7. Summary of the challenges related to distributed RE process

Challenges	Demands for RE process development
Optimized cooperation in the RE process with the supplier	Cooperation with the supplier in the early phases was seen as beneficial in many projects to transfer knowledge for implementation.
Distribution of RE work between the customer and a supplier	Based on the study, customer organizations should have internal or external requirements analysts to produce high quality requirements for procurement of large-scale projects. Also, internal RE processes and tool support were needed by the practitioners. The supplier's skilled requirements analysts were important for project success.
High quality requirements for RFQ/RFP and procurement	For RFQ (Request for Quote) or RFP (Request for Proposal), customer organizations need to define requirements and their own or external RE resources are needed. Requirements direct suppliers to provide comparable bids – all suppliers must receive the same information.
Iteratively improving requirements in cooperation with suppliers	Requirements definition is a learning process; from 2–4 iterations were performed in the studied projects. The customer learns from the solutions available and the supplier learns from the customer's needs and environment.
Common understanding of the project scope and complexity	In addition to written requirements, discussions and clarifications are needed to build common understanding and trust. Customers need to understand how the solution meets their requirements and suppliers must to understand business needs and the whole complexity of the project.
Requirements vital part of the project contract	Requirements are a vital part of a contract between a customer and a supplier and thus a baseline of the scope. Also, agile projects demand high-level scoping.
Negotiation of RE practices	The system work models, modeling techniques, tools, responsibilities and distribution of work varied based on the supplier. RE practices need to be negotiated.
Design specifications defined by the supplier specify the solution	Requirements are further specified during the system specifications. Customer organizations define the requirements and suppliers have documentation responsibility for design specifications in cooperation with the customer.

4.7   IT Environment, Enterprise Architecture and Development Portfolio

Program portfolio and the size and complexity of the project bring demands to RE processes. Requirements modeling techniques varied in the projects studied, as the modeling demands in different application domains are different. In the customer organizations, each project is somewhat unique and implemented only once, whereas software suppliers may learn from previous projects with certain software products, technology and application domains.

Also, the importance of enterprise architecture has increased, as the number of technologies and complexity of solutions has grown rapidly. Projects hardly ever begin from scratch and the solutions made must fit into the company's technical environment – requirements from the enterprise architecture and other systems to be integrated must be collected. In addition to the enterprise architecture approach, solution architecture is needed in mapping the requirements to solutions. Also, a solution may fit the business need, but it may cause high maintenance costs if it is unsuitable for the IT environment. The customer organization must have a lifecycle approach. Sustainable long-term solutions are needed, not just fast and cheap solutions from the project scope. Challenges and related demands are summarized in Table 8.

Table 8. Summary of the challenges related to company IT environment, enterprise architecture and development portfolio

Challenges	Demands for RE process development
Development program portfolio, size and complexity of the projects	Complex large-scale projects require different practices, tools and support from the RE process than small maintenance projects. The RE process, practices and tools were developed in the case study organization to better support large projects.
Enterprise architecture, IT environment and maintenance	Enterprise architecture, current IT environment and maintenance of the systems bring limitations and requirements. Negotiation of the technical or non-functional requirements is essential as they often have an impact upon the selected solutions and may add costs.
Different types of projects and solutions	RE process and practices must be flexible to support the needs of different types of projects, whether it is about renewing service production processes, ERP implementation or mandatory changes to legacy systems. However, the core of the RE process may be similar in all the projects.
Other development methods, models and frameworks utilized	RE processes should fit into the methods, models and frameworks utilized in the company that are related to business development, program and project management, enterprise architecture, procurement, risk management and other related processes.
Modeling comprehensive requirements from the enterprise context	Requirements modeling should cover comprehensively different aspects from the enterprise context: service design, business processes, business logic and functionality, data, integrations, IT solution should also fit into enterprise architecture.

5   Discussion

We identified seven categories of challenges that establish demands to the customer organization's RE process. This case study describes a complex environment in which the customer organization develops IT systems, and it systematically defines challenges related to the RE process. The results of the study are based on the 17 interviews of practitioners from different roles, experiences gathered from the 15 strategic large outsourced projects and the in-depth analysis of the current state in one customer organization. Here we discuss the main findings of the case study and relate them to existing RE literature.

Our results emphasize the importance of understanding the current state of resources available, organizational capabilities and knowledge in the RE process development. It is important to select RE practices and tools that support the needs of the customer organization. *The customer organization has the business knowledge and ownership of requirements, but it was unclear what capabilities and roles customer organization should have and which RE activities can be outsourced in the distributed RE process.* Our previous case studies have also highlighted the importance of human factors, and the usefulness and practicality of the RE process [15]. Furthermore, adequate RE processes and role awareness [3] and high-level customer involvement [6] have enhanced the success of RE processes.

The business focus is an important characteristic of the customer organization's RE process. Instead of just IT systems development, the development of the whole operating model (business processes, services, organization and IT systems) was emphasized in this study. Business development sets requirements to system development and vice versa. Furthermore, a business requirement may often be fulfilled by both system requirements and business development tasks. The business process focus has also been identified as a current RE trend by Hansen, Berente and Lyytinen [4]. *In the case study company, two important questions are: 1) how can business and IT development be combined effectively in the RE process and 2) can business-driven development [22] bring IT and business closer together?* Combining process modeling to service design and service blueprinting [24] might be a good combination in the future development projects.

From the point of view of the case study organization, requirements were an essential tool to ensure that the expected benefits are received with the accepted costs. A critical question is *how to connect the RE process to business case estimation, project scoping, procurement and other decision-making processes of the company.* Studies related to scoping projects effectively [6] and requirements prioritization, for example, extreme prioritization [12] may be useful. Strategy steering and goal orientation were also identified as notable themes. Also a relevant question is *how to steer projects to achieve strategic development goals?* The goal-oriented RE [24] [25] could bring business goals closer to the RE process of the case study organization.

RE processes in the outsourced environment requires close co-operation between the customer and the supplier. Requirements evolve iteratively during requirements definition, procurement and implementation of projects between the customer and the supplier. The importance of communication between the stakeholders in addition to high quality documentation, handshaking and discussions between the customer and supplier were emphasized in the study. In practice, *what kind of RE process should be used to transfer knowledge between the customer and the supplier efficiently in outsourced projects during procurement and implementation of the project?* Agile RE practices such as iterative RE and face-to-face communication [12] might yield solutions. Furthermore, shared goal, culture, process, responsibility and trust between the customer and the vendor were identified as success factors of offshore outsourcing projects [5]. Tiwana suggests that totally novel projects require extensive client-vendor communication across all phases of the development projects; customer should have more technology knowledge and vendor more business knowledge [26].

Based on the study, the sourcing model has a major impact upon the RE process in the outsourced environment. In the literature, distributed requirements and interdependent complexity have been identified as RE trends [4], and a long-term relationship with a service provider organization, domain knowledge, communication and trust as success factors of the RE process [14]. Our findings indicate that the complexity of the requirements management increased in the projects with multiple suppliers. In the studied projects, the number of suppliers climbed as high as 15 due to the highly integrated systems and a business requirement was fulfilled by several solutions delivered by different suppliers. The customer acted as an integrator and had a responsibility to coordinate all suppliers to deliver implementation matching the requirements. The question is *how to deal with RE challenges in complex multi-supplier projects with suppliers with software development methods, processes and tools?*

In the literature, packaged software and integration focus have been identified as current RE trends [5]. These were also a trend in the studied projects. Our findings also support the findings of Sadraei et al. who report that the RE process is highly dependent upon the context [3]. Based on the study, type of the solution had an impact upon the RE workload, RE activities needed: tailored software solutions needed detailed RE models, whereas in the projects related to software products, understanding of how products features meet the requirements was considered essential.

The number of available requirements modeling techniques, frameworks and tools is high and it is challenging to select the most suitable technique for the project context. Based on our study, requirements modeling should cover different aspects: strategic development goals, business processes, service design, functionality, information and data, system integrations and IT infrastructure. Typically, several modelling techniques, tools and extensive modelling skills were needed to model requirements for procurement. One of the open questions is *how to support needs of the customer organization in requirements modeling?*

Centrality of architecture has been identified as a current RE trend [4] and modelling system environment and architecture have been identified as significant RE practices for outsourced projects [18]. Our findings also indicate that both enterprise and solution architectures are important in the context of RE processes.

6   Threats to Validity

Threats to validity were analyzed based on the framework by Runeson et al. [27]. The first author of the paper is an employee of the case study organization, which is both a strength and a possible threat to validity of the results. Based on the practical experience of the case study organization's RE process and projects, the author has background information to deeply understand the research context. Also, interviewees were comfortable and motivated to discuss challenges as results were also used in the case study organization's RE process development and the researcher had access to all necessary project documentation. As a threat, the researcher's own experience may have affected the interpretation of the results. To improve reliability of the results and avoid biased interpretation, we used investigator triangulation. Two external researchers participated in the case study planning and the analysis of the results. To avoid construct validity threats, we organized validation workshops where the practitioners of the case study company reviewed the findings iteratively.

As an external validity threat, the results of a single organization may not be generalized as such to other customer organizations. To validate the results further, studies of RE challenges in other customer organizations would be beneficial. However, similar kind of organization structures, processes and sourcing models are used by other organizations in the banking and insurance sector as well as in many public sector organizations, and thus, the challenges and further research topics identified may be relevant for a large number of organizations. The identified demands for RE process development may bring useful viewpoints for RE process developers and practitioners participating in IT development projects. In addition, the findings may be useful for supplier organizations to understand better customers' challenges and to improve cooperation in the RE process.

7   Conclusions

Our case study suggests that the development of the customer organization's RE process in the outsourced environment is both critical and challenging. We identified 42 challenges that bring demands to the RE process. It is very important that the RE process supports a company's development processes such as procurement, software project management and business process development. The RE process should also satisfy demands that come from the IT environment and enterprise architecture. In the customer organization, the focus is more on the strategic business goals, business process development and stakeholder needs, and IT is one of the tools to develop business. The RE process documentation and good RE practices must be understandable for business personnel without extensive RE training and skills.

The RE process must also be flexible. The sourcing model and the type of the solution have a significant impact on how requirements work is done in projects. Close cooperation with suppliers is also a vital part of the distributed RE process. Requirements evolve iteratively during collaboration. Therefore, requirements should be actively managed with the supplier throughout requirements definition, procurement and implementation of projects.

This paper is both an experience report from a case study organization and a problem statement of the RE challenges that a customer organization can have in the outsourced environment. We hope that the results of this case study serve as an inspiration for other RE researchers who are interested in solving complex challenges. We also hope that the results are useful to other customer organizations and software suppliers. In the future, we will focus on two research questions. Firstly, we will investigate how to combine business and IT development in the RE process. Secondly, we will study more closely the distribution of the RE process between the customer and supplier in the outsourced environment.

References

1. McKincey&Company, Business technology office, Delivering large-scale IT projects on time, on budget, and on value (2012)
2. Hofmann, H.F., Lehner, F.: Requirements Engineering as a Success Factor in Software Projects. IEEE Software 18(4), 58–66 (2001)
3. Sadraei, E., Aurum, A., Ghassan, B.: A field study of the requirements engineering practice in Australian sofware industry. Requirements Engineering 12(3), 145–162 (2007)
4. Hansen, S., Berente, N., Lyytinen, K.: Requirements in the 21st century: current practice and emerging trends. In: Lyytinen, K., Loucopoulos, P., Mylopoulos, J., Robinson, B. (eds.) Design Requirements Engineering. LNBIP, vol. 14, pp. 44–87. Springer, Heidelberg (2009)
5. Bhat, J.M., Gupta, M., Murt, S.N.: Overcoming requirements engineering challenges: Lessons from offshore outsourcing. IEEE Software 23(5), 38–44 (2006)
6. Verner, J., Cox, K., Bleistein, S., Cerpa, N.: Requirements engineering and software project success: an industrial survey in Australia and the U.S. Australian Journal of Information Systems 13(1), 225–238 (2005)
7. Verner, J.M., Abdullah, L.M.: Exploratory case study research: Outsourced project failure. Information and Software Technology 54(8), 866–886 (2012)
8. Abdullah, L.M., Verner, J.M.: Outsourced strategic IT systems development risk. In: Third International Conference on Research Challenges in Information Science, pp. 275–286 (2009)
9. IEEE, Std 1362™ - IEEE Guide for Information Technology—System Definition Concept of Operations (ConOps) Document, (R2007) (1998)
10. Wiegers, K.E.: Software Requirements. Microsoft Press, Redmond (2003)
11. IEEE/EIA, 12207.0-1996 Standard for Information Technology - Software life cycle processes (1998)
12. Cao, L., Ramesh, B.: Agile Requirements Engineering Practices: An Empirical Study. IEEE Software 25(1), 60–67 (2008)
13. Houdek, F., Pohl, K.: Analyzing requirements engineering processes: a case study. In: Proceedings of 11th International Conference on Database and Expert Systems Applications (2000)
14. Herbsleb, J.D., Paulish, D.J., Bass, M.: Global software development at siemens: experience from nine projects. In: Proceedings of 27th International Conference on Software Engineering (2005)

15. Kauppinen, M., Vartiainen, M., Kontio, J., Kujala, S., Sulonen, R.: Implementing requirements engineering processes throughout organizations: success factors and challenges. Information and Software Technology **44**(14), 937–953 (2004)
16. Kauppinen, M.: Introducing Requirements Engineering Into Product Development: Towards Systematic User Requirements Definition, Doctoral Thesis, Helsinki University of Technology, Espoo (2005)
17. Hull, E., Jackson, K., Dick, J.: Requirements Engineering. Springer, London (2011)
18. Iqbal, I., Ahmad, J., Nizam, R., Nasir, M.H., Noor, M.A.: Significant Requirements Engineering Practices for Softwre Development Outsourcing. In: IEEE Australian Conference of Sofware Engineering, pp. 132–144 (2013)
19. Sabherwal, R.: The evolution of coordination in outsourced software development projects: a comparison of client and vendor perspectives. Information and Organization **13**(3), 153–202 (2003)
20. Hiisilä, H., Kauppinen, M., Kujala, S.: Interview guide and report. http://cse.aalto.fi/en/research/empirical_software_engineering/product_requirements/publications/publication_attachments/refsq15_interview_guide/(2014)
21. Lazar, J., Feng, J., Hochheiser, H.: Research methods in human-computer interaction. Wiley, Chichester (2010)
22. Koehler, J., Hauser, R., Küster, J., Ryndina, K., Vanhatalo, J., Wahler, M.: The Role of Visual Modeling and Model Transformations in Business-driven Development. Electronic Notes in Theoretical Computer Science **211**, 5–15 (2008)
23. Ojasalo, J.: Contrasting theoretical grounds of business process modeling and service blueprinting. In: Global Conference of Business and Finance Proceedings, pp. 410–420 (2012)
24. Ullah, A., Lai, R.: Modeling business goal for business/IT alignment using requirements engineering. Journal of Computer Information Systems **51**(3), 21–28 (2011)
25. van Lamsweerde, A.: Goal-oriented requirements enginering: a roundtrip from research to practice. In: Proceedings of the 12th IEEE Joint International Requirements Engineering Conference (RE 2004), pp. 4-7, Kyoto (2004)
26. Tiwana, A.: Beyond the black box: knowledge overlaps in software outsourcing. IEEE Software **21**(5), 51–59 (2004)
27. Runeson, P., Host, M., Rainer, A., Regnell, B.: Case study research in software engineering: Guidelines and examples. John Wiley & Sons (2012)

A Case Study Evaluation
of the Guideline-Supported QUPER Model
for Elicitation of Quality Requirements

Richard Berntsson Svensson[1]([✉]) and Björn Regnell[2]

[1] Department of Computer Science and Engineering,
Chalmers | University of Gothenburg, Gothenburg, Sweden
richard@cse.gu.se
[2] Department of Computer Science, Lund University, Lund, Sweden
bjorn.regnell@cs.lth.se

Abstract. [**Context & motivation**] For market-driven software product developing organizations operating on a competitive open market, it is important to plan the product's releases so that they can reach the market as early as possible with a competitive level of quality compared to its competitors' products. Hence, quality requirements can be seen as a key competitive advantage. The QUPER model was developed with the aim to support high-level decision-making in release planning of quality requirements. [**Question/problem**] As a follow up on previous studies on QUPER, this study investigates: What are practitioners' views on the utilities of QUPER extended with guidelines including domain-specific examples? [**Principal ideas/results**] In the presented case study, a set of detailed guidelines of how to apply QUPER in practice, including how to handle cost dependencies between quality requirements, was evaluated at a case company in the mobile handset domain with 24 professionals using real quality requirements. [**Contribution**] The results point to the importance of having concrete guidelines combined with instructive examples from real practice, while it is not always obvious for a practitioner to transfer cost-dependency examples into the domains that are different from the example domain. The transferability of guidelines and examples to support methodology adoption is an interesting issue for further research.

Keywords: Software engineering · Requirements engineering · Release planning · QUPER · Quality requirements · Empirical case study

1 Introduction

In market-driven software product development, humans make decisions based on both explicitly and implicitly known objects and constraints. Any computational technique, in isolation, is unlikely to provide meaningful results since only a small part of the reality can be captured in these techniques [20]. Release planning, the process of deciding which features and quality level should be

© Springer International Publishing Switzerland 2015
S.A. Fricker and K. Schneider (Eds.): REFSQ 2015, LNCS 9013, pp. 230–246, 2015.
DOI: 10.1007/978-3-319-16101-3_15

included in which release [3], which is both a cognitively and computationally difficult problem [20], is classified as a wicked problem [9] since different kinds of uncertainty make it difficult to formulate and solve the problem. Moreover, the objective of release planning is to 'maximize the benefit'; however, the difficulty lies in how to give a measurable definition of 'benefit' [20].

An especially challenging problem for organizations developing software-intensive incremental products offered to a market is to set the right quality target in relation to future market demands and competitor products. When is the quality level good enough? When is the quality level a competitive advantage? Several methods and approaches supporting strategic release planning are reported in the literature. For example, Release Planning Prototype [10] and EVOLVE [15]. These techniques use generic algorithms to resolve the release planning issue. Using generic algorithms may not be worthwhile if the input data to the process is highly uncertain.

To the best of our knowledge, only few studies have looked into strategic release planning of quality requirements (QR), despite their importance for market success [4], [16]. According to the survey by Svahberg et al. [32], only two strategic release planning methods address quality constraints: The quantitative Win-Win model [28] addresses effort and time constraints, but not the quality level of QR, while the only method to address quality and cost constraints of QR is the QUPER model [32].

This paper is based upon previous work published in [6], [8], [22], [24] where different aspects of the QUPER model were introduced. This paper adds the following contribution to our previous investigations of QUPER, (1) the detailed practical guidelines of how to apply QUPER in practice, with an illustration of a QR, (2) the added step of how to incorporate cost dependencies between QR., and (3) Two new evaluations of the complete version of the QUPER model with 11 professionals in the first evaluation and 13 professionals in the second evaluation at a case company to evaluate QUPER's applicability using the detailed guidelines with real QR.

The remainder of this paper is organized as follows. Section 2 offers an overview of related work, while background and motivation are presented in Section 3. Section 4 offers an introduction and exemplification of the QUPER model. Section 5 presents how QUPER was evaluated at the case company, and lessons learned are discussed in Section 6. Limitations of the study are discussed in Section 7, while Section 8 gives a summary of the main conclusions.

2 Related Work

There are several release planning methods in the literature, varying from informal approaches such as planning games in agile development [11] to more rigorous and formal methods as described in [15], [29], [31]. Svahnberg et al. identified 24 methods for strategic release planning, where 10 methods are extensions of others, thus 14 original methods were identified [32]. Of the 24 identified methods, 16 are related to the EVOLVE-family [15], [19], [29]. In addition to the

EVOLVE-family, other release planning methods include, e.g. software product release planning through optimization and what-if analysis [2], combining optimized value and cost with requirements interdependencies [9], and an approach using linear programming [1].

In Saliu and Ruhe [31], seven different release planning methods using algorithms are compared and evaluated. The evaluated methods are: estimation-based management framework for enhancive maintenance, incremental funding method, cost-value approach for prioritizing requirements, optimizing value and cost in requirements analysis, the next release problem, planning software evolution with risk management, and EVOLVE*. The main difference between the methods is in how many properties that are considered. In addition, three main deficits in the evaluated methods were discovered: (1) no major focus on system constraints, (2) not enough decision support tools that are fully developed (except for Release-Planner, which is a tool based on the overall architecture of EVOLVE*), and (3) largely focused on 'fixed release intervals'.

In 'traditional' release planning, FR are favored, while quality aspects, such as performance and reliability, are missing in related products [27]. One approach to include quality aspects in release planning is to use EVOLVE II to generate alternatives for cost devoted to functional versus quality requirements [27]. For example, one alternative devotes 100% of the resources to functionality, while a second alternative devotes 90% to functionality and 10% to quality. Although this approach includes the cost for QR in release planning, what level of quality the next release should have on a continuous quality scale for specific quality aspects is not considered. It may be possible to combine QUPER with EVOLVE II by using QUPER to decide the needed level of quality and then use this as an input to EVOLVE II for resource allocation. However, such combinations are out of scope of this study and may be objects of further studies.

Software quality is not only defined by the relevant perspectives, but also by the context in which it exists [17]. For example, just as each line of cars has a target market, software quality must be planned to allow a development company to meet its business objectives. Less than perfect software quality may be ideal [33], but deciding what is good enough can only be decided in a given business context [17]. Thus, the tough question to answer is 'when is the quality level good enough'? This question is one of the motives behind the development of QUPER, and the study of its applicability in a real-world context with domain-specific examples to illustrate guidelines.

3   Background and Motivation

The development of QUPER was prompted by the faced challenges of rapid technology development in combination with increasing market demands on expanding product portfolios targeting a wide scope of different capabilities and price ranges in the mobile device industry [25]. Moving towards rapidly changing market requirements and environmental regulations has urged dramatic changes in software companies for future economic survival. Moreover, global competition forces companies to become more competitive and responsive to consumers and market developments, and creating value for software companies is more important than ever before.

The need for a supporting model for handling and working with QR in this context was explicitly identified during an investigation of the cross-company requirements engineering (RE) process between two case companies [25]. Furthermore, the companies explicitly stated the importance of having a handle on QR, which has been confirmed by Berntsson Svensson et al. [5].

Two main factors motivated the creation and evolvement of QUPER: (1) a direct need identified in industry and (2) a suitable model was not found in the literature, i.e. a model for supporting release planning of QR (see Section 2).

Regarding the industry need, there was an expressed interest from the two cross-companies to improve the way of working with QR towards the needs of the market. The actual need for this type of model has become even more apparent after the initial development of QUPER. A different organization in a different domain than the mobile handset showed an interest in applying QUPER to their organization [8], due to which they experienced similar challenges as the two cross-companies.

Looking at the state of art, there is research being conducted in the area of release planning in a market-driven development situation. Although there is an identified need in industry to support QR in release planning, and it is important to have a handle on QR [5], there is a lack of an appropriate model. Offering support for release planning of QR prompted the effort to develop QUPER in a generic way for organizations faced with certain issues, rather than tailoring the model towards on organization.

4   QUPER Guidelines with Examples

This section describes the guideline-supported QUPER model for elicitation of QR. The main new contribution of this paper is the practical guidelines (see Steps 1-7 below) with an illustration of a QR when applying QUPER in practice. Moreover, the detailed guidelines include an added step of how to identify cost dependencies between QR (see Step 7 below). For a more detailed description of the QUPER model, see e.g. [24], [22]. An overview of the detailed guidelines are described in the following sub-sections, while a more detailed and complete description of the guidelines are available in [21].

The reason for adding the cost dependency step is because dependencies may have a major impact on the estimated cost for other QR. The cost to improve the quality level for one QR may imply an improved level of quality for other QR. This may lead to a change of other QR cost barriers and which QR to select for the coming release. Therefore, it is important incorporate a cost dependency step in the QUPER model.

Step 1 - Identify candidate QR. When defining QR, it is important to consider relevant features, market segment, competitor, and hardware platform capability. Once such feature has been identified, the consequences for the particular QR should be consider, for example:

- Different mobile phones offered to different market segments may have different requirements on image quality
- A competitor may recently have released a mobile phone with better gaming performance changing the perception of gaming quality
- Today's hardware is not the same as tomorrows, features may run much faster
- Users' evolving expectations, expects better performance in the latest mobile phones

    If several QR have been identified, it may not be useful to apply QUPER's steps on all of them. Quality requirements where QUPER may not be relevant include, for example:

- Quality requirements that refers to a certain standard
- Quality requirements where a certain level of quality is always the same, e.g. in mobile TV where 28 frames per second is standard

Step 2 - Define scale and unit. For the selected QR, define a scale and a measurement unit that can be used to express the level of quality of QR. A scale can for example be *"time"* and the measurement unit can be *"minutes"*.

Step 3 - Identify reference levels. For each QR, it is useful to identify reference levels based on actual products. Reference levels can be based on competing as well as own products (Qref). Estimates can be given in three forms, depending on how the potential uncertainty in the estimates should be captured:

- Point estimates including a single figure, e.g. 3 minutes
- Interval estimates including a [min, max] interval, e.g. 3-4 minutes
- Triangle distribution estimates including a three-tuple of [low bund, most probable, high bound] figures that show the estimated probability distribution, e.g. low: 3 minutes, high: 5 minutes, probable 4 minutes.

    The reference levels further calibrate the estimates and provide objective measures to relate the QR to. Figure 1 illustrates added reference levels for the QR *Time shift buffer size.*

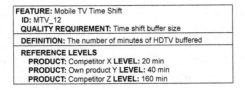

Fig. 1. Illustration of added reference levels

Step 4 - Elicit quality breakpoints. When all reference levels have been identified, for each QR, *the market expectations* should be defined in terms of the values of quality breakpoints. First, determine the utility breakpoint, which is the lowest acceptable value *on the market* for a given segment.

    How to judge what is lowest acceptable value:

- Is it possible to sell this feature at this quality? If not, then below utility
- Will this quality generate a too high return rate? If yes, then below utility

Then, determine the saturation breakpoint, representing quality levels that are clearly considered excessive *by the market*.

How to judge what is excessive quality:
- Over this breakpoint will not sell any more products
- Over this breakpoint will not give any market advantages
- Will enhance the user experience

Finally, the differentiation breakpoint somewhere between utility and saturation is determined. Values above this quality level gives market advantage compared to the current products of your competitors.

How to judge differentiation quality:
- The quality will be better than competitors
- The quality can be used in marketing the product

Similar to step 3 (Identify reference levels), estimates can be given in three forms; however, point estimates are the preferred form (see Step 3 for more details).

Figure 2 shows the identified quality breakpoints for *Time shift buffer size*.

FEATURE: Mobile TV Time Shift **ID**: MTV_12 **QUALITY REQUIREMENT**: Time shift buffer size
DEFINITION: The number of minutes of HDTV buffered
REFERENCE LEVELS **PRODUCT**: Competitor X **LEVEL**: 20 min **PRODUCT**: Own product Y **LEVEL**: 40 min **PRODUCT**: Competitor Z **LEVEL**: 160 min
QUALITY BREAKPOINTS **UTILITY**: 15 min **RATIONALE**: all products are able **SATURATION**: 200 min **RATIONALE**: films are shorter **DIFFERENTIATION**: 50 min **RATIONALE**: high price point

Fig. 2. An illustration of quality breakpoints have been defined

Step 5 - Estimate cost barriers. When market expectations have been identified, for each QR, estimate the cost in terms of the values of cost barriers (CB). To identify the CB, practitioners with good domain and architectural knowledge may be needed. If possible, identify similar quality requirements' CB from previous projects and use as input. Although it is possible to identify and estimate one, two, or several CB for each QR, the recommended number of CB is two. The first CB is mainly related to software changes, while a second CB is mainly related to new hardware components, or affects the entire software architecture.

First, estimate the first CB in terms of cost (C1) and at what quality level (Q1) where an increase in quality has a high cost penalty.

How to identify the first cost barrier:
- Q1: May relate to software changes, for example, requires a change in one or a few parts of the architecture, extensive optimization of code, or a major re-work of the code
- Q1: May only affect your own and/or closely related projects' code/architecture
- C1: Represents the cost penalty of raising the quality level from the current quality level (Qref) to Q1

Then, estimate the second CB in terms of cost (C2) and at what quality level (Q2) where an increase in quality has a high cost penalty.

How to identify the second cost barrier:
- Q2: May affect major (if not all) parts of the entire products' architecture
- Q2: The hardware's physical constraints may be used as Q2
- Q2: May require major infrastructure (e.g. code optimization) changes in several projects
- C2: Represents the cost penalty given that the C1 investment has been made, when raising the quality from Q1 to Q2

In Figure 3, cost barriers have been identified for *Time shift buffer size.*

Step 6 - Set candidate requirements. Now, make estimations, propose candidate requirements, discuss and decide actual requirements for coming releases, where estimates can be given in three forms (see Step 3). One way to specify a requirements quality interval is by using both a *Good* and a *Stretch* target. The actual QR is the interval that is specified by the two *targets*. It is possible to define the requirement interval in the following ways:
- With both a Good target and a Stretch target
- With *only* a Stretch target, which means the highest value is specified
- With *only* a Good target, which means the lowest accepted value is specified

Figure 4 shows the identified target, as an interval using *Good* and *Stretch*, for *Time shift buffer size.*

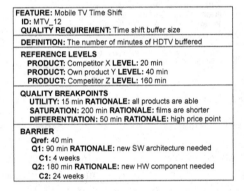

Fig. 3. Illustration of feature with cost barriers

Step 7 - Identify cost dependencies. If cost dependencies among QR are considered important to identify for cost estimations, then, for each top-n QR, identify which modules (architectural components/parts) that needs to be changed if that QR is to be improved beyond the "next" breakpoint (either utility or differentiation depending on its current position).

How to identify potential dependencies:
- If two (or more) QR affect the same architectural part(s), they may be dependent on each other.
- Identify dependencies by already existing dependency tools/models, e.g. by a traceability tool or a Feature Dependency Model.

When potential cost dependencies among the top-n QR have been identified, for each top-n QR: (1) list which other top-n QR that are easier/cheaper to

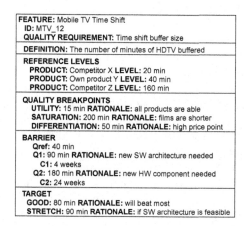

Fig. 4. Illustration of feature with targets

improve if this QR is improved, and (2) list which other top-n QR that are more difficult/expensive to improve if this QR is improved.

Then, an expert subjectively (based on experience and "gut feeling") select m QR (e.g. the ones that will be implemented, the most important QR to improve the level quality) that is a subset of the top-n QR ($m \leq n$) and set a quality level target for each of these m QR that seem to provide a reasonable cost increase.

Then, for this set of m QR; make an effort estimation in weeks or months informed by the above, by first making individual effort estimates of each m QR given that all of the targets are implemented by subjectively taking into account the "synergies" and the "counter working" in step 5, and the sum all up to a complete effort for the m QR.

Finally, if the total effort is too high or too low compared to available resources then change the subset in a "smart way" (this new candidate set is derived subjectively based on "gut feeling" and the experience of the expert) to arrive at another "better" effort estimate.

5   QUPER Case Study Evaluation

This section describes the evaluation methodology of QUPER as it was evaluated in industry with a case company. The evaluation is guided by this research question:

RQ: What are practitioners' views on the utilities of QUPER extended with guidelines including domain-specific examples?

5.1   Case Company Description

The development of the detailed practical guidelines of how to apply QUPER in practice in this paper was developed and evaluated at a large company operating in a market-driven RE context using a product line approach. The company has about 5,000 employees and develops embedded systems for a global market. A typical project has around 60-80 newly added features, from which 700-1000 system requirements are produced. The company has a very large and complex requirements legacy database with requirements at different abstraction levels in orders of 20,000 requirements, which makes it an example of a very large-scale RE context [23]. About 25% of the system and legacy requirements are QR, i.e. either 'pure' QR [7] or a requirement that has both functional and quality aspects mixed [7]. A typical project at this company lasts for about 2 years and is implemented by 20-25 teams with about 40-80 developers per team.

5.2   Evaluation Methodology

Two evaluations of the complete QUPER model was carried out using a qualitative research approach, namely in-depth semi-structured interviews [26] and self-administrated questionnaires [13], [26]. Each of the two evaluations are described in detail below.

First evaluation *Planning/Selection:* The first step was to plan the study and how to evaluate the QUPER model at the case company. The interview instrument (see Table 1) was design with inspiration from [8], while the self-administrated questionnaire (see Table 2) was inspired by [6]. The self-administrated questionnaire used a seven-point Likert scale, representing levels of agreement from 'strongly disagree' to 'strongly agree'. When conducting research using self-administrated questionnaires, it is possible to test the internal consistency [12] (a type of reliability) and the shared variance through, e.g. a factor analysis [14]. However, these tests are dependent on how many responses obtained per item (over-determination of factors). In this case we have a very low variable/factor ratio (only 24 responses for 11 factors), therefore we believe that such an analysis is not feasible in this case[12], [18]

To test the interview instrument and the questionnaire, two pilot interviews were conducted to improve the instruments prior to the industry evaluation. The two pilot studies led to improved wording of a number of questions, one question was removed due to that it would give the same answer as another question, and two questions were completely rewritten in accordance to feedback.

The selection of practitioners for participating in the first evaluation was conducted in cooperation with two managers at the case company. The two managers identified the subjects that he/she thought were the most suitable and representative of the company to participate in this study. That is, the researchers did not influence the selection of subjects, nor did the researchers have any personal relationship to the subjects. Eleven practitioners, representing different roles and areas were chosen. The roles chosen are: 4 product managers, 2 project managers, 1 software architect, 1 test manager, 1 head of software quality, and 2 senior software engineers.

Table 1. The Interview Instrument

Questions about the QUPER model
What is your general view of using QUPER?
What was helpful compared to the previous way of working?
Was it easier to coordinate the decision process?
What were the challenges in applying QUPER
Do you think the estimates (targets) will be more accurate with QUPER?
Can the use of QUPER improve the decision-making process?
Final question
Is there anything else you would like to add that we have not mentioned

Table 2. The Questionnaire

Q	Do you agree that...?
Q1	QUPER is easy to understand
Q2	QUPER's guidelines work in an industrial setting
Q3	QUPER improves the understanding of needed level of quality
Q4	QUPER improves the understanding of QR
Q5	QUPER improves the decision-making process, e.g. release planning, of QR
Q6	QUPER's benefit view is helpful when specifying QR
Q7	It is difficult to identify the breakpoints
Q8	QUPER's cost view is helpful when specifying QR
Q9	It is difficult to identify the cost barriers
Q10	QUPER's roadmap view is helpful when specifying QR
Q11	Applying QUPER takes too much time to be useful

Applying QUPER in practice: The second step involved applying the QUPER model in practice. The practitioners received the detailed practical guidelines to follow the steps using real QR from their projects. The variation of how many QR each practitioner applied QUEPR's steps to range from a few QR up to 20 (the actual QR are not revealed for confidentiality reasons). The main goal of the second step was to achieve an understanding of the detailed practical guidelines usefulness and applicability in an industrial environment.

Data collection: The third step was carried out using semi-structured interviews [26] in the offices of the practitioners and lasted between 40 and 60 minutes each. During the interviews, the purpose of the evaluation was explained. Then, the practitioners answered the self-administered questionnaire, followed by questions (from the interview instrument) about applying the complete QUPER model in practice, which was discussed in detail. We took records in the form of written extensive notes in order to facilitate and improve the analysis process. In addition, the interviewer had the chance to validate the questions with the interviewee lessening changes of misunderstandings. That is, the interviewer went back to the interviewee to validate the interviewers interpretation of the results to minimize misinterpretations and validate the results.

Analysis: The collected data was analyzed using content analysis [26]. The content analysis involved marking and discussing interesting sections of the transcripts. The first author examined the sections individually. The category analysis included examination of the content from different perspectives and a search for explicitly stated or concealed pros and cons in relation to the usefulness and applicability of the model. For the self-administrated questionnaire data given by the subjects, descriptive statistic was performed.

Second evaluation *Planning/Selection:* A second evaluation of the QUPER model was conducted with 13 new practitioners. The researchers contacted a "gate-keeper" at the case company who identified the subjects that he/she thought were the most suitable and representative of the company to participate in this study. The roles chosen are: 6 product managers, 3 project manager, 2 senior software engineers, 1 test manager, and 1 software developer. We continued with the sampling strategy developed in the first evaluation.

Applying QUPER in practice: The second step, similar to the first evaluation, involved applying QUPER in practice. We followed the same structure as in the first evaluation, i.e. the practitioners received detailed practical guidelines of how to use the model. These guidelines were used when applying QUPER to real QR from the practitioners real projects. The number of applied QR varies from 2 to 8 (the actual QR are not revealed for confidentiality reasons).

*Data collection:*The semi-structured interview approach was continued. The interviews varied between 50-65 minutes in length. Extensive written notes were taken in the same manner as in the first evaluation.

*Analysis:*Since we sought after a comprehensive view of the complete data set, the data from the first evaluation was analyzed together with the data from the second evaluation. In the final analysis we used the four categories (Sections 6.1 - 6.4) that emerged in the first evaluation. The extensive notes from the entire data set were analyzed by the first author were interesting quotations were marked with one or more of the four categories. For the analysis, all related note quotations for each category were complied and printed into a readable format. The results from the analysis are found in Section 6.

6   Lesson Learned

Below, lessons learned and the results from the self-administrated questionnaire are discussed. The results from the self-administrated questionnaire are shown in Table 3.

Table 3. Distributions of questionnaire answers

ID	Strongly disagree	Disagree	Slightly disagree	Neutral	Slightly agree	Agree	Strongly agree
Q1	0	0	0	4	7	11	2
Q2	0	0	0	0	3	16	5
Q3	0	0	0	0	6	12	6
Q4	0	0	0	2	11	7	4
Q5	0	0	0	10	0	10	4
Q6	0	0	0	4	9	9	2
Q7	0	4	7	7	2	4	0
Q8	0	0	0	11	2	9	2
Q9	0	0	2	9	5	6	2
Q10	0	0	0	0	0	11	13
Q11	2	12	2	6	2	0	0

6.1 Ease of Use

In general, the practitioners agree that the QUPER model is easy to understand (Q1 in Table 3), that the detailed guidelines work in an industrial environment (Q2), and the model does not take too much time to apply in practice (Q11).

During the interviews, several practitioners explained that the detailed guidelines (Section 4) are very helpful due to easy steps to follow, and in particular the provided examples (see Figures 1-4) for each step. Moreover, the steps in the detailed guidelines have about enough information, not too much or too little to be applicable in industry. Several practitioners stressed another important issue in relation to QUPER's applicability in industry, all steps are not mandatory to use. According the practitioners, if they are "forced" to go through all steps, some people may be too scared to use the model. One practitioner explained further, "a model cannot be too big or too complicated, it must be a 'light model' to be applicable in industry, which QUPER fulfills". In addition, the steps in the detailed guidelines were seen as following a logical order when applied to QR.

Although the practitioners viewed QUPER as easy to use and understand, there were two main concerns about the detailed guidelines. First, a need for more examples, in particular of other QR than performance requirements, e.g., usability requirements. One practitioner asked, how do you specify a usability requirement using the QUPER model when the usability is not related to performance requirements? The second main concern was related to inconsistent usage of the model. The practitioners believed that some people may use the concepts of the QUPER model in different ways, and a special concern was related to that higher quality is sometimes related to higher value, while other times a lower value means higher quality.

6.2   Importance of the Three Views

In Table 3, the results show that the roadmap view is the most important view of the QUPER model (Q10 in Table 3). In addition, the benefit view may be helpful when specifying QR (Q6 in Table 3), while the cost view is the least important (Q8) of the three views. One explanation of why the roadmap view is seen as the most important view was discovered during the interviews. The information from both the benefit and cost view is visualized in the roadmap view. Hence, the other views are not seen as important.

In Table 3, the results show that the identification of breakpoints in the benefit view is viewed as neither difficult, nor easy (Q7). The reason may be explained by the different approaches of identifying the breakpoints. During the interviews, four different approaches of how to identify the breakpoints were discovered: (1) using their own subjective estimate, i.e., the practitioner has an understanding, based on his/her experience and "gut feeling", of the estimates for the breakpoints, (2) to perform several new tests of the competitors' products level of quality, and use these values as input when estimating the breakpoints, (3) if these tests (as described above) have all ready been performed, it is easy to access a database with this information, and (4) to use advanced and extensive market analysis techniques to identify the breakpoints.

The cost view was viewed as the least important among the three views, which is related to the perceived difficulties on estimating the cost of requirements according to the practitioners. Several practitioners explained that cost estimation, in general, is always difficult regardless if it is for FR or for QR. The difficulties lie in the ability to estimate the cost and map that cost to a real value, i.e., not only using cost estimations for resources planning, but actually estimate the actual cost of implementing QR. This may explain why the practitioners viewed it slightly difficult to estimate the cost barriers (Q9 in Table 3). In addition, one practitioner explained, to estimate a cost barrier, an extensive estimation analysis work may be needed, which will be time consuming and therefore not useable in practice.

6.3   Applicability of the Cost Dependency Step

The cost dependency step in the QUPER model (see Section 4), was viewed as easy to follow, and at the same time detailed enough to be useful in practice. The detailed guidelines provided the practitioners with a good enough understanding of potential dependencies between QR. According to several practitioners, the detailed guidelines for the cost dependency step are similar to their approach of dealing with dependencies between features. However, one practitioner believed that this step might be difficult to follow and apply for some practitioners.

6.4   Supporting Release Planning

In general, all practitioners agreed that QUPER improves the understanding of QR (Q3 in Table 3), and that the model would improve the decision-making process in, e.g., release planning of QR (Q5 in Table 3). In addition, the roadmap view is seen as the central part of the improvement in the decision-making process (Q10 in Table 3).

During the interviews, the practitioners explained the importance of the roadmap view. The roadmap view provides the decision-makers with an overview, which is a good basis for discussions of which quality level to aim for in the coming releases. One practitioner further explained, it is easier to understand the thought behind, and the need for a certain level of quality when it is presented on the roadmap view since it is related to the market and the competitors.

The importance of relating the needed level of quality to the market and the competitors was expressed by several of the interviewed practitioners. One practitioner explained, "the relation to the market and our competitors is very important for our 'selling features' since we will have a better understanding if we are market leaders or not". Furthermore, the decisions about the needed level of quality will have a better substance compared to just presenting a metric of the quality level. In addition to the decision-making process, the practitioners believe that the QUPER model could improve the communication between the people. For example, the concepts of QUPER provide them with a "common language" that everybody (that has used QUPER) understands and make sure they are talking about the same things.

Although this first evaluation of the complete QUPER model shows promising results, the practitioners had a few concerns. First, there may be difficulties to convince others at the case company to use the model. It is easier to just decide the level of quality out of the blue instead of learning a new model and follow a set of guidelines. Some of the practitioners suggested to have a workshop to teach the QUPER model to the employees of the case company where a "QUPER expert" should be present at the first time. Second, according to one practitioner, it is important to choose the right QR to apply QUPER. The QUPER model cannot be applied to all QR, e.g., certain QR must have a specific level of quality to fulfill a certificate or a standard. Third, as several practitioners stated, to fully understand and evaluate the improvements of the decision-making process, the QUPER model should be used in a project from the start of a project until the product is launched to the market.

7   Limitations

Threats to validity are outlined and discussed based on the classification by Runeson et al. [30].

One threat is related to the selection process of subjects for interviews (construct validity). Selection bias is always present when subjects are not fully randomly sampled. A possible bias may be that only subjects that have a positive attitude towards QR and the QUPER model are selected. However, the subjects were selected based on their role and experience of using QUPER by a "gate-keeper" at the case company. Moreover, the use of very enthusiastic or skeptical subjects could be a threat. In this study, several of the subjects have been involved during the entire, or part of the evolvement of the QUPER model. Hence, they may have a positive attitude towards the model from the beginning. To minimize this threat, several subjects that had not been part of the evolvement of the model were included in the sample size. In addition, the presence of a researcher may influence the behavior of the subjects, more specifically, subjects being afraid of being evaluated. This threat was alleviated by the guarantee of anonymity as too all information divulged during the interviews, and the answers were only to be used by the researchers.

Since this study is of empirical nature, incorrect data (internal validity) is a validity threat. In case of the interviews, taking records in form of written extensive notes assured the correct data. In addition, the researchers had the chance to validate the questions and answers with the subjects lessening the chances of misunderstandings. The reliability of the study relates to whether the same outcome could be expected with another set of researchers. To increase the reliability of this study, a systematic and documented researcher process has been applied where a trace of evidence has been retained for each analysis step. The traceability back to each source of evidence is documented.

The ability to generalize the results beyond the actual study (external validity) is a threat to validity. Although the case company is large and develops technically complex embedded systems, it cannot be taken as a representative for all types of large companies developing embedded systems. Hence, the results should be interpreted with some caution. However, some of the problems introduced as motivation behind the conception of QUPER, to some extent could be general for organization faced with developing embedded products for a market. In addition, from a perspective of the concepts and practical application of QUPER as described in this paper can give an overview of the challenges facing the companies where QUPER has been implemented.

8   Conclusions

This paper presents the first complete version of the QUPER model, including the detailed guidelines of how to apply QUPER in practice. As part of QUPER's development, evolvement, and refinement, parts of the model has been validated in a series of steps in prior industry validation [6], [8], [22], [24]. During these prior validations, QUPER has matured, and improvements have been made. In this paper, the complete version of QUPER was evaluated in industry at one case company with 24 industry professionals using real QR.

The results point to the importance of having concrete guidelines combined with instructive examples from real practice, while it is not always obvious for a practitioner to transfer cost-dependency examples into the domains that are different from the example domain.

Future work includes evaluations in industry in different domains where the long-term effects of using QUPER need to be investigated to fully validate its feasibility and scalability. Furthermore, to replicate this empirical study in the same domain, but in different companies to compare the usefulness and applicability of the QUPER model is an interesting future work. Moreover, the transferability of guidelines and examples to support methodology adoption, and the use of analogy-based estimations are interesting issues for further research.

References

1. van den Akker, M., Brinkkemper, S., Diepen, G., Versendaal, J.: Determination of the next release of a software product: an approach using integer linear programming. In: Proc. of the 11th International Workshop on Requirements Engineering Foundation for Software Quality, pp. 119–124 (2005)
2. van den Akker, M., Brinkkemper, S., Diepen, G., Versendaal, J.: Software Product Release Planning through Optimization and What-if Analysis. Information and Software Technology **50**, 101–111 (2008)
3. Al-Emran, A., Pfahl, D., Ruhe, G.: Decision support for product release planning based on robustness analysis. In: Proc. of the 18th IEEE International Requirements Engineering Conference, pp. 157–166, September-October 2010
4. Barney, S., Aurum, A., Wohlin, C.: A product management challenge: Creating software product value through requirements selection. Journal of Systems Architecture **54**, 576–593 (2008)
5. Berntsson Svensson, R., Gorschek, T., Regnell, B., Torkar, R., Shahrokni, A., Feldt, R.: Quality Requirements in Industrial Practice - an extended interview study at eleven companies. IEEE Transaction on Software Engineering **38**, 935 (2012)
6. Berntsson Svensson, R., Lindberg Parker, P., Regnell, B.: A Prototype tool for QUPER to support release planning of quality equirements. In: Proc. of the 5th International Workshop on Software Product Management (IWSPM 2011), August 2011
7. Berntsson Svensson, R., Olsson, T., Regnell, B.: An investigation of how quality requirements are specified in industrial practice. Information and Software Technology **55**(7), 1224–1236 (2013)
8. Berntsson Svensson, R., Sprockel, Y., Regnell, B., Brinkkemper, S.: Cost and benefit analysis of quality requirements in competitive software product management: A case study. In: Proc. of the 4th International Workshop on Software Product Management, pp. 40–48. IEEE Compt. Soc., September 2010
9. Carlshamre, P.: Release planning in market-driven software product development: Provoking an understanding. Requirements Engineering **7**, 139–151 (2002)
10. Carlshamre, P., Regnell, B.: Requirements lifecycle management and release planning in market-driven requirements engineering. In: Proc. on the 11th International Workshop on Database and Expert Systems Applications, pp. 961–965. IEEE Comput. Soc., September 2000
11. Cockburn, A.: Agile Software Development. Addison-Wesley (2002)
12. Cronbach, L.: Coefficient alpha and the internal structure of tests. Psychometrika **16**(3), 297–334 (1951)
13. Fink, A.: The survey handbook. Sage Publications (2003)
14. Fabrigar, L.R., Wegener, D.T.: Exploratory Factor Analysis. OUP, USA (2012)
15. Greer, D., Ruhe, G.: Software release planning: an evolutionary and iterative approach. Information and Software Technology **46**, 243–253 (2004)
16. Jacobs, S.: Introducing measurable quality requirements: A case study. In: Proc. of the 4th IEEE International Symp. on Requirements Engineering (ISRE 1999), pp. 172–179. IEEE CS Press, June 1999

17. Kitchenham, B., Pfleeger, S.: Software quality: The elusive target. IEEE Software **13**, 12–21 (1996)
18. MacCallum, R.C., Widaman, K.F., Zhang, S., Hong, S.: Sample size in factor analysis. Psychological Method. **4**, 84–99 (1999)
19. Maurice, S., Ruhe, G., Saliu, O., Ngo-The, A.: Decision support for value-based software release planning. In: Biffl, S., Aurum, A., Boehm, B., Erdogan, H., Grunbacher, P. (eds.) Value-Based Software Engineering, pp. 247–261. Springer, Berlin (2006)
20. Ngo-The, A., Ruhe, G.: A systematic approach for solving the wicked problem of software release planning. Soft Computing - A Fusion of Foundations, Methodologies and Applications 12, 95–108 (2008)
21. QUPER model. http://www.quper.org
22. Regnell, B., Berntsson Svensson, R., Olsson, T.: Supporting Roadmapping of Quality Requirements. IEEE Software **25**, 42–47 (2008)
23. Regnell, B., Svensson, R.B., Wnuk, K.: Can we beat the complexity of very large-scale requirements engineering? In: Rolland, C. (ed.) REFSQ 2008. LNCS, vol. 5025, pp. 123–128. Springer, Heidelberg (2008)
24. Regnell, B., Höst, M., Berntsson Svensson, R.: A quality performance model for cost-benefit analysis of non-functional requirements applied to the mobile handset domain. In: Sawyer, P., Heymans, P. (eds.) REFSQ 2007. LNCS, vol. 4542, pp. 277–291. Springer, Heidelberg (2007)
25. Regnell, B., Olsson, H.O., Mossberg, S.: Assessing requirements compliance scenarios in system platform subcontracting. In: Münch, J., Vierimaa, M. (eds.) PROFES 2006. LNCS, vol. 4034, pp. 362–376. Springer, Heidelberg (2006)
26. Robson, C.: Real World Research. Blackwell, Oxford (2002)
27. Ruhe, G.: Product release planning - Methods, Tools and Applications. CRC Press (2010)
28. Ruhe, G., Greer, D.: Quantitative studies in software re-lease planning under risk and resource constraints. In: Proceedings of the International Symposium on Empirical Software Engineering (ISESE), pp. 262–271. IEEE, Los Alamitos (2003)
29. Ruhe, G., Ngo-The, A.: Hybrid Intelligence in Software Release Planning. International Journal of Hybrid Intelligent Systems **1**, 99–110 (2004)
30. Runeson, P., Höst, M., Rainer, A., Regnell, L: Case study research in software engineering - guidelines and examples. Wiley (2012)
31. Saliu, O., Ruhe, G.: Supporting software release planning decisions for evolving systems. In: Proc. of the 29th Annual IEEE/NASA Software Engineering Workshop, pp. 14–26 (2005)
32. Svahnberg, M., Gorschek, T., Feldt, R., Torkar, R., Saleem, S.B.: A systematic review on strategic release planning models. Information and Software Technology **52**, 237–248 (2010)
33. Youdon, E.: When good enough is best. IEEE Software **12**, 79–81 (1995)

Towards Crowd-Based Requirements Engineering

A Research Preview

Eduard C. Groen$^{(\boxtimes)}$, Joerg Doerr, and Sebastian Adam

Fraunhofer Institute for Experimental Software Engineering (Fraunhofer IESE)
Fraunhofer-Platz 1, 67663 Kaiserslautern, Germany
{eduard.groen,joerg.doerr,sebastian.adam}@iese.fraunhofer.de

Abstract. **[Context and motivation]** Stakeholders who are highly distributed form a large, heterogeneous online group, the so-called "crowd". The rise of mobile, social and cloud apps has led to a stark increase in crowd-based settings. **[Question/problem]** Traditional requirements engineering (RE) techniques face scalability issues and require the co-presence of stakeholders and engineers, which cannot be realized in a crowd setting. While different approaches have recently been introduced to partially automate RE in this context, a multi-method approach to (semi-)automate all RE activities is still needed. **[Principal ideas/results]** We propose "Crowd-based Requirements Engineering" as an approach that integrates existing elicitation and analysis techniques and fills existing gaps by introducing new concepts. It collects feedback through direct interactions and social collaboration, and by deploying mining techniques. **[Contribution]** This paper describes the initial state of the art of our approach, and previews our plans for further research.

Keywords: Requirements engineering · Requirements elicitation · Crowdsourcing · Text mining · Data mining

1 Introduction

Offering services and applications online opens the way to a potentially large market, but competition is high in this field. This pressures developers and service providers into continuously exciting their customers with positive interactions and innovations in order to prevent them from switching to competitive solutions. Requirements engineering (RE) plays a pivotal role in mapping and anticipating the stakeholders' needs. However, traditional RE techniques depend on co-presence (i.e., on the analyst(s) and stakeholder(s) gathered at the same time and place) and therefore do not scale well to settings with many distributed stakeholders [1]. As online users are physically distributed, remote RE techniques are required that allow the analyst(s) and the many stakeholders to be active in different places and at different times [2].

Existing techniques in the area of remote RE techniques rely on (semi-)automating aspects of RE (e.g., [2, 3]), but the greatest challenge is to bridge the gaps between them in an integrated approach. We argue in this paper that research has so far focused on particular sub-domains and has not approached this field holistically

© Springer International Publishing Switzerland 2015
S.A. Fricker and K. Schneider (Eds.): REFSQ 2015, LNCS 9013, pp. 247–253, 2015.
DOI: 10.1007/978-3-319-16101-3_16

enough, even though automation has lifted the limits on the quantities of data, or the number of stakeholders these data are collected from. This is why we propose an integrative approach coined "Crowd-based Requirements Engineering"; a semi-automated RE approach for obtaining and analyzing any kind of "user feedback" from a "crowd", with the goal of deriving validated user requirements. The domain of RE should consider the crowd as a pool of current and potential stakeholders wherever customers share or exchange their experience with a particular product and the extent to which it meets their needs, because requirements can be derived from such statements (i.e., user feedback).

However, to elaborate such an approach, a comprehensive taxonomy of user feedback is needed first, as current RE tools for obtaining requirements through remote techniques focus on specific feedback types and typically use just one interaction method [4]. Additionally, because these tools do not gather the various types of user feedback systematically, they potentially overlook relevant data and are prone to fostering selection bias [4]. Thus, only if data are gathered across all dimensions and match the different user preferences regarding feedback will these data be representative of the crowd as a whole.

In order to develop a crowd-based RE platform and overcome known challenges, we first need to get a better understanding of the state of the art and the concepts that are central to this approach. Hence, this paper addresses the following research questions:

- **RQ1.** *Which solutions have been suggested and/or developed to counter the deficits of traditional RE in crowd settings through the use of automation?*
- **RQ2.** *How can user feedback be categorized into relevant dimensions?*

In Section 2, we discuss work related to the key concepts of Crowd-based RE, and we present a brief overview of related work on existing solutions (RQ1) in Section 3. In Section 4, we provide an outline of our research including a first taxonomy of user feedback dimensions (RQ2). Finally, in Section 5, we conclude and describe our next steps.

2   Related Work: Conceptualization

This section considers the key terms underpinning Crowd-based RE. Central to this approach is the crowd, which generates user feedback across multiple dimensions through a wide range of communication channels and media. This user feedback can be obtained through techniques such as crowdsourcing, and analyzed through text mining and data mining, as will be discussed in Section 3.

The concept of a crowd originates from psychological observances of social contagion and other behavioral patterns that occur among large and inherently heterogeneous groups of people who are physically aggregated in an environment [5]. Reciprocal relationships and powerful group behavior develop through a chain reaction, and are propagated through particular triggers [6]. The displayed behavior of an online crowd, where people are explicitly not gathered in one place, is remarkably similar to that of a real crowd, though varying in speed, size and scope [6]. As a result, we define a crowd as "a group of current and/or potential stakeholders, large enough in size to display group behavior, who have a common interest in a particular service".

The user feedback that a crowd provides can be analyzed to derive needs, wishes, ideas, bug reports, and clues about trends in order to anticipate new innovations. As this information is provided by many stakeholders, problems frequently encountered with small sample sizes can be overcome. For example, as stakeholders from different cultures and with different backgrounds will have different attitudes towards a particular subject, this may cancel out the deliberate withholding of information by other stakeholders due to political, social, or emotional reasons [2].

Fundamental research into the characterization of user feedback is scarce, although several works provide important insights. An analysis of feedback behavior in Apple's AppStore [7], among others, revealed that few users write more than one review; that more reviews are written directly following a new release, and that applications with which users build a "relationship" (e.g., social media apps, games) receive considerably more reviews. In [4], four clusters of user types are presented by their attitude towards providing feedback (see Figure 1), differing in such factors as openness towards being asked or reminded to provide feedback; the extent to which privacy outweighs allowing (anonymized) data mining, and whether feedback is provided out of an intrinsic motivation or because of social factors. Finally, user feedback was characterized in [8], while [9] provides a user feedback ontology to clarify the concepts of this domain.

3   Related Work: Tooling

In this section, we discuss existing tools that collect and/or analyze types of user feedback obtained from a crowd. Socially oriented collaboration tools primarily make use of crowdsourcing techniques, collaborative solutions, and participatory design [2]. Crowdsourcing solutions such as CrowdREquire [10] offer a bounty to the crowd member(s) who provide(s) the best requirements specification at the request of a client (i.e., a software developer), while other solutions focus on error detection (denoted "crowdtesting") or usability testing [11], for which A/B testing is often very suitable. According to [2], web-based approaches should be augmented with social network analysis and recommender systems in which stakeholders write, prioritize, and vote for requirements. Examples are presented in [12–14]. Requirements may also be organized and linked automatically, for example based on their semantic similarity [15].

Mobile apps provide a front-end that guides users through a reporting process through which they can provide additional media besides written language, while data analysis takes place on a server (e.g., [16–17]). OpenProposal is a toolbar plug-in through which users can annotate screenshots of desktop software [18].

Text mining tools predominantly focus on analyzing presently available data without actively involving stakeholders, thereby not supporting elicitation directly [2]. Rather, they determine the relevance and importance of a sentence or statement through natural language (NL) algorithms, usually based on app store reviews (e.g., [19–20]). Forum discussions, for example in a bug-tracking system, can be analyzed by calculating the strength of a proposed idea based on the quantity and valence of the responses [21].

Finally, data mining techniques such as usage mining provide support for uncovering 'unknown unknown' requirements [2]. These requirements are not expressed, articulated, or even accessible in the stakeholders' minds, even though they are the most likely to provide innovative and radically new ideas [2]. Usage mining can discover and predict patterns such as typical and deviant workflows, associations, shortcuts, and bottlenecks [22], which might point to the existence of an 'unknown unknown' requirement.

4   Research Outline

Currently existing tools gather statements either through social collaborations, text mining, or data mining, but a systematic practice is still missing [4]. To date, no known tool integrates multiple approaches or caters to the various ways in which different user personality clusters prefer to provide user feedback, thereby potentially excluding groups of stakeholders. Realizing a multi-method solution would greatly expand the amount of data gathered, reduce selection bias, and enable more statistically sound comparisons to be made. This is why in this section, we propose an integrative solution that combines the existing approaches and also covers dimensions so far neglected.

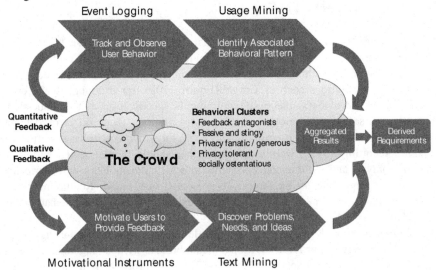

Fig. 1. A tentative model of Crowd-based RE. The behavioral clusters are adapted from [4].

Figure 1 shows how our proposed model processes user feedback by data type. Quantitative feedback (upper process chain) is tracked and observed by logging events, and analysis patterns subsequently select and sort the data. For qualitative feedback (lower process chain), users have either already provided feedback, or need to be motivated to do so through interactions and incentives. Relevant statements are filtered and analyzed through NL analysis. Some data can be analyzed through both processes, for example by both identifying (quantitative) patterns in a video and processing the (qualitative) transcript of the audio recording or an observer's notes. The results of the two processes can be aggregated and validated to obtain requirements.

In order to develop suitable analysis methods to take all types of crowd members into account, and to understand in which ways they prefer to provide user feedback, we have so far identified five feedback dimensions from the literature (see Table 1). The "mode" dimension is similar to the "communication" of feedback described in [8]. The "awareness" dimension uses different terms than the "explicit" and "passive" types of feedback presented in [4, 8] due to possible confusion over the different applications of the word "explicit", and because a stakeholder can never be passive when generating feedback. These types of feedback are covered by combinations of our dimensions.

Existing tools either ask users to provide (targeted, qualitative) feedback, crawl presently available (non-targeted, qualitative) feedback, or collect usage data (non-targeted, quantitative feedback), which means that many other configurations of the user feedback dimensions are not being covered at this point, which our approach aims to resolve. Statements containing tacit requirements (e.g., "This is a crap app" [19]), which are often considered non-informative, are inherently relevant to our approach. As the author of such a statement was sufficiently (dis)satisfied to make the effort of providing feedback, requesting further clarification would yield targeted feedback. By logging the source of a statement, dimensions such as online or offline feedback, or the type of stakeholder who provided the feedback, can be implicitly captured by our dimensions.

Table 1. Taxonomy of user feedback dimensions

Dimension	Type	Description
Awareness	Targeted	Intentionally provided to improve the product or with a reasonable expectancy it will be used for that purpose
	Non-targeted	Relevant information without such intention or expectancy
	Tacit	Too unclear to understand what it refers to
Mode	Direct	Provided in an interaction with the developer as addressee
	Indirect	Left at or communicated through another medium
Data Type	Qualitative	Natural language expressions (including transcripts)
	Quantitative	Statistically analyzable as well as quantifiable data
Intention	Rating	With a particular valence
	Justifying	Explaining why the user has a particular opinion
	Demanding	Clearly verbalizing a need
Homogeneity	Public crowd	Expressed in an open setting
	Private crowd	Expressed in a closed group

5   Conclusion and Next Steps

In this paper, we have proposed Crowd-based Requirements Engineering, our umbrella term for all automated RE techniques, including crowdsourcing, text mining, and data mining. This approach is unique in that it attempts to create a holistic approach in which all RE activities are represented. We have described how we plan to involve the crowd and the user feedback we obtain from them in all its facets. We have given a summary of existing concepts and tools in this field (RQ1) and introduced an initial taxonomy of user feedback (RQ2). Besides refining our concepts and taking smaller steps such as expanding tools that crawl only one app store with interfaces to other app stores, our next research steps will mainly be concerned with overcoming the challenges faced to develop such a platform. In particular, we would like to investigate:

- How to solve the reticence or concerns of stakeholders regarding the provision of feedback through the use of suitable motivational instruments and appropriate levels of intrusiveness?
- How to deal with legal and intellectual property considerations?
- How to extract requirements from user feedback for each configuration of the five dimensions through suitable algorithms that do not interfere with one another?
- How to classify, prioritize, cluster, and validate robust requirements, using algorithms, data validity measurements, and direct interactions with users?
- How to present the vast number of requirements and statements clearly, displaying only relevant data and using aggregations such as graphical visualizations?
- How to secure data traceability for effortless rollback using data attributes?

Acknowledgements. This work is supported by the RESCUER project, funded by the European Commission (Grant: 614154) and by the Brazilian National Council for Scientific and Technological Development CNPq/MCTI (Grant: 490084/2013-3).

References

1. Todoran, I., Seyff, N., Glinz, M.: How cloud providers elicit consumer requirements: an exploratory study of nineteen companies. In: 21st IEEE International RE Conference, pp. 105–114. IEEE International (2013)
2. Sutcliffe, A., Sawyer, P.: Requirements elicitation: towards the unknown unknowns. In: 21st IEEE International RE Conference. Research track (2013)
3. Goldin, L., Berry, D.M.: AbstFinder: A Prototype Natural Language Text Abstraction Finder for Use in Requirements Elicitation. Automat. Softw. Eng. **4**(4), 375–412 (1997)
4. Almali, M., Ncube, C., Ali, R.: The design of adaptive acquisition of users feedback: an empirical study. In: 8th International Conference on Research Challenges in Information Science, pp. 1–12. IEEE International (2014)
5. Henein, C.M., White, T.: Information in crowds: the swarm information model. In: El Yacoubi, S., Chopard, B., Bandini, S. (eds.) ACRI 2006. LNCS, vol. 4173, pp. 703–706. Springer, Heidelberg (2006)

6. Russ, C.: Online crowds: extraordinary mass behavior on the internet. In: I-Media 2007 and I-SEMANTICS 2007 (2007)
7. Pagano, D., Maalej, W.: User feedback in the appstore: an empirical study. In: 21st IEEE International RE Conference, pp. 125–134. IEEE International (2013)
8. Morales-Ramirez, I.: On exploiting end-user feedback in requirements engineering. In: 19th International Working Conference on Requirements Engineering: Foundations for Software Quality, Doctoral Symposium Programme, pp. 223–230 (2013)
9. Morales-Ramirez, I., Perini, A., Guizzardi, R.: Providing foundations for user feedback concepts by extending a communication ontology. In: 33rd International Conference on Conceptual Modeling. Submitted (2014)
10. Adepetu, A., Ahmed, K.A., Abd, Z.A., Al Zaabi, A.A., Svetinovic, D.: CrowdREquire: A Requirements Engineering Crowdsourcing Platform. AAAI Technical Report SS-12-06, The 2012 AAAI Spring Symposium Series (2012)
11. Liu, D., Lease, M., Kuipers, M., Bias, R.: Crowdsourcing for Usability Testing. Technical Report, American Society for Information Society and Technology (2012)
12. Castro-Herrera, C., Duan, C., Cleland-Huang, J., Mobasher, B.: Using data mining and recommender systems to facilitate large-scale, open, and inclusive requirements elicitation processes. In: 16th IEEE International RE Conference. Workshop paper (2008)
13. Dheepa, V., Aravindhar, D.J., Vijayalakshmi, C.: A Novel Method for Large Scale Requirement Elicitation. Int. J. Innov. Res. Sci. Eng. Technol. 2(7), 375–379 (2013)
14. Renzel, D., Behrendt, M., Klamma, R., Jarke, M.: Requirements Bazaar: social requirements engineering for community-driven innovation. In: 21st IEEE International Requirements Engineering Conference, pp. 326–327. IEEE International (2013)
15. Natt och Dag, J., Gervasi, V., Brinkkemper, S., Regnell, B.: Speeding up requirements management in a product software company: linking customer wishes to product requirements through linguistic engineering. In: Proceedings of the 12th Requirements Engineering Conference, pp. 283–294 (2004)
16. Gärtner, S., Schneider, K.: A method for prioritizing end-user feedback for requirements engineering. In: 5th International Workshop on Cooperative and Human Aspects of Software Engineering. IEEE International (2012)
17. Seyff, N., Graf, F., Maiden, N.: Using mobile re tools to give end-users their own voice. In: 18th IEEE International RE Conference, pp. 37–46. IEEE, Sydney (2010)
18. Rashid, A., Wiesenberger, J., Meder, D., Baumann, J.: Bringing developers and users closer together: the OpenProposal story. In: Heinzl, A., Appelrath, H.-J., Sinz,, E.J., et al. (eds.) Proceedings of the Primium Subconference at the Multikonferenz Wirtschaftsinformatik (MKWI), CEUR-WS 328, pp. 9–26 (2008)
19. Chen, N., Lin, J., Hoi, S.C.H., Xiao, X., Zhang, B.: AR-Miner: mining informative reviews for developers from mobile app marketplace. In: 36th International Conference on Software Engineering. In press (2014)
20. Iacob, C., Harrison, R.: Retrieving and analyzing mobile apps feature requests from online reviews. In: 10th International Conference on Mining Software Repositories, pp. 41–44 (2013)
21. Morales-Ramirez, I., Perini, A.: Argumentation-based discussion for user forum: a research preview. In: Salinesi, C., van de Weerd, I. (eds.) REFSQ 2014. LNCS, vol. 8396, pp. 232–238. Springer, Heidelberg (2014)
22. Pachidi, S., Spruit, M., Van de Weerd, I.: Understanding Users' Behavior with Software Operation Data Mining. Computers in Human Behavior 30, 583–594 (2014)

Functional Requirements Modelling
for Interactive TV Applications

Sergio Canchi[✉] and Juan Eduardo Durán

FaMAF Universidad Nacional de Córdoba, Córdoba, Argentina
scanchi@famaf.unc.edu.ar, duran@mate.uncor.edu

Abstract. **[Context and motivation]** There is a scarcity of proposals for functional requirements modelling for the interactive TV applications (iTV); this is a complex problem due to several fields/factors/dimensions/trends involved; therefore, it is necessary to give support to model iTV requirements. **[Question/problem]** We have found in the literature some iTV task classifications; some of their limitations are: classifications of actions were not proposed, the action classes found are not enough, it was not explained for each functionality kind how to systematically describe its members in terms of action classes of a taxonomy of actions, and the task classes are not enough for practical iTVs. **[Principal ideas/results]** For iTV applications we defined two UML profiles: one extending use case diagrams (UCD), and another extending activity diagrams (AD) for describing use cases (UC); 4 real iTVs were (partially) considered to illustrate the use of both profiles. **[Contribution]** Both profiles describe useful classifications with tasks/actions classes not found in the literature; for the identification of UCs we consider using few criteria instead of considering a lot of task classes; for every UC kind we indicate which action kinds must be used (for describing UCs of this kind); our approach allows to answer the question: to what kind of stakeholder a UC implementation should be assigned.

Keywords: Interactive TV applications · Enhanced TV applications · Functional requirements · Use cases · UML

1   Introduction

In [1] an *iTV* is a user experience that involves at least one user and one or more audiovisual and networked devices. According to [7] an *enhanced* iTV (eTV) is a service which directly enhances a particular TV program or event, considering look and feel - graphic design -, user-journey – navigation - and user-experience – functionality. A *social TV system* supports distant or collocated viewers to communicate with each other. A *second screen* in [8] is an additional device that connects viewers to complementary content, while they watch TV via applications, derivative content and features that are synchronized with TV programs. According to [12] a *task* describes an activity that has to be carried out to fulfil the user's goals. In [5] an *action* is the fundamental unit of behaviour specification; an action takes a set of inputs, and con- verts them into a set of outputs.

© Springer International Publishing Switzerland 2015
S.A. Fricker and K. Schneider (Eds.): REFSQ 2015, LNCS 9013, pp. 254–261, 2015.
DOI: 10.1007/978-3-319-16101-3_17

In some works of the area of iTV development it was stated the importance of a requirements phase for iTV construction, e.g. see [2, 3, 4]. For iTV development it is important to use knowledge of areas such as HCI, multimedia systems and infor- mation systems; some growing trends concerning iTVs are: the use of a *second screen*; the development of *social TV systems*; the *collaborative TV systems*, e.g. col- laborative rating and filtering systems; *context-awareness*. The reasons to have a sys- tematic approach to model iTV requirements are: to manage the complexity, to use important concepts with a clear meaning, to reduce gaps in requirements, to reveal conflicting or unfeasible requirements; to better understand the requirements. It is not enough to use only a generic notation for requirements (e.g. task diagrams, UML diagrams), because it is necessary to give more support to analysts, e.g. using iTV taxonomies/criteria for tasks/actions, using precisely defined concepts, and using patterns for describing tasks of a given type in terms of actions. There is a scarcity of proposals for describing iTVs functional requirements; we have only found some iTV task taxonomies - see [6, 7, 8, 9]; these proposals have the following limitations: 1) action classifications for iTVs were not proposed; 2) the task classes found for actions are not enough - for lacking action types see Sec. 2; 3) it was not explained how to systematically describe non-basic tasks of a given class in terms of action classes of a taxonomy of actions; 4) they did not consider how to organize tasks and functionali- ties, e.g. for distributing their development to specialized stakeholders, and to decom- pose a system into subsystems; 5) we did not find some important functionality clas- ses - see Sec. 2 for examples.

We have found several taxonomies of iTVs in the literature (between them, [6], [7], [10], [11] are the relevant ones), they present some criteria/dimensions that can be used to classify an eTV; however, as we will see some important criteria/dimensions are lacking.

We needed to choose between using task diagrams (e.g. CTTs), and using UML profiles extending requirements diagrams. Due to the complexity of iTVs, to give enough support to the analyst it is necessary to have too many task classes; another idea is to characterize a task according to some relevant criteria; with this approach a few criteria need to be considered instead. UML profiles (and not task diagrams) are prepared for associating several criteria to elements; therefore, we decided to work with UML; other reasons for using UML are: UCDs allow organizing functionality into packages (we use this facility in this paper), and UCDs allow associating several actors to a UC.

In this paper we define: a classification of eTVs by considering existing and new dimensions/criteria, a UML profile extending UCDs considering the relevant crite- ria/dimensions for iTVs (these criteria are enough to consider all the task classes found), and a classification of actions to describe UCs. For each type of UC, we ex- plain what kinds of actions are mandatory for describing UCs of this stereotype. Both UML profiles for requirements were tested with 4 real case studies of different eTV types (see [13, 14, 15, 16]).

2   Taxonomy for eTVs and UML Profiles

We consider criteria for eTVs that affect either functionality identification (i.e. with an impact on the types of tasks needed) or functionality organization, e.g. groups of functionality to be assigned to different kinds of developers. In Table 1, we evaluate the relevant iTV application taxonomies found in the literature according to 5 criteria. For the case of social iTV systems we have the following criterion: If the iTV allows synchronous communication between users (i.e. in real time) or not (with a time lag). From [6] we take a classification for social iTV systems.

Table 1. Comparison of taxonomies for iTVs in the literature

	Criterion	Kunert [7]	Rodriges [10]	Soares [11]	Cesar [6]
C1	Semantic relationship with the program´s content	Yes	Yes	yes	no
C2	Temporal synchronization with the TV Program	Yes	Yes	yes	no
C3	The viewer participates in the program	Yes	No	no	no
C4	The iTV is social	No	No	no	yes
C5	The iTV allows synchronous communication between the users	No	No	no	yes

In this work, we consider the 5 criteria of Table 1, and we add 3 new criteria. The iTV classes found that are a combination of some of the 8 criteria were excluded from our criteria selection. **C6**) the viewer creates content, e.g. application in [16]; **C7**) the viewer involves himself in commercial processes, e.g. shopping, apply for event tickets as spectator (e.g. ITV the X Factor – see [13] - in redeem UC); **C8**) there is a second screen, e.g. applications in [13], [17], [18].

In the literature about iTVs we have found classifications of tasks in which the user participates; such classifications have several classes, are incomplete, and are not appropriate UC taxonomies, because there exist UCs that need to include tasks of more than one task class; for these reasons, we considered different criteria for UC development; these criteria cover the topics considered by the task classes found and new topics not found. A UC may consider more than one criterion for functionality classification. We use the word information with the meaning: content associated to the program, media, data about users, data about the system state, data in data sources.

CF1: One or more CRUD operations requested by the user (in [9]). Stereotypes: «view»: The user either involves in information search, or browses information, or looks at notifications. «modify»: The user creates/edits/deletes information; the result of a modification is stored in persistent/volatile media, locally (i.e. in the viewer's device) or externally. «transaction»: The user inputs some data, a transaction is exe- cuted, and its results are displayed. **CF2**: («interaction between persons») the viewer interacts with somebody (motivated by [8] that uses socializing), e.g. communication between users, game playing. **CF3**: («change state») A transition is performed that changes the application's state. **CF4**: («sync») The UC is temporarily synchronized with the TV program.

CF5: («external») The UC contains a task that is performed outside the iTV, e.g. by an external application. **CF6**: («sysCreate») the system cre- ates automatically some information without user participation.

Criteria from CF3 to CF6 are not present in the found taxonomies of iTV tasks. Stereotypes for actors: «user»: a human user role. «broadcaster»: the broadcaster; it is used when some broadcaster's information arrives. «timer»: a timer; it is used for periodic tasks that are triggered by a timer's timeout. «externalApp»: an external application; it is used either when an external application triggers a UC using a notification, or when a UC sends a service request to an external application.

To organize the UCs, and to assign their development to the different stakeholders we considered the stereotypes (not found in the literature): «first screen»: the UC package contains the accessible UCs from the first screen, i.e. TV set showing a pro- gram. To implement such UCs is needed experience in iTV middleware, e.g. DVB- GEM, SBTVD-Ginga, HbbTV. «second screen»: the UC package contains the acces- sible UCs from the second screen. To implement such UCs is needed experience in a mobile platform, e.g. Android and iOS. These UC packages are needed for the appli- cation prototype in [19].

For each iTV criterion some UCs stereotypes are mandatory for iTVs respecting the criterion: stereotypes for CRUD operations for C1; «sync» for C2; «modify» for C3; «interaction between persons» for C4 and C5; «modify» for C6; «transaction» or «modify» for C7; think if «second screen» and «first screen» are necessary for C8.

UCD of the ITV the X Factor (see [13]): «change state» *Log in*, «modify» *Register, Login* is extended by *Register*. «broadcaster» *iTV* triggers «sync» «modify» *Rate performance* (the viewer rates the performances in real-time during each show to earn a spot on our coveted leader board), «view» *Biggest performances* (the viewer watches the biggest performances minutes after they appear on TV); «view» «external» *Check offers* (the viewer views current offers from the partners of ITV – e.g. Domino that sells pizzas - in the wallet), «transaction» «external» *Redeem* (the viewer redeems a selected offer - some earned points are given in exchange for the selected offers). *Check offer* is extended by *Redeem*. *Check offer* and *Redeem* are associated to «externalApp» *partner*. The ITV the X-Factor considers all the UCs in only a second screen.

We consider two kinds of action classes: actions to be developed by UI designers for user-system interaction (e.g. for input and output of information), and actions to be implemented by developers (autonomous actions, i.e. performed by the system without user intervention); as a consequence, each role group will develop the actions for which they are more experienced, and there is no interaction between UI designers and developers for developing an action. The action classes were obtained by figuring out how to decompose relevant classes of tasks in the literature into more basic actions, and by considering the push and pull strategies (see [20]).

Action stereotypes for UI designers: «input»: for either input of data, or interaction of the user for functionality/content access (in [6], [7], [9] there are only some specific input tasks). «edit»: (in [9]) for the user edition of content that is present in the UI. «output»: (in [9]) for the system presenting content/data/collection. «feedback»: for the system provision of feedback to the user in answer to a user initiated action/activity (in [12]) The following stereotype is not present in the iTV task taxonomies found: «**prompt**»: for the system presenting a call to action, or asking for the provision of data by the user. **Action stereotypes for developers: «search**»: (in [7]) for the search of content in a repository. «**control**»: for control of media content (e.g. start, pause, rewind, resume, stop, record, enable/disable accessibility features - e.g. closed caption, audio description, sing language) – [9] presents some tasks for control. The following stereotypes are not present in the iTV task taxonomies found. «**notification**»: for only the reception of an event notification. «**participate**»: after the viewer answers a question (e.g. of a quiz, poll, voting), his (perhaps processed) answer is sent. «**communicate**»: to send information entered by the viewer to another person. «**job**»: for autonomous actions not respecting the previous stereotypes.

Table 2 lists for each UC stereotype the action stereotypes that are mandatory to describe a UC of this kind, in the order that should appear in the UC description. UCs of stereotype «sync» usually start their execution with a «notification» action. A UC may have more than one stereotype in the table's rows; in such cases the behaviours of stereotypes can be combined in sequence.

Table 2. Mandatory action stereotypes for use case stereotypes

UC stereotype	mandatory
«view»	Search inside the application: «prompt», «input», «search», «output»
	Search in external source: «prompt», «input», «job», «output»
	Media playing: «control»
«modify»	«prompt», («input» or «edit»), «job», «feedback»
«transaction»	«prompt», «input», «job», «feedback»
«interaction beteween persons»	Communicate: «prompt», «input», «communicate», «job»
	Playing: «prompt», «input», «job», «output»
	Receive communication: «notification», «output»
«change state»	«prompt», «input», «job»
«sysCreate»	«job»

In UC *rate performance* of ITV The X factor ([13]), the user is notified to rate a performance («notification»); the user chooses a value («input»); finally, the selected option is sent («participate») and stored by the system («job»). In UC *share rate* of [13], the user requests to share the performance's rate («input»); the system prompts a friends list («prompt»); the user chooses a friend («input»), and selects share («input»); finally, the data for sharing is sent («communicate») and stored («job»). In UC *make caption* of CW The Vampire Diaries ([16]) the user chooses to insert caption («input»); the system takes a screenshot of the episode («job»), and shows it («output»); finally, the user edits a caption («edit») that is added to the screenshot.

3   Related Work

For functionality identification, the relevant task classes for us are those whose instances need for their description at least one autonomous action, and one user-system interaction action. For action identification the relevant task classes for us are those whose instances are either autonomous actions or user-system interaction actions. Table 3 compares the found relevant literature according to 8 requirements. For each requirement (named with its identifier – 1st column) a cell's (identified with the cite number - instead of author's name) rating is justified giving the extent of consideration of the requirement or some lacking task classes (considered by us).

Table 3. Evaluation of approaches in the literature for classification of tasks/actions

REQ	Topic	Kunert [7]	Cesar [6], [9]	Roy [8]
R1	CRUD	R: yes, CUD: reg	yes	CR: yes
R2	Interaction between persons	Communicate, play game.	Communicate	yes
R3	State change	reg -	no	no
R4	Temporal synchronization	No	no	no
R5	Inclusion of external tasks	reg -	reg -	no
R6	System creates information	No	no	reg
R7	Autonomous action types	reg -	reg -	no
R8	User-system interaction action types	reg -	reg	no

For our work we rate all the requirements with yes. Justification of the ratings: R1: [7]: not delete and edit; R3: [7]: a few specific tasks for state change and not the criterion. R5: [7] only *shopping* and *additional videos* (they may include external tasks) and not the criterion; [6], [9] only *view extra material* (it may include external task) and not the criterion. R6: [8]: only *recommendation* and not the criterion. R7: [7]: search and only *download* for job, not considered: notification, control, send participation, and send communication; [6], [9]: some tasks for control, session transfer for job; not considered: search, notify, send communication, and send participation; R8: [7]: some tasks for input, output; not considered: edit, prompt, and feedback. [6], [9]: some tasks for input, edit, output; not considered: prompt and feedback.

4   Conclusion

Our UML profiles were designed for iTV in general and with emphasis on eTVs. We have not considered context aware iTVs and non-functional requirements.

We define some tasks for the systematic description of requirements: classify the application according to some dimensions/criteria, which allows us to analyse an eTV in terms of dimensions that are important for its development; apply rules that for an eTV criteria tell what UC stereotypes are needed, this is to help the novice analyst in the iTV domain to identify functionality; identify the UCs according to criteria, and analyse a UC in terms of the needed criteria for it, in order to give support to the analyst to identify and understand UCs nature; describe UCs with ADs using an action taxonomy, this allows the analyst to describe UCs systematically; use guidelines for describing UCs of a given stereotype in terms of actions, this is to help the novice analyst in the iTV domain to describe UCs.

For the 4 case studies, for the UC descriptions covered, the set of action stereotypes we have defined are enough. In addition, we checked that our action taxonomies/UC taxonomies take into account the classes of tasks found in the literature.

The eTV classification criteria are useful to suggest 4 of the UC stereotypes (that is 50 % of them); we suspect that «view» and «change state» (25% of the UC stereotypes) are frequently present in eTVs (this is confirmed by our case studies). We explained only for 6 UC stereotypes (75 % of them) what actions are mandatory; for the «external» stereotype we only needed to explain how to describe an external search; the requirements of «sync» were only explained for the case of a synchronized notification by the system (it demands the use of «notification» at start of a UC).

Acknowledgements. This work is supported by Córdoba TDT Consorcio de Cooperación FSTICs 2010/04 and Agencia Nac. de Promoción Científica y Tecnológica.

References

1. Cesar, P., Chorianopoulos, K.: Interactivity and user participation in the television life cycle: creating, sharing, and controlling content. In: UXTV 2008, pp. 125-128 (2008)
2. Gawlinski, M.: Interactive Television Production. Focal Press, Oxford (2003)
3. Kunert, T.: Interaction design patterns in the context of interactive TV applications. In: Proceedings of the 9th IFIP TC13 Intl. Conf. on HCI (2003)
4. Wang, J., Li, H., Xie, T., Wang, Y.: UCD-process-driven UI Design and Development Toolkit for ITV Interactive Application. JIC 8(12), 2359–2365 (2011)
5. Unified Modelling Language Superstructure. http://www.omg.org/spec/UML/2.4.1/
6. Cesar, P., Chorianopoulos, K.: The Evolution of TV Systems, Content, and Users Toward Interactivity. Foundations and Trends in HCI 2(4), 373–395 (2009)
7. Kunert, T.: User-Centered Interaction Design Patterns for Interactive Digital Television Applications. Human-Computer Interaction Series. Springer, London (2009)
8. Roy, C.: The Second Screen and Television - Overview and Growth Perspectives. Whitepaper Series Nro 1 co-published by Evolumedia Group and the CMF (October 2012)
9. Cesar, P., Bulterman, D.C.A., Jansen, J.: Leveraging user impact: an architecture for secondary screens usage in interactive television. Multimedia Systems 15(3) (July 2009)
10. Rodrigues, R.F., Soares, L.F.: Produção de Conteúdo Declarativo para TV Digital. SEMISH - Seminário Integrado de Software e Hardware (2006)
11. Gomes Soares, L.F., Ferreira Moreno, M., Monteiro de Resende Costa, R.: Towards the convergence of digital TV systems. JISA 1(1), 69–79 (2010)
12. Concurrent Task Trees. http://www.w3.org/TR/task-models/
13. ITV The X Factor. http://www.itv.com/xfactor
14. BBC Antiques Roadshow. http://www.bbc.co.uk/antiquesroadshow

15. BBC The Voice. www.bbc.co.uk/programmes/b01nnfdd (accessed December 23, 2014)
16. Vampire Diaries. https://itunes.apple.com/us/app/the-vampire-diaries/id398107676?mt=8
17. Viggle. http://get.viggle.com (accessed December 23, 2014)
18. Snappy TV. http://www.snappytv.com (accessed December 23, 2014)
19. Simon, H., Comunello, E., Von Wangenheim, A.: Enrichment of Interactive Digital TV using Second Screen. IJCA **64**(22), 258–264 (2013)
20. Trehan, M., Trehan, R.: Advertising and Sales Management. V. K. Publications (2008)

FlexiView: A Magnet-Based Approach for Visualizing Requirements Artifacts

Parisa Ghazi[(⊠)], Norbert Seyff, and Martin Glinz

Department of Informatics, University of Zurich, Zurich, Switzerland
{ghazi,seyff,glinz}@ifi.uzh.ch

Abstract. **[Context and motivation]** Requirements engineers create large numbers of artifacts when eliciting and documenting requirements. They need to navigate through these artifacts and display information details at points of interest for reviewing or editing information. **[Question/problem]** Traditional visualization mechanisms such as scrolling and opening multiple windows lose context when navigating and can be cumbersome to use, hence. On the other hand, focus+context approaches can display details in context, but they distort the data shown (e.g., fisheye views) or result in a large display canvas which again requires scrolling (e.g., zooming in ADORA). **[Principal ideas/results]** We are developing a novel method for displaying just the information needed to perform an intended task. Our method partitions the available screen space into regions. The boundaries of regions are simulated with a model consisting of virtual magnetic balls and springs that behaves like a physical system. This model supports the requirements engineer in selecting how the relevant information should be displayed. **[Contribution]** In this paper, we present preliminary results on how our conceptual solution works and what benefits are expected.

Keywords: Requirements engineering · Visualization · Focus+context · Physics-based interface · Magnet

1 Introduction

When eliciting and documenting requirements, requirements engineers create a large number of artifacts (e.g., documents, models, or sketches). Creating and working with these artifacts on electronic devices entails two visualization problems, particularly when working with displays of limited size (e.g., tablets): (i) There are artifacts such as large models or sketches that are larger than the available display. (ii) A requirements engineer frequently needs to view more than one artifact concurrently in order to comprehend or edit these artifacts.

Today's tools employ traditional techniques for tackling these visualization problems: the first problem is typically addressed by scrolling and the second one by opening multiple windows [1]. These techniques work well for focusing on individual pieces of information, but they do this at the expense of losing the information about the context that those pieces are embedded in. Therefore, working with traditional visualization mechanisms is cumbersome when the elements to be displayed in detail

© Springer International Publishing Switzerland 2015
S.A. Fricker and K. Schneider (Eds.): REFSQ 2015, LNCS 9013, pp. 262–269, 2015.
DOI: 10.1007/978-3-319-16101-3_18

are part of a network of interconnected elements, which is typically the case in Requirements Engineering (RE). On the other hand, there are so-called focus+context visualization approaches that can display details in context [1], [6]. However, the existing approaches distort the data shown (e.g., fisheye views) [4], [10] or result in a large display canvas which requires scrolling (e.g., zooming in ADORA) [8].

In our research we are developing a new visualization mechanism called *FlexiView* which solves, in a unified way, both visualization problems mentioned above. Based on a *physical metaphor of magnets and springs* [2], [9], [11], FlexiView shall be able to flexibly visualize detailed requirements artifacts without losing the surrounding context within a display canvas of fixed size. In contrast to existing visualization mechanisms, FlexiView will be designed such that it can be used for visualizing both single artifacts (e.g., a graphic model diagram or a sketch) and a network of multiple different artifacts.

The rest of the paper is organized as follows. In Section 2, we briefly discuss the goals of our approach. Section 3 reviews the relevant literature. In Section 4, we present our approach and discuss its features and benefits. Section 5 concludes the paper.

2   Research Goals

Our goal is to develop a unified focus+context visualization mechanism which is tailored to requirements engineering. With our approach, we aim at overcoming the problems of existing visualization approaches for RE artifacts, thus allowing the construction of innovative RE tools (e.g., for supporting lightweight requirements modeling [5]) as well as improving the way how existing RE tools visualize information. We envisage that such tools will (i) reduce the time and energy spent on navigating among various artifacts, (ii) prevent users (requirements engineers as well as stakeholders and developers) from getting lost in the navigation space, and (iii) make the set of RE artifacts better comprehensible for users. We expect that our visualization mechanisms will be useful also for visualizing other artifacts, e.g., in software architecture, but we will concentrate on RE artifacts in our research.

3   Related Work

Scrolling and opening multiple windows are traditional ways to deal with a large number of artifacts. They have been used in almost all available user interfaces. However, they lose context and create visual discontinuities, thus causing cognitive overhead for the user [1].

Focus+context visualization techniques display the focus within its context in a single continuous view. The theoretical foundation for focus+context interfaces was established by Furnas [4], who describes generalized fisheye views. This is a general interaction framework for information filtering according to the user's current point of interest. This concept was later used for creating Graphical Fisheye Views (GFV) [10]. GFV is a non-linear distortion-oriented graphical visualization technique and supports multiple foci. The results are sometimes reported as too distorted. Many derivations of fisheye views can be found in literature, such as JellyLens [7] that morphs around arbitrary geometric features in the data. In the ADORA project, a fisheye zoom algorithm for visualizing and manipulating hierarchical graphical ADORA models was developed [8]. The algorithm provides an editable layout which is stable under multiple zooming operations. However, zooming in multiple points may result in a large canvas which requires the user to scroll again.

In the field of graph visualization, many techniques and algorithms have been created for viewing large graphs. A particular thread of work deals with manipulating graph visualizations based on a physical metaphor [9], treating graph nodes as metal balls and edges as springs that are flexibly attached to those balls [2]. By applying forces to such a network of balls and springs, for example by placing magnets, interesting parts of a graph can be highlighted or magnified [11], thus allowing the construction of intuitive, user-friendly graph visualization and navigation mechanisms.

4   FlexiView: A Magnet-Based Visualization Approach

FlexiView combines the concepts of fisheye zooming and magnet-based graph visualization into a new technique for visualizing and manipulating requirements artifacts. We have chosen this technique due to its potential for solving both visualization problems mentioned in Sect. 1 (visualizing large individual artifacts as well as sets of interconnected artifacts) in a uniform way on display devices of limited size. Subsequently, we illustrate the idea using a typical scenario occurring in early stages of requirements engineering: we have a set of interconnected artifacts, each artifact being a chunk of text, a sketch, a model fragment, an image, etc.

4.1   Conceptual Solution

FlexiView partitions the whole working space into regions in such a way that each region contains just one element (i.e., a single artifact in the scenario mentioned above). For the sake of simplicity, we will call these elements objects. Unlike other visualization techniques, users interact with regions instead of objects. The interactions of the users affect the regions and any change in the regions affects the objects consequently. To manipulate the size of the regions, we model the region boundaries with a physical spring model [2] (Fig. 1a) and apply forces to that model using virtual

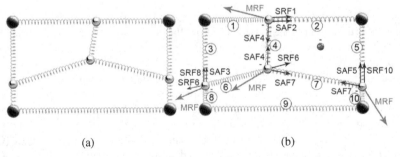

(a)   (b)

Fig. 1. (a) A sample of regions modeled by metal balls and springs. (b) The positions of the balls are determined by three forces: the Spring Repulsive Force (SRF), the Spring Attractive Force (SAF), and the Magnet Repulsive Force (MRF).

magnets [11] (Fig. 1b). The four balls in the corners of the display space are considered to be fixed and neutral. All other balls can move and are considered to be magnetic, having a negative pole on their surface. The balls positioned on a horizontal or vertical edge of the display space can only move horizontally or vertically, respectively. The other balls can move in any direction.

In its initial position, the model is in balance. Users can now manipulate the size of regions by creating virtual magnets anywhere on the screen. These magnets have a single pole on their surface. The position, strength and polarity of these magnets determine how the regions change: any magnet repels the balls of the same polarity and attracts the balls of the opposite polarity. The placement of virtual magnets on the drawing space applies forces to the movable balls and makes them move, thus compressing or stretching the springs attached to the balls. Springs apply forces to the balls in return. The balls move until the forces of springs and the magnet(s) applied to them neutralize each other. The system is in balance again until the user changes the layout by creating or removing a magnet, moving an existing magnet, or altering its strength. Creating multiple magnets affects multiple regions simultaneously.

Figure 1b shows the forces and the resulting repositioning of balls when a magnet of negative polarity is placed in the top right region. Compressed springs apply repulsive forces and stretched springs apply attractive forces. The directions of spring forces are aligned with the directions of the springs. The direction of the force that the magnet applies is given by the straight line between the magnet and the ball. The balls on the boundaries of the drawing space behave in a restricted way as described above.

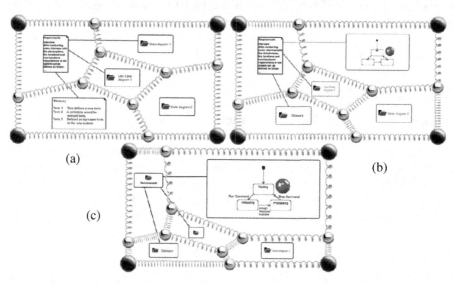

Fig. 2. (a) RE artifacts and their regions. (b) The user has placed a magnet in the top right region, resulting in the enlargement of this region and the appearance of more details. In the shrunk region at the bottom left, fewer details are displayed. (c) The user has increased the strength of the magnet, so the the corresponding region grows and the other ones shrink.

The size and the position of the objects are controlled by the regions they reside in. When the position or the size of a region is changed by the user, the new position or size of the objects residing in that region will be calculated accordingly. The result will be the enlargement or shrinkage of objects. Eventually a new view of the original information is produced. Figure 2 shows three steps of a user interaction. The first image (2a) shows some objects representing requirements artifacts, their relations and their regions. The regions are modeled by our balls and springs model. In the second image (2b), the user has created a virtual magnet with negative polarity (the red ball) in the region of interest. The magnet has repelled the balls and caused the region of interest to increase in size. The object in this region is enlarged and can be displayed with more detail, hence. Conversely, the bottom left region has become too small to display its object in detail, so this object is replaced by a more abstract representation. In Figure 2c the user has increased the power of the magnet, resulting in a larger region of interest and further shrinkage of the other regions.

In order to replace objects in shrunk regions with more abstract representations and those in enlarged regions with more detailed ones, we keep display metadata for all objects [3]. We assume that we have at least a three-level hierarchy: project – artifact – contents of artifact. If an artifact, for example, is a symbol-and-line drawing, the symbols in that drawing constitute another level of hierarchy.

The applications used to create and edit artifacts store them in their own file format on local or remote storages or in repositories. We assume that these applications provide a kind of plug-in of FlexiView such that FlexiView can access the information required to display the artifacts and/or their constituents. Thus, users can explore information by navigating in and between artifacts with FlexiView while they can still manipulate and modify the content shown using the corresponding applications.

4.2   Algorithms for FlexiView

We are currently exploring existing graph manipulation algorithms that can be adapted for implementing the FlexiView approach. As in other work [11], we do not strive for physical accuracy, modeling exactly Hooke's law for the springs and the laws of magnetism for the magnets, but use the physical model as a *metaphor* for guiding algorithm design. The users of FlexiView will not have to bother with physics. For them, using a magnet will feel like having a wizard that magnifies the region of interest on the display by a user-controlled factor and shrinks the rest accordingly.

4.3   Expected Benefits

Keeping the overview. A strong magnet can enlarge a region up to almost the whole working space and consequently shrink the other regions and their residing objects down to almost a dot. However the overview still exists. Although the undersized objects may be unclear, showing their relations and their positions keeps the complete image of the information in the user's mind.

Minimizing distortion. All focus+context techniques distort the image of the information. In FlexiView the information inside each region alone is not distorted.

The overall distortion available gradually increases when moving away from the current foci and decreases reaching far regions. Furthermore, the neighboring structure and relative position of the regions is kept intact. This way, the user is still capable of mapping the produced view to the original one, thus causing less disorientation.

Editing ability. Distorted views may improve the visualization, but are not pleasant when it comes to editing tasks. In our approach each region acts as an undistorted drawing canvas which enables users to edit information conveniently.

Being reversible. The altered views of the information are temporary views which are produced during specific tasks. The benefit of using magnets as tools of interaction is that by removing them, the original view reappears on the screen immediately. Moreover, the sequence of creating magnets on the screen can be undone not only in the reverse order but any magnet can be removed regardless of existing magnets created after it.

4.4 An Application Scenario

We illustrate the expected benefits of FlexiView with an application scenario from RE. Imagine a requirements engineer works on a requirements change request concerning the behavior of a component X. Let's follow this engineer's work through a sequence of steps. (1) The engineer starts from an overview that displays an interconnected set of requirements artifacts. (2) She places a magnet on the component X icon so that the constituents of component X appear. (3) She then places the magnet on the state machine icon of component X and increases the strength of the magnet until the state diagram appears. (4) Now she can study this diagram and figure out how it would be impacted by the requested change. (5) Next she wants to know the corresponding stakeholders. Placing another magnet on the pre-tracing link, she follows that link to the list of stakeholders, where she intensifies the strength of this magnet to see the actual stakeholders for the state machine of component X (the size of the state machine will shrink when displaying the stakeholder list, but it will remain a focus area on the display as its magnet is still there). (6) For a critical stakeholder, the engineer now wants to view this stakeholder's business goals. She moves the second magnet from the stakeholder list to the business goal specification, following the corresponding link. The stakeholder list disappears as soon as the magnet is moved and the region containing the business goal specification is enlarged. (7) By controlling the intensity of the magnet, she can now navigate into the business goals. (8) Having studied this information, she now wants to modify the state machine of component X. As the magnet on the state machine of component X is still there, she just removes the magnet from the business goal specification and the display reverts exactly to the situation that she had in step (4), thus allowing her to make the intended modification.

4.5 Research Status

We started this research in spring 2014 with conducting a thorough literature review. Based on the results of this review as well as an analysis of navigation and visualization problems identified in our FlexiSketch project [12], we have developed the concepts of FlexiView as a new technique for visualizing and manipulating requirements artifacts. We are currently investigating algorithms for implementing our approach. Our research will continue with actually implementing FlexiView and creating a test environment which will allow us to evaluate our approach against other approaches for visualizing and editing a set of requirements artifacts. We will evaluate the usefulness of FlexiView for performing typical RE tasks such as creating and understanding artifacts, tracing and change management. Additionally, we will deploy our approach on FlexiSketch [12], where we plan to conduct real-world evaluation studies.

5   Conclusions

In this paper we have previewed FlexiView: a novel visualization technique which aims at enabling requirements engineers to work with multiple interconnected artifacts on screens of limited size and, using the very same visualization technique, enabling them to navigate in artifacts that are larger than the available screen. Based on its underlying physical metaphor of springs and magnets, we expect FlexiView to provide seamless and natural looking multi-focus zooming. Due to its generic nature, FlexiView will be embeddable in both existing and novel tools that manipulate requirements artifacts such that these tools deliver their services through the FlexiView visualization mechanisms.

References

1. Cockburn, A., Karlson, A., Bederson, B.B.: A review of overview+detail, zooming, and focus+context interfaces. ACM Computing Surveys **41**(1), 1–31 (2008)
2. Eades, P.: A heuristic for graph drawing. Congresses Numerantium **42**, 149–160 (1984)
3. Frisch, M., Dachselt, R., Brückmann, T.: Towards seamless semantic zooming techniques for UML diagrams. In: 4th ACM Symposium on Software Visualization (SoftVis 2008), pp. 207–208 (2008)
4. Furnas, G.W.: Generalized fisheye views. In: SIGCHI Conference on Human Factors in Computing Systems (CHI 1986), pp. 16–23 (1986)
5. Glinz, M.: Very lightweight requirements modeling. In: 18th IEEE International Requirements Engineering Conference (RE 2010), pp. 385–386 (2010)
6. Kagdi, H., Maletic, J.I.: Onion graphs for focus+context views of UML class diagrams. In: 4th IEEE International Workshop on Visualizing Software for Understanding and Analysis (VISSOFT 2007), pp. 80–87 (2007)
7. Pindat, C., Pietriga, E., Chapuis, O., Puech, C.: JellyLens: Content-aware adaptive lenses. In: 25th Annual ACM Symposium on User Interface Software and Technology (UIST 2012), pp. 261–270 (2012)
8. Reinhard, T., Meier, S., Stoiber, R., Cramer C., Glinz, M.: Tool support for the navigation in graphical models. In: 30th International Conference on Software Engineering (ICSE 2008), pp. 823–826 (2008)
9. Rzeszotarski, J.M., Kittur, A.: Kinetica: Naturalistic multi-touch data visualization. In: SIGCHI Conference on Human Factors in Computing Systems (CHI 2014), pp. 897–906 (2014)

10. Sarkar, M., Brown, M.H.: Graphical fisheye views. Communications of the ACM **37**(12), 73–84 (1994)
11. Spritzer, A.S., Freitas, C.M.D.S.: A physics-based approach for interactive manipulation of graph visualizations. In: Working Conference Advanced Visual Interfaces (AVI 2008), pp. 271–278 (2008)
12. Wüest, D., Seyff, N., Glinz, M.: Semi-automatic generation of metamodels from model sketches. In: 28th IEEE/ACM International Conference on Automated Software Engineering (ASE), pp. 664–669 (2013)

Requirements Engineering in the Bidding Stage of Software Projects – A Research Preview

Kai Breiner[1], Michael Gillmann[2], Axel Kalenborn[3(✉)], and Christian Müller[1]

[1] Fraunhofer IESE, Kaiserslautern, Germany
{Kai.Breiner,Christian.Mueller}@iese.fraunhofer.de
[2] Insiders Technologies GmbH, Kaiserslautern, Germany
M.Gillmann@insiders-technologies.de
[3] Wirtschaftsinformatik, Universität Trier, Trier, Germnay
Axel.kalenborn@uni-trier.de

Abstract. **[Context and motivation]** Before a software project officially starts, there is a stage that has not received much consideration in literature: the precontract or bidding stage. **[Question/problem]** In this phase, basic Requirements Engineering (RE) activities are conducted without having a budget, yet. In this paper, the SmartOffer project is described, which aims on improving RE during this precontract phase. **[Principal idea/results]** Therefore, bidding processes of several organizations were analyzed and commonalities/differences were identified. The consolidated process is described in this paper. It consists out of four abstract phases: assessment of demand, conception, proposal, and actual project conduction. Mandatory and optional process steps within these phases allow for being tailored to different companies and products. **[Contribution]** The consolidated bidding process provides the potential for automation and tool support. In consequence the precontract phase will be more efficient and effective. Building a tool supporting this process as well as evaluating this tool will be addressed in future work to complement this research preview.

Keywords: Software projects · Precontract phase · Bidding phase · Proposal · Requirements engineering

1   Motivation

Software Development is characterized through a deficit of resources. At the same time, the importance of software is growing, as digital equipment is used in more and more business and private areas. Because of this, the software development has to be efficient and in the majority of cases, software projects are developed by external partners [1]. To be able to work with an external partner, the placing of a software project is a buying process, consisting of a proposal and the acceptance of this proposal.

So before a software project starts, there is a phase that has not received much consideration in requirements engineering literature yet: the precontract or bidding phase

© Springer International Publishing Switzerland 2015
S.A. Fricker and K. Schneider (Eds.): REFSQ 2015, LNCS 9013, pp. 270–276, 2015.
DOI: 10.1007/978-3-319-16101-3_19

during which a rough concept of the software to be implemented has to be established in the form of a bid or proposal.

An important part of a bid is a cost estimate that should be as precise as possible. For this cost estimate, an initial requirements analysis and documentation is necessary, because nobody is able to calculate a project without knowing what to implement. The proposal is used to enhance the comprehension of the project and provides a basis for the contract to be concluded with a prospective customer. So it has to be written and presented in an understandable way especially for the decision makers that are not willing and able to read a complex IT documentation.

The problem is that during the bidding stage, detailed requirements analyses are not yet possible because the analysis is not paid and the bidders are competing with other suppliers. If a bidder is not awarded the contract for the software project, the incurred expenses are not covered. As software budgets are running short, an efficient approach for preparing a bid is needed, to reduce this unclear investment.

On the other hand the preparation process involves risks and uncertainties for both, the purchaser and the service provider. There is an asymmetry of information between the two parties. The potential service provider doesn't know the requirements and the budget, the purchaser only has a limited notice of the provider's actual reputation in the project field [2].

Therefore, both partners try to exchange the information required for decision-making. For the service provider, this means that he has to prepare a bidding document and demonstrate his capacity.

Bidding documents have to convince the customer of the bidder's competence and of the idea that he is the right partner for the respective project [10]. This can only be reached with professional and elaborate bids, the implementation of which, however, causes great effort. To be able to do this, we are looking into the process of bid preparation in our partner companies.

The SmartOffer project is focused on the problems in this phase of a software project especially from the view of small and medium-sized enterprises (SMEs). The main goal of the SmartOffer project is to develop an innovative tool-based methodology for the improvement of the pre-project phase (especially for SMEs) looking at the development of dialogue-oriented, Internet-based systems and Web applications.

In the next section, the state of the art in this area is described, while Section 3 summarizes the methodology and first results. Future work is described in Section 4.

2   State of the Art: Preparation of Software Projects

The purpose of the precontract phase is the preparation of a bid. A bid contains the scope and conditions of a software project and defines the legal framework for its implementation.

In the common process models of software engineering, the precontract phase is not integrated in a suitable way [4], [13]. The projects generally begin with a detailed stage of requirements engineering and then pass on to conception and realization [5]. Only the V-Modell XT and the CMMI Standard include an adequate precontract phase but have the main view on the purchaser and not on the service providers [6]. Also many known requirements engineering methods, are not applicable for the preparation of software projects in the context of the bidding stage. Methods like an opinion surveys or customer monitoring are to cost intensive for the requirements exploitation. And functional descriptions or documentation models like the UML are too abstract and thus not suitable to convince decision makers [6].

Especially in SMEs, bids often cannot be prepared as carefully and detailed as necessary, because they are prepared by the company management itself and the margins of these projects are lower than in large-scale enterprises [12]. So time and money that they are able to spend for creating a bid is very limited. Further, to successfully sell a project, it does not only need to be understandable, but also communicate confidence that attracts customers and transports the project ideas.

To transport ideas to the decision makers on customer side, a visualization of what you want to do is not only helpful, but often necessary [9]. This is especially the case in the area of dialog oriented systems, where usability and look and feel have great influence on the project success. This phenomenon is known as IKIWISI ("I know it, when I see it") and deals with the problem that the software users do not understand the requirements until they see them [8]. Thus, the presentation view is an important basis for the dialog with the customer [7]. This is due to the fact that the decision makers are often no IT specialists themselves and cannot understand abstract models or descriptions.

So in the SmartOffer project we want to spend attention on the precontract phase and develop a method that enables SMEs to efficiently create attractive and competitive bids that satisfy the need of the potential customers.

3   Research Preview: Methodology and First Results

The first goal of the SmartOffer project was to analyze the process of bid preparation in the companies being partners of SmartOffer. To achieve this goal three 1-day workshops (one with each company participating in the SmartOffer project[1]) took place to see how their current work in bidding processes look like, which tools they use and how we can make the bid preparation faster and more efficient in the future. The industry partners participating in the SmartOffer project represent a wide bandwidth of software developing domains, from developing individual Web pages over Web-based applications up to highly multipliable configurable software products. All of these project partners have several years of market experience in a bunch of customer as well as software product development projects.

3.1   Methodology for Process Definition

All the workshops were conducted using the IESE business process elicitation method [11], which consists of the following activities:

---

[1] Official Web page of the SmartOffer project: http://www.smartoffer-projekt.de

- **Element selection** – Identification of: activities, artefacts, roles, and tools.
- **Process forming** – Participants had to create a process covering all their activities.
- **Evaluation** – Feedback about advantages and disadvantages regarding their own process, as well as change requests were collected.

While sharing many commonalities, all the individual elicited processes were consolidated and put into an as-is reference process. Depending on their organization, different terminology, tools, or even execution orders were used for describing similar facts. This leveraged the consolidation of a unified process.

Identified weaknesses and improvement ideas regarding the individual processes that were shared by at least 2/3 of the project partners were considered for further improvement. Stepwise these weaknesses and improvement ideas were used to adapt the activity descriptions or the process flow of the unified process accordingly. In this way, all the deficiencies were addressed and aggregated into a so-called to-be reference process.

Finally, this to-be process has been stressed by an expert review, in which representatives of the companies, but those who were not involved in the elicitation process before, judged the adequateness and suitability of the to-be process based on their past project experience. First, they assessed the overall applicability of the to-be process in their company before they described their expected performance improvements (e.g., more cost efficient, but also other quality attributes such as degree of reusability, or the overall quality of the potential resulting proposal). The results of these reviews were provided via email and consolidated by the paper authors.

Important threats of validity for this methodology include the fact that all companies came from a similar domain prohibiting a generalization of the to-be process applicability for other bidding processes. Furthermore, the to-be process was only evaluated by expert review and not actually applied in a case study, or, at least, a controlled experiment.

3.2   The Pre-Project (To-be) Reference Process

In total, the developed to-be process consists of 40 activities (mandatory and optional) which cover all actions and their results necessary in order to create a valid bid. Fig. 1 shows the overall process. On an abstract level, the activities can be grouped into four logical project phases depending on the position within the process:

- **Assessment of demand** – all activities to gather information and requirements
- **Conception** – all activities that are conducted for internally creating the bid.
- **Proposal** – all activities to submit the bid.
- **Project** – the final phase in which the project itself – if granted – is executed.

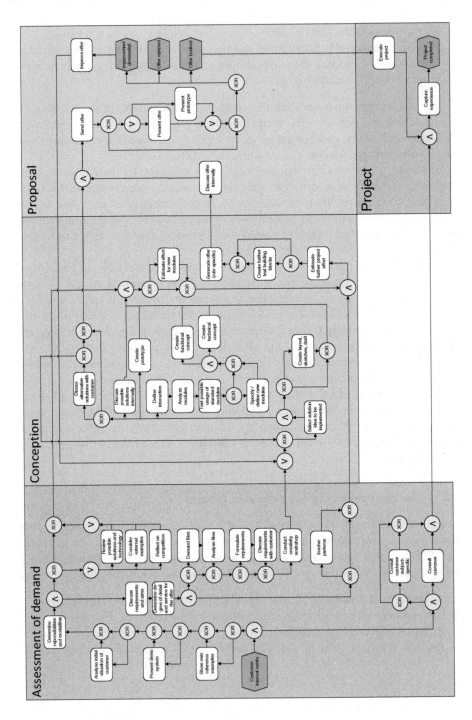

Fig. 1. The pre-project process

Beginning of the process is the state "customer interest exists" (Fig. 1). To understand the problem domain a set of actions aim on gathering information about the initial problem and to evaluate the findings (Assessment of Demand). Result is a set of basic requirements to be used for all further activities. The second phase (Conception) is conducted to consider plausible solution ideas and to determine the degree of possible proposal reusability (less expensive) and which parts have to be built from scratch (more expensive). After an iterative expert based estimation, the bid is generated. The third phase (Proposal) includes all activities to sell the bid to the potential customer, which can be support by personal presentations, dialogs, or even by a running prototype. The conduction of the final project is represented in the last phase (Project). Experience gained during the execution of a project provides valuable feedback regarding its offer. Such lessons learned need to be processed and considered for future project offers (e.g., adjusted templates, realistic estimates).

4   Summary and Prospects

The SmartOffer project investigates in the bidding phase of a software project especially from the view of small and medium-sized enterprises (SMEs). Short-term goal is to identify a unified process, which can (partly) be supported by a tool in the long-term.

So far a common process (including mandatory and optional activities) could be identified, shared by all the industrial project partners. This was possible due to the fact that these companies already unintentionally prepared bids in a systematic manner, which were overlapping in between all parties. Taking disadvantages and change requests into account the shared process could be restructured and evaluated within the participating industrial partners. This process was presented in this paper.

After identifying all necessary steps of the process, potential for automation will evaluated and implemented in future work: (1) Currently, the process is characterized by media disruptions as well as by the usage of a plethora of different tools. The idea is to automate frequently used steps (e.g., reusing building blocks) and provide a more efficient workflow by one holistic tool. (2) Hence, the tool will support the pre-requirements process to guarantee completeness, collect and compare success indicators of several bids over time, and generate the bid, i.e., final document to be sent to the to-be customer. (3) At the end, we will evaluate the best-practice process as well as the tool by comparing the results (i.e. resulting bids generated by and with them at the industrial partner's sites) against the bidding processes of the industrial partners used at the beginning of the project

Acknowledgment. This work was funded by the German Federal Ministry of Education and Research (BMBF) in the SmartOffer project under grant number 01IS13024. The authors assume responsibility for the content.

References

1. Bergner, K., Jacobi, C., Rausch, A., Sihling, M., Vilbig, A.: Make-or-Buy von Software-komponenten. In: OBJEKTspektrum, p. 17, January 2001
2. Weiber, R., Jacob, F.: Kundenbezogene Informationsgewinnung. In: Kleinaltenkamp, M., Plinke, W. (eds.) Technischer Vertrieb - Grundlagen, 2nd edn, pp. 523–612. Springer, Berlin (2000)
3. Pohl, K.: Requirements-Engineering: Grundlagen, Prinzipien, Techniken, 2nd edn. Depunkt-Verlag, Essen (2008)
4. Ludewig, J., Lichter, H.: Software-Engineering: Grundlagen, Menschen, Prozesse, Techniken, Stuttgart, Aachen (2010)
5. Robertson, S., Roberston, J.: Mastering the Requirements Process, 2nd edn. Upper Saddle River (2006)
6. Kalenborn, A., Timm, I.: Der Einfluss der Vorvertragsphase auf die Qualität von IT-Projekten. In: Linssen, O., Kurmann, K. (Hrsg.): Qualitätsmanagement und Vorge-hensmodelle - 19. Workshop der Fachgruppe Vorgehensmodelle im Fachgebiet Wirt-schaftsinformatik, pp. 91–100 (2012)
7. Lauesen, S.: User interface design: a software engineering perspective. Addison Wesley, Copenhagen (2005)
8. Boehm, B.: Requirements that Handle IKIWISI, COTS, and Rapid Change. IEEE Computer 33(7), 99–102 (2000)
9. Flinders, K.: Using pictures to explain software requirements could save billions (2010). http://www.computerweekly.com/Articles/2010/10/25/243517/Using-pictures-to-explain-software-requirements-could-save-billions-says.htm (August 5, 2013)
10. Paech, B., Heinrich, R., Zorn-Pauli, G., Jung, A., Tadjiky, S.: Answering a request for proposal – challenges and proposed solutions. In: Regnell, B., Damian, D. (eds.) REFSQ 2011. LNCS, vol. 7195, pp. 16–29. Springer, Heidelberg (2012)
11. Adam, S., Riegel, N., Koch, M.: A methodological framework with lessons learned for introducing business process management. In: Nurcan, S., Proper, H.A., Soffer, P., Krogstie, J., Schmidt, R., Halpin, T., Bider, I. (eds.) BPMDS 2013 and EMMSAD 2013. LNBIP, vol. 147, pp. 78–93. Springer, Heidelberg (2013)
12. Meffert, H.: Marketing: Grundlagen marktorientierter Unternehmensführung, 9th edn. Gabler-Verlag, Münster (2000)
13. Kalenborn, A.: Angebotserstellung und Planung von Internet-Projekten. Springer-Vieweg, Trier (2014)

Research Preview: Supporting Requirements Feedback Flows in Iterative System Development

Eric Knauss[1]([✉]), Andreas Andersson[1], Michael Rybacki[1], and Erik Israelsson[2]

[1] Department of Computer Science and Engineering,
Chalmers | University of Gothenburg, Gothenburg, Sweden
eric.knauss@cse.gu.se
[2] Volvo Car Corporation, Göteborg, Sweden

Abstract. *Context & motivation:* Today, embedded systems are increasingly interconnected and operate in a rich context of systems and internet-based services. Iterative development is one strategy of developing such cyber-physical systems. It enables exploration of early prototypes of a feature in the context of its intended use and collecting telemetric data from test-runs. This is a rich data source that can be leveraged for learning behavioural requirements for a feature. *Question/problem:* However, we found practitioners struggling with deriving requirements for the next iteration from such test-runs in a systematic and repeatable way. *Principal ideas/results:* We allow test drivers to add markers when the system behaves unexpectedly by introducing a dedicated feedback tool. Preliminary evaluation shows that these markers lead to better feedback to the development team and indicates a positive impact on the development cycle. *Contribution:* We give an example, report experiences, and discuss industrial implications of feedback systems and in situ requirements gathering in iterative system development.

Keywords: In situ requirements · Feedback system · Requirements and continuous integration

1 Introduction

In the automotive industry, recent advances in connected car technology – i.e. connecting vehicles to the internet – have led to development of internet-augmented driver assistance systems. These systems utilise the car's internet connection to assist the driver by providing them with live updates on information that is potentially important to their safety, such as traffic and weather conditions. Consequently, requirements are context dependent and upfront analyzis of requirements needs to be complemented by iterative development and learning in a realistic context. The success of in situ requirements approaches (such as [4,6]) indicates that such exploratory testing in iterative development can lead to a better understanding of requirements.

This paper reports on the introduction of a feedback system to facilitate collecting context-specific, spontaneous feedback in situ with the goal to support

© Springer International Publishing Switzerland 2015
S.A. Fricker and K. Schneider (Eds.): REFSQ 2015, LNCS 9013, pp. 277–283, 2015.
DOI: 10.1007/978-3-319-16101-3_20

development engineers of the Active Safety Division at Volvo Car Cooperation (VCC) in iterative system development. Its purpose is to allow systematic gathering of requirements from field tests and provide analysts with data reported directly by test drivers to plan for the next iteration. Preliminary evaluation based on a prototype of the feedback system and interviews with developers indicates that the approach is indeed valuable: The feedback system supports development engineers in collecting and understanding requirements based on observations about how driver assistance systems behave in the field.

While introducing the feedback system, we followed a design science approach [10], which implies iterative design, development, and evaluation of our candidate solution in close collaboration with its stakeholders. Thus, our lessons learnt from integrating a feedback system into industrial iterative system development are incorporated into our solution design to a large extent. We will describe the feedback system with its intended context of use as well as its central features in the next section. Then, we will report on our preliminary evaluation and discuss how a feedback system can impact the effectivity of learning requirements (discovering new or refining existing requirements) in iterative system development.

2   Concept: Learn Requirements During Test Drives

Recent research indicates that some requirements only emerge in operational contexts: Seyff et al. argue that capturing the needs of users in the field strengthens user participation in requirements engineering activities [6]. Schneider shows how raw user feedback on a running system can be transformed into requirements [4]. Different approaches of capturing context during requirements elicitation have been proposed, such as a model-based approach by [7], which models the system context with aspects such as participants, activities and environments. Another option is to unobtrusively observe users engaging with the system in the intended context of use [1] or to provide them with focused feedback channels allowing stakeholders to provide feedback *when and where* a situation worth reporting is encountered [5]. All these approaches imply a certain alignment to the system under development. Therefore, we start by describing the specific context in which we introduce the feedback system for iterative requirements gathering, before we highlight its important concepts and features.

2.1   Research Context: Active Safety at Volvo Cars

We aim at supporting requirements gathering during test-drives for the Road Friction Information system (RFI), developed by Active Safety Devision at Volvo Car Corporation (VCC). RFI is a warning system for sharing information about low road friction [8]. RFI uses the Connected Car technology (i.e. Volvo cloud services, [2]) for sending data about low road friction to the cloud when cars enter a slippery road patch. A warning message is then sent to other connected cars in the area to which the information is relevant, and is displayed to drivers on the car's digital instrument panel. Since the RFI system is a new technology,

Fig. 1. From left to right: The center console (Volvo XC90[2]), the first suggested solution design, and its implementation

it has to undergo a thorough examination in different driving conditions to learn its exact operational requirements and to avoid a large number of situations where the RFI system would either warn when it should not, or not warn when it should. Therefore, it is important to continuously collect experience with the system and to use it systematically during development.

At Active Safety, a project usually starts with a list of the planned driver assistance system's requirements. Systems with high safety-criticality, such as collision mitigation systems, require well-defined requirements. Other systems, such as RFI, are initially only defined by a rough outline and requirements are iteratively refined by the development team. In this study, we are especially interested in qualitative testing between iterations, where the system is tested under realistic conditions in its intended context of use. After such tests, test-drivers pass information on the test orally to developing engineers, less frequently a co-worker on the passenger seat takes notes.

2.2 Critical Features of the Feedback System

Our implementation is based on four iterations through the regulative cycle proposed for design science research [10]. Thus, the features presented here are the result of close cooperation between researchers (moderating the process, proposing initial designs and prototypes of the system) and practitioners (sharing experiences from daily work, testing prototypes in a realistic context). We worked with four engineers at VCC: The fourth author, an experienced engineer, promoted the idea of the feedback system internally and interfaced the researchers as a product owner. Two other experienced engineers provided feedback on the different versions of the feedback system from the context of their project work. A fourth engineer helped as an expert in HMI design.

The product owner envisioned the feedback system to be installed in a touch screen located in the car's center console, which usually offers an interface for

---

[2] http://www.kbb.com/car-news/all-the-latest/volvo-concept-coupe-previews-2015-xc90-design-cues/2000009640/

Table 1. Critical features of a feedback system for the Road Friction System

Modes of Operation. Due to safety considerations, the system should provide two modes: In *Driving Mode*, test-drivers can *tag* events (e.g. receiving a slippery road warning) for which they would like to give feedback. Drivers will not be asked to perform any more operations at the time to avoid diverting their attention from the road. Instead, they would be prompted for feedback to tagged events at the end of the drive in *Parking Mode*. In this mode, the driver is required to select the entity (e.g. the Road Friction Information system) to give feedback on, before selecting feedback from predefined feedback options, adding a comment, and finally selecting a mood icon to indicate the positive, neutral, or negative nature of feedback.

Feedback Facilities. The interplay of the two modes of operations as well as the information needs of developing engineers for planning the next iteration sets the stage to optimize which feedback to request in what situations. As a starting point, we offered users to give free text feedback together with mood icons, which were well received and preferred over neutral tagging (i.e. without indication whether the event was positive or negative) by practitioners. However, we discovered the need of visual reminders of the situation, when post-processing feedback in parking mode. Two types of reminders were suggested by practitioners. Firstly, a small map could be shown in the corner, while adding more details to a tagged event. Secondly, to enable users to discern many events on the map, a *mindshot* should be taken during the event. Suggestions included taking a picture of the driver, additional mood icons, and short audio recordings right after tagging. Complementing free-text fields, test-drivers requested predefined text blocks for different events and feedback types.

Integration in Development Cycle. To provide useful requirements related information to VCC engineers planning the next iteration, we decided to use a cloud database to store and share tagged events. For each event, the database stores all user choices, e.g. mode, focal entity, feedback option, and free text message. Additional metadata includes the test-car's ID, information about the test-drive (name of test-driver, start and finishing time, route, duration, and version number of the driving assistance system under test), as well as date, time, and GPS positions of the events. VCC engineers emphasized the potential of reliable and automatic collection of metadata to support and speed up the use of feedback from test-drives, e.g. by facilitating triangulation with telemetric data.

Critical Quality Attributes. Crucial quality attributes for the feedback system are simplicity and non-intrusiveness, thus allowing users to focus on their test activities without jeopardising the driver's or the passengers' safety. We carefully designed the feedback tree (as suggested by Schneider [4]) to reduce the need of typing text and to balance the amount of information shown on the screen with the number of interactions needed to give feedback (see Fig. 1, right).

infotainment and navigational support (see Fig. 1, left). Table 1 shows the critical features of the feedback system we developed, organized in four categories: *Modes of Operation*, *Feebdack Facilities*, *Integration in Development Cycle*, and *Critical Quality Attributes*.

3 Preliminary Evaluation

In our preliminary evaluation, we were guided by two research questions:

1. Does the feedback system increase the quality of feedback from test-drives?

2. Will the feedback system positively impact the iterative development of connected systems?

To answer Question 1, we conducted four realistic test-drives with two VCC test-drivers – each driver performed a *normal test-drive* (i.e. gave feedback after the drive was finished) and a *tool-supported* test-drive, where the feedback system was used. For Question 2, we interviewed the test-drivers after the test-drives.

3.1 Findings from Test-Drives

To test the RFI system in the field, VCC engineers generate a number of low friction events along a certain route. Then, a test-driver drives along that route with a development car, looking for warning signals, and noting deviations from expected behaviour. For our evaluation, we choose a 10km long route in Torslanda, Sweden, which is often used for test-drives by Volvo engineers. It includes industrial area streets, intersections, and a stretch of highway. Low friction events were simulated by the interviewer using tools developed for the RFI system. Although simulated, these events come from the same cloud server as real events, and are displayed in the car in the same way. The interviewer generated a number of simulated low friction events per route, informing the test driver whenever an event should be displayed to the driver as a low friction alert. We then compared the reported feedback with the road events generated by the interviewer (see Table 2).

Normal Drive. We interviewed the test-persons after the test-drives (test-person 1: 3h after the test-drive, test-person 2: 20min after the test-drive). With this delay we simulated a real situation, where VCC developers are often not able to evaluate a test-drive within short time after the drive. Both test-drivers and researchers were surprised on the inaccuracy of this recollection (Table 2). Our test-persons recalled three out of four events. The first test-person was misjudging the time of an event up to 30 min after it really occurred, while the second test-person was able to give the correct time with acceptable accuracy (i.e. good enough to allow later analysis). Despite this accuracy and the shorter delay, even test-person 2 was unsure about the circumstances of the events. Only one test-person could correctly localize one event with acceptable accuracy. In other cases, they were able to name the street on which the event occurred (which is 16km long) or misplaced it altogether. In some cases, they were unable to state what kind of event occurred (warning, when none should have been given; no warning, when a warning should have been given).

Tool-Supported Drive. In the tool-supported drive, we did not check for the event location, as this was automatically captured from the GPS. Instead we investigated if the correct mood icon was selected (happy, neutral, or sad) and if the event type was correctly identified (e.g. too many warnings at the same time). During the drive, the test driver tagged a number of events using the feedback system (operated by the interviewer for safety reasons), and then used the prototype again after the finished drive to specify these events by selecting entities and giving free text feedback. We created a larger number of friction events in tool-supported drives (9 per drive, compared to 4 in normal drives) in order to explore whether there was a limit to the number of events remembered by the engineers in tool-supported drive. No such limit was found, which we attribute to the fact that the test drivers did not have to concentrate on remembering time and location of the feedback events, only the type of occurrence.

3.2   Findings from Interviews.

Metadata is an Important Asset. Our interviewees acknowledged that the observed inaccuracies (especially of the event time) in *normal test-drives* would significantly impact the workload of engineers, e.g. by increasing the amount of

Table 2. Comparing the test-drivers' recollection about events during test-drives with and without feedback system ('+' = correct, '!' = not correct, '–' = forgotten)

Test-driver	Normal test-drive		Tool-supported test-drive	
	Characteristic	Event 1 2 3 4	Characteristic	Event 1 2 3 4 5 6 7 8 9
1	Time	! ! ! –	Time	+ + + + + + + + +
	Location	! ! ! –	Mood icon	+ + + + + + + + +
	Event type	+ ▨ + –	Event type	+ + + + + + + + +
2	Time	+ + + ▨	Time	+ + + + + + + + +
	Location	▨ ! + –	Mood icon	+ + + + ! ! + + ! +
	Event type	+ + + ▨	Event type	+ + ▨ ! ! ! ▨ + ▨ +

data that a developer would need to analyze for refining system requirements from observations. It is even possible that developers would discard observations as false positives when looking at a wrong time span.

Speed-up Through Explicit Tool Support. The interviewees emphasized the overall simplification of the process of gathering information on the RFI system's behaviour in the field. This includes automatic saving of metadata about the car (contextual data), but also simplifying the development cycle by eliminating the need to take notes while driving. With the system, test-drivers will be able to leave the office, go for a test drive, and report accurate data with minimal overhead (i.e. without bringing a laptop or another person's assistance).

4   Discussion and Future Work

Detailed requirements of complex, connected embedded systems often surface only when the system is used in its intended context, e.g. during field-tests between iterations. In this paper we report experiences and a preliminary evaluation from introducing a feedback system into iterative system development with the goal to facilitate systematic collection of requirements-related data during field-tests. Our findings indicate that efficient communication of test-drive results to development engineers can be a crucial factor in the development of driver assistance systems in the automotive industry. When developing such highly connected systems, the ability to automate the process of getting test-driver feedback together with contextual information to the developing team promises to increase the quality of feedback and to speed up the development cycle, as it allows engineers to focus on resolving issues instead of on searching their causes.

Our solution is very specific to the case at hand and tailoring it to exploring features around self-driving and inter-connected cars during test-drives is probably one reason for the very positive feedback from our interviewees. However, other industrial settings can profit from this blue-print for improving requirements management in continuous integration. In our case, both researchers and VCC engineers were surprised to see how clearly test-drives with the feedback system outperformed ad-hoc approaches. Being able to tag events as they happen and then to refine them later based on a dedicated tool can have a strong impact on the quality of feedback that is obtained from testing a system in its intended context of use. In addition, automatically storing metadata such as test-car ID and date of trip can improve the workflow significantly.

Based on our experience, we believe that using such metadata to synthesise and triangulate observations with other means of data-collection (such as telemetry) would be a good direction for future research. An engineer could then explore in the collected data what exactly happened prior to an unexpected event, which allows extracting new or changed requirements. Especially in the light of growing data volume collected by systems during usage, the timestamp of an observation will help in selecting the data that can be related to the event. Future work should focus on special workflows and tool support to analyze requirements with data visualization support (as suggested by Wehrmaker et al. [9]) as well as to mine requirements from telemetric data (as discussed by Rook et al. [3]) to enable continuous integration.

Acknowledgments. We thank the VCC engineers for support and encouragement, as well as K. Schneider and M. Tichy for their valuable feedback.

References

1. Brill, O., Knauss, E.: Structured and unobtrusive observation of anonymous users and their context for requirements elicitation. In: 19th Intl. Requirements Engineering Conf. (RE), pp. 175–184 (2011)
2. Holloway, J.: Gizmag takes a ride in volvo's most autonomous car yet. http://www.gizmag.com/volvoautonomouscars/28161/ ((2013) (last access: April 28, 2014)
3. Rook, A., Knauss, A., Damian, D., Thomo, A.: A case study of applying data mining to sensor data for contextual requirements analysis. In: Intl. WS on Artificial Intelligence for Requirements Engineering (AIRE 2014), Karlskrona, Sweden (2014)
4. Schneider, K.: Focusing spontaneous feedback to support system evolution. In: 19th Intl. Requirements Engineering Conf. (RE), pp. 165–174 (August 2011)
5. Schneider, K., Meyer, S., Peters, M., Schliephacke, F., Mörschbach, J., Aguirre, L.: Feedback in context: Supporting the evolution of it-ecosystems. In: Ali Babar, M., Vierimaa, M., Oivo, M. (eds.) PROFES 2010. LNCS, vol. 6156, pp. 191–205. Springer, Heidelberg (2010)
6. Seyff, N., Graf, F., Maiden, N.: Using Mobile RE Tools to give End-users their Own Voice. In: 18th Intl. Requirements Engineering Conf. (RE), pp. 37–46 (2010)
7. Sitou, W., Spanfelner, B.: Towards requirements engineering for context adaptive systems. In: 31st Annual Intl. Computer Software and Applications Conference (COMPSAC 2007), vol. 2, pp. 593–600 (2007)
8. VCC: Volvo car group initiates scandinavian pilot using cloud-based communication to make driving safer (2014). https://www.media.volvocars.com/global/en-gb/media/pressreleases/141041/volvo-car-group-initiates-scandinavian-pilot-using-cloud-based-communication-to-make-driving-safer (last access: April 7, 2014)
9. Wehrmaker, T., Gärtner, S., Schneider, K.: Contexter feedback system. In: Proc. of Intl. Conf. on Software Engineering, pp. 1459–1460. IEEE Press (2012)
10. Wieringa, R.J.: Design science as nested problem solving. In: 4th Intl. Conf. on Design Science Research in Inf. Sys. and Techn., Philadelphia, pp. 1–12 (2009)

User-Constrained Clustering in Online Requirements Forums

Chuan Duan, Horatiu Dumitru,
Jane Cleland-Huang$^{(\boxtimes)}$, and Bamshad Mobasher

DePaul University, Chicago, IL 60422, USA
{macduan,dumitru.horatiu}@gmail.com, {jhuang,mobasher}@cs.depaul.edu

Abstract. [**Context & motivation:**] Software development projects involving geographically dispersed stakeholders often use web-based discussion forums to gather feature requests. Our previous study showed that users have a tendency to create redundant threads as well as large unfocused mega-threads. [**Question/problem:**] In this paper we propose novel solution for integrating user feedback into the process of dynamically and iteratively clustering features into discussion threads. [**Principal ideas/results:**] We integrate feed back in the form of *stick-together* and *move-apart* advice, plus *user-defined tags* into our consensus based clustering process. [**Contribution:**] Experimental results demonstrate that our approach is able to deliver high quality and stable clusters to facilitate forum-based requirements elicitation.

1 Introduction

Software development projects are typically initiated through a requirements gathering phase in which business analysts work with project stakeholders to elicit the functional and behavioral requirements of the system [17]. This is a critical phase of every software project, and numerous case studies and surveys have shown that incomplete or incorrect requirements are one of the primary causes of project failure, and lead to millions of dollars in lost revenue every year [14]. Traditionally the process of requirements elicitation is performed using face-to-face techniques such as interviews, brainstorming sessions, and other interactive workshop activities. However, recent advancements in technology have led to a growing trend towards using online forums and wikis to facilitate the requirements gathering process [9]. In these forums and wikis, project stakeholders gather in a virtual meeting place, often asynchronously, to explore and specify the project requirements. Generally, topic-based discussions take place within discussion threads, which are created on demand by the project stakeholders [6]. For this forum process to effectively support the requirements process, the discussion threads need to work in much the same way as in-person meetings by drawing together stakeholders with similar interests so that they can explore and articulate their needs for the product under development. In practice, this does not happen very effectively. A prior survey we conducted of feature request forums for seven open source projects, demonstrated that human users do not do a very good job in creating cohesive,

S.A. Fricker and K. Schneider (Eds.): REFSQ 2015, LNCS 9013, pp. 284–299, 2015.
DOI: 10.1007/978-3-319-16101-3_21

and distinct user defined threads [5,16]. Our study showed that almost all of the forums contained one or more mega-threads which were used to discuss a broad variety of topics, while at the same time over 50% of the discussion threads contained only one or two feature requests or comments [6].

Problems associated with allowing users to define and manage their own threads can be partially addressed through utilizing data-mining techniques to manage both the creation of threads and the placement of new feature requests into threads. However, the requirements elicitation phase of a project is fast-moving and volatile with feature requests arriving as a continual or intermittent stream of ideas. Furthermore, in some projects these feature requests arrive in a random order so that early requests are representative of the full range of potential discussion topics, while in other projects features are explored sequentially by topic and arrive in a more orderly manner. The clustering algorithm must deliver high quality clusters despite the incremental arrival of feature requests in order to create highly-focused discussion threads which at least partially replace the need for face-to-face requirements gathering and/or analysis meetings. Furthermore, the adopted algorithm must incorporate user feedback to improve cluster quality and minimize unnecessary reorganizations of topics. Additionally the algorithm must have a fast running time so as to not interfere with visible forum activities. These objectives give rise to the first research question of whether it is possible to increase the stability of the incremental clustering process without negatively affecting its performance or quality, and secondly, the somewhat paradoxical question of whether user feedback can be incorporated in the clustering process in order to change and improve the structure of the clustering, without negatively impacting stability. In addition to evaluating the stability of the clustering algorithm and its suitability for use in a requirements forum, the novel contribution of this paper is the integration of various forms of user feedback into the clustering process.

The remainder of the paper is laid out as follows. Section 2 briefly summarizes our approach to requirements clustering and our novel approach for integrating user feedback. Section 3 reports on a series of experiments that were conducted to evaluate whether the requirements clustering algorithm delivers all three objectives of high cluster quality, stability, and high performance. It then evaluates several approaches for integrating user constraints to improve cluster quality. Section 4 investigates the impact of tagging on clustering. Section 5 discusses threats to validity of our study while Sections 6 and 7 describe related work and summarize our findings.

2   The Clustering Framework

The framework, which is depicted in Fig. 1, includes three distinct phases of start-up, classification, and re-clustering. The architecture of the framework and its default parameters were designed and determined empirically through prior work [6,11]. During the start-up phase of a project, a web-based collection tool is used to gather an initial set of feature requests from project stakeholders.

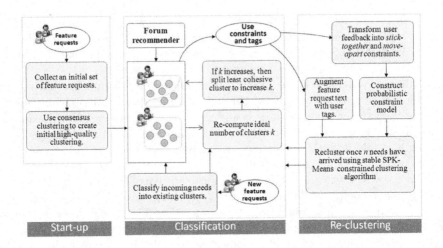

Fig. 1. The requirements clustering framework with user constraints

Consensus-based clustering is then used to generate the first set of clusters and subsequent feature requests are then classified into these existing clusters. The framework continually monitors the data to determine when a new topic has been introduced. It then identifies the least cohesive cluster, splits it into two parts, and moves closely related feature requests into the appropriate new cluster. After a predetermined number of new feature requests have arrived, the feature requests are re-clustered using a seed-preserving version of Spherical K-Means that is designed to increase stability while maintaining quality of the clusters. The remainder of this section describes these processes and their underlying algorithms.

2.1   Preprocessing of Feature Requests

Following standard information retrieval techniques [12], feature requests are first preprocessed to remove common words such as "this" and "because" which are not useful for identifying underlying themes. The remaining terms are then stemmed to their morphological roots. Given the final dictionary of terms $T = \{t_1, t_2, ..., t_w\}$, each feature request x is represented as a vector over $T : x = (f_{x,1}, f_{x,2}, ..., f_{x,w})$, where $f_{x,i}$ is the weight associated with term t_i in request x. The weights are typically computed using the standard tf-idf approach from information retrieval. Specifically, $f_{x,i} = tf_{x,i} \cdot log_2(N/df_i)$ where N represents the number of feature requests in the forum, $tf_{x,i}$ represents the term frequency of t_i in the feature request x, and df_i represents the number of feature requests containing t_i. The similarity between each pair of request vectors $a = (a_1, a_2, ..., a_w)$ and $b = (b_1, b_2, ..., b_w)$ is then computed using the Cosine similarity measure:

$$sim(a, b) = \frac{\sum_{i=1}^{w} a_i \cdot b_i}{\sqrt{\sum_{i=1}^{w} a_i^2 \cdot \sum_{i=1}^{w} b_i^2}} \tag{1}$$

2.2 Clustering

Our clustering framework utilizes a technique proposed by Can [4] to predict the appropriate number of clusters for the current dataset, and then utilizes a consensus clustering approach, described in our prior work [11]. In each of R runs, a proportion α of the whole dataset is randomly extracted and then partitioned into K clusters using Spherical K-means (SPK) [10]. Based on prior experiments α was set to 0.8. The remaining feature requests are then classified into their most closely related clusters.

Our ensemble integration is based on the concept of an N by N co- association matrix M. Let $\chi = \{x_1, x_2, ..., x_n\}$ be the set of instances to be clustered. A clustering ensemble $P = \{P^1, P^2, ..., P^R\}$ represents R partitionings of χ where the partitioning $P^i = \{C_1^i, C_2^i, ..., C_{k_i}^i\}$ represents a set of clusters such that $\bigcup_{j=1}^{k_i} C_j^i$. Then each element of the co-association matrix M represents a voting score between a pair of instances

$$M(i, j) = \frac{n_{ij}}{R} \tag{2}$$

where n_{ij} is the number of times the instance pair x_i, x_j is assigned to the same cluster over the ensemble. The underlying assumption is that pairs of feature requests that truly belong together in a cluster, are likely to be placed together in more of the individual clusterings, than pairs that do not belong together. The final partitioning is usually generated from M using either hierarchical clustering to cluster over the co-association matrix [13], or graph partitioning algorithms [18], which transform the co-association matrix into a weighted graph and then partition the graph into K parts through finding the K disjoint clusters of vertices that minimize the multi-cut. In our framework we adopted the hierarchical clustering approach. Although consensus clustering has a relatively long running time, it delivers clusters that are consistently of higher quality than the average SPK clustering, and invariably close to the optimal quality achievable by an individual SPK clustering. Experiments validating this finding for software requirements and feature requests are reported in a prior paper [11].

2.3 Managing New Feature Requests

Following the arrival of each new feature request the ideal granularity is recomputed to determine if a new cluster should be added. To add such a cluster in a way that preserves stability of existing clusters while minimizing clustering time, our approach identifies the least cohesive cluster, and then bisects it using SPK with K = 2. The cohesion is measured by the standard SPK objective function as $CH(C_i) = \sum_{x \in C_i} sim(x, \mu_i)$ where μ_i represents the centroid of cluster C_i. After the split, feature requests from neighboring clusters are re-evaluated to determine if they exhibit closer proximity to one of the two new centroids than to their own currently assigned centroids. If this is the case, they are reassigned to the relevant cluster. To ensure continued clustering quality, the entire dataset is re-clustered periodically after a fixed number of new feature requests have arrived. Re-clustering is performed using a modified SPKMeans algorithm that we name the Seed-Preserving SPKMeans, designed to minimize the movement of feature requests between clusters, through re-using the current set of centroids as seeds for the new clustering.

2.4   Incorporating User Feedback

The requirements clustering framework also takes advantage of the interactive nature of the discussion threads in order to gather user feedback about the quality of each of the clusters. Users who feel that a particular feature request does not belong in a given thread can vote for its removal. Likewise, users who want to encourage a set of feature requests to stay together in future re-clusterings can vote to keep them together. In related work, several researchers have investigated the use of semi-supervised clustering techniques, in which the clustering process is guided by prior knowledge or constraints collected through expert user feedback [2,7,8,19,21]. The most commonly adopted user-generated constraints are pair-wise Must- Link (ML) and Cannot-Link (CL) constraints, indicating respectively whether a pair of instances should be placed in the same or in separate clusters. Due to inconsistencies when constraints are gathered from real users these constraints cannot be treated as hard and fast rules. Our framework adopts a consensus-based constrained clustering algorithm [11] which uses COPK-means [21] to generate multiple constrained partitions and then combines them using a consensus algorithm. In our implementation of COPK-means the constrained instance assignment is not only applied to the usual batch assignment stage of spherical K-means, but also to the incremental optimization stage.

The feedback provided by the users in a forum is used to generate pair-wise constraints such that any two feature requests that users specify as belonging together in the cluster will be transformed into an ML link, and any pair of feature requests for which one belongs and one does not belong will be transformed into a CL link. However, one potential limitation of this approach is that gathering user feedback within the context of a discussion forum means that only two of four possible scenarios can be captured. These four scenarios could be described as *stick-together*, representing feature requests that are already correctly clustered together, *move-apart* representing feature requests that are incorrectly clustered together, *stay-apart* representing feature requests that are correctly placed in different clusters, and *move-together* representing those that are incorrectly clustered apart and should be placed together. By capturing constraints within the context of a forum, our mechanism captures only stick-together and move-apart constraints.

We illustrate our approach in Fig. 2 using posts extracted from the Sugar-CRM discussion forum. In Fig. 2(a), a thread has emerged around the topic of customer surveys. However, over time the topic has branched into a discussion about online voting making the thread relatively incohesive. Four of the active thread participants provide advice in terms of move-apart and stick-together directives. For example, Flo advises that four of the posts must stay together and that one should be moved apart. She offers no opinion on the other posts.

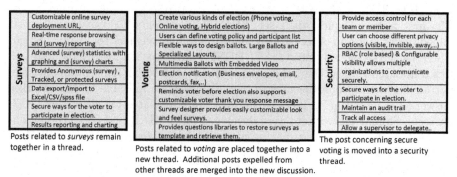

Key:
→ Move-apart from other posts in the thread
● Group together ■ Group together into a different group   🏷 User defined tag

		Flo	Jim	Sally	Yong
	Customizable online survey deployment URL, 🏷dashboard		●	●	●
	Real-time response browsing and (survey) reporting	●	●		●
	Advanced (survey) statistics with graphing and (survey) charts	●	●		●
	Provides Anonymous (survey) , Tracked, or protected surveys		●		●
	Create various kinds of election (Phone voting, Online voting, Hybrid elections)		■		
	Users can define voting policy and participant list		■		
Surveys	Flexible ways to design ballots. Large Ballots and Specialized Layouts,		■	●	
	Multimedia Ballots with Embedded Video		■		
	Data export/import to Excel/CSV/spss file	●			●
	Secure ways for the voter to participate in election. 🏷privacy	→	■		●
	Results reporting and charting	●			
	Election notification (Business envelopes, email, postcards, fax,..)		■		■
	Reminds voter before election also supports customizable voter thank you response message		■		■
	Transcript Voicemail to Email			●	
	User can record and play back a meeting				→

(a) Stakeholders provide grouping advice in the form of move-apart and stay-together votes. They can also add user defined tags to each post. This feedback is used by the clustering algorithm to maintain stability of the discussion forums.

Surveys	**Voting**	**Security**
Customizable online survey deployment URL,	Create various kinds of election (Phone voting, Online voting, Hybrid elections)	Provide access control for each team or member
Real-time response browsing and (survey) reporting	Users can define voting policy and participant list	User can choose different privacy options (visible, invisible, away,...)
Advanced (survey) statistics with graphing and (survey) charts	Flexible ways to design ballots. Large Ballots and Specialized Layouts,	RBAC (role based) & Configurable visibility allows multiple
Provides Anonymous (survey) , Tracked, or protected surveys	Multimedia Ballots with Embedded Video	organizations to communicate securely.
Data export/import to Excel/CSV/spss file	Election notification (Business envelopes, email, postcards, fax,..)	Secure ways for the voter to participate in election.
Secure ways for the voter to participate in election.	Reminds voter before election also supports customizable voter thank you response message	Maintain an audit trail
Results reporting and charting	Survey designer provides easily customizable look and feel surveys.	Track all access
	Provides questions libraries to restore surveys as template and retrieve them.	Allow a supervisor to delegate..

Posts related to *surveys* remain together in a thread.

Posts related to *voting* are placed together into a new thread. Additional posts expelled from other threads are merged into the new discussion.

The post concerning secure voting is moved into a security thread.

(b) The clustering algorithm is rerun. The algorithm follows the advice provided by the users and produces new and/or refined discussion threads.

Fig. 2. The user-guided clustering process applied to posts extracted from the Sugar-CRM discussion forum. Individual posts are summarized for clarity purposes.

Jim suggests separating the majority of posts into two groups (depicted by the blue circle and red square respectively). Sally suggests that the two posts related to online surveys and ballot design should stay together, and Yong outlines a plan for creating two groups. Yong's groups are similar to, but not the same as Jim's. In addition, two user-defined tags have been added. The clustering algorithm takes this partial, and somewhat conflicting, advise into consideration and produces the three threads shown in Fig. 2(b). The first thread represents the subset of posts from the original thread that refer to *surveys*. The second thread contains posts related to *voting* and includes posts from the original thread plus additional ones drawn from other threads. Finally, the post related to secure voting gets moved into an existing thread discussing security.

Experiments reported in the following section of this paper evaluate the impact of the user advice to improve quality, and also to determine if in fact, the stick-together constraints increase stability. Furthermore, to compensate for the lack of *move-together* links, which are considered relatively informative for improving cluster quality, the requirements framework also allows users to tag the feature requests in order to augment their meaning and further improve the benefits of incremental and constrained re-clustering.

3   Experimental Evaluation

This section presents a series of experiments that were designed to evaluate the clustering framework's ability to quickly and efficiently deliver cohesive, distinct, and stable clusters.

3.1   Data Sets

The experiments utilized 8 datasets including six well-known TREC data sets Tr11, Tr12, Tr23, Tr45, Tr41, and Tr31 [20] and two sets of real feature requests. The first feature request data set, SUGAR, represents 1000 feature requests mined from the forum of a customer relationship management tool named Sugar-CRM, while the second dataset, STUDENT represents 366 feature requests collected from students at DePaul describing their needs for an Amazon-like student portal. The main properties of each data set are listed in Table 1. Benchmarked answer sets, representing ideal clusterings, were available for all of the TREC datasets. Similar answer sets were developed for SUGAR and STUDENT. The SUGAR answer set was created by modifying the threads created by SUGAR users, in order to merge very small threads, and by decomposing mega-threads into more meaningful clusters. The STUDENT answer set was built from scratch by three researchers at DePaul University.

Table 1. Data set properties: n_d = number of documents, n_w = total number of words, K = number of clusters, and $|d|$ = average number of terms per document

Data	n_d	n_w	$|d|$	K
STUDENT	366	908	8	29
tr11	414	6429	281	9
tr12	313	5804	273	8
tr23	204	5832	385	6
tr31	927	10128	268	7
tr41	878	7454	1957	10
tr45	690	8261	280	10
SUGAR	1000	3463	27	40

3.2   Validation Metrics

For purposes of the experiments described in this paper, cluster quality was measured using the Normalized Mutual Information (NMI) metric [13]. NMI measures the level of agreement between two different clusters, in this case between the generated clustering and the answer set. More precisely it measures the extent that the knowledge of one clustering reduces uncertainty of the other. For two clusterings P^a and P^b, NMI normalizes the mutual information between them $I(P^a, P^b)$ as the average sum of their entropies $H(P^a)$ and $H(P^b)$

$$NMI(P^a, P^b) = \frac{I(P^a, P^b)}{[H(P^a) + H(P^b)]/2} \tag{3}$$

Two different metrics were used to measure stability. They are described using the following notation. T and T' represent two consecutive incremental stages during clustering, P and P' represent clusterings generated during T and T' respectively, and C_i and C'_j are the clusters in P and P'. For most of the experiments, the well-known Jaccard index (JAC) is used to measure stability. In P and P', pairs of feature requests fall into 4 classes labeled from a-d respectively as follows: a: those assigned together in both P and P', b: those assigned together in P but not in P', c: those assigned together in P' but not in P, and finally d: those assigned separately in both P and P'. JAC is then defined as

$$JAC = a/(a + b + c) \tag{4}$$

A second metric measures the Percentage of feature requests Moving Per Iteration (PMPI), and is computed as the number of feature requests that change cluster from one increment to the next over the total number of feature requests in the current dataset.

NMPI provides a more intuitive notion of stability than JAC. However, when new seeds are used to re-cluster a dataset there is no simple way to determine whether a feature request moves a cluster between P and P', and so measuring movement is difficult. In contrast, the seed-preserving approach retains the original centroids of P in P', and so it is possible to determine whether a feature request stays in the same cluster or not.

3.3   Improving Stability

The first series of experiments compared the performance, quality, and stability of the seed-preserving approach, versus the standard approach in which new seeds were created at each re-clustering. The basic algorithm follows the incremental re-clustering process described in Section 2 of this paper. Each experiment was repeated 10 times, and the average result is reported. Although experiments were conducted using varying sized increments, the increment size did not significantly affect the results and so most of the results are reported at increment sizes of 25, i.e. re-clustering is performed following the arrival of each 25 feature requests.

Performance. Table 2 reports the performance of the seed-preserving incremental approach versus using new seeds for each re-clustering, and clearly demonstrates that the seed-preserving method significantly decreased the running time of the algorithm. For example, the running time of the SUGAR data was decreased from almost 109 seconds to just under 7 seconds.

Table 2. Total Time Spent Clustering for Seed Preserving Clustering versus re-seeding (secs)

Dataset	Increment Size				Single clustering
	1	10	25	50	
STUDENT: (366 feature requests)					
Seed Preserving Increments	7.49	0.98	0.62	0.41	0.04
Standard Increments	101.82	10.78	4.74	2.92	0.73
SUGAR: (1000 feature requests)					
Seed Preserving Increments	85.54	13.24	6.66	4.27	0.22
Standard Increments	2347.31	249.92	108.62	57.83	6.69

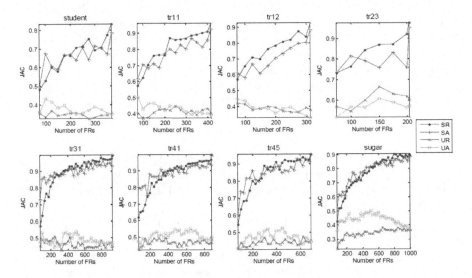

Fig. 3. Stability of different orderings of feature requests using seed-preserving and standard re-clusterings

Stability. The next experiment used the JAC metric to compare the stability of the seed preserving re-clustering versus standard re-clustering. In addition, each approach was evaluated for two different arrival orders of feature requests in order to determine if stability was achieved in each of these potential scenarios. In the first case, the ordering of feature requests was randomly selected, while in the second case feature requests were clustered using standard SPK, and then placed into a randomly ordered queue. Feature requests were then randomly selected from the first cluster in the queue until no more remained. They were then randomly selected from the next cluster, and so on. This second case simulated the scenario in which the arrival of feature requests followed some logical ordering of topics.

Results reported in Fig. 3 plot the stability of the clusterings measured using the JAC index, against the number of feature requests in the current dataset for seed-preserving clustering with random arrival (SR) and ordered arrival (SA), and standard clustering with random arrival (UR) and ordered arrival (UA). In each of the eight datasets, the seed-preserving approach was demonstrated to

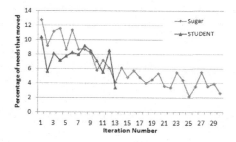

Fig. 4. Percentage of Feature Requests moved per iteration (PMPI)

outperform the standard method. A comparison of the results from the random arrival versus ordered arrival of feature requests showed that feature requests that arrived randomly initially exhibited lower levels of stability, but then after several increments matched or outperformed the stability of the ordered arrivals. This suggests that in the case of random arrival ordering, early feature requests caused some initial reorganization, but that once the primary topics were discovered, the clusters began to stabilize. A second observation is that in the case of random arrival order, the clusters stabilized significantly after arrival of approximately 20-30% of the total feature requests. This suggests that the initial instability might be avoided if there were a longer start-up period for gathering feature requests before the initial clusters are formed.

To provide a more intuitive view of stability, Fig. 4 depicts the PMPI metric showing the percentage of feature requests that changed cluster from one increment to the next for SUGAR and STUDENT datasets. As can be seen from the graph, in early iterations there is movement of 10-13%, while in later iterations of the SUGAR data this decreases to 2-6%. STUDENT did not entirely stabilize, however this is probably due to the small size of the dataset.

Quality. The NMI scores of the final clusterings in comparison to the answer sets were then computed to determine whether the seed-preserving algorithm was detrimental to the quality of the clustering. Again, results are reported for both ordered and random arrival orderings of the feature requests. Results are reported in Table 3 for seed-preserving in random order, seed-preserving with ordered arrival, standard with random arrival, and finally standard with ordered arrival. These results showed insignificant differences between the quality of seed-preserving versus non-seed preserving clusterings for both the ordered and random arrival orderings. However, in 75% of the cases tested the seed-preserving approach had slightly higher NMI scores than the traditional clustering method, indicating no general loss in cluster quality when this approach was used.

Analysis of Results. These results demonstrated that the seed-preserving algorithm effectively maintained the quality and performance of the clustering, while significantly improving stability.

Table 3. Cluster quality, measured using NMI, comparing the seed-preserving versus standard clustering methods.

Dataset	Increments of 10				Increments of 25			
	Seed Rand	Seed Ordered	Standard Rand	Standard Order	Seed Rand	Seed Order	Standard Rand	Standard Order
STUDENT	0.593	0.590	0.597	0.590	0.592	0.580	0.589	0.589
tr11	0.602	0.593	0.589	0.590	0.615	0.596	0.604	0.594
tr12	0.581	0.584	0.576	0.567	0.578	0.582	0.585	0.579
tr23	0.476	0.470	0.464	0.471	0.465	0.482	0.477	0.481
tr31	0.512	0.520	0.511	0.512	0.517	0.517	0.512	0.510
tr41	0.615	0.614	0.604	0.611	0.609	0.607	0.607	0.609
tr45	0.649	0.654	0.640	0.638	0.653	0.651	0.638	0.640
SUGAR	0.559	0.557	0.554	0.556	0.560	0.550	0.553	0.554

3.4 Improving Quality Through User Feedback

The second series of experiments evaluated whether user feedback could be used to increase the quality of the clusters without negatively impacting quality. As previously explained, the requirements gathering forum provides a natural context for gathering feedback from users in an incremental fashion as users interact with the discussion forums. However, this feedback creates a tension in the clustering process. On one hand, the user feedback should cause restructuring of unfocused clusters or misplaced feature requests, but on the other hand, unnecessary change, especially changes which negatively impacts cluster quality, should be minimized. This series of experiments therefore studied the impact of pair-wise constraints inserted during the process of incremental clustering. For these experiments, the increment size was fixed at 25, feature requests arrived in random order, and 25 constraints were inserted at each increment.

Three different methods of constraint generation were explored. The first approach served as a baseline and defined constraints by randomly selecting two feature requests and generating an ML if both artifacts were assigned together in the answer clustering, and a CL otherwise. The second method used bounded constraint generation, by selecting constraints that lie at the boundaries of clusters in order to maximize the benefits of constrained clustering. Boundary constraints are found by clustering the entire dataset using the consensus clustering method described in Section 2.3, and then selecting pairs of feature requests with scores in the co-association matrix within a given interval window. Based on initial experimentation, the window was set to [0.1, 0.5] for this experiment.

The third method selected constraints only if both feature requests had been placed in the same cluster. This simulated the more realistic case for the requirements domain, in which feedback was elicited from users during their real-time interactions with the discussion threads. As previously discussed, this approach limits the potential constraints to *stick-together*, and *move-apart*, while failing to capture move-together, and stay-apart constraints.

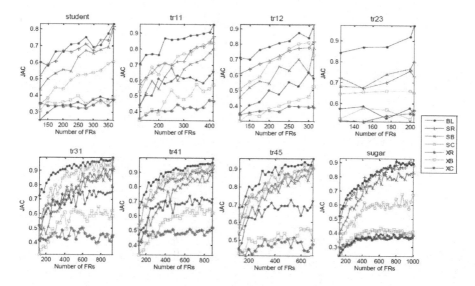

Fig. 5. Stability of seed-preserving re-clustering algorithm using different constraint generation methods at increment sizes of 25

These three approaches were implemented for both seed-preserving and standard re-clustering methods, resulting in the following six cases: seed-preserving random (SR), seed-preserving boundary (SB), seed-preserving cluster-based (SC), standard random (XR), standard boundary (XB), and standard cluster-based (XC) respectively.

Performance. Incorporating constraints into the re-clustering process increased the runtime of each algorithm. For example the total clustering time for STUDENT using the seed-preserving algorithm and random arrival order increased from 0.62 seconds to 10.28 seconds, and in SUGAR data from 6.66 seconds to almost 262 seconds. As this time is dispersed across multiple clusterings this level of increase in running time is not problematic within the requirements domain.

Stability. Stability results are reported in Fig. 5 and show that in general the seed-preserving method outperformed the traditional algorithm when user feedback was incorporated into the re-clustering process. The bounded constraint selection technique outperformed the random approach when the standard clustering algorithm was used, but interestingly failed to outperform the random approach when the seed-preserving algorithm was used. This observation might be explained by the fact that boundary conditions are more stable in the seed-preserving approach, and so only considering boundary constraints failed to unearth some of the structural changes that needed to occur.

A second interesting observation is that the cluster-based method that utilized only stick-together and move-apart constraints returned mixed results. In datasets, such as TR31 and TR41 it outperformed the other constraint selection techniques, while in other datasets, notably including the two sets of feature requests SUGAR and STUDENT, it performed significantly worse than the other two methods.

Fig. 5 also includes a baseline plot labeled (BL), which represents the case of the seed-preserving clustering with random arrival ordering of feature requests without constraints. In all eight datasets, the use of constraints decreased the stability of the incremental re-clustering; however this decrease was significantly less marked when the seed-preserving algorithm was used. In other words, although stability decreased when user constraints were incorporated, the seed-preserving algorithm still maintained relatively high levels of stability in all three cases.

Table 4. NMI Scores with various user constraints

Name	BL	SR	SB	SC	XR	XB	XC
STUDENT	0.592	0.610	0.650	0.656	0.611	0.636	0.642
tr11	0.615	0.641	0.700	0.675	0.624	0.702	0.683
tr12	0.578	0.610	0.692	0.682	0.622	0.676	0.681
tr23	0.465	0.499	0.509	0.532	0.523	0.504	0.539
tr31	0.517	0.547	0.582	0.568	0.542	0.583	0.573
tr41	0.609	0.639	0.698	0.67	0.633	0.693	0.672
tr45	0.653	0.682	0.719	0.724	0.673	0.721	0.718
SUGAR	0.560	0.571	0.611	0.598	0.571	0.609	0.608

Quality. The NMI scores of the final clusterings compared to the answer sets were computed to determine whether the use of constraints improved the quality of the clustering. Results are reported in Table 4. The first column represents the baseline case of seed-preserving clustering with random ordered arrival of feature requests but no user feedback. In every single dataset, all of the user constraint techniques returned higher NMI scores than this baseline case. Seed-preserving, randomly ordered algorithms showed an average NMI increase of 11.3

Analysis of Results. These results demonstrate that the stick-together and move-apart constraints performed unexpectedly well in improving the quality of the clusters, but also had some negative impact on the stability of the incremental clustering algorithm. Despite the slightly higher stability of the bounded approach, it is disadvantaged by the time-consuming pre-processing stage and the need for users to participate in a series of training sessions. In contrast, the cluster-based technique requires no special pre-processing and collects feedback from users within the natural context of their regular forum activities.

4   Improving Quality Through User Tags

The final series of experiments were designed to evaluate whether user tags might help increase the quality of the clusterings. As the use of tags does not significantly impact performance, this experiment is evaluated with respect to quality and stability only. A group of five DePaul MS students and faculty were each asked to look through ten randomly assigned clusters from the STUDENT dataset and to tag feature requests. They were instructed that these tags would be used to help improve the placement of feature requests into correct clusters. As a result, 141 of the 366 feature requests were tagged with additional information. Some feature requests were tagged by more than one person, and on average each of the tagged feature requests were assigned 9.2 distinct terms. Terms from each tag were then added to the text of the feature request, and subsequent incremental reclusterings were based on the combined text of the feature request plus the user contributed tags. Results, reported in Fig. 6, indicate that there was almost no change in stability when tags were combined with each of the three individual constraint generation methods. NMI scores were computed for each of the final clusterings produced using tagged feature requests. Results, reported in Fig. 7, indicate that the use of tags led to a significant improvement in cluster quality. For example, the NMI score for cluster-based constraints improved by 12.4% when tagging was used.

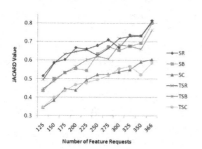

Fig. 6. Stability of STUDENT data when user tags are added

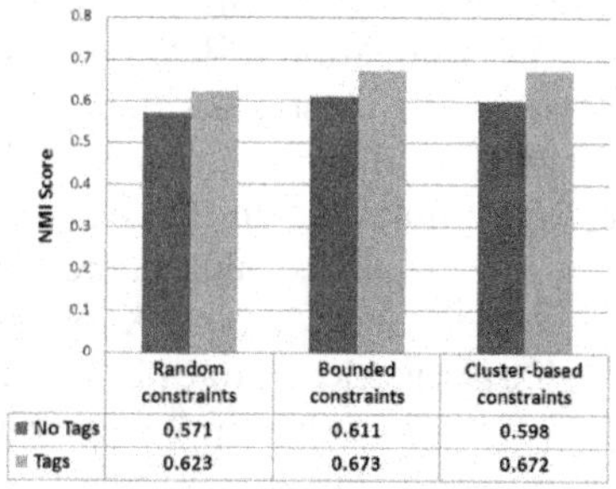

Fig. 7. NMI scores of tagged feature requests clustered incrementally with user constraints

5   Threats to Validity

The primary threat to validity for our work is introduced by the scarcity of golden-standard sets of clustered requirements, and the fact that there are several valid clusterings for any particular dataset. It is extremely time consuming to manually cluster meaningfully sized set of feature requests and/or requirements, and furthermore such datasets would not have been validated over time. To address the first problem, we supplemented the requirements datasets with publicly available datasets including validated clusterings from the TREC dataset [20]. Datasets with small document sizes were selected as they were most similar in nature to requirements. Utilizing the TREC datasets and their previously validated answer sets introduces greater external validity to our experiments. At the same time, we included two datasets "student" and "SUGAR" which were built specifically from feature requests. In general, the results from the feature request datasets supported the findings from the TRECdatasets. A second threat to validity emerges from the fact that user feedback was simulated for several of the experiments, and so the results do not take into consideration the nuances of individual behaviour and the willingness of users to provide feedback.

6   Related Work

Constrained clustering has been investigated across a wide variety of algorithms, including hierarchical clustering, non-negative matrix factorization, and partitioned clustering, especially the variants based on K-means which can be further categorized as constraint enforcement, learning distance metric, seeding, violation penalty, and hybrid approaches. One representative technique for the constraint enforcement algorithm is COPK-means [21], which strictly enforces both ML and CL constraints during the cluster assignment stage. The algorithm proposed by Xing [22] tries to learn a diagonal or full covariance matrix from the constraints. Seeded-Kmeans proposed in [1] utilizes labeling information that is more specific than standard ML/CL, of partial points to initialize the centroids and constrain the cluster assignment. PCKmeans, which is a violation penalty algorithm [2], modifies the objective function in K-means by adding a penalty for constraint violations in the form of a weighted number of violations. MPCK-means [3] is a metric learning-enhanced violation penalty algorithm, which combines ideas from Basu [2] and Xing [22].

The characteristics of data in the domain of clustering feature requests differ from the contexts of these previous studies, primarily with respect to the nature of the data being clustered and the interactive user-feedback process enabled in an online forum. Hariri et al., developed the Incremental Diffusive Clustering (IDC) approach for creating high quality clusters of features [15]; however, their approach is too slow for the dynamic environment of a requirements discussion forum because it produces only one cluster per iteration.

7   Conclusions

The clustering algorithm in this paper was designed to address several problems we observed in online forums that are used to elicit and discuss feature requests. The redundant discussion threads and often isolated comments makes it difficult for forums to take the place of in-person meetings. The experiments we conducted demonstrated that our seed-preserving approach to incremental clustering can deliver high quality, and relatively stable discussion threads throughout the incremental re-clustering process. This is of particular importance when forums are used to support requirements gathering activities. Our experimental results also demonstrated that incorporating user feedback in the form of stick-together and move-apart links, and augmenting the feature requests with user tags increases the quality of the generated clusters while maintaining much of the stability provided by the seed-preserving clustering algorithm.

Acknowledgments. The work described in this paper was partially funded by National Science Foundation Grant IIS-0916852.

References

1. Basu, S., Banerjee, A., Mooney, R.: Semi-supervised clustering by seeding. In: Conference on Machine Learning, pp. 27–34 (2002)
2. Basu, S., Bilenko, M., Mooney, R.J.: A probabilistic framework for semi-supervised clustering. In: KDD, pp. 59–68 (2004)
3. Bilenko, M., Basu, S., Mooney, R.J.: Integrating constraints and metric learning in semi-supervised clustering. In: ICML (2004)
4. Can, F., Ozkarahan, E.A.: Concepts and effectiveness of the cover-coefficient-based clustering methodology for text databases. ACM Trans. Database Syst. 15(4), 483–517 (1990)
5. Castro-Herrera, C., Cleland-Huang, J., Mobasher, B.: A recommender system for dynamically evolving online forums. In: ACM Conference on Recommender Systems, RecSys 2009, pp. 213–216. ACM, New York (2009)
6. Cleland-Huang, J., Dumitru, H., Duan, C., Castro-Herrera, C.: Automated support for managing feature requests in open forums. Communications of the ACM 52(10), 68–74 (2009)
7. Cohn, D., Caruana, R., Mccallum, A.: Semi-supervised clustering with user feedback. Technical report (2003)
8. Davidson, I., Ravi, S.S.: Identifying and generating easy sets of constraints for clustering. In: AAAI, pp. 336–341 (2006)
9. Decker, B., Ras, E., Rech, J., Jaubert, P., Rieth, M.: Wiki-based stakeholder participation in requirements engineering. IEEE Software 24(2), 28–35 (2007)
10. Dhillon, I.S., Modha, D.S.: Concept decompositions for large sparse text data using clustering. In: Machine Learning, pp. 143–175 (2000)
11. Duan, C., Cleland-Huang, J., Mobasher, B.: A consensus based approach to constrained clustering of software requirements. In: CIKM, pp. 1073–1082 (2008)
12. Frakes, W.B., Baeza-Yates, R.A.: Information Retrieval: Data Structures & Algorithms. Prentice-Hall (1992)
13. Fred, A.L.N., Jain, A.K.: Combining multiple clusterings using evidence accumulation. IEEE Trans. Pattern Anal. Mach. Intell. 27(6), 835–850 (2005)
14. Glass, R.L.: The standish report: does it really describe a software crisis? Commun. ACM 49(8), 15–16 (2006)
15. Hariri, N., Castro-Herrera, C., Mirakhorli, M., Cleland-Huang, J., Mobasher, B.: Supporting domain analysis through mining and recommending features from online product listings. IEEE Trans. Software Eng. 39(12), 1736–1752 (2013)
16. Laurent, P., Cleland-Huang, J.: Lessons learned from open source projects for facilitating online requirements processes. In: Glinz, M., Heymans, P. (eds.) REFSQ 2009 Amsterdam. LNCS, vol. 5512, pp. 240–255. Springer, Heidelberg (2009)
17. Robertson, S., Robertson, J.: Mastering the Requirements Process: Getting Requirements Right, 3rd edn. Pearson Educational (2012)
18. Strehl, A., Ghosh, J.: Cluster ensembles - a knowledge reuse framework for combining multiple partitions. Machine Learning Research 3, 583–617 (2002)
19. Tang, W., Xiong, H., Zhong, S., Wu, J.: Enhancing semi-supervised clustering: a feature projection perspective. In: KDD, pp. 707–716 (2007)
20. TREC. Data collection from Text REtrieval Conference. http://trec.nist.gov/
21. Wagstaff, K., Cardie, C., Rogers, S., Schrödl, S.: Constrained k-means clustering with background knowledge. In: ICML, pp. 577–584 (2001)
22. Xing, E.P., Ng, A.Y., Jordan, M. I., Russell, S.J.: Distance metric learning with application to clustering with side-information. In: NIPS, pp. 505–512 (2002)

A Systematic Literature Review of Requirements Prioritization Criteria

Norman Riegel[✉] and Joerg Doerr

Fraunhofer IESE, Fraunhofer Platz 1, 67663 Kaiserslautern, Germany
{norman.riegel,joerg.doerr}@iese.fraunhofer.de

Abstract. **[Context & motivation]** Requirements prioritization is typically applied in order to determine which requirements or features should be included in a certain release or implemented first. While most requirements prioritization approaches prescribe a fixed set of prioritization criteria that have to be assessed during the prioritization process, there is often a need for criteria that are customized to the specific project situation. **[Question/problem]** However, determining customized prioritization criteria is a time-consuming and laborious task. Instead of an in-depth analysis, criteria are often identified by gut feeling, which is error-prone and bears the risk of choosing misleading criteria. **[Principal ideas/results]** This paper aims at identifying and categorizing prioritization criteria discussed in the vast body of prioritization literature for software development. We describe a systematic literature review and, as a result, present a consolidated prioritization criteria model. **[Contribution]** Besides a comprehensive overview of prioritization criteria discussed in the literature, this paper introduces a classification schema that allows researchers and practitioners to identify prioritization criteria and related literature in a time-saving manner.

Keywords: Requirements prioritization criteria · Systematic literature review

1   Introduction

Requirements prioritization is an important aspect of any software development process. Requirements prioritization approaches are typically applied in order to determine which requirements or features should be included in a certain release or which should be implemented first [1]. Beyond that, recent approaches even utilize prioritization in order to identify the requirements that shall be refined next during a requirements elicitation process [2] [3].

In all prioritization approaches, one or more criteria are taken into consideration in order to determine the value of the requirements. Criteria may be, for example, "business value", "implementation cost" or "risk". Depending on the concrete prioritization approach used, the criteria are rated explicitly by different stakeholders (e.g., on Likert scales) or determined automatically based on other information (e.g., by analyzing system usage protocols).

© Springer International Publishing Switzerland 2015
S.A. Fricker and K. Schneider (Eds.): REFSQ 2015, LNCS 9013, pp. 300–317, 2015.
DOI: 10.1007/978-3-319-16101-3_22

Most requirements prioritization approaches prescribe a fixed set of criteria that have to be assessed during the prioritization process. Wiegers, for example, proposes in his method the use of the criteria "value", "cost", "risk", and "penalty" [1]. Only a handful of approaches do not prescribe the use of any criteria: in the value-oriented prioritization (VOP) approach [4], for example, core business values have to be determined first in order to assess the requirements against them.

The benefit of predefined criteria is that they can be used quickly out-of-the box. However, they often do not fit well into the given context [5]. Hence, there is a need for criteria that are customized to the specific project situation, but determining customized prioritization criteria is a time-consuming and laborious task. Instead of an in-depth analysis, criteria are often identified by gut feeling, which is error-prone and bears the risk of choosing misleading criteria. Berander [5] already remarked that research should focus on finding efficient methods for the determination of criteria (and developing prioritization approaches that can be used flexibly with different criteria), rather than spending effort on optimizing the calculations of prioritization approaches.

This paper aims at identifying and categorizing prioritization criteria discussed in the vast body of prioritization literature for software development. We describe a systematic literature review and, as a result, present a consolidated prioritization criteria model which consists of around 280 criteria. Several systematic literature reviews have already been performed in the context of requirements prioritization (e.g., [6][7][8][9]). In contrast to these studies, the goal of our work is not to identify certain prioritization approaches but to identify the criteria that are discussed in the prioritization literature. Our study is also not limited to any particular application domain, specific prioritization techniques, or special types of criteria (e.g., benefits). Furthermore, the goal of our study is not to merely collect these criteria, but to consolidate them and integrate them into a complete criteria model. We introduce a classification schema that allows researchers and practitioners to identify suitable prioritization criteria and related literature references in a time-saving manner. Thus, it is a first step towards the efficient selection of prioritization criteria for more flexible prioritization approaches.

The remainder of this paper is structured as follows: Section 2 describes our reseearch approach, i.e. the systematic literature survey and the creation of the prioritization criteria model, section 3 discusses the details of the criteria model, and section 4 finally concludes the paper and gives an outlook on future work.

2   Research Approach

In order to identify requirements prioritization criteria from the literature, we conducted a systematic literature review according to the guidelines of Kitchenham [10]. Thus, the first step (1) was the definition of a review protocol that defines the rationale for the survey, the research question, the search strategy, and the selection and assessment criteria (see Figure 1). The research question to be answered was: "Which prioritization criteria are discussed in the requirements prioritization literature?" In order to answer this question, a search string (i.e., "requirements AND (value OR criteria OR metrics OR attributes OR measures OR factors) AND (prioritization OR negotiation OR "release planning" OR "decision making")") was developed, tested, and applied to Scopus[1] as well as to the ACM digital library[2] in title, abstract and keywords. The reason for using these two libraries was that they cover most of the content from relevant publishers or databases [11] (e.g., from IEEE Xplore [12], Springer, Elsevier) and thus include most of the relevant work in the requirements engineering area (e.g., proceedings of the International Requirements Engineering Conference, proceedings of the REFSQ conference, the Requirements Engineering Journal, ICSE conference proceedings), as well as, for instance, the LNCS proceedings, where many related papers are published. Thus, a direct search at IEEE Xplore, Springer Link or other sources was not deemed necessary. The search was limited to computer science and related fields and included all available publication years, publication channels (e.g., conference and workshop proceedings, dissertations, journals, etc.), and publication types (e.g., method papers, experience reports, case studys, etc.). Although the tested search strings were used, it was found that many hits were not relevant for the research question. Those that do not deal with software requirements prioritization (e.g., construction material selection, prioritization in networks, etc.) or do not fit the search terms (i.e., listed in the search result, but does not include the search terms) were excluded. By reading the publications' titles and abstracts and comparing them with the exclusion criteria defined, we were able to dismiss many papers directly (2).

In the third step (3), the remaining publications were accessed and classified into two categories in order to get an overview of the prevailing publication types:

- Category 1: (Software) Requirements prioritization and negotiation approaches and release planning models (i.e., publications where a concrete approach is described)
- Category 2: Non-methodological publications in the context of requirements prioritization (e.g., empirical studies and literature reviews)

Then the publications were analyzed in detail in order to identify prioritization criteria mentioned in the text. If necessary (i.e., if references to prioritization criteria from other resources were mentioned), secondary resources from the references were also accessed (4) and analyzed according to the defined review criteria.

---

[1] http://www.scopus.com/
[2] http://dl.acm.org/

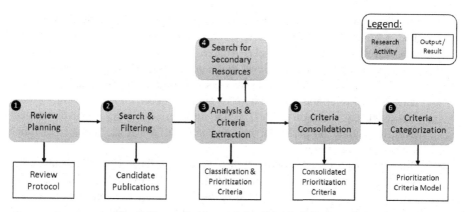

Fig. 1. Research Approach for Criteria Collection

The systematic literature review resulted in a set of 83 publications (narrowed down from around 1750 initial search hits) from which prioritization criteria could be extracted (the complete list of literature sources can be found in [13]). We classified 61 publications in category 1 and 22 publications in category 2. From the 83 publications, we extracted around 760 criteria in total.

In the next step (5), these criteria were then analyzed in order to remove duplicates and identify synonyms and homonyms. During the consolidation of the criteria, we experienced the following challenges:

- Most of the publications we analyzed do not describe the contained criteria in detail; rather, they just list them in the text without any description or further discussion. Thus, it is often not clear for the reader what exactly is meant by the criterion. Only a few papers (e.g., [14], [15]) describe the mentioned criteria in more detail. As a consequence, identifying synonyms or homonyms across the different publications was difficult and not always possible.

- In general, there is no consensus regarding the meaning of a criterion across publications and among different authors. For example, in some publications the criterion "implementation cost" is synonymous with "development cost", i.e., the authors do not distinguish between these two terms. However, in other publications, "development cost" (and further cost types) is seen as merely a part of "implementation cost". Thus, "implementation cost" is rather used as an umbrella term in the latter. As a consequence, the classification of a criterion in the hierarchy of our criteria model (see step (6)) might not accurately reflect the original meaning of this criterion intended by certain authors. Thus, the classification of a criterion in the criteria model reflects our interpretation of its meaning, which is also defined in the model. Furthermore, due to the similar nature of some criteria, not all criteria are independent of each other.

- Due to the nature of the different publications (e.g., concrete prioritization method descriptions, empirical surveys, etc.), the criteria that we found were on very different abstraction levels. Whereas the criteria applied in method descriptions are typically on a level that can be assessed on a scale by a stakeholder, the criteria discussed in surveys are on a level where an assessment scale is hard to apply. Furthermore, some criteria are on a very abstract business level (e.g., "market value"), while others are on a very detailed technical level, depending on particular requirements artifacts (e.g., "number of times use case appears in model").

- Often, publications use generic terms for the criteria, e.g. "risk". In this case, we tried to find out from the surrounding text what exactly the authors meant with this term. Often it was possible to find a more concrete interpretation, such as "technical risk". However, in some of the publications, it was not possible to find a concrete interpretation. Thus, only the generic term could be referenced.

Finally, we were able to consolidate the vast number of criteria into a smaller set of around 280 criteria. Similar to a thematic analysis approach [16], we categorized them into several abstract categories during this consolidation. The clusters were built by browsing the criteria and identifying and naming themes to which the criteria belong. As a starting point, we named the major categories according to the structuring in [1].

In the last step (6), this categorization was iteratively refined, creating further subcategories. In addition, a definition was provided for each criterion in order to foster a common understanding of the criteria. Finally, the model was discussed with several requirements engineering experts. Based on their feedback, the model was slightly restructured into its final structure, which is described in section 3.

Concerning the threats to validity, we consider two threats to be the most prominent ones. First of all, despite the rigorous search strategy, there exists the possibility that we may have missed important publications. Publications might exist that are not indexed in the databases we used. Also, we might not have extracted all relevant publications using the search terms in their titles, abstracts, or keywords. However, we noticed during the extraction of the criteria that after a certain number of publications, no new criteria could be identified anymore. Thus, the integration of missing publications might not have a large impact on the model, as only few new criteria might exist. The second threat arises due to the challenges descibed above. As we had to consolidate the vast number of criteria into a smaller set, the possibility exists that some criteria were seen as synonyms, even if their meaning might actually be different. Thus, some criteria might have been discarded inadvertently. This is due to the fact that mostly no definitions for criteria were provided in the literature. However, we tried to minimize this threat by not eliminating questionable criteria, rather trying to integrate them into our taxonomy. Furthermore, due to the structure of the model and the definitions we created, it should be easy to integrate other criteria into the model.

3   Prioritization Criteria Model

The prioritization criteria model consists of six major categories, which are further refined into different subcategories. The major categories are: (1) benefits, (2) costs, (3) risks, (4) penalties & penalty avoidance, (5) business context, and (6) technical context & requirements characteristics. The largest group is the benefits category, containing 93 criteria, which represent 33% of all criteria contained in the model (see Figure 2).

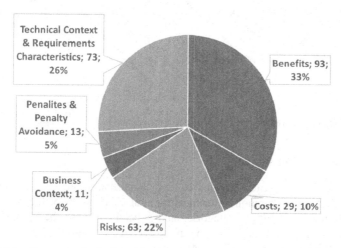

Fig. 2. Major Categories in the Prioritization Criteria Model and the included Number of Criteria

Figure 3 shows the Top Ten of the most frequently mentioned criteria in the literature. The most frequent criterion is "implementation effort" with 54 occurrences. Three of the Top Ten criteria are from the benefits category ("business value", "customer satisfaction", and "stakeholder satisfaction"), two criteria are from the costs category ("implementation effort" and "development effort"), four criteria are from the technical context & requirements characteristics category ("resource availability", "implementation dependencies", "requirements dependencies", and "staff competence"), and one criterion is from the risks category ("requirements volatility").

In the next sections, the prioritization criteria model will be described in more detail. Section 3.1 describes the structure of the model and basic terminology necessary to understand its structure. Section 3.2-3.7 describe the different categories and subcategories of the model, as well as some examples of criteria included in them.

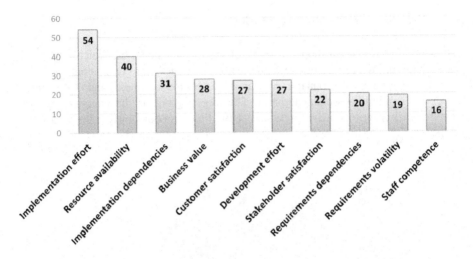

Fig. 3. Top Ten Prioritization Criteria mentioned in the Literature

3.1 Structure and Terminology

During the creation of the criteria model we recognized that in order to create a meaningful categorization, a common understanding is also necessary of the basic terms needed to describe the different categories and subcategories of the model. In the following, an overview of the most important terms used in the model and their conceptual relationships is given (see Figure 4).

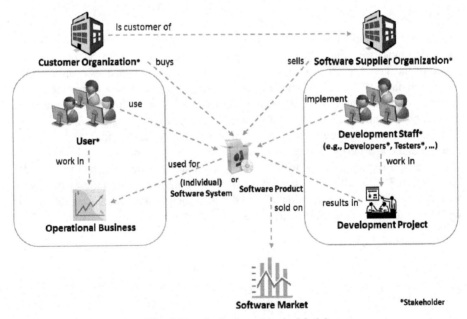

Fig. 4. Terminology used in the Model

Typically, the requirements are prioritized either by a software supplier organization (software development organization) or by a customer organization (receiver/beneficiary of the software system to be developed). Thus, both are also the main stakeholder groups of the criteria model. The prioritized requirements serve as a basis for developing either a software product/system to be sold on a software market or an (individual) software system for a certain customer organization. Whereas in the former case, the software supplier prioritizes the requirements based on market needs, in the latter the customer organization does so based on their operational business needs. The software product is implemented in development projects by development staff (e.g., developers, testers, user interface designers) of the software supplier. The software product (either bought on the market or individually developed) is finally used by the end users in the customer organization in order to support the operational business of the organization. Organizations, and mainly particular roles like user or developer, which are typically involved in or affected by the prioritization, are summarized under the term stakeholder.

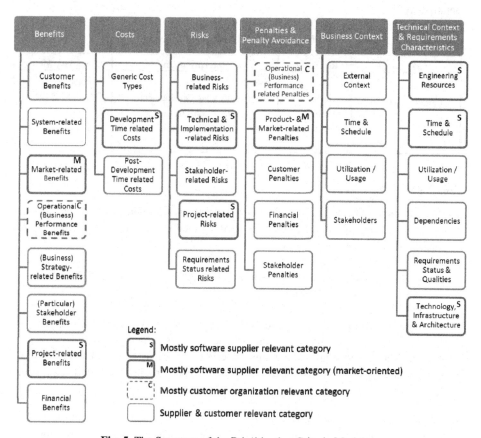

Fig. 5. The Structure of the Prioritization Criteria Model

The model contains criteria that are useful in different requirements prioritization contexts. Thus, it is not customized for any specific point of view. Depending on the situation and the perspective of the decision maker (i.e., software supplier or customer organization), particular subcategories (and the included criteria) are more appropriate for the concrete prioritization than others. An overview of the structure of the model is given in Figure 5. In order to provide guidance, we included some indicators to facilitate navigation in the model based on the prioritization perspective. As it can be seen, the number of subcategories is not balanced between the different major categories. The reason for this is that the type and number of subcategories depend on the criteria found in the literature.

In part, the criteria are also structured hierarchically, i.e., more specific criteria are subordinated under more generic criteria, if appropriate[3]. Furthermore, the criteria themselves are described in detail in a tabular form; an example is shown in Table 1. In the following sections, we will present the criteria that are included in the different categories. However, due to their vast number, we are not able to provide all their details here.

Table 1. Criterion Description Scheme

Criterion	References	Interpretation	Exemplary Metric
Example: Implementation cost / effort	Example: [Wie99] [Moh08] [Fir04]	Example: Costs of any kind (development, testing, integration, etc.) that are incurred if the requirement is implemented.	Example: E.g., effort in [person-days]

3.2   Benefits

In this category, criteria are included that express or are related to benefits that are realized if the respective requirement[4] is implemented (see overview in Table 2). We further divided this category into the following subcategories:

- Customer Benefits: contains criteria that express or are related to benefits for a customer (e.g., "efficiency gains for customer, "competitive gains for customer").
- System-related Benefits: contains criteria that express or are related to benefits with regard to a software system/product (e.g., "product quality").
- Market-related Benefits: contains criteria that express or are related to benefits with regard to the market to which a software product is related (e.g., "customer loyalty").

---

[3] However, the subordinated criteria typically do not completely describe the superordinate criterion.

[4] Although the term *feature* is sometimes used in the literature instead of the term *requirement*, we do not distinguish between these two terms in our model.

- Organizational (Business) Performance Benefits: contains criteria that express or are related to operational performance benefits with regard to the operational business of an organization (e.g., "cost saving", "process efficiency").
- (Business) Strategy-related Benefits: contains criteria that express or are related to business-strategy related benefits (e.g., "contribution to business goals", "long-term strategic value").
- (Particular) Stakeholder Benefits: contains criteria that express or are related to benefits for stakeholders in general (e.g., "stakeholder satisfaction") or particular stakeholder groups, e.g., users of the software product or system (e.g., "end user satisfaction").
- Project-related Benefits: contains criteria that express or are related to benefits for a software development project (e.g., "relevance to project success", "contribution to overall release goal").
- Financial Benefits: contains criteria that express or are related to financial benefits (e.g., "ROI", "NPV").

Table 2. Overview of the Criteria in the Benefits Category

Benefits
❖ Business value / business importance / gain for organization

System-related Benefits	Market-related Benefits
❖ Product / system value	❖ (Product) Market value
➢ Linkage to overall system goals	❖ Customer loyalty / retention
❖ Product / system quality	❖ Marketability / ability to sell
➢ Ease of use / convenience	❖ New business potential / product and service enhancement
➢ Scalability	➢ Additional customer sales
➢ Sustainability of solution	➢ Extra cost customer will spend
➢ Changeable solution	❖ Market percentage
➢ Uniform solution	❖ Competitiveness
➢ Performance	➢ Creation of competitive advantage
➢ Stability	➢ Status of competitors with respect to the requirement
➢ Security	➢ Innovativeness
➢ Integrity	❖ Market technology trends
➢ Availability	❖ Brand protection
➢ Testability	❖ (Feature) Influence on buying decision
➢ Accuracy	❖ Resalable solution
	❖ (Long term) Product strategy
	❖ Fit with / effects on other products

Table 2. (*continued*)

Project-related Benefits

- ❖ Project value
  - ➢ Relevance to project success
  - ➢ Importance wrt. / contribution to overall re-lease goal
  - ➢ Release theme
  - ➢ Feature contribution to project vision
- ❖ Synergy effects by combining tasks

(Particular) Stakeholder Benefits

- ❖ Personal preference & stakeholder priority / preference / value / satisfaction / desire
  - ➢ End user value / satisfaction
  - ➢ Value creation for developer
  - ➢ Relevance to stakeholders' goals
- ❖ Fit with skills / training

Financial Benefits

- ❖ Financial benefit / revenue
  - ➢ Return on investment (ROI)
  - ➢ Net present value (NPV)
  - ➢ Internal rate of return (IRR)
  - ➢ Payback period

(Business) Strategy-related Benefits

- ❖ Strategic alignment / suitability to business strategy
  - ➢ Importance / contribution to business goals
  - ➢ Criticality to mission success
- ❖ Long term strategic value / strategic benefit
- ❖ Tactical usefulness

Customer Benefits

- ❖ Customer value / satisfaction / preference
  - ➢ Efficiency gains for customer
  - ➢ Competitive gains for customer
  - ➢ Intermediary satisfaction

Operational (Business) Performance Benefits

- ❖ Organizational effectiveness
  - ➢ Support of work
    - • Fit with business processes
    - • Contribution to user task
    - • Feature / requirement support for main (usage) scenario
- ❖ Organizational efficiency / productivity improvement
  - ➢ Cost saving / reduction
  - ➢ Economies of production
  - ➢ Cost reduction of IT operation
  - ➢ Process / workflow efficiency
  - ➢ Speed
  - ➢ Throughput
- ❖ Operational risk reduction
  - ➢ Countermeasure benefit
- ❖ Inbound logistics
- ❖ Supplier relations
- ❖ Customer relations
- ❖ Competitor relations
- ❖ Business innovation
- ❖ Deliveries
- ❖ Third party relations
- ❖ Marketing support
- ❖ Decision making
- ❖ Learning and knowledge
- ❖ Organization culture
- ❖ Information
- ❖ Technology / tools
- ❖ Strategy formulation and planning
- ❖ Communication
- ❖ Flow of products / services
- ❖ Control and follow-up (improved reporting)
- ❖ Change management
- ❖ Integration and coordination
- ❖ Flexibility

3.3   Costs

In this category, criteria are included that express or are related to costs that are incurred if the respective requirement is implemented (see overview in Table 3). The category is divided into the following subcategories:

- Generic Cost Types: contains criteria that express or are related to generic cost types (e.g., "life-cycle costs", infrastructure").
- Development Time related Costs: contains criteria that express or are related to costs related to the development phase of a system or software product (e.g., "development cost", "testing cost").
- Post-Development Time related Costs: contains criteria that express or are related to costs that are incurred after the development phase of a system or software product (e.g., "maintenance cost", operational costs").

Table 3. Overview of the Criteria in the Costs Category

Costs	
Generic Cost Types	**Development Time related Costs**
❖ Life-cycle costs	❖ Implementation cost / effort
❖ Total ownership cost	➢ Development cost / effort
❖ Money / finances / budget	• Task size
❖ Time	➢ Documentation cost
❖ Labor	➢ Functional implementation effort
❖ Overhead	➢ Technical implementation effort
❖ Infrastructure	➢ Quality cost
➢ Hardware unit costs	• Testing cost
❖ Travel	▪ Integration testing cost
❖ Material	▪ User acceptance testing cost
Post-development Time related Costs	• Cost for fixing defects detected during testing
❖ Post-development cost	➢ Quality (attribute) implementation effort
➢ Maintenance cost	➢ Risk mitigation effort / cost
➢ Support costs	❖ Product costs
➢ Operational costs	
➢ Shipping	

3.4 Risks

In this category, criteria are included that express or are related to risks regarding the implementation of a requirement (see overview in Table 4). The category is divided into the following subcategories:

- Business-related Risks: contains criteria that express or are related to risks with respect to the business (e.g., "loss of customers", "sales barriers").
- Technical & Implementation-related Risks: contains criteria that express or are related to risks with respect to technology and implementation (e.g., "architecture conflict", "implementation difficulty").
- Stakeholder-related Risks: contains criteria that express or are related to risks for and induced by stakeholders (e.g., "personnel risks", "risks of acceptance").
- Project-related Risks: contains criteria that express or are related to risks in a software development project (e.g., "overrun risk", "over budget risk").
- Requirements Status related Risks: contains criteria that express or are related to risks due to the changes and imprecision of a requirement (e.g., "market changes", "changes from technical perspective").

Table 3. Overview of the Criteria in the Risks Category

Risks

Technical & Implementation-related Risks
- ❖ Technical risks
  - ➢ Architecture conflict
    - • Severe redesign of architecture
    - • Impact on essential non-functional requirements
  - ➢ Database risks
  - ➢ Product quality loss
    - • Performance risks
    - • Risk of maintenance
    - • Loss of confidential data
  - ➢ Technical risk in current system
  - ➢ Technical risk in proposed system
  - ➢ (Technical) Complexity
- ❖ Implementation risk
  - ➢ Implementation technology risks / technical uncertainty
  - ➢ Scope loss
  - ➢ Risk of buggy implementation
  - ➢ Implementation difficulty
    - • Development risk
    - • Difficulty of programming language used
    - • Large Size
    - • Tedium
    - • Uncertainty
    - • Novelty
    - • Number of people involved
    - • Organizational constraints
  - ➢ Implementation feasibility
    - • Ease of realization (technical feasibility)
  - ➢ External risks

Requirements Status related Risks
- ❖ Vague story
- ❖ Requirements volatility / stability
  - ➢ Changes from business perspective
  - ➢ Changes from technical perspective
  - ➢ Market changes
  - ➢ Legislative changes
  - ➢ Users change
  - ➢ Requirements become more clear during software life cycle

Business-related Risks
- ❖ Business risks
  - ➢ Productivity loss
  - ➢ Loss of reputation
  - ➢ Loss of customers
  - ➢ Negative value of undesired event inherent in a feature
    - • Security related risks / misuse case risk
    - • Safety risks
  - ➢ Ease of realization (economic feasibility)
  - ➢ Ease of realization (social feasibility)
  - ➢ Ease of realization (political feasibility)
  - ➢ Market uncertainty
  - ➢ Sales barriers
  - ➢ Commercial concerns

Project-related Risks
- ❖ Overrun / schedule risk / loss
- ❖ Over budget risk
  - ➢ Fixing cost (losses)
- ❖ (Implementation) Process risk
- ❖ Environmental factor (development context)
- ❖ Project duration
- ❖ Project dependencies
- ❖ Impediment of attaining the requirement in the project

Stakeholder-related Risks
- ❖ Personnel risks
- ❖ Estimation risks (in size & team productivity)
- ❖ Risks of acceptance
- ❖ (Decision) uncertainty
- ❖ Part time team member use

3.5   Penalties & Penalty Avoidance

In this category, criteria are included that express or are related to penalties that occur if the respective requirement is not implemented (e.g., "negative value"), as well as criteria that express or are related to penalty avoidance (e.g., "harm avoidance") if the respective requirement is implemented (see overview in Table 5). The category is divided into the following subcategories:

- Operational (Business) Performance related Penalties: contains criteria that express or are related to penalties for the operational business of an organization (e.g., "penalty in operation").
- Product- & Market-related Penalties: contains criteria that express or are related to penalties for a software product or with regard to the market to which the software product is related (e.g., "damage to product").
- Customer Penalties: contains criteria that express or are related to penalties for customers (e.g., "customer dissatisfaction").
- Financial Penalties: contains criteria that express or are related to financial penalties (e.g., "contractual commitment").
- Stakeholder Penalties: contains criteria that express or are related to penalties for stakeholders (e.g., "stakeholder dissatisfaction").

Table 4. Overview of the Criteria in the Penalties & Penalty Avoidance Category

Penalties & Penalty Avoidance
- ❖ Negative value / loss / damage / penalty to business / loss of value
- ❖ Harm avoidance

Operational (Business) Performance related Penalties
- ❖ How complicated would workaround be
- ❖ Penalty in operation / performance impact

Product- & Market-related Penalties
- ❖ Detraction from product's value / damage to product
- ❖ Market share aspect (penalty)

Customer Penalties
- ❖ Negative value / damage / penalty for / loss to customer
- ❖ Customer dissatisfaction

Financial Penalties
- ❖ Cost of not implementing
- ❖ Financial penalty / profit aspect (penalty)
- ❖ Legal mandate / regulations
- ❖ Promised / contractual commitment

Stakeholder Penalties
- ❖ (Stakeholder) Dissatisfaction

3.6   Business Context

In this category, criteria are included that are related to the business context of a requirement (see overview in Table 6). These criteria do not express any concrete benefit or loss that is realized when implementing a requirement, but rather describe context factors that have a positive or negative influence on the requirement's value. For example, if two requirements are equally beneficial, a context factor may help to distinguish them and help to decide which one to prefer. An example of such a criterion is "urgency". Two requirements might be of the same benefit, but one is more urgent than the other. Thus, the more urgent one is preferred. The category is divided into the following subcategories:

- External Context: contains criteria that express or are related to the external context of an organization (e.g., "external dependencies", "customer demand").
- Time & Schedule: contains criteria that express or are related to business-relevant time & schedule contexts (e.g., "urgency", "time to market").
- Utilization/Usage: contains criteria that express or are related to the business usage context (e.g., "frequency of use").

- Stakeholders: contains criteria that express or are related to the stakeholder context (e.g., "originator of requirement", "stakeholder agreement").

Table 5. Overview of the Criteria in the Business Context Category

Business Context	
External Context	**Utilization / Usage**
❖ After sale support	❖ Frequency of use
❖ External dependencies	❖ Actor priority / weight
➤ Customer demand	
➤ Formal governmental demand	
Time & Schedule	**Stakeholders**
❖ Urgency	❖ Originator of requirement
➤ Time to market	❖ Stakeholder agreement
	❖ Likelihood of success

3.7   Technical Context & Requirements Characteristics

In this category, criteria are included that are related to or based on the technical context of a requirement (e.g., "architecture impact"), as well as particular requirements characteristics (e.g., "readiness for implementation"). Just like the business context criteria, these criteria do not express any concrete benefit or loss that is realized when implementing a requirement, but rather describe context factors that have a positive or negative influence on the decision in favor of or against a requirement. An overview is shown in Table 7. The category is divided into the following subcategories:

- Engineering Resources: contains criteria that express or are related to engineering resources, i.e., basically human resources (e.g., "staff competence", "resource availability").
- Time & Schedule: contains criteria that express or are related to implementation time and schedule (e.g., "development lead time", "delivery date").
- Utilization/Usage: contains criteria that express technical usage requirements characteristics (e.g., "reuse potential").
- Dependencies: contains criteria that express or are related to dependencies of and between requirements (e.g., "implementation dependencies", "cost dependencies").
- Requirements Status & Qualities: contains criteria that express or are related to the status of requirements and the (specification) quality of the requirements (e.g., "traceability", "completeness").
- Technology, Infrastructure & Architecture: contains criteria that express or are related to the technological, infrastructural, and architectural context of a requirement (e.g., "importance for product architecture", "infrastructure criticality").

Table 6. Overview of the Criteria in the Technical Context & Requirements Characteristics Category

Technical Context & Requirements Characteristics

Engineering Resources
- ❖ Staff competence / skills
  - ➤ Familiarity of the life-cycle model during the project
  - ➤ Experience on the area
  - ➤ Experience on development methodology used
  - ➤ Ability of analyzer
- ❖ Motivation of the team
- ❖ Balanced workload
- ❖ Resource availability / capacity
  - ➤ Developer productivity
    - • Velocity
  - ➤ Key resources
    - • Resources for specification
    - • Functional resources
    - • Analysis and design
    - • Implementation / Development
    - • Testing
    - • User interface
    - • Research

Dependencies
- ❖ Requirements dependencies
  - ➤ Technical & functional dependencies
  - ➤ Number of requirements that depend on requirement
    - • Number of use cases this use case includes
    - • Number of use cases that includes this use case
    - • Number of use cases this use case extends
    - • Number of use cases that extend this use case
    - • Number of use cases inherited by this use case
  - ➤ Feature weight from use cases
  - ➤ Revenue dependencies
  - ➤ Cost / effort dependencies
  - ➤ Inter-domain dependencies
  - ➤ Dependencies among user stories
  - ➤ Dependencies among delivery stories (between non-functional requirements and architectural choices)
- ❖ Implementation dependencies
  - ➤ Intra-domain dependencies
  - ➤ Dependencies due to downstream activities
  - ➤ Team-based dependencies

Time & Schedule
- ❖ (Implementation) time / schedule
  - ➤ (Development) Lead time
- ❖ Delivery date / release date
- ❖ Project deadline / temporality

Utilization / Usage
- ❖ Object usage for a particular scenario of the use case
- ❖ Actor usage for a particular scenario of the use case
- ❖ Reuse potential / reuse frequency
- ❖ Number of times use case appears in model

Requirements Status & Qualities
- ❖ Readiness for implementation
- ❖ Adequate / Sufficient detail in specification
- ❖ Requirements quality / requirements specification factors
  - ➤ Modifiability
  - ➤ Traceability
  - ➤ Testability
  - ➤ Completeness
  - ➤ Consistency
  - ➤ Understandability
  - ➤ Within Scope
  - ➤ Non-redundant

Technology, Infrastructure & Architecture
- ❖ System impact (changes to existing system)
  - ➤ Keep legacy system alive
  - ➤ (Impact on) Maintenance (of current system)
  - ➤ (Long term) architecture Impact
    - • Importance for product architecture
    - • Technical debt
    - • (Impact on long-term) Evolution (of system)
  - ➤ (Short term) Architectural / development impact
  - ➤ Infrastructure (criticality)
  - ➤ Preferred operating architecture
  - ➤ Technology opportunities
  - ➤ Technology should support current functionality
  - ➤ Integration to external systems
- ❖ System value of a feature (impacted components)
- ❖ Use case weight (transactions)
- ❖ Adherence to corporate software design parameters
  - ➤ IT departments technical guidelines
- ❖ Technical priority

4   Conclusion and Future Work

In this paper, we presented a prioritization criteria model as the result of a systematic literature review. It consists of about 280 prioritization criteria extracted from the literature and allows identifying prioritization criteria in a time-saving manner. It is a first step towards the efficient selection of prioritization criteria for more flexible prioritization approaches. It can be used as a basis for the further development of domain-specific criteria models. Future work on the model should include customization for certain application domains to facilitate its usage. Also it cannot be ruled out that criteria might exist that were not identified during the survey and that must be integrated in the future. As a next step, we will customize the model for the business application domain in order to apply it in our prioritization framework [2].

References

1. Wiegers, K.E.: First Things First: Prioritizing Requirements. Software Development **7**(9), 48–53 (1999)
2. Riegel, N.: Guiding requirements elicitation using a prioritization framework. In: REFSQ 2013 Workshop Proceedings, pp. 133–144 (2013)
3. Riegel, N., Doerr, J.: An analysis of priority-based decision heuristics for optimizing elicitation efficiency. In: Salinesi, C., van de Weerd, I. (eds.) REFSQ 2014. LNCS, vol. 8396, pp. 268–284. Springer, Heidelberg (2014)
4. Azar, J., Smith, R.K., Cordes, D.: Value-oriented requirements prioritization in a small development organization. IEEE Software **24**(1), 32–37 (2007)
5. Berander, P.: Evolving Prioritization for Software Product Management. Blekinge Institute of Technology. Doctoral Dissertation Series (2007)
6. Daneva, M., Herrmann, A.: Requirements prioritization based on benefit and cost prediction: An agenda for future research. In: Proc. of RE 2009, pp. 125–134 (2009)
7. Pitangueira, A.M., Maciel, R.S.P., de Oliveira Barros, M., Andrade, A.S.: A systematic review of software requirements selection and prioritization using SBSE approaches. In: Ruhe, G., Zhang, Y. (eds.) SSBSE 2013. LNCS, vol. 8084, pp. 188–208. Springer, Heidelberg (2013)
8. Svahnberg, M., Gorschek, T., Feldt, R., Torkar, R., Saleem, S.B., Shafique, M.U.: A systematic review on strategic release planning models. Information and Software Technology **52**, 237–248 (2010)
9. Achimugu, P., Selamat, A., Ibrahim, R., Mahrin, M.N.: A systematic literature review of software requirements prioritization research. Information and Software Technology **56**(6), 568–585 (2014)
10. Kitchenham, B.: Procedures for Performing Systematic Reviews. Keele University Technical Report TR/SE-0401. Keele University (2004)
11. Elsevier: http://www.elsevier.com/online-tools/scopus/content-overview. (last accessed on October 16, 2014)
12. IEEE: https://supportcenter.ieee.org/app/answers/detail/a_id/510/~/is-ieeexplore-digital-library-content-indexed-in-scopus%3F. (last accessed on October 16, 2014)

13. Riegel, N.: Prioritization Criteria Collection and Literature Sources. IESE-Report, 048.14/E (2014)
14. Wohlin, C., Aurum, A.: What is important when deciding to include a software requirement in a project or release? In: Int. Symp. on Empirical SE, pp. 246–255 (2005)
15. Barney, S., Aurum, A., Wohlin, C.: Quest for a silver bullet: Creating software product value through requirements selection. In: Proc. of SEAA 2006, pp. 274–281 (2006)
16. Cruzes, D.S., Dybå, T.: Research synthesis in software engineering: A tertiary study. Information & Software Technology 53(5), 440–455 (2011)

Embedding Stakeholder Values in the Requirements Engineering Process

Maaike Harbers[1]([✉]), Christian Detweiler[1], and Mark A. Neerincx[1,2]

[1] Interactive Intelligence Group, Delft University of Technology,
Delft, The Netherlands
{M.Harbers,C.A.Detweiler}@tudelft.nl
[2] TNO Human Factors, Soesterberg, The Netherlands
mark.neerincx@tno.nl

Abstract. Software has become an integral part of our daily lives and should therefore account for human values such as trust, autonomy and privacy. Human values have received increased attention in the field of Requirements Engineering over the last few years, but existing work offers no systematic way to use elicited values in requirements engineering and evaluation processes. In earlier work we proposed the Value Story workshop, a domain-independent method that connects value elicitation techniques from the field of Human-Computer Interaction to the identification of user stories, a common requirements specification format in Requirements Engineering. This paper studies whether user stories obtained in a Value Story workshop 1) adequately account for values, and 2) are usable by developers. The results of an empirical evaluation show that values are significantly better incorporated in user stories obtained in a Value Story workshop than through user stories obtained in regular requirements elicitation workshops. The results also show that value-based user stories are deemed valuable to the end-user, but rated less well on their size, estimableness and testability. This paper concludes that the Value Story workshop is a promising method for embedding values in the Requirements Engineering process, but that value-based user stories need to be translated to use cases to make them suitable for planning and organizing implementation activities.

1 Introduction

Software systems affect human values such as trust, autonomy and security. For instance, software systems that are password-protected support security, and social network services promote friendship. Values can be defined as "what a person or group of people consider important in life" [16]. Software affects the values of its direct users, but also those of indirect stakeholders. For example, parents often do not directly interact with the video games their children play, but the software can still affect the parents' values. Software systems can affect human values in positive and negative ways. A negative effect, for example, is that systems storing a lot of user data may hinder their users' privacy. In other words, software affects the values of direct and indirect stakeholders, either by

© Springer International Publishing Switzerland 2015
S.A. Fricker and K. Schneider (Eds.): REFSQ 2015, LNCS 9013, pp. 318–332, 2015.
DOI: 10.1007/978-3-319-16101-3_23

supporting or hindering these values. The effects of software on human values are not always foreseeable, and this can yield solutions that are, for example, secure but impossible to use, or efficient but not trustworthy.

We argue that, in order to minimize these undesired effects, values should be accounted for in the Requirements Engineering process. We believe that explicitly identifying and considering stakeholder values during requirements elicitation, identification and analysis will lead to software that better supports human values. Furthermore, when values are systematically addressed in the Requirements Engineering process, general knowledge about value-based design solutions can be gathered, e.g., by developing value sensitive design patterns [9].

Recently, human values have been receiving some attention in the field of Requirements Engineering. This work mostly focuses on eliciting values [19,29, 33], but does not account for incorporating elicited values in the Requirements Engineering process in a systematic way. Another research area that considers values in software development is Human-Computer Interaction. In that field, over the last two decades, several methodologies have been proposed to account for values in design, e.g. [14,16,26]. In particular the Value Sensitive Design (VSD) framework [16] contains a rich collection of tools and techniques for the elicitation and analysis of values in the light of technology. However, also in the field of Human-Computer Interaction, the process of translating elicited values to actual requirements is not extensively addressed [10,22].

In earlier work, we began developing a workshop format that aims to bridge the gap between value elicitation and analysis on the one hand, and software requirements on the other hand [11,17]. This workshop format, called the Value Story workshop, is a domain-independent method that uses techniques from VSD to identify stakeholders and elicit their values, and combines these with a few novel steps, in such a way that the results of the workshop can be captured in the form of user stories. User stories are often used in Agile software development to capture initial requirements, and can be used as a starting point for a full requirements specification [4].

The Value Story workshop has potential as a way to embed stakeholder values into the Requirements Engineering process, but this requires that the user stories collected in a Value Story workshop indeed account for values, and that they are usable by developers who will work with them. In this paper, we describe an evaluation study that examines whether the above two requirements are satisfied. In the study, user stories collected in a Value Story workshop (value-based user stories) and user stories obtained through regular requirement elicitation workshops (regular user stories) were evaluated by 14 experts, both from a Requirements Engineering and a VSD perspective. To successfully embed values in the Requirements Engineering process, the value-based user stories should better account for values than the regular user stories, and they should be at least as usable to developers as the regular user stories.

The outline of this paper is as follows. In Section 2, we will provide an overview of related work on values in software development in the fields of Requirements Engineering and Human-Computer Interaction. In Section 3, we describe the Value

Story workshop and its imagined use in the Requirements Engineering process. In Section 4, we describe the goals and the Requirements Engineering process of the project in which the evaluation study was performed. In Section 5, provide the methods, results and a discussion of the evaluation study. In Section 6, we end the paper with a conclusion and suggestions for future work.

2   Related Work

Over the last 20 years, a considerable body of work has focused on developing theoretical and methodological frameworks to deal with values in designing information systems. Much of this work has emerged in the field of Human-Computer Interaction (e.g., [3, 13, 16]). In this section we will discuss VSD, one of the most elaborate of these frameworks. Furthermore, values have been studied in the field of of Requirements Engineering. In the second part of this section we will discuss approaches in the field of Requirements Engineering that address human values.

2.1   Value Sensitive Design

VSD is "a theoretically grounded approach to the design of technology that accounts for human values in a principled and comprehensive manner throughout the design process" [16]. Key concepts in most work on VSD are values, stakeholders, and value tensions. Values are defined as "what a person or group of people considers important in life" [16]. Examples include human welfare, ownership and property, privacy, trust and autonomy. Values can be *explicitly supported values* (those the system is required to support), *designer values* (those held by the system's designers), and *stakeholder values* (those held by various stakeholders). VSD distinguishes between *direct stakeholders*, who interact directly with the system or its output, and *indirect stakeholders*, who are impacted by the system without interacting with it directly. More recent work on VSD (e.g, [6, 8, 23]) has addressed *value tensions*, which can arise when supporting one value, such as awareness, comes at the expense of another, such as privacy.

The VSD methodology contains three parts: conceptual, empirical and technical investigations. Conceptual investigations involve the analysis of direct and indirect stakeholders, their values, and how the envisioned technology affects their values. Empirical investigations involve the elicitation of stakeholders' views and values, and evaluations of prototypes. Technical investigations involve the assessment of existing technologies and solutions, and the development of prototypes. VSD provides a number of specific techniques that support the conceptual and empirical investigations, such as Value Scenarios [24], Value Dams and Flows [23], and Envisioning Cards [15].

Many of these techniques focus on identifying or discovering values (and issues related to those values). Other work on values in design has argued that value discovery is not the only activity involved in systematically incorporating values in the design process. Translation and verification are also required [13]. Translation involves operationalization (defining values in concrete terms) and implementation (specifying design features that correspond to identified values). VSD has been criticized for lacking clarity on the concept values and their realization [7, 22, 28], which suggests that translation is an underdeveloped activity in the VSD framework. Thus, though Requirements Engineering might benefit from VSD techniques to elicit and analyze values, VSD does not offer guidance on specifying requirements to support identified values.

Van de Poel addresses the issue of translating values into design requirements with his notion of a *values hierarchy*, a hierarchical structure of values, norms and design requirements [28]. Van de Poel proposes a two-step process to translate a general value to more specific design requirements: 1) translate a general value into one or more general norms 2) translate these general norms into more specific design requirements. Though this approach addresses the need for a technique to translate values into requirements, Van de Poel does not describe how values should be identified or elicited, nor does he offer suggestions on how to incorporate the approach into a Requirements Engineering process.

De Greef and colleagues' sCEthics method [7] also addresses VSD's lack of explicit and systematic elicitation of requirements by incorporating VSD techniques in the situated Cognitive Engineering methodology [25]. sCEthics incorporates VSD's stakeholder analysis into situated Cognitive Engineering's analysis of operational demands, and links identified values to situated Cognitive Engineering's human factors considerations. This information is used to specify a requirements baseline, which includes a design rationale that consists of claims to justify and use cases to contextualize the requirements. An evaluation of the sCEthics tool revealed that though the tool was seen as useful in many ways, the part that links ethical values to requirements needs to be improved [7].

2.2 Values in Requirements Engineering

Within Requirements Engineering, it has long been recognized that it is common for systems to be created that are technically sound but do not meet the needs of their human operators [12]. It is argued that this stems from a failure to view information technology from a wider perspective and consider requirements that arise from placing a system in a social context. Failure to distinguish between user requirements and system requirements (and treating user requirements as system requirements) can lead to problems [20]. It has often been acknowledged that 'soft issues', such as politics and people's feelings, motivations and values, are important in the Requirements Engineering process, but relatively little guidance is offered on how to deal with them [33].

Among these soft issues, human values have received relatively little attention, with only a few approaches in Requirements Engineering explicitly aimed at dealing with values. Values such as privacy and safety might be dealt with as non-functional requirements among other non-functional requirements, such as performance and accuracy. However, this risks reducing human values to system attributes, thereby missing the reflective understanding of these values and how they function in stakeholders' lives. That understanding is required to soundly incorporate values into a technical design [13].

Thew and Sutcliffe [33] introduced a method that aims to improve the elicitation and analysis of soft issues, which include users' motivations, emotions and values. Though this method deals with values, it focuses on how values influence the Requirements Engineering process. The method identifies the Requirements Engineering process management implications that values bring about, rather than specifying system features to support those values.

Koch and colleagues [19] described a method (initially proposed in [29]) to approximate users' values while preserving their privacy. The method consists of a research process in which key tasks are identified, and an application process in which the users' preferences for these tasks are inquired into and used to approximate their values. This method helps elicit user values, but specifying requirements based on these values is an open challenge. Furthermore, the authors intend to use values elicited with their method to adapt existing systems rather than discover requirements for new systems or features. Neither this method, nor Thew and Sutcliffe's, considers indirect stakeholders and their values.

Ramos and colleagues [30] argue that issues surrounding emotions, values and beliefs in the Requirements Engineering process can prevent successful deployment of computer-based systems. To address this, they propose a *constructionist requirements elicitation process*, which aims to create knowledge about emotions, values and beliefs in the Requirements Engineering process. Though they mention values and beliefs, the authors focus on eliciting emotions (and emotional issues) that affect requirements, and offer little guidance on eliciting values or translating them into requirements.

3   The Value Story Workshop

The Value Story workshop is the result of a series of workshops inspired on the Value Dams and Flow method [23], in which we experimented with different formats [11,17]. In its current format, the Value Story workshop contains the following steps:

1. Identify direct and indirect stakeholders of an envisioned system
2. Identify the values of each stakeholder group
3. Provide one or more concrete situations for each value
4. Identify a stakeholder need for each concrete situation.

A concrete situation is an illustration of a possible effect (positive or negative) on a stakeholder value, e.g. 'if I am continuously recorded by video my privacy is hindered'. A stakeholder need describes specific system features that support these positive effects and/or diminish or remove the negative effects, e.g., 'these video recordings should not be stored'. In this workshop format, participants need not refer to specific system features, which encourages them to maintain a broad scope and leaves space to identify alternatives. Furthermore, the participants get the opportunity to fill in themselves what the system should look like in step 4. The

Value Story workshop was tested and positively received in two large European projects: COMPEIT [5] and IQmulus [18].

The results of the Value Story workshop can be used to create user stories. User stories are used in Agile software development to capture (high-level) requirements [4]. User stories normally have the following format: *As a <role>, I want <something> so that <benefit>* (where the last part of the user story (so that <benefit>) is optional). This format is suitable for representing the results of the Value Story workshop because it involves the actor who issued the desire (<role>) and the rationale behind the desire (<benefit>). The slightly adapted version of the user story template has the following form: *As a <stakeholder>, I want <stakeholder need> in order to support <value>*. Creating user stories according to this template yields value-based user stories, also called Value Stories, to which the workshop owes its name.

The user story template connects value-oriented techniques with existing approaches in Requirements Engineering because of the relationship between user stories and concepts in Requirements Engineering. There are different views on this relationship. It has been argued that user stories, which describe "valuable system functionality from [the] user perspective", can be used to capture user requirements [31]. Others compare user stories to use cases [27] or requirements packages [34], both of which are familiar concepts in Requirements Engineering.

We suggest collecting value-based user stories in the early Requirements Engineering phase (requirements elicitation or gathering), and using them as a starting point to derive *scenarios* and *use cases*. Scenarios are narratives that include a setting, actors with goals, and a sequence of actions and events [25], and a use case is a description of the possible sequences of interactions between the system under discussion and its external actors, related to a particular goal [2]. There are multiple approaches that systematically incorporate scenarios and use cases in their Requirements Engineering process, such as Requirements Engineering with Scenarios for User Centered Engineering (RESCUE) [21], scenario-based requirements engineering [32], and situated Cognitive Engineering (sCE) [25]. It is beyond the scope of this paper to provide a detailed discussion of the relation between user stories, scenarios and use cases. Our main point here is that by representing Value Story workshop results as user stories, they relate to existing concepts in Requirements Engineering, and can as such be used in existing Requirements Engineering processes.

4   Requirements Engineering in IQmulus

The study presented in this paper evaluates the outcomes of a Value Story workshop and of other requirements elicitation activities, both conducted in the IQmulus project [18]. IQmulus is a 4-year European project that aims to make large geospatial data sets more accessible to decision makers. In this section, we describe the regular (i.e. not value-sensitive) and value-sensitive requirements elicitation activities in the IQmulus project.

4.1   Regular Requirements Elicitation

The regular requirements elicitation and identification process used in the IQmulus project consists of three steps: collecting user stories, filtering and prioritizing user stories, and deriving use case from the selected set of user stories. In this section, we focus on the first step, the elicitation of user stories.

The collection of user stories was performed by the user partners of the IQmulus consortium, potential future users of the system being developed in the IQmulus project. User stories were collected through workshops with local stakeholders. These semi-structured workshops were guided by a questionnaire that was specifically developed for this purpose. The questionnaire consists of four parts. Part A contains questions about the stakeholder's general background, such as 'What is your role?' and 'How many years of experience do you have in that role?'. Part B contains questions about how decisions are made today and what is needed additionally to make better decisions. Part C of the questionnaire contains questions about the limitations and possible improvements for the functionality and usability of the system that is currently used, for example, 'What are limitations for the functionality of your current infrastructure with respect to visualization?' These questions address different aspects of the system, including performance, data integration, and visualization. In part D of the questionnaire, local stakeholders were asked for general comments and remarks.

The user partners of the consortium used the results of these workshops to identify user stories that captured the stakeholders' desires with regard to the system to be developed. An example of a collected user story is: "As a GIS expert I want to delineate slopes steeper than a given threshold so that I can support the definition of erosion risk areas." A total of 14 user workshops were organized by 5 consortium partners, with a participant number ranging from 4 to 12. This resulted in a total of 139 regular user stories, 58 in the first round and 81 in a second round.

4.2   Value-Sensitive Requirements Elicitation

Parallel to the regular requirements elicitation process described above, a Value Story workshop was conducted [11]. The workshop had 9 participants from 5 of the user partners of the consortium, and followed the format as described in Section 3. None of the participants was familiar with VSD before their participation in the Value Story workshop, so the workshop started with a presentation to introduce them to the concept of values and the VSD framework.

In the first step of the workshop, the participants identified 13 direct and indirect stakeholders. Due to time constraints, it was not possible to analyze all of the identified stakeholder groups extensively. Therefore, the following three stakeholder groups were selected for further analysis: geographic information system (GIS) expert (direct stakeholder), decision maker (indirect stakeholder), and resident of an area with flood risk (indirect stakeholder). The decision maker is identified as an indirect stakeholder, which means that he does not directly interact with the system, but instead, requests and receives information from GIS experts.

In the second step, for each of these stakeholder groups one or more values were identified. This resulted in a total of 31 values. In the third step, the workshop participants provided at least one concrete situation for each value to illustrate the relevance of that value for that stakeholder group. This step produced 50 concrete situations. In the fourth step of the workshop, the participants identified one or more stakeholder needs with respect to the system to be developed for each concrete situation. This yielded 94 stakeholder needs.

Subsequently, user stories were created, for instance, "As a decision maker I want visualization of information, legend making, semiology, symbology in order to support understandability and efficient communication." In total, 72 value-based user stories were created. The number of user stories is smaller than the number of stakeholder needs because some of the stakeholder needs overlapped.

5   User Story Evaluation by Experts

The study presented in this section provides an evaluation of the user stories obtained in the IQmulus project through regular requirement elicitation workshops (Section 4.1) and a Value Story workshop (Section 4.2). In this section, we discuss the methods, results and a discussion of the study.

5.1   Methods

In the evaluation study, the 10 regular and 10 value-based user stories were evaluated by 14 experts with different backgrounds. The first group of evaluators consisted of 7 software developers with an average of 7.5 years of experience as a software developer. They evaluated the user stories on their usability. The other 7 evaluators were VSD experts with an average of 4.3 years of active contribution to the VSD field. The VSD experts evaluated the user stories on the extent to which they accounted for values. All 14 experts evaluated all 20 user stories, without knowing that there were two types of user stories.

Table 1. Evaluation criteria for VSD experts

Question	Type of answer
1. Which values, if any, does this user story concern?	list up to three values
2. Indicate for each value whether the user story hinders, supports or does not affect the value.	h, s or n
3. After reading this user story, the developer will understand how the desired feature will affect the value(s) at stake.	5-point Likert scale
4. The value perspective is explicitly addressed in this user story.	5-point Likert scale

The aim of the Value Story workshop is to structurally address values in the Requirements Engineering process. This requires that its output, user stories, account for values and are usable by developers. We used VSD experts to evaluate user stories with respect to the first requirement, and developers to evaluate them with respect to the second. There were no existing evaluation criteria to evaluate user stories on the extent to which they account for values, so we developed our own questions. Table 1 shows the questions for the VSD experts. For the evaluation by developers, we used the INVEST (Independent, Negotiable, Valuable, Estimable, Small, Testable) criteria [1], an existing set of criteria for the evaluation of user stories, shown in Table 2. The software developers evaluated each user story according to all 6 criteria on a 5-point Likert scale, where 1 represents a low and 5 a high score on the respective criterion.

Table 2. Evaluation criteria for software developers

Criterion	Description
Independent	Stories are easiest to work with if they are independent. That is, they are self-contained, and can be scheduled and implemented independent from other features of the system.
Negotiable	A good story is negotiable. It is not an explicit contract for features; rather, details will be co-created by the customer and programmer during development. A good story captures the essence, not the details.
Valuable	A story needs to be valuable to the customer. Developers may have (legitimate) concerns, but these should be framed in a way that makes the customer perceive them as important.
Estimable	A good story can be estimated. An exact estimate is not needed, but it should be enough to help the customer rank and schedule the story's implementation.
Small	Good stories tend to be small. Stories typically represent at most a few person-weeks worth of work. Above this size, it seems to be too hard to know what's in the story's scope.
Testable	A good story is testable. A story should only be considered done, if it was tested successfully. Therefore, a user story must provide the information that is needed to write a test for it.

At the time the evaluation study was performed, there were 58 regular user stories (of the first round of workshops) and 72 value-based user stories available. In a pilot study we tested the amount of time it took to evaluate a user story, and found that the evaluation of 20 user stories was acceptable for one person. We randomly selected 10 regular user stories and 10 value-based user stories from the two sets. The evaluation was performed using a questionnaire in which the 20 user stories were presented in a random order, with either the developers or VSD criteria. The evaluators were not informed that there were two types of user stories. After evaluating the 20 user stories, the experts rated their capability of filling in the questionnaire.

5.2   Results

Figure 1 shows the average evaluations of 20 user stories on the INVEST criteria by 7 software developers on a 1-5 scale. The evaluators indicated that their ability to evaluate user stories on these criteria was fair to good. In numbers, the means and standard deviations (*sd*) for regular user stories are I=3.0 (*sd=0.4*), N=3.5 (*sd=0.3*), V=4.1 (*sd=0.3*), E=3.4 (*sd=0.6*), S=3.2 (*sd=0.7*), and T=3.8 (*sd=0.8*), and for value-based user stories I=2.8 (*sd=0.4*), N=3.5 (*sd=0.5*), V=3.8 (*sd=0.6*), E=2.5 (*sd=0.3*), S=2.3 (*sd=0.2*), and T=2.6 (*sd=0.4*). The results show that regular and value-based user stories have similar scores on the criteria Independent, Negotiable and Valuable, but that the regular user stories have significantly (T-test, α <0.0001) higher scores than value-based user stories on the criteria Estimable, Small and Testable.

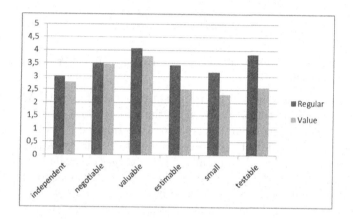

Fig. 1. Software developers' (n_e=7) evaluation of regular (n_r=10) and value-based (n_v=10) user stories on the INVEST criteria

VSD experts were asked to list, for each user story, a maximum of 3 values addressed by that user story (see Table 1). We will not present all values that were identified, but discuss some notable cases. Of the 10 regular user stories, there were 3 user stories for which the majority of the evaluators (at least 4) identified *safety* as an underlying value, and there was 1 user story for which *efficiency* was listed by the majority of evaluators. For the remaining 6 user stories, there was no value upon which the majority of evaluators agreed. There were 2 regular user stories, however, for which the majority did not list any value. Other values that were mentioned relatively often were *reliability* and *accuracy*.

Of the 10 value-based user stories, there were 7 user stories for which the majority of the evaluators identified the same value. These majority values are *personal safety* (twice), *accountability* (twice), *autonomy*, *trust* and *solidarity*. For 5 user stories, the value identified by the majority matched to the value explicitly mentioned in the user story. Interestingly, this was not the case for the two user stories for which the majority listed personal safety as an underlying value. The explicitly mentioned values in these two user stories were communication and availability of information. It only happened twice that one evaluator did not list a value for a value-based user story. For all other value-based user stories, all evaluators identified at least one value.

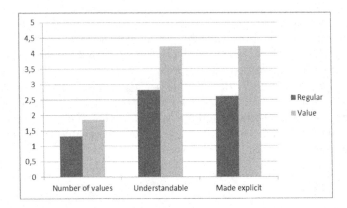

Fig. 2. VSD experts' (n_e=7) evaluation of regular (n_r=10) and value-based (n_v=10) user stories on the VSD criteria

Figure 2 shows the quantitative results of the evaluations of 7 VSD experts, who rated the 20 user stories according to the VSD criteria on a 1-5 scale. The graph shows the averages of all 7 experts for 10 regular and 10 value-based user stories. The evaluators indicated that their ability to evaluate user stories on these criteria was fair to very good. In numbers, the averages of regular user stories are Nr. of values = 1.3 (sd=0.6), Understandable = 2.8 (sd=0.8), and Made explicit = 2.6 (sd=0.6), and the averages of value-based user stories are Nr. of values = 1.9 (sd=0.5), Understandable = 4.2 (sd=0.5), and Made explicit = 4.2 (sd=0.6). The results show that the VSD experts were able to come up with more values for the value-based user stories than for the regular user stories. This difference, however, is not significant (T-test, α <0.5) after a Bonferroni correction of the α <. Furthermore, the VSD experts scored the understandability and explicitness of values significantly (T-test, α <0.0001) higher for value-based user stories than regular user stories.

5.3   Discussion of the Results

This study involves evaluations by software developers and VSD experts. The results of the developers' evaluation shows that regular user stories have positive scores (higher than 3 on the 1-5 Likert scale) on all INVEST criteria, though only slightly positive (3.0 and 3.2) for the criteria of independence and size. These results suggest that, according to the INVEST criteria, the regular user stories are of fair to good quality.

Value-based user stories received similar scores to regular user stories on the first three INVEST criteria, but score less well on their size, estimableness and testability. A likely explanation for these relatively low scores is that value-based user stories express, on average, more abstract stakeholder needs. The desires expressed in regular user stories tend to be more specific in comparison. That is to be expected since the process of generating regular user stories explicitly focused system features from the onset. Abstractness of user stories is problematic when they are used to schedule and organize implementation activities. However, as explained in Section 3, we recommend using user stories to identify use cases. It may be that the step from user stories to use cases is larger for value-based user stories than regular user stories. But once use cases are derived, these should be sufficiently detailed and concrete to form appropriate elements to plan and organize development activities.

These results seem to be in line with the values that the VSD experts listed for each user story. Values identified for regular user stories (safety, reliability, accuracy) are often related to the system, e.g., the system should be reliable and accurate. In contrast, values identified for value-based user stories (personal safety, accountability, autonomy, trust, solidarity) more often concern societal and personal human values, not directly related to the system.

The VSD experts gave higher scores to value-based than regular user stories on questions that address the VSD perspective. This was as expected, since the value-based stories were collected in a workshop that paid explicit attention to stakeholder values, which was not the case for the regular user stories. The scores on questions 3 ('After reading this user story, the developer will understand how the desired feature will affect the value(s) at stake.') and 4 ('The value perspective is explicitly addressed in this user story') are only slightly positive for regular user stories and clearly positive for value-based user stories, that is, 2.8 and 2.6, and 4.2 and 4.2 on a scale of 1-5, respectively. This seems to indicate that the Value Story workshops was successful with respect to these criteria.

There are a number of limitations to the present study that potentially impact its internal validity. The evaluation criteria for VSD experts were designed for this study specifically. We noticed several potential problems with the criteria. For question 1 ('Which values, if any, does this user story concern?'), one of the evaluators indicated that she became tired of coming up with values towards the end of the questionnaire, which may have affected the results. However, this effects both regular and value-based user stories to the same extent, since they were presented in a random order. For question 2 ('Indicate for each value whether the user story hinders, supports or does not affect the value.'), none of the experts identified hinder relations. It might have been beneficial to explicitly ask for potential negative effects of software on humans values, e.g., to obtain information on which features to avoid. In question 3, VSD experts were asked to adopt the perspective of a developer, which may have been difficult for them. We did not ask VSD experts about their experience as developers, if any. Moreover, this question could have been asked to developers themselves, which was not done in the current study. Question 4 may appear to be trivial for value-based user stories. However, inclusion of a value in a user story does not necessarily mean that the value perspective is completely addressed. Addressing the value perspective also requires a reflective understanding of the values in question and the role they play in stakeholders' lives [13]. Indeed we found that the experts rated some of the value-based user stories more positively than others with regard to the value perspective. The evaluation criteria for developers were not new. However, one of the experts remarked that the criteria Estimable and Small are hard to distinguish from one another.

Despite these potential problems and unclarities, as mentioned before, all of the 14 experts rated his/her ability to evaluate user stories on these criteria above fair.

Another potential limitation is that the developers were all familiar with the project in which the user stories were elicited, whereas none of the VSD experts were involved in that project. Ideally, the VSD experts would have had the same contextual knowledge of the project that the developers had. Nevertheless, none of the VSD experts indicated insufficient ability to evaluate the user stories.

Finally, it is important to note that the study involved a limited number of evaluators and user stories. It is therefore impossible to give conclusive answers regarding the quality and usefulness of the Value Story workshop based on these results. Nevertheless, the results are in line with our expectations that user stories obtained in a Value-Story workshop better address values than user stories obtained in a regular workshop. Furthermore, experts indicated that value-based user stories are valuable to the end-user. The results thus suggest that the Value Story workshop is a promising technique for embedding values in the Requirements Engineering process.

6   Conclusion

The Value Story workshop is a domain-independent method that aims to connect VSD elicitation techniques to the identification of user stories, a common requirements specification format in Requirements Engineering. In this paper, we investigated whether user stories obtained in a Value Story workshop adequately account for values, and are usable by developers. For that, we performed an a study in which 14 experts on software development and VSD evaluated and compared user stories gathered in a Value Story workshop and in more traditional workshops. The results show that values are significantly better addressed in value-based user stories than in regular user stories. Furthermore, the results show that value-based user stories score well on delivering value to the end-user, but less well on their size, estimableness and testability.

In future work, we will address several points. First, we will further discuss and develop criteria to evaluate the extent to which values are accounted for in user stories. This will include directly asking developers about their understanding of values and the relation between values and stakeholder needs in user stories. Second, regarding the Value Story workshop itself, we plan to include a step to prioritize value-based user stories, to make it possible to express that some values are more important to consider than others, and to provide a systematic approach to detect and resolve tensions between conflicting stakeholder needs. Third, we will explore ways to account for values throughout subsequent steps in the Requirements Engineering process, for example, by using user stories to specify scenarios, use cases and system requirements, as suggested in Section 3. Fourth, we will develop a tool to support the Requirements Engineering process in which the Value Story workshop is embedded.

To conclude, the Value Story workshop is a promising, domain-independent technique for embedding values in the Requirements Engineering process. We hope that this approach will contribute to the development of technologies that better respect human values.

Acknowledgments. The authors would like to thank all participants of the various Value Story workshops for their valuable input, and all evaluators for their insightful feedback. This research is part of the RAILROAD project and is supported by ProRail and the Netherlands organization for scientific research (NWO) (under grant 438-12-306).

References

1. Buglione, L., Abran, A.: Improving the user story agile technique using the invest criteria. In: Proceedings of IWSM, pp. 49–53. IEEE (2013)
2. Cockburn, A.: Writing effective use cases. Pearson Education (2001)
3. Cockton, G.: Designing worth is worth designing. In: Proceedings of the 4th Nordic Conference on Human-Computer Interaction: Changing Roles, NordiCHI 2006, pp. 165–174. ACM, New York (2006)
4. Cohn, M.: User stories applied: For agile software development. Addison-Wesley Professional (2004)
5. COMPEIT: (2014). http://www.compeit.eu/
6. Czeskis, A., Dermendjieva, I., Yapit, H., Borning, A., Friedman, B., Gill, B., Kohno, T.: Parenting from the pocket: value tensions and technical directions for secure and private parent-teen mobile safety. In: Usable Privacy and Security, pp. 15:1–15:15. ACM (2010)
7. de Greef, T., Mohabir, A., van der Poel, I., Neerincx, M: sCEthics: embedding ethical values in cognitive engineering. In: Proceedings of the 31st European Conference on Cognitive Ergonomics, p. 4. ACM (2013)
8. Denning, T., Borning, A., Friedman, B., Gill, B.T., Kohno, T., Maisel, W.H.: Patients, pacemakers, and implantable defibrillators: human values and security for wireless implantable medical devices. In: Proceedings of the SIGCHI Conference on Human Factors in Computing Systems, pp. 917–926. ACM (2010)
9. Detweiler, C., Hindriks, K.: Value-sensitive design patterns for pervasive health care. In: 2012 IEEE International Conference on Pervasive Computing and Communications Workshops (PERCOM Workshops), pp. 908–913. IEEE (2012)
10. Detweiler, C., Hindriks, K., Jonker, C.: Principles for value-sensitive agent-oriented software engineering. In: Weyns, D., Gleizes, M.-P. (eds.) AOSE 2010. LNCS, vol. 6788, pp. 1–16. Springer, Heidelberg (2011)
11. Detweiler, C.A., Harbers, M., Hindriks, K.: Value stories: putting values into requirements engineering. In: Proceedings of CREARE (2014)
12. Dobson, J., Strens, R.: Organisational requirements definition for information technology systems. In: Proceedings of the First International Conference on Requirements Engineering, pp. 158–165, April 1994
13. Flanagan, M., Howe, D.C., Nissenbaum, H.: Embodying Values in Technology: Theory and Practice, pp. 322–353. Cambridge University Press (2008)
14. Flanagan, M., Nissenbaum, H.: A game design methodology to incorporate social activist themes. In: Proceedings of the SIGCHI Conference on Human Factors in Computing Systems, pp. 181–190. ACM (2007)
15. Friedman, B., Hendry, D.: The envisioning cards: a toolkit for catalyzing humanistic and technical imaginations. In: Proceedings of the 2012 ACM Annual Conference on Human Factors in Computing Systems, pp. 1145–1148. ACM (2012)

16. Friedman, B., Kahn Jr., P.H., Borning, A., Huldtgren, A.: Value sensitive design and information systems. In: Early Engagement and New Technologies: Opening up the Laboratory, pp. 55–95. Springer (2013)
17. Harbers, M., Neerincx, M.A.: Value sensitive design of automated workload distribution support for traffic control teams. In: Proceedings of HCII (2014)
18. IQmulus: (2014). https://www.iqmulus.eu/
19. Koch, S.H., Proynova, R., Paech, B., Wetter, T.: How to approximate users' values while preserving privacy: experiences with using attitudes towards work tasks as proxies for personal value elicitation. Ethics and Information Technology 15(1), 45–61 (2013)
20. Maiden, N.: User requirements and system requirements. IEEE Software 25(2), 90–91 (2008)
21. Maiden, N., Robertson, S.: Developing use cases and scenarios in the requirements process. In: Proceedings of the 27th International Conference on Software Engineering, ICSE 2005, pp. 561–570. ACM, New York (2005)
22. Manders-Huits, N.: What values in design? the challenge of incorporating moral values into design. Science and Engineering Ethics 17(2), 271–287 (2011)
23. Miller, J.K., Friedman, B., Jancke, G.: Value tensions in design: the value sensitive design, development, and appropriation of a corporation's groupware system. In: Proceedings of the 2007 International ACM Conference on Supporting Group Work, pp. 281–290. ACM (2007)
24. Nathan, L.P., Klasnja, P.V., Friedman, B.: Value scenarios: a technique for envisioning systemic effects of new technologies. In: CHI 2007 Extended Abstracts on Human Factors in Computing Systems, pp. 2585–2590. ACM (2007)
25. Neerincx, M.A., Lindenberg, J.: Situated cognitive engineering for complex task environments. In: Naturalistic Decision Making and Macrocognition, pp. 373–390 (2008)
26. Nissenbaum, H.: Values in the design of computer systems. Computers and Society 28(1), 38–39 (1998)
27. Paetsch, F., Eberlein, A., Maurer, F.: Requirements engineering and agile software development. In: 2012 IEEE 21st International Workshop on Enabling Technologies: Infrastructure for Collaborative Enterprises, p. 308 (2003)
28. Poel, I.: Translating values into design requirements. In: Michelfelder, D.P., McCarthy, N., Goldberg, D.E. (eds.) Philosophy and Engineering: Reflections on Practice, Principles and Process. Philosophy of Engineering and Technology, vol. 15, pp. 253–266. Springer, Netherlands (2013)
29. Proynova, R., Paech, B., Wicht, A., Wetter, T.: Use of personal values in requirements engineering – a research preview. In: Wieringa, R., Persson, A. (eds.) REFSQ 2010. LNCS, vol. 6182, pp. 17–22. Springer, Heidelberg (2010)
30. Ramos, I., Berry, D., Carvalho, J.: Requirements engineering for organizational transformation. Information and Software Technology 47(7), 479–495 (2005)
31. Savolainen, J., Kuusela, J., Vilavaara, A.: Transition to agile development - rediscovery of important requirements engineering practices. In: Requirements Engineering Conference (RE), pp. 289–294. IEEE (2010)
32. Sutcliffe, A.: Scenario-based requirements engineering. In: Requirements Engineering Conference, pp. 320–329 (2003)
33. Thew, S., Sutcliffe, A.: Investigating the role of 'soft issues' in the re process. In: International Conference on Requirements Engineering, pp. 63–66. IEEE (2008)
34. Waldmann, B.: There's never enough time: doing requirements under resource constraints, and what requirements engineering can learn from agile development. In: Requirements Engineering Conference (RE), pp. 301–305. IEEE (2011)

Author Index